Reconstructing the Canon: Russian Writing in the 1980s

STUDIES IN RUSSIAN AND EUROPEAN LITERATURE

A series edited by

Peter I. Barta
University of Surrey

and

David Shepherd
University of Sheffield

Editorial Board

Patricia Brodsky, *University of Missouri at Kansas City*
Pamela Davidson, *University of London*
Galya Diment, *University of Washington, Seattle*
John Elsworth, *University of Manchester*
Julian Graffy, *University of London*
Joan Grossman, *University of California, Berkeley*
Lindsey Hughes, *University of London*
Vyacheslav Ivanov, *Moscow State University* and
University of California at Los Angeles
Michael Katz, *University of Texas at Austin*
Catriona Kelly, *University of Oxford*
Roger Keys, *University of St. Andrews, Scotland*
William Leatherbarrow, *University of Sheffield*
Arnold McMillin, *University of London*
Bernice Glatzer Rosenthal, *Fordham University Bronx, New York*

Volume 1

Russian Literature and the Classics
Edited by Peter I. Barta, David H. J. Larmour, and Paul Allen Miller

Volume 2

The Contexts of Bakhtin: Philosophy, Authorship, Aesthetics
Edited by David Shepherd

Volume 3

Reconstructing the Canon: Russian Writing in the 1980s
Edited by Arnold McMillin

Forthcoming titles

Iurii Dombrovskili: Freedom Under Totalitarianism, Peter Doyle
Carnivalizing Difference: Bakhtin and the Other
Edfted by Peter I. Barta, Paul Allen Miller, Chuck Platter, and David Shepherd
Discourse and Ideology in Nabokov's Prose, Edited by David H. J. Larmour
Polish Literature in the European Context, Edited by Patricia Pollock Brodsky
Gender and Sexuality in Russian Civilization, Edited by Peter I. Barta

EDITED BY

ARNOLD MCMILLIN
UNIVERSITY OF LONDON

Reconstructing the Canon: Russian Writing in the 1980s

harwood academic publishers
Australia • Canada • France •
Germany • India • Japan • Luxembourg •
Malaysia • The Netherlands • Russia •
Singapore • Switzerland

Amsteldijk 166
1st Floor
1079 LH Amsterdam
The Netherlands

British Library Cataloguing in Publication Data

Reconstructing the Canon : Russian writing in the 1980s —
    (Studies in Russian and European literature ; v. 3 — ISSN 1024-8021
    1. Russian literature – 20th century – History and criticism
    I. McMillin, Arnold B.
    891.7'90'0044

                    1003256394

    ISBN: 90-5702-593-0

T

CONTENTS

INTRODUCTION TO THE SERIES

Change and difference have become the cliched watchwords of Slavic studies in recent years. There is surely no need for further cataloguing — whether celebratory or cautionary — of the transformations in the practices and potential of our discipline wrought by the political, social, and economic turmoil of the former Soviet Union and the Eastern Bloc, not to mention the sweeping changes in interpretive practices within the study of the humanities in Western countries.

A series such as *Studies in Russian and European Literature* must in large degree be a response to those transformations; it cannot, however, be reduced to their mere product or reflection, and does not set out to impress by superficial novelty. In seeking to promote a comparative approach, with particular emphasis on the ties between Russian and other European literatures, and on the relationship between Western and Eastern European cultures, the series will extend long-established paths of inquiry. There will also be continuity in the embrace it offers theory, to which Russia and Eastern Europe are no strangers.

At the same time, such a venture must recognize that much of what passes for change and difference is all too often nothing more than an exchange of negative for positive which leaves old categorizations and oppositions in place, their valencies inverted by a mechanical operation of a kind characteristic of a world and a system which are supposed to have been discredited. The demise of one conceptual framework and the concomitant vindication of another might well hold out the prospect of rapid and dispiriting ossification. *Studies in Russian and European Literature* will resist this possibility. Like its global counterpart, literary history has not yet come to an end.

Peter I. Barta
David Shepherd

vii

PREFACE

In 1993-94 the Russian Department of the School of Slavonic and East European Studies of London University took "Russian literature in the 1980s" as the theme of its Russian Literature Seminar series, which attracted a number of interesting papers and provoked lively topical discussion. Some, but in the event only a minority, of the papers given in that programme have found their way into this volume where they are supplemented by contributions from visiting and foreign lecturers during that year, as well as studies commissioned from other British, American and continental scholars working on literature of the 1980s.

The editor acknowledges with thanks the grant from the Publications Fund of the School towards the cost of making the Index. He particularly wishes to express his gratitude to the founders of Studies in Russian and European Literature, Peter Barta and David Shepherd, for encouraging him to submit the volume to their series and for their many helpful suggestions; to Barbara Wyllie for her excellent work on the Index; to Ben Chatterley for his invaluable technical assistance at various stages of production; and, far from least, to his wife Svetlana who provided comfort and inspiration at all stages.

INTRODUCTION

Arnold McMillin

The restructuring of the Russian literary canon in the 1980s, although a welcome and exciting development in itself, has hardly been a cause for wonderment against the backdrop of almost unprecedented political change. The canon has, of course, been de- and re-constructed many times during the last two centuries, and reputations have come and gone in even shorter order than in most Western countries. Amongst obvious examples are the temporary eclipse of Pushkin by the rise of the mid-nineteenth-century novel, the critical silencing of Fet, Futurism's total rejection of the cultural past, and the highly selective acknowledgment of what is now the classical literary canon by the Bolsheviks. The latter political prejudice cut whole generations of Russians off from large sections of their national literature: Dostoevskii, Berdiaev and other non-socialist writers, for example, or major émigrés like Bunin and Nabokov, to say nothing of the myriad poets, playwrights and prose writers who remained in Russia for better or worse, often having to wait decades for grudging and not infrequently posthumous rehabilitation.Purges and the GULag, we may hope, belong firmly in the past, but emigration, mainly of the Third Wave, has continued to play a large role in Russia's cultural process, not least in the changing literary canon of the 1980s; indeed, it forms a recurrent theme in several of the essays in the present volume. With the approach of the millennium there increases the temptation to chop literary history, like other historical periods, into artificially discrete segments. But it is difficult not to feel — even without the contrast of the preceding age of Brezhnevian stagnation — that time has accelerated in the 1980s (like the Volga/Itil´ in Sokolov's *Mezhdu sobakoi i volkom* which flows at different speeds according to season and location), the literary current moving with remarkable rapidity

1

from the vestiges of socialist realism, via re-born *molodaia proza*, "alternative prose", "other prose", "bad prose" (much of Soviet criticism's broad brush has remained untrimmed), *andergraund*, *sverkhrealizm*, conceptualism, the neo- and post-avant-garde, and, in the most general terms, postmodernism, to say nothing of the rash of *chernukha* and *pornukha*. Even this variety, however, is only part of the picture, and many other writers are at last beginning to be recognized at their true worth. They include such novelists as Sokolov and Zinik, who have appeared in emigration, or poets like Aizenberg, Sedakova and Shvarts who, without leaving Russia, found themselves even further from a broad Russian readership in the obscurity of inner exile and ostracism. Still other writers, like Slavkin, have built and maintained high reputations by works which owe much to the classical heritage, and nothing to either political conformity or, more recently, radical innovations and taboo-breaking.

Reconstructing the Canon aims to cover certain characteristic aspects of a period which began with the gerontocracy of Chernenko and ended with the disintegration of Communism, which began with a peak in the emigration of writers and other intellectuals from the Soviet Union and ended with their rehabilitation and, in some cases, return home. It was, indeed, a period of great political and cultural diversity, and it is intended that some of that variety should be reflected in these pages. Particularly important was that the uncompromising maximalist criticism which carried over from the previous decade was still fully in operation during the early eighties, with many émigré and Soviet critics alike unwilling or unable to see the whole picture of Russian literature.[1] Six of the contributions here are devoted to novelists, three to poets, and two to "para-literary" surveys of changing perceptions of the major literary trends of the recent past. It seems fitting that the volume should open with an essay on the towering figure of Iurii Lotman, the most significant literary scholar and theoretician of the age. The interview with Ol´ga Sedakova, which occupies a central place in this collection, is the first such presentation of a poet who, since the death of Brodskii, seems to many readers to be the most luminous figure in present-day Russian poetry. The interview attempts to capture the spirit of the poet's responses by reproducing, so far as is possible in print and in translation, her natural manner of discourse, rather than turning it into a series of literary statements.

Apart from the interview, several different literary approaches are represented here, ranging from personal memoir to overviews of periods and genres, from carefully documented studies of individual writers to highly technical formalist investigations of literary structures. Inevitably, the volume represents a sampling — albeit a highly original one — rather than full coverage of the decade in question, and many writers, far from neglected elsewhere, are conspicuous by their absence here, most notably Brodsky, Bitov and Tat´iana Tolstaia — the list could easily be extended.[2]

Above the vulgarity of both Communist political dogmatism and the cacophonous fray of competing literary fashions in the market place, stands the magisterial figure of Iurii Lotman, Russia's greatest critic since Bakhtin, and the man who, as an inspiration to many of Russia's finest philological minds, maintained the highest cultural traditions outside the devalued literary culture of his time. In the words of Ol´ga Sedakova in her interview: "The academic avant-garde was then playing the role formerly played by Russian literature (and that, as everyone knows, was a lot more than literature). It was asking all the really important questions of the time — cultural, spiritual, even political." Thus it is that David Bethea's study of Lotman's biographical work is more than just a commentary on commentaries: it is also a timely tribute to the broad genius who in the seventies and eighties provided an inspiration to many, and who was without doubt one of the very greatest luminaries of the period. As such it makes an eminently suitable opening to a volume attempting to present a picture of a broad and varied period.

No vaulting claims for herself are made by Ol´ga Sedakova, but her extended interview with Valentina Polukhina does offer an excellent insight into her own poetry, which came to maturity in the 1980s at the same time as it emerged from long years of samizdat and official ostracism, but which still lacks an adequate critical response. That alone would warrant the publication of her first major interview. In addition to the many insights into her own poetry and her response to other writers, however, it also presents a valuable personal overview of the period with which this volume is concerned, touching on many of the themes developed by other contributors. It is notable that in addition to her great admiration for critics like Lotman and Sergei Averintsev, she singles out for particular praise the brilliant, elusive poetry of Evgeniia Shvarts, a writer who has very much come to the fore in the eighties, but whose verse, like Sedakova's own work, has hitherto also been accorded less critical attention than it deserves. Stephanie Sandler's close analysis of four of Shvarts's short poems also surveys some of the other young poets of the period. It is difficult to imagine a reconstructed canon in which either Sedakova or Shvarts did not occupy a prominent place.

Mikhail Aizenberg, described by Zinovy Zinik as an "odd man out", also knows what Sedakova calls the "salt" of exile within one's own country. As an émigré himself, Zinik shows through his friend Aizenberg the problems that *not* emigrating can bring, and illuminates the question of emigration as well as of literary groupings and of cultural leadership (almost patronage) through the work of a worthwhile, but difficult and somewhat neglected poet. Zinik himself has treated with great perspicacity and wit the problems of emigration in many works of fiction and criticism. Robert Porter discusses the nature of his writing on the basis of three key works and his articles. Although, like Sedakova and Shvarts, Zinik has received far less critical attention than canonical writers of the previous decade such as Evtushenko and Voznesenskii (to say nothing of, for example, the *derevenshchiki*), he is now well respected by a new generation of readers in metropolitan Russia and has undoubtedly re-entered the Russian literary canon.

Several articles in this volume are concerned with emigration in various forms — a natural consequence of Brezhnev's deeply destructive policies in the late seventies and early eighties. One of the most distinguished émigrés of the Third Wave was, of course, Andrei Siniavskii (Abram Tertz) who died on 25 February 1997, during this book's gestation. In her study Jane Grayson illustrates the problems of self-vindication faced by this protean figure, attacked in the West and (since *glasnost'* and the re-publication of his work) in Russia too. Politics seem to be an inevitable concomitant of émigré life, and, dogged by rumours of youthful collaboration with the KGB, Siniavskii had to defend himself vigorously. More difficult, but no less important to the writer, was defending himself against what may be the almost more heinous charge (brought by metropolitan and émigré readers alike) that he had slandered Pushkin in his highly individual *Progulki s Pushkinym*. Typically for this writer, the defence against taboo-breaking was made through the life of Pushkin himself and his novel *Kapitanskaia dochka*. Whatever else the hounding of Siniavskii for his brilliant whimsy shows, it is clear that, despite all the distractions of a country in political and economic chaos, for many Russians literature remains a matter of primary importance.

Aleksandr Zinov´ev (as he himself would be the first to say) is unique, not only amongst writers of the Third Wave, but in Russian literature as a whole. As it happens, the essay devoted to him is also unique, as the sole example in this volume of a formal, statistical analysis. It goes a long way towards showing not only that Zinov´ev's books have far more system to them than many readers first suspected, but also precisely how his highly individual manner of writing has enabled him to adapt successfully to the new conditions which have arisen in the course of the 1980s.

Sasha Sokolov's novel *Mezhdu sobakoi i volkom* was awarded a prize by the underground Leningrad journal *Chasy* for the best prose of 1981. Hanna Kolb's close analysis of the dissolution of reality in this Gothic picture of degraded provincial Russia is the most substantial piece of critical work yet addressed to what is a major postmodernist text, a work which at the beginning of the eighties could only have been published outside

Russia, but which now, together with Sokolov's other novels, occupies a distinct place in the reconstructed literary canon.

The *derevenshchiki*, darlings of the Soviet Establishment in the sixties and seventies, did not prosper after their movement had passed its heyday, but several of them appeared to adopt ever more extreme political positions, turning themselves from mild critics of the regime into extreme nationalist ideologues. Kathleen Parthé considers to what extent it is fair to blame writers like Belov and Rasputin for the wave of anti-Semitism and chauvinism in Russia of the 1980s, and — in general — how far it is justified to re-assess writers in the way that is going on in Russia today. Reconstructing the canon, she argues, must not involve wholesale rejection of writers' valuable earlier work on account of their behaviour in "para-literary space". Rasputin, the Siberian, also figures in Ewa Thompson's analysis of the unconscious or subconscious nationalist and imperialist attitudes she finds prevalent in Russian literature of the eighties and earlier. Her indictment also includes Solzhenitsyn (no longer concerned with literature in the 1980s) and Astaf´ev (another writer whose best works contrast startlingly with some of what he has produced in this age of transition), to say nothing of Jane Austen, Dickens and Conrad.

Drama, and in particular its postmodernistic "new wave", is represented here by the intriguing plays of Viktor Slavkin which maintain many links with Russia's literary past, not least in his best known work to date, *Serso*. Thus, we have examples of both younger and older writers developing in the 1980s whilst remaining steeped in a rich classical tradition.

The somewhat indeterminate genre of urban prose took a particularly depressing turn in the 1980s, with a strong new tendency towards naturalism and dirty realism dominated by pessimism and squalor. Such writing reaches a logical culmination in the controversial, shocking work of Vladimir Sorokin which, written in the eighties, has had to wait until the nineties to be published. The deeply spiritual Sedakova refers with disgust to a "gala parade of all the obscenities", and another dignified poet of the older generation, Iunna Morits, has said "literature wants to vomit", comparing the contemporary literary situation to "a revolt of slaves given absolute freedom".[3] Indeed, a casual reading of almost any Russian book catalogue nowadays reveals such Limonovesque titles as *Odnokhuistvennyi Uliss* (Eduard Kulemin) and *Kak ia zanimalsia onanizmom* (the third part of an autobiographical trilogy by Igor´ Iarkevich), to give but two examples. By comparison, Sorokin is a writer of high seriousness, whose challenge to (rapidly disappearing) taboos has a clear and specific literary purpose. His novel *Norma* is described by David Gillespie as a postmodern protest against the now departed Soviet norm. He represents, amongst other things, the breaking of linguistic norms, both through *mat* and trans-sense, something that distinguishes him from the type of new urban realism epitomized as Kavalerovs and coffins by Sally Dalton-Brown. Whether or not Sorokin's writing is to one's personal taste, his belief in the importance of literature cannot be gainsaid.

In applying a number of different literary approaches to a wide range of literature, this collection hopes to cast light on some of the new and characteristic features of a decade which has been remarkable in literature, as in all aspects of Russian life. Regardless of chronology, almost all the authors and works selected reflect the move out of and away from Soviet literature, and particularly its Brezhnevian manifestation. Norman Shneidman wrote in 1989: "The Soviet literary scene is today volatile, and prose is at a cross-roads." It is hard, however, to agree with his assertion that there are "few young names deserving positive mention" (Shneidman, 22). Many writers and poets to whom he does not even allude in his study, such as Sedakova, Shvarts and Sorokin, to name but a few, along with other writers who are passing through a period of critical re-assessment and personal development, point the way to a rapidly moving and rich literary period of great contrasts. Few would challenge Lotman's belief that "literature is not a shelf of books, it is a living organism (and this organism survives on the unity of its atmosphere, on the presence of indisputable values)" (Lotman 1987, 320). The false unity of Communist purpose, once broken, was bound to lead to fragmentation, and the indisputable values may indeed be contested and disputed, but the organism continues to live. Little helped by critics who, with rare exceptions, lag well behind the new development of literature, and unattracted by groups ("they have changed the decor of literary life", as Sedakova says, "but the leading characters on stage remain the same"), the creators of new Russian literature bring diverse gifts to a post-Soviet generation of readers ready to respond to the new as well as to re-assess the literature of the past. At every level, the reconstruction of the canon proceeds apace.

REFERENCE

Lotman, Iu. M., 1987. *Sotvorenie Karamzina*, "Pisateli o pisateliakh" series (Moscow: Kniga).

NOTES

1. This question, one of the principal issues to be debated in the late seventies and early eighties, was addressed at a conference in Geneva in 1978 and in a subsequent book, Georges Nivat (ed.), *Odna ili dve russkikh literatury* (L'Age d'Homme: Lausanne, 1981).

2. Amongst other English-language books devoted to presenting a broader and more general survey of the eighties may be mentioned the following: N.N. Shneidman, *Soviet Literature in the 1980s: Decade of Transition* (Toronto, Buffalo and London: University of Toronto Press, 1989) (hereafter Shneidman); Sheelagh Duffin-Graham (ed.), *New Directions in Soviet Literature* (New York: St Martin's Press, 1992); Deming Brown, *The Last Years of Soviet Russian Literature* (Cambridge: Cambridge University Press, 1993); Robert Porter, *Russia's Alternative Prose* (Berg: Oxford and Providence, 1994) (hereafter Porter); and Rosalind Marsh, *History and Literature in Contemporary Russia* (Macmillan: Basingstoke, 1995). Other critics have chosen specific authors or themes from or including the eighties: see, for example, Cynthia Simmons, *Their Master's Voice: Vassily Aksyonov, Venedikt Erofeev, Eduard Limonov, and Sasha Sokolov* (Peter Lang: New York, 1993); Edith W. Clowes, *Russian Experimental Fiction: Resisting Ideology after Utopia* (Princeton: Princeton University Press, 1993); and Katherine L. Ryan-Hayes, *Contemporary Russian Satire: A Genre Study* (Cambridge: Cambridge University Press, 1995).

3. Quoted from Porter, 31.

IURII LOTMAN IN THE 1980s:
THE CODE AND ITS RELATION
TO LITERARY BIOGRAPHY

David M. Bethea

Perhaps no two thinkers in the latter decades of the twentieth century have changed more our ability to conceptualize Russian literature, the Russian literary context, and ultimately verbal reality regardless of national origins, than Mikhail Bakhtin (1895–1975) and Iurii Lotman (1922–1993). Lidiia Ginzburg, to cite the most obvious counter example, certainly belongs to the ranks of the greatest scholar-critics of her generation, but in the final analysis her mind was less far-ranging and less endlessly *probing* than either Bakhtin's or Lotman's. Indeed, one might go so far as to make the point that, in late twentieth-century Russian culture *tout court*, Bakhtin and Lotman are phenomena of the very first importance, in terms of their cognitive capaciousness and the uniquely productive trajectories of their insights undisputed geniuses — two huge, majestic mountains against a cultural and literary backdrop of lesser peaks and, beyond that, flatlands. True, one does not want to overstate the case: Brodsky, Solzhenitsyn, Siniavskii-Tertz, and others among the "primary creators", and Ginzburg, Boris Uspenskii, V.V. Ivanov, Mikhail Gasparov, and others among the "secondary creators" — all these are without doubt writers and thinkers of major proportions, even (one has to use the word sparingly) "geniuses". And yet, one is struck by the sense that Bakhtin and Lotman are, by some "Hamburg account" measuring the ability of the human mind to mimic the speed of light, comparable to no one of their time and place except each other. Not by chance was Lotman often compared, both in how he looked and how he thought, to Albert Einstein.

The purpose of the present essay is modest. In the first part I will try to show how Lotman learned from Bakhtin in the 1980s, adapting the latter's "dialogism" (in its various incarnations) to open up the more mechanical structural-semiotic "modelling systems" made famous in the works of the Moscow-Tartu School of the 1960s and 1970s. This shift in Lotman has been duly noted by several commentators. What has not been noted, however, is the potentially positive or "energy-releasing" aspects of the one concept Bakhtin found most "closed" and "deadening" about structural analysis — the so-called *code*,[1] which stood to a given text or cultural moment as the Saussurean *langue* stood to the *parole* of individual utterance. My main interest in this first part is simply to demonstrate that, while Lotman learned from Bakhtin and thus under the power of the latter's arguments was able to, as it were, organize and "soften up" the harder edges of the structuralist-semiotic worldview,[2] he still remained very much his own thinker, and he did so precisely in this area of the *creative potential* in what might be termed "code wrestling". In this, as I will suggest, Lotman remained true to the genres and the literary period he began with and was our greatest pioneer in (re)discovering: Russian *poetry* and *poetic consciousness* of the Karamzin-Pushkin era. Lotman emerges then as the antipode to Bakhtin, our greatest theorist of the novel and of the novelistic consciousness associated with Dostoevskii and (by Bakhtin's distinguished students) Tolstoi. And the divide, crudely put, between these two thinkers rises up over their orientations, positive and negative respectively, towards the categories of "code", "model", "structure".

Thereafter, in the second part of the essay, I will turn to the major works of Lotman's last decade — his books on Pushkin and Karamzin — all of which apply in non-specialist language the lessons of "code wrestling" to concrete examples of what might be called "poetic thinking". It is my hypothesis that Lotman, who has learned from Bakhtin but has also learned where he departs from his antipode, is trying to use his method to get as close as possible to the headwaters of poetic creativity itself: how poets use the material of life, beginning with its implicit codes, not only to write but to *live* creatively. The connection between life and art, text and code, can be, Lotman comes more and more to see, — the ultimate semiotic gesture. In this context, Pushkin and Karamzin were Lotman's greatest exemplars, models, and, not by chance, *personal* sources of inspiration. In other words, Lotman kept growing as a thinker at a truly astonishing rate: at the end he was returning to the concrete lives and texts studied by the literary historian and critic not so much as an expression of the entropy of his conceptualizing ardour (quite the opposite in fact, to judge by his more adventuresome 1980s pieces on the semiosphere and its relation to intracranial function), but as an expression of his most real, most living, and, one might foretell, most durable idea: poets need the biologically, existentially, and aesthetically *encoded* constraints of a single life lived in time in order to create something whose exemplary ("modelling") power appears *greater than* the constraints giving rise to it.

How, on one level, does the strait-jacket of the rhyme scheme, say the Onegin stanza, *enable* the verbal movement standing in for the physical grace of Istomina dancing on stage? How, on another, do the duelling or gambling or nobleman's honour codes of Pushkin's milieu shape but also challenge, *bring out not automatically but through struggle*, the behaviour we have come to associate with the quintessential poet's life? In short, what *choice* is there in a life that takes codes seriously? By discussing these matters in a language that itself was simpler, more direct, and at the same time more metaphorical, expressive, and *multiply coded* than the metalanguage of the semiotician, Lotman was taking a risk, but one he could not apparently in good conscience avoid. He was, courageously, testing the limits of his own codes and sense of generic propriety (the scholar/scientist who has the right only to reconstruct faithfully, but not to invent). He was bending the sharp edges of his structural-semiotic model as far as they could legitimately go in the direction of "life". He was trying to touch the hot core of "creativity" across the threshold of a cognitive lucidity perhaps unmatched in the history of Russian culture. And so, the actual lives of Pushkin and Karamzin became the necessary ballast, the compelling exempla, making the "castles in the air" of scientific/semiotic theory real, alive, *non-repeating*, and therefore inspiring. Very few Russian thinkers, or any thinkers for that matter, have dug as deeply and broadly in the past for Mandel´shtamian horseshoes, that is, the chance discovery that casts a poetically lived life in a new, meaningful light (see below Lotman's repeated trope of the archaeological site). If the rather technical discussions about culture as semiosphere, functionally asymmetrical hemispheres of the brain, neurolinguistics, and so on, were the dialectic scaffolding, the "rhyme scheme" that allowed mature Lotmanian thought to soar across interdisciplinary boundaries into the outer reaches of scientific speculation, then here was Istomina's dance, the beauty of an individual life that does not merely replicate a model/code but itself *generates meaning* against those codes.

*

One of the core components of Bakhtinian thought is its relentless emphasis on the dialogic, uniquely specific and unreplicatable nature of an utterance (*vyskazyvanie*), broadly defined.[3] It is the very *ongoing, in-process, interpersonal* (*mezhlichnostnyi*) aspect of dialogue that makes it, in Bakhtin's language, forever unfinalizable, open. Thus, if the process of semiosis requires signs to generate thought and meaning in the first place, then the originary pivot of the Bakhtinian position is away from Saussurean *langue* and towards his (Bakhtin's) somewhat eccentric version of *parole*, or *vyskazyvanie*. As has been pointed out by Ponzio and Grzybek, in this orientation Bakhtin is virtually of one mind with the American pragmatist and pioneering semiologist Charles Sanders Peirce: "for Bakhtin (as well as for Peirce) these signs [creating meaning/semiosis — DMB] 'belong not to the closed and defined system, the code (*langue*), but rather engage each other in the process of interpretation'" (Ponzio 1984, 274; cited Grzybek 1995, 252). It is completely logical, therefore, that Bakhtin would be critical of the mechanical, "artificially intelligent" (linguistic competence *predicted* by codes) trajectory of structuralism, from Saussure's positings of a codifying *langue* to Chomsky's transformational unpackings of "deep structure": "My attitude towards structuralism: I am against enclosure in a text" (1979a, 372); and "a code is a deliberately established, killed [*umershchvlennyi*] creative context" (1979b, 352).[4] Like any philosopher, Bakhtin was interested in what could be generated *that was genuinely new* out of a dialogic encounter, and so, in his thinking, because a "context is potentially incomplete [*nezavershim*]", while "a code should be complete/finished off [*zavershim*]", "the code [. . .] does not have cognitive, creative significance" (1979b, 352).

There is a potentially subtle paradox here in Bakhtin's thought, not so much in its logic (which is unerring) but in its, at times, eccentric application. Crudely speaking, one might phrase the contradiction thus: Bakhtin's exclusive emphasis on — indeed, his obsession with — openness meant that his ideas, however rich and provocative, could never be "tightened up", made more "scientific", even the slightest bit "closed". They attach to real texts and contexts (that is, to Bakhtin's rather specialized use of literary and cultural history) only in the most general way. Why? Because their chief goal was to trace the human being's cognitive drive towards greater communicative openness: of verbal forms (dialogism), of novelistic structure (polyphony), of space-time relations (chronotope), of language that breaks down stylistic boundaries and argues with itself (heteroglossia), of the "authorizing" process (*chuzhaia rech'*/another's speech), of bodies that celebrate their multiple orifices (carnival). Bakhtin assumed that little could be learned by studying how the human personality interacted with the "closed" or coded aspects of certain verbal forms. Poetry became in his thinking, which in the end could not do without its own binary oppositions, the necessary monologic antipode to the genre chosen by history for its dialogic adaptability and closeness to "life", the novel. However, as one of Bakhtin's most perceptive students has recently suggested, his spirited defence of the living context is itself strangely decontextualized, bereft of *real biography*: "Bakhtin embraces struggle, but at the level of words, not personal fates. For him, the novel is above all the home of many wonderful, unwinnable, unloseable *wars with words*" (Emerson [forthcoming], 47). In this sense, Bakhtin had something to learn from Lotman.

Lotman's orientation to the code/text/context force field of course differed fundamentally from Bakhtin's. To the end of his life he did not reject the principal scientific assumptions of Saussurean linguistics, beginning with the notion that there was a dialectical tension between *langue* and *parole*, code and text, in every formal discursive encounter.[5] It took someone of Lotman's immense curiosity, flexibility, common sense, tact, and unparalleled concrete knowledge both about the history of literary forms and the history of social behaviour to see this complex tension in a way that was more than Saussure-Jakobson and less than Bakhtin-Peirce. Here one might argue that, precisely because Lotman was less of a speculative phenomenologist with one powerful idea (history's drive towards novelization) and more of a pragmatic "enlightener" and scientific thinker, he could in a way utterly alien to Bakhtin and indeed rare for any tradition conjoin the roles of code-taxonomer, text-reader, and context-reconstructor. My point here is simply that, to use the same metaphor, Lotman could "loosen up", "organicize" his original Saussurean stance, which he did in the late 1970s and especially in the 1980s, whereas Bakhtin, who saw semiotics as *only* interested in the "transmission of a *ready-made* message with the help of a *ready-made* code" (1979b, 352; my emphasis — DMB), could not see a reason for "tightening up" his. Bakhtin could not move — paradoxically, the "maximalism" of his dialogism would not permit it — from the position that "[i]n living speech the message, strictly speaking, is created *in the process* of communication, and so, in essence, *there is no code*" (1979b, 352; my emphasis — DMB). But Lotman could move, and why is a tantalizing imponderable.[6] It is to this move that we now turn in the second part of the essay.

*

Lotman authored and/or edited four works on Pushkin and Karamzin in the 1980s: *Roman A.S. Pushkina "Evgenii Onegin": Kommentarii* (A.S. Pushkin's novel *Eugene Onegin*: commentary, 1980), *Aleksandr Sergeevich Pushkin: Biografiia pisatelia* (Aleksandr Sergeevich Pushkin: A biography of the writer, 1981), the "Literaturnye pamiatniki" (Literary Monuments) edition of Karamzin's *Pis'ma russkogo puteshestvennika* (Letters of a Russian traveller, 1984), and *Sotvorenie Karamzina* (The creation of Karamzin, 1987). These works are among Lotman's most significant and it is clear from his correspondence of the time that they are also dear to their author/editor and, the biographies of Pushkin and Karamzin especially, summational or "stock-taking" with regard to his career.[7] It was here that Lotman, now often reminded of his own deteriorating health, set out to demonstrate the full human potential of his semiotic science.[8] What is striking from our point of view is that these works provide their own *textual* evidence of Lotman's turn, begun in the late 1970s and fully realized in the 1980s,[9] towards a modified Bakhtinian position with regard to code: in other words, these works are textually oriented both in terms of their subjects (the concrete "texts" of Karamzin's and Pushkin's lives and works) and in terms of the more "natural" (thus multiply coded, potentially *personal*)[10] language of Lotman's own writing. Two documents, virtually contemporaneous, are particularly useful to us as we examine Lotman's mature application of code: the until recently unpublished preface to the Polish edition of the Pushkin biography (1995a, 85–88) and the first chapter of the Karamzin biography, "Roman-rekonstruktsiia" (1987, 11–14).

In the preface to the Polish edition, Lotman begins in his characteristically tactful fashion by appealing to his Polish readership: his work was not written with the present audience in mind, so he begs the Poles' indulgence for his own potential cultural bias and points them to an excellent biography in Polish (by W. Woroszylski) for additional "context". Then he proceeds — in a way that is never made so explicit in the Russian edition — to explain the challenge he set himself in writing such a biography: he was trying to show the human, personal (as in *lichnoe, lichnost´*) element in the science of semiotics.

> I have come to hear more than once that semiotic research, by occupying itself with the analysis of texts, loses sight of the complexity of the living human personality [*zhivaia chelovecheskaia lichnost´*]. History, say the opponents of semiotics, is the history of people, and not of texts and codes. And it is precisely this — the human — aspect of history that remains, in their opinion, outside the possibilities of semiotic research. (1995a, 85)

This is the bias that Lotman is trying to overturn by telling Pushkin's story: "social man" or the "man mixing with others" (*obshchaiushchiisia chelovek*) is also, whether we like the scientific pretensions of the language or not, "semiotic man" (*semioticheskii chelovek*). But the humanizing element in this scientific approach comes through the presence of dialogue, and here Lotman must have known for certain that his words had a definite Bakhtinian ring to them: "The life of man is a continuous dialogue with those around him and with himself, and it can be examined according to the laws of the dialogic text" (1995a, 86).

Thus, technically speaking, Lotman has set himself the task of examining the writer's "biography as the object of semiotic culturology" (86). But the fact of the matter is that Lotman does not, in this most important of cultural cases (Pushkin's biography!), want to speak technically. Indeed, he imposes a genre on himself — a "textbook for pupils" (*posobie dlia uchashchikhsia*) at the publishing house "Prosveshchenie" (Enlightenment) — that is maximally "simple", straightforward, non-technical:

> Assuming that any scientific truth can be, once it has attained a certain level of maturity, expressed in a generally accessible language, and [assuming as well] that a complex system of specialized metalanguage can be likened to scaffolding around a building — it is necessary while the building is being constructed, but can be removed when the latter is ready — I wanted to attempt to write a book in such a way that to read it one would not need any specialized training in semiotics, and that to the reader a semiotic view towards life would seem not only natural but for this very same reader long since familiar [lit. "characteristic"]. (1995a, 86)

Lotman was hoping, at least explicitly, that by writing such a biography he would be demonstrating that semiotic science had come of age. This was the actual test case to prove all the semiotic calculations and "formulas". However, in taking on this genre, much the same way that Pushkin would take on a genre as a test of his own ingenuity, Lotman was simultaneously moving in the opposite direction: towards the personal, as opposed to the abstract and purely descriptive; towards the unique, as opposed to the predictable and replicable; and finally towards the creative (the linguistically heterogenous and potentially *unpredictable*), as opposed to the monologic and "closed" (his semiotic metalanguage). In other words, the "protean" nature of Lotman's experiments with "scholarly" genres in the 1980s had a familiar ring to it.

But Lotman had yet another challenge in mind when he undertook to write the Pushkin biography, and it is at this point that we come face to face with his simultaneous convergence on, and divergence from, the Bakhtinian animus towards codes. First, the distinction:

The study of cultural semiotics introduces us to two possible situations:

(1) General codes for the given collective determine the nature of texts generated by the personality. [Such] texts do not have an individual character and present themselves merely as the automatic realization of the laws of socio-cultural grammars.

(2) Texts are generated by the personality according to the laws of a grammar arising *ad hoc*. With respect to already existent socio-semiotic norms, [these] texts present themselves as a shift, a violation, a "scandal". (1995a, 86)

It was of course the first category of *texts determined by codes* that Bakhtin had taken issue with in his "Iz zapisei 1970–1971" and that Lotman had come to realize was not sufficently flexible to cover all situations in cultural semiotics. Bakhtin saw, a priori, the dialogic situation as happening between the two (or more) concrete, actual consciousnesses involved. A person, say a Decembrist like Lunin or Pestel´, could model his behaviour on that of the Romans or Spartans, but the "dialogue" that ensued from this modelling process would necessarily be different, if in terms of nothing other than its "context" (Russian, nineteenth-century, post-Napoleonic, and so on) from the original source (for example, Caesar's death, Cato's glorious deed, Hector's leaving for battle) (see Lotman 1985, 110; 1992–1993, I: 307).

But what Lotman had pointed out, and correctly, in his pathbreaking work on the Decembrists, is that much of these young nobles' behaviour *did* have a monologic/monolithic cast to it: consciously, because the situation demanded resolve, they were inserting their own lives into ancient *plots* which obliged them to act in certain honourable, brave, chivalrous ways, neither playful nor "double-voiced". Hence they were creating texts, to use Lotman's formulation, not of "individual character" (except that each would, as a member of the collective, enter history in this significant way) but ones that "automatically realized the laws of socio-cultural grammars". To be sure, there were numerous plots, whose variations meant that this behaviour was never absolutely predictable or marionette-like, but all the same the use of a "modelling" approach to the "texts" of these lives appeared entirely appropriate. The pathos of the Decembrists' situation was that they *willingly* emplotted their lives after such ancient types of heroic civic duty.[11] This was their romanticism, their "poetic" as opposed to "novelistic" behaviour: their lives, even their everyday lives, had to signify in precisely this *emplotted* manner. All else was insignificant and thus not worthy of comment/inclusion, which is to say, for these individuals the "prosaic" could not yet "mean".[12] In this case, the unfinalizable speech act did not encompass the urge for an integral, finalizable biography, but the other way around.

That Lotman could study this type of behaviour in context and not see it as something inevitably to be overcome on the path to "novelization" is one of his distinctive accomplishments. However, it is his second formulation that for us deserves special attention because in it he broaches more explicitly than heretofore a biographically generative definition of code. In this instance, the texts (of art, of a life) are not determined beforehand by a plot or code, but *created individually, on an ad hoc basis, according to an emerging grammar*. This shift sounds almost Bakhtinian, but is it really? As Lotman continues in the following paragraph:

> It is precisely this second instance that can be characterized as the activity of semiotic creation [*semioticheskoe tvorchestvo*]. As applied to the "text of life" these instances can be characterized as alternatives: either circumstances impose norms of behaviour and a type of action on the individual [i.e., the Decembrist model — DMB], or the individual transforms [lit. "transfigures"

— *preobrazuet*] circumstances according to the laws of his own internal norm. In the first instance, the person's life acquires the character of a "model biography" [*tipovaia biografiia*], while in the second, even when what finally awaits him is defeat or destruction, the person becomes a creative participant in his own life. (1995a, 86)

Lotman is suggesting that the second type of personality (here Pushkin, later Karamzin) has a special orientation towards the text of its life. It finds a way *to use* the codes and behavioural norms for its own benefit, as an artist works with his medium:

One can liken him [the creative personality] to a sculptor and the circumstances of life to the stone with which he enters into struggle, opposing the stubbornness of his design to the stubbornness of the material. A sculptor cannot complain of the fact that the granite presented to him is too hard, because the resistance of the material enters into the energy-supplying [*energeticheskii*] moment of creation. (1995a, 86)[13]

This is, I would submit, one of Lotman's most profound insights. For the genuinely creative personality the "code" exists only as precondition, firm footing from which to push off, but after that it exists *to be overcome*. Whether metre or rhyme scheme or strophic design in a poem or rules for duelling or gambling in life, the code is not a ready-made plot (as in the case of the Decembrists' modelling from Roman sources). It is not a totalizing model to follow. Rather it is a formal occasion that guarantees *in advance* that the emerging plot (that is, the finished poem, the completed duel or card game) will produce a change, *but one that is itself not necessarily predictable*. Signifying turning-points in a biography, which to a literary sensibility always evoke the spectre of pre-existing codes, are perceived as belonging more to the authoring personality than to the modelling codes. Pushkin and Karamzin were creative precisely because the literary roles/masks they routinely donned at various stages of their careers (for example, that of Byronic apprentice in Pushkin's case, that of student and naive, sentimental traveller in Karamzin's) allowed them freedom in the privacy of their own thoughts to develop personalities that had little to do with those masks and indeed could be seen in retrospect to actually oppose them. Also fascinating in this connection is the fact that the only way the lucid and always reasonable Lotman can himself tap the "energy-supplying moment of creation" is by bending his own language towards the slightly "murky" pole of poetic expressiveness, the metaphor of the sculptor and his stone.

While certain of Bakhtin's students could successfully apply the philosopher's ideas to aspects of Pushkin's work (for example, Sergei Bocharov on voice zones in *Evgenii Onegin*), Bakhtin appeared less original, less "himself", when the topic was Pushkin. The reason is that Bakhtinian thought, with its concealed (almost Hegelian?) teleology, its drive towards ever emerging novelization, cannot account for the poetic *use* of codes: the idea that a personality can fully acknowledge the arbitrariness of a fixed form and yet willingly adopt that form to generate energy and construct a life that is, yes, open. Pushkinian thought, in Bakhtinian terms, is balanced *between* the epic and the novel, understanding both yet giving itself fully to neither: as opposed to the Decembrists, it already sees the potential for "prosaic" signification, but as opposed to the great realists of the next generation, it is not yet ready to "monologize" fully the "poetic", that is, to expose artistic convention as not only arbitrary but *false* and *wrong* because it is so. The visual *ostranenie* (making-strange) of Natasha Rostova's visit to the opera or the verbal/psychological "double-voicedness" of Ippolit Terent´ev's confession, where one can plead in public for one's own dignity, is unthinkable to Pushkin.

The mark of the mature Pushkinian hero is an awareness of the necessity of codes together with the inability of any one "plot" to encompass "life". This is what Lotman grasps. To repeat, a set of rules for behaving in a conventional situation (such as a duel) is not the same as a literary plot or the ancient recording of a heroic life. The one is merely a *point d'appui*, the other an actual "situational" template.[14] One reason Pushkin as authoring consciousness of *Pikovaia dama* (The queen of spades) cannot allow his character German to win is that the latter wants to cheat the code: to gamble is just that, to follow the code in the *chance* that one's fortunes might improve. A change will take place that one is not allowed to know in advance. Likewise with Masha Mironova and Petr Grinev in *Kapitanskaia dochka* (The Captain's daughter): here the code, the starting point, is a nobleman's honour and his oath to his sovereign, while the "game", a brutal peasant rebellion, is much more complex and much less formalized. As long as the code is followed in good faith, however, the plot will take care of itself. In Pushkin's "purer" fiction, say *Povesti Belkina* (Tales of Belkin), where the historical theme is less pronounced and characters are allowed to engage in metaliterary games, we find examples such as Aleksei and Liza in "Baryshnia-krest´ianka" (Mistress into maid), who know all along they are *acting out* aspects of other writers' *siuzhety*, but use those various emplotments to get at their genuine, exuberant natures. They end up being *greater than* the ability of any one plot to contain them. "Life" emerges triumphant, but it is a life uniquely aware of literary role-playing and conventions.

This logic, which Lotman more than any other recent commentator was aware of, was applied by him with inspiring elegance to Pushkin's own biography. Together with Stella Abramovich, whose outstanding work on the last year of Pushkin's life confirmed his own hypotheses,[15] Lotman came to the view that the Pushkin who duelled with d'Anthès was neither "seeking death" (the romantic fallacy) nor at the moment of his fatal encounter any longer "at the mercy" of the court society that had been threatening his reputation over the final months (the sociological fallacy) (see 1981, 245–46). In other words, Pushkin forced the use of the duelling code on the other side, knowing that *some change* (for example, exile to the country with his wife and family or death on his terms) would take place. And far from causing anxiety, this turning of his fate over to an artificial code gave him, for the first time in months, peace of mind and, possibly (had he lived), renewed *creative energy*. What Pushkin was willing to do was *gamble,* in the true spirit of gambling; under no circumstances, however, was he willing to be the pitiful figure, the cuckolded husband, in someone else's lowbrow comedy of manners. This, for example, is how Lotman describes Pushkin at the time of the final duel:

> Having taken the decisive step [i.e., having written Baron Heckeren such an insulting letter that the latter's adoptive son d'Anthès would have no choice but to answer the challenge], Pushkin immediately, according to the accounts of contemporaries, calmed down and became "especially jovial". He was planning to live, full of literary projects; setting off for the duel, he wrote the children's writer A.O. Ishimova a business letter asking for translations for *Sovremennik*. The letter, written just hours before the fatal duel, ended with the words, "Today I accidentally opened your *History in Stories* [*Istoriia v rasskazakh*], and, not intending to, fell to reading it. That's how one should write!" These were the last lines written by Pushkin's hand. (1981, 244)

Pushkin, then, was using the code, not the finished plot, in order to be the author of his life *up to the end*. As terrifying as it sounds, it really did not matter what happened: in any case, it would be on Pushkin's terms. There were things that mattered to Pushkin more than merely staying alive (his honour, his family's privacy, his reputation in the eyes of history). But the code, itself a closed set of rules, guaranteed a "poetic" merging of text and context because Pushkin had both the cognitive awareness and the daring to gamble on a new meaning. Lotman's language towards the end of the biography, his use of elevated diction when describing the hero ("Pushkin died not defeated [*pobezhdennym*], but victorious [*pobeditelem*]" [1981, 245]) and of emotionally tinged, even sarcastic terms when describing the court and the Heckeren faction ("light vaudeville" [*legkii vodevil*], "young good-for-nothings" [*molodye shalopai*], "their pygmy-like nonentity" [*ikh nichtozhestvo pigmeev*] [1981, 248]), shows to what extent he himself has been drawn into this drama, how much he personally is *inspired* by it. Thus, the code, rather than being synonymous, in Bakhtin's phrasing, with "an intentionally fixed, killed context", is that formal unit which, while not determining the outcome, enables poetic behaviour in life. It gives back to the authoring *lichnost´* an element of choice, not the free choice of result but the opportunity to provoke change.

In his work on Karamzin, Lotman goes farther still in the direction of poetic language. By now there is clearly something to lose in this gamble, beginning with the scholar-theoretician's reputation for rigour, objectivity, and "good taste", as Lotman tells his friend Egorov in a moment of touching self-deflation:

> The publishing house ["Kniga" — DMB] has set as a condition that the book [*Sotvorenie Karamzina*] be "literary" (in the agreement there is even the phrase "artistic prose" — may they all go to hell!). But "artistry" [*khudozhestvennost´*] fits me like a foxtrot fits an elephant. I'm so afraid that it will turn out vulgar [*poshlo*] and bad, just like I can't stand in others. (Letter of 12 July 1985; 1995d, 74)

Yet still Lotman persists. He even devises a new genre, something he calls a "novel of reconstruction" (*roman-rekonstruktsiia*), in order to penetrate that narrow space between Karamzin's literary masks and the always partially concealed actual biographical face of the writer beneath.

The story opens with an extended allegory, a dramatically announced *artistic* trope, about an archaeological site. Once upon a time there was a master builder who wanted to create a beautiful temple (*khram*), but one that was, paradoxically, "free" (*svobodnyi*). That is, the temple would be built not according to a fixed design, but according to an ideal that itself would change as the actual edifice rose up out of the chosen island site. But now many centuries have passed, and it is the job of the archaeologist, with his specialized tools (books, maps, shovel) and his specialized language (the draughtsman's), to return to the site and reconstruct, shard by moss-covered shard, what was once the magnificent building: "Reconstruction is never uncontested and final: after all, one has to re-erect not a model barracks [*tipovaia kazarma*], but a creation of individual genius, one has to guess not only what *was* done by the builder, but what *was not*, what he rejected, what he did not want to do or what he wanted to, but could not" (1987, 12).

As Lotman's allegory quickly makes clear in the following paragraphs, the creative biography of Karamzin is just such a "free temple" and he, Iurii Lotman, has come upon its site as just such an archaeologist-biographer.[16] Nowhere in all his hundreds of articles, books, editions, commentaries, and notes, does Lotman speak so openly and so freely, with such conscious aesthetic framing, about the educated guesswork required to retrieve the *tvorcheskaia lichnost´* (creative personality). He tells the reader that this new genre is "special" (*osobyi*): its practitioner must possess a "combination of precise knowledge and intuition and imagination [. . .]. The researcher and the novelist serve equally as co-authors in the creation of the biographical novel of reconstruction" (1987, 12–13). As opposed to Tynianov in his biographical novels, Lotman's novelist-reconstructor does not have the right, based on tangential evidence, to "invent" certain of his hero's thoughts or speeches (the most notorious example being Tynianov's novelizing Pushkin's "secret love" as Karamzin's wife).[17] The quarry is not a compelling story based on new "dramatic" discoveries,[18] but something else: "the recreation of that integral ideal of personality [compare the earlier image of the *"free* temple"], which the hero of the biography created in his soul" (1987, 13). What is specifically poetic about Lotman's approach, what brings it closer than ever to primary creation from the vantage of pure reconstructive scholarship, is its emphasis on the integrity and beauty of the personality studied and on the not unrelated fact that Lotman himself is made "free" (inspired) by his own self-imposed generic constraints. "The novel of reconstruction is sterner and in a way poorer than the biographical novel. But it has one primary advantage, the urge to come maximally close to a reconstructed reality, to the genuine personality of the one on whom the author has focused his attention" (1987, 13).

The plot of Karamzin's life is, Lotman argues, not merely pre-Pushkinian (the temporal principle), but the very foundation on which the archetypal Russian poet's life became possible in the first place (the causal, enabling principle). This plot was not about creating his (Karamzin's) own fully poeticized life (a romantic concept that had to await Napoleon and Byron); it was rather about creating a Russian reader who for the first time could sit at the feast of European culture not as a bumbling, xenophobic outsider, but as someone with his (or, as was more often the case, her) honour and dignity intact. In this respect, Karamzin's "reforms" — of language, of sensibility, of standards of civility — were no less epochal than Peter's, a fact of which the publicly self-effacing Karamzin was no doubt aware (see 1987, 228–30). The drama in Karamzin's biographical plot, which Lotman's combing of the "archaeological site" brings out brilliantly, had little to do with the writer's personal fate: Karamzin did not maintain diaries, never spoke of the shape of his own life openly, and indeed kept his inner world "hermetically sealed" (17) from outsiders, which included virtually everyone.

No, the drama in Karamzin's story came from his use of literary masks — especially those of the naive, sentimental traveller, of the dandy, and of the pedant — to *create his reader*, to coax him into the world of European culture, letters, politics, and science without reminding him that he does not "belong". To do this, Karamzin had to devise a persona, as he does in *Pis'ma russkogo puteshestvennika*, who effortlessly shifts between positions of "less than" (less perceptive, less worldly, less self-absorbed) and "more than" (more knowledgeable, more educated, on equal footing with the great minds of Europe) his reader, with the result that the latter becomes civilized along the way. Over and over again Lotman demonstrates the inner workings of this mystification: the dates in the *Pis'ma* that do not "fit" the actual itinerary, the submerged biographies behind fleeting initials, the "impressions" of a great cultural or historical figure that the actual Karamzin knew much better, from works or deeds, than his "simple" surrogate. Again, why? Because in this way Karamzin's silly speaker could suddenly become, without anyone really noticing it (in fact, everyone naturally assumed this speaker was Karamzin himself), "a worthy interlocutor not only of Swiss innkeepers and Parisian 'nymphs of joy'", but also of Kant, Lavoisier, Herder (1987, 24). Aesthetic play acquired moral, heuristic value, while the "real" Karamzin, always tactful, always more than any mask and any emerging reader, remained behind the scenes as history's witness: "This [the incompatibility of the masks] gave the image thus created great inner freedom and unpredictability of behaviour for the reader" (1987, 24).

In conclusion, I would like to suggest, in the spirit of "responsible speculation", how Karamzin's biography was especially significant to Lotman, perhaps even more than Pushkin's. For Karamzin, like Lotman himself, was above all an enlightener, one who believed that the literary and aesthetic codes available to us exist *to civilize*, to generate new information and more informed readers. But this is, ultimately, a very difficult process *inside which* to shape, to synchronize, to nourish one's own life: the successful civilizing of one's readers.[19] It is not by chance, I suspect, that Lotman came back to Karamzin this way at the end of his own career[20] and that he reserves some of his warmest commentary for this man who, unlike Pushkin, was somehow more than his written texts. (Logically speaking, Pushkin's words themselves are always so full of creative energy — the verbal equivalent of a fire without ash — that it is impossible to say he is more than they are.) But Karamzin's combination of enlightened scepticism meant that at the end, unlike the great poet and the great poetic life his presence would enable, he could not personalize his triumph. Why? Because the codes Karamzin used to generate meaning — the etiquette of the salon, a daily regimen oriented towards intellectual labour, a family life that ran smoothly, a position as court historian whose role was honest, independent witness — all pointed to *invisibility*, to the absence of *personal drama*, to the outside position of a moderating consciousness (less primarily "poetic" than "enlightening") that wanted its work to speak for it. So, while he was a man of impeccable honour, decency, and independent thought, Karamzin felt most at home with those codes of the enlightenment that "smoothed over" and patiently, tactfully explained, thereby creating not the presence but the absence of drama and explosive change. The codes to which Pushkin had recourse in moments of crisis, on the other hand, duelling and gambling in particular, were society's ways of civilizing *disruption*: they were tailor-made, in the wake of the new romantic biography, for dramatizing turning-points and denouements.

Inasmuch as the modest Lotman was able to do so, he made a special plea for Karamzin — a plea that Pushkin was in no need of — that was potentially self-referential. What he said in this case was what his reminiscences of perhaps the "dryest" Pushkinist, Boris Tomashevskii, intimated as well: "In order to study the creative work of a writer, even as one consciously strives to the limits of objectivity, the scholar must find in his subject something that resonates with him, a kind of mirrored space, in which he himself can be reflected" (1995b, 58). One reason, I suspect, Lotman was so moved by the example of Karamzin was that, while Karamzin still *created himself*, he did so *without a poetic life*; Pushkin, on the other hand, created himself with and through one. Karamzin entered Russian culture, much like Lotman will by the way, as a *principle* of honour, dignity, fair play and tact, hard work, truly awesome knowledge, respect for the past, and so on, but not as a biography that could dramatize this accomplishment. Thus, at strategic moments of the book, especially at the beginning and the ending, Lotman uses utterly non-scientific language to bond with his hero and, presumably, *his own future reader*, in the name of Russian culture, in the name of a spiritual generosity Lotman knows is virtually "untellable" as plot.

First, the beginning:

> Karamzin created Karamzin. He created him his entire life as a writer. He created him consciously and steadfastly. Creating literary works and creating for the reader an authorial image, Karamzin simultaneously created a reader. He created a type of new Russian cultural man. [...] The defining trait of Karamzin's personality became precisely his wholeness/integrity [*tsel'nost'*]. Various masks blended, joined into a unity. Its basis was a unity of the writer's and reader's honour. Karamzin entered into Russian culture as a man and writer who was not subject to circumstances and who stood above them. (1987, 29)

While Lotman himself would never make the connection, we, his students, can: is this not also a picture of another author's remarkable self-creation, of the unity behind his personality's many "masks": "simple" soldier and comrade,[21] viewer of history's catastrophes from ground level, brilliant scientist, founder of a school of thought, family man, inventive *cuisinier*, gracious host, witty interlocutor, lover of all manner of verbal game-playing,[22] self-deprecating cartoonist, indefatigable lecturer, generous mentor to scores of students, literary historian/biographer/close reader extraordinaire, "in spirit and behaviour, one of [his] country's last noblemen [*odnim iz poslednikh dvorian*]" (Vl. Uspenskii 1995, 102)?[23] Is this also not the creator of a type of new Russian cultural man, *homo semioticus*, the quintessential *obshchaiushchiisia chelovek*?

Then, the ending:

> Several months before his death Mikhail Mikhailovich Bakhtin uttered the splendid words: "There is nothing that is absolutely dead: every idea will have its holiday of rebirth." [...] Karamzin is returning to our literature *as a personality*. [I have in mind] his living countenance, his soul — and may I be forgiven for this not very stylish idea, perhaps almost as necessary to contemporary literature as his works themselves. [...] Literature is not a shelf of books, it is a living organism, and this organism survives on the unity of its atmosphere, on the presence of indisputable values. [...] The atmosphere of honourability, of spiritual nobility, of the fearless search for truth: this is the air of literature. Without it, literature will die.
> But this atmosphere is created only at the cost of great and difficult personal efforts.
> Karamzin created many works, among them the marvellous *Pis'ma russkogo puteshestvennika* and the magnificent *Istoriia gosudarstva Rossiiskogo*. But Karamzin's greatest creation was himself, his life, his inspired personality [*odukhotvorennaia lichnost'*]. (1987, 319–20)

Is this not also an appropriate epitaph for Bakhtin's greatest interlocutor, the one whose *odukhotvorennaia lichnost'* split the poetic codes of Russian culture the way his alter-ego Albert Einstein taught us to split the atom?

REFERENCES

Abramovich, S., 1994. *Predystoriia poslednei dueli Pushkina: Ianvar' 1836 – ianvar' 1837* (St Petersburg: Petropolis).

Bakhtin, M. M., 1979a. "K metodologii gumanitarnykh nauk", in *Estetika slovesnogo tvorchestva* (Moscow: Iskusstvo), 361–73.

———, 1979b. "Iz zapisei 1970-1971", in *Estetika slovesnogo tvorchestva* (Moscow: Iskusstvo), 336–60.

Daniel', S. M., 1995. "Iz memuarov byvshego studenta-zaochnika", in E.V. Permiakov (ed.), *Lotmanovskii sbornik 1* (Moscow: Its-Garant), 151–59.

Eco, U., 1990. "Introduction", in Yuri M. Lotman, *Universe of the Mind: A Semiotic Theory of Culture*, trans. Ann Shukman (Bloomington: Indiana University Press), vii-xiii.

Egorov, B. F., 1994. "Polveka s Iu.M. Lotmanom", in *Iu.M. Lotman i tartusko-moskovskaia semioticheskaia shkola* (Moscow: Gnozis), 475–85.

Emerson, C., (forthcoming). "Russian Theories of the Novel", in Malcolm V. Jones and Robin Feuer Miller (eds), *Cambridge Companion to the Russian Novel* (Cambridge: Cambridge University Press).

Grzybek, P., 1995. "Bakhtinskaia semiotika i moskovsko-tartuskaia shkola", in E.V. Permiakov (ed.), *Lotmanovskii sbornik 1* (Moscow: Its-Garant), 240–59.

Kamenskaia, V. A., 1995. "O Iurii Mikhailoviche Lotmane — snizu vverkh", in E.V. Permiakov (ed.), *Lotmanovskii sbornik 1* (Moscow: Its-Garant), 160-74.

Karamzin, N. M., 1984. *Pis'ma russkogo puteshestvennika*, Iu.M. Lotman, N.A. Marchenko, B.A. Uspenskii (eds), "Literaturnye pamiatniki" series (Leningrad: Nauka).

Lotman, L. M., 1995. "Moi vospominaniia o brate Iurii Mikhailoviche Lotmane: Detskie i iunosheskie gody", in E.V. Permiakov (ed.), *Lotmanovskii sbornik 1* (Moscow: Its-Garant), 128–50.

Lotman, Iu. M., 1980. *Roman A.S. Pushkina 'Evgenii Onegin': Kommentarii* (Leningrad: Prosveshchenie).

_____, 1981. *Aleksandr Sergeevich Pushkin: Biografiia pisatelia* (Leningrad: Prosveshchenie).

_____, 1983. "Kul'tura i tekst kak generatory smysla", in *Kiberneticheskaia lingvistika* (Moscow), 23–30.

_____, 1985. "The Decembrist in Daily Life (Everyday Behavior as a Historical-Psychological Category)", in Alexander D. Nakhimovsky and Alice Stone Nakhimovsky (eds), *The Semiotics of Russian Cultural History*, intro. Boris Gasparov (Ithaca: Cornell University Press), 95–149.

_____, 1986. "K sovremennomu poniatiiu teksta", *Uchenye zapiski Tartuskogo gosudarstvennogo universiteta*, 736: 104–08.

_____, 1987. *Sotvorenie Karamzina*, "Pisateli o pisateliakh" series (Moscow: Kniga).

_____, 1990a. "Autocommunication: 'I' and 'Other' as Addressees", in Yuri M. Lotman, *Universe of the Mind: A Semiotic Theory of Culture*, trans. Ann Shukman, intro. Umberto Eco (Bloomington: Indiana University Press), 20–35.

_____, 1990b. "Preface", in Yuri M. Lotman, *Universe of the Mind: A Semiotic Theory of Culture*, trans. Ann Shukman, intro. Umberto Eco (Bloomington: Indiana University Press), 1–7.

_____, 1990c. "Three Functions of the Text", in Yuri M. Lotman, *Universe of the Mind: A Semiotic Theory of Culture*, trans. Ann Shukman, intro. Umberto Eco (Bloomington: Indiana University Press), 11–19.

_____, 1992. *Kul'tura i vzryv* (Moscow: Gnozis).

_____, 1992-1993. *Izbrannye stat'i*, 3 vols. (Tallinn: Aleksandra).

_____, 1994a. "O dueli Pushkina bez 'tain' i zagadok", in Stella Abramovich, *Predystoriia poslednei dueli Pushkina: Ianvar´1836 – ianvar´1837* (St Petersburg: Petropolis), 326-38.

_____, 1994b. "Zametki o tartuskikh semioticheskikh izdaniiakh", in *Iu.M. Lotman i tartusko-moskovskaia semioticheskaia shkola* (Moscow: Gnozis), 497–501.

_____, 1994c. "Zimnie zametki o letnikh shkolakh", in *Iu.M. Lotman i tartusko-moskovskaia semioticheskaia shkola* (Moscow: Gnozis), 295–98.

_____, 1995a. "'Aleksandr Sergeevich Pushkin: Biografiia pisatelia'. Predislovie k pol´skomu izdaniiu", in E.V. Permiakov (ed.), *Lotmanovskii sbornik 1* (Moscow: Its-Garant), 85-88.

_____, 1995b. "Dvoinoi portret", in E.V. Permiakov (ed.), *Lotmanovskii sbornik 1* (Moscow: Its-Garant), 54–71.

_____, 1995c. "Ne-memuary", in E.V. Permiakov (ed.), *Lotmanovskii sbornik 1* (Moscow: Its-Garant), 6–53.

_____, 1995d. "Pis´ma o Karamzine", in E.V. Permiakov (ed.), *Lotmanovskii sbornik 1*, notes and commentary B.F. Egorov (Moscow: Its-Garant), 72–78.

Mandelker, A., 1994. "Semiotizing the Sphere: Organicist Theory in Lotman, Bakhtin, and Vernadsky", *PMLA* 109 (May): 385–96.

Ponzio, A., 1984. "Semiotics Between Peirce and Bakhtin", *Recherches Semiotiques — Semiotic Inquiry* 4: 273-92.

Reid, A., 1990. "Who is Lotman and Why is Bakhtin Saying Those Nasty Things About Him?", *DISCOURS SOCIAL/Social Discourse* 3 (Spring-Summer): 311–24.

Uspenskii, V. A., 1995. "Progulki s Lotmanom i vtorichnoe modelirovanie", in E.V. Permiakov (ed.), *Lotmanovskii sbornik 1* (Moscow: Its-Garant), 99–127.

Voloshinov, V. N., 1930. *Marksizm i filosofiia iazyka: Osnovnye problemy sotsiologicheskogo metoda v nauke o iazyke*, 2nd ed. (Leningrad: Priboi).

NOTES

1.   "In the course of his research Lotman realized that a code identified in a culture is much more complex than that which can be identified in a language and his analyses became increasingly subtle and took on a rich, complex historical awareness" (Eco 1990, xii). For a succinct description of Lotman's own understanding of how "code" functions in Saussurean versus Jakobsonian linguistics, see "Three Functions of the Text" (1990c, 11–19). It is here, *inter alia*, that Lotman, expanding on Jakobson's "poetic function", speaks about a semiotic code as potentially including "not only a certain binary set of rules for encoding and decoding a message, but also a multi-dimensional hierarchy",

which can have a "creative function" — that is, it can do more than transmit ready-made messages, it can "serve as a generator of new ones" (13). Lotman then shows in "Autocommunication: 'I' and 'Other' as addressees" how the Jakobsonian communication model can be modified, precisely at the level of code, in certain "I-I" situations involving complex or "secondary-modelling" speech (the poetic speaker delivering a "message" to himself): "the 'I-I' system qualitatively transforms the information, and this leads to a restructuring of the actual 'I' itself" (1990a, 22). It is the element of human *choice* and *self-creation* in this "recoding" that we will be examining in the essay below. All translations of texts are my own.

2. For more on the later Lotman's turn towards "organicist" models under the influence of Vernadskii ("biosphere") and Bakhtin ("logosphere"), see Mandelker 1994.

3. See, for instance: "Every utterance is only a moment of continuous discursive interaction" (Voloshinov 1930, 97); or "There is no such thing as an isolated utterance" (Bakhtin 1979b, 340); or "Every word (every sign) of a text leads beyond its boundaries. Any understanding is the correlation of a given text to other texts [...] and their reinterpretation [*pereosmyslenie*] in a new context (mine, the present's, the future's). [...] We emphasize that this contact is the dialogic contact between texts (utterances)" (Bakhtin 1979a, 364).

4. Bakhtin mentions Lotman at least twice in these late writings, both times somewhat critically. See, for example, the following from "Iz zapisei 1970–1971": "The understanding of multiplicity of styles [*mnogostil´nost´*] in *Evgenii Onegin* (see Lotman) as a *recoding* [*perekodirovanie*] (of romanticism to realism, etc.) leads to the falling away of the most important *dialogic* moment and to the transforming of a dialogue of styles into the simple existence of different versions of the same thing. . . . The code assumes some sort of ready state of content and the realization of a choice among *given* codes" (1979b, 339). Elsewhere Bakhtin complains that, while Lotman sees the "logical" categories of "opposition" and "shift in codes", he "hears voices" (1979a, 372). For a useful discussion of Bakhtin's comments about Lotman, see Reid 1990.

5. See, for example, his "Preface" to *Universe of the Mind* (1990), which he concluded with a section entitled "After Saussure". In these pages, Lotman cites all the advances in "scientific thought" about language made by those such as Bakhtin, Propp, Jakobson, and Peirce, but he reserves a special place for Saussure, "whose works [...] remain in force as the foundation stones of semiotics" (1990b, 5). Thus, even at this late date Lotman is absolutely comfortable speaking about semiotics both as a "scientific discipline" and a "method of the humanities" (4). By the same token, two of Saussure's ideas remain valid to Lotman, undergirding his work as theorist (i.e., explorer of semiotic *langue*) and literary scholar/

historian/critic (i.e. explorer of semiotic *parole*), right to the end: "the opposition language [*langue*] and speech [*parole*] (or code and text)", and "the opposition: synchrony and diachrony" (1990b, 5).

6.   Perhaps because he never doubted the fundamental ("scientific") truth of the Saussurean oppositions? Perhaps because these first truths belonged to Saussure and to science "in general", and so their refinement over time was natural and expected (Lotman was apparently not threatened with the loss of intellectual "copyrights", whereas Bakhtin, who was not possessive with regard to his own "authorship", could not imagine his own thought developing outside its original dialogic framework)? In fairness to Bakhtin, however, it needs to be stressed that his critical comments about semiotics and Lotman come in random *notes* he wrote near the end of his life and may never have intended to publish.

7.   As Lotman confides to his friend B.F. Egorov in a letter of 18 February 1986: "In general I researched and wrote the book [*Sotvorenie Karamzina* — DMB] for income ('such am I in the nakedness of my cynicism', as Pushkin said), but it turned out as something not devoid of meaning, a kind of summing-up of my works [*itog rabot*] over a number of years" (1995d, 77).

8.   See Lotman's comments in the same letter cited in note 7: "For some reason I've gone down hill seriously over the last months. I look calmly at the approaching far shore of the crossing" (1995d, 78).

9.   "In the second half of the 1970s the concept of the text was reconsidered by the Moscow-Tartu School, especially in a series of articles by Lotman [e.g. 'Kul'tura kak kollektivnyi intellekt' (1977), 'Mozg — tekst — kul'tura — iskusstvennyi intellekt' (1981), 'Semiotika kul'tury i poniatie teksta' (1981), 'Kul'tura i tekst kak generatory smysla' (1983), 'K sovremennomu poniatiiu teksta' (1986)]. It is noteworthy that in these articles the original [i.e. that given by the Moscow-Tartu School] definition of the text is subjected to some adjustments in the spirit of Bakhtinian semiotics" (Grzybek 1995, 247). It is not fortuitous, in my opinion, that the later and more explicit of these theoretical articles were written contemporaneously with the text-oriented biographies of Pushkin and Karamzin.

10.   Lotman places "natural language" (*estestvennyi iazyk*), as in normal, everyday speech, in a position of "inside-between" (*vnutri-mezhdu*), which is to say, it can be located somewhere between artificial/meta-languages, on the one hand, and artistic or complex semiotic ("secondary modelling") languages, on the other. In this sense, "natural language" by nature is heterogenous and thus more "dialogic" (the connection here with Bakhtin's notion of heteroglossia should be obvious) than the metalanguage of the semiotician. (See Lotman 1983, 26; 1986, 104; 1990c, 14; and Grzybek 1995, 248–49.) By writing the biographies in a version of "natural language", Lotman was aesthetically complicating (not simplifying) his texts in order to bring them (and himself)

closer to the threshold of personal "meaning *generation*", which in the language of the poets is called inspiration. Not by chance, the "explosion" of inspiration will be one of the central topics of Lotman's last book, *Kul'tura i vzryv* (Culture and explosion, 1992).

11. "The difference [between 'routine behaviour' and 'signifying activity' — DMB] is essential: individuals do not select routine behaviour but rather acquire it from their society, from the historical period in which they live or from their psychological or physiological makeup; there is no alternative to it. Signifying behaviour, on the contrary, is always the result of choice. It always involves individuals' free activity, their choice of the language they will use in their relations with society" (Lotman 1985, 129; 1992–1993, I:321).

12. Lotman gives the illustrative example of Ryleev's semiotically marked *Russian* lunches (for example, in the "Spartan", pre-December 14 climate it was considered "effete" to stress "Gallic" values): one of the participants in these lunches, Mikhail Bestuzhev, remarks how he would see his colleagues pacing around the room with *cigars* and appetizers of *cabbage* while criticizing Zhukovskii's "obscure romanticism". The non-Russian cigars were semiotically "invisible", which is to say there was no bad faith in smoking them, because they were *just there*, as part of the non-signifying background. The Russian cabbage, on the other hand, had a semiotically loaded, ideological import. See Lotman 1985, 137; 1992–1993, I:327.

13. Lotman uses this same metaphor of the sculptor working with stone — he even uses the concrete image of Michelangelo — in an October 1986 letter (unpublished) to Boris Egorov explaining the central idea behind the Pushkin biography: everything the poet touched in life he, like King Midas, turned with fabulous alchemical efficiency to the gold of art. But King Midas's story ends sadly, as did Pushkin's, because he turned his food to gold as well, and by so doing starved. Lotman is in this letter quite passionate and even moving in defense of his idea: the fact that Pushkin worked with, struggled with, codes did not seem to him a matter of facile or cold-blooded "manipulation". Nor did it make Pushkin's biography less "tragic", quite the opposite in fact, so that Pushkin's story emerged as a "tragedy of strength" rather than a "tragedy of weakness". Lotman had been responding to his friend Egorov, who himself had argued that Lotman's Pushkin came across as too conscious, too predetermined: once again, the notion of codes as "fixed, mechanical". I might add that this, significantly, is not the only time Lotman resorts to the King Midas metaphor for creative behaviour: in his Preface to *Universe of the Mind*, he writes of the semiotic researcher (including of course himself!) that the latter "has the habit of transforming the world around him/her so as to show up the semiotic structures. Everything that King Midas touched with his golden hand turned to gold. In the same way, everything which the semiotic researcher turns his/her attention to becomes semioticized in his hands" (1990b,

5). My thanks to Mikhail Lotman and Boris Egorov for providing me a copy of the October 1986 letter.

14. Lotman was apparently approaching this idea when he applied A. Zorin's distinction between "role" and "situational" behaviour, between a mask affixed to a persona as opposed to a mask attached to a *bytovaia situatsiia* (everyday situation), in the closing pages of *Sotvorenie Karamzina* (1987, 318-19).

15. See Lotman's afterword ("O dueli Pushkina bez 'tain' i zagadok"), in Abramovich, *Predystoriia poslednei dueli Pushkina* (1994a, 326–38). This piece, first published as a review of Abramovich's 1984 edition of the same book, is important not only as a statement of Lotman's ideas *vis-à-vis* the "plot" of Pushkin's death but also as perhaps his most eloquent defence of the proper "rules" for undertaking biographical research.

16. Lotman uses this same extended archaeological metaphor towards the end of the Pushkin biography. See 1981, 226.

17. In this respect, it would be interesting to compare Lotman's methodology in *Sotvorenie Karamzina* to Khodasevich's in his *Derzhavin*.

18. See Lotman's opening comments in his afterword to Abramovich's *Predystoriia poslednei dueli Pushkina* (1994a, 326–28).

19. At risk of a crude biographism, I would like to propose that the ageing Lotman saw something quite concrete in common between himself and the hero of *Sotvorenie Karamzina*: a position that might be termed the "discarding of final illusions". Karamzin's had to do with his efforts to create an enlightened reader during his lifetime (Alexander I being the most important) who would make a difference (December 14 and its harsh Nikolaevan aftermath was the proof that the primary message of the great *Istoriia* — respect the past, learn from the past — had not been heeded); Lotman's had to do with his efforts to create a school of thought that would remain vital in the absence of *his* personality. As Lotman argues about Karamzin and as various memoirs and letters suggest about Lotman, both figures accepted the fact that they were coming to the end of their lives "without hope" and without what normally passes for religious faith (see 1987, 311; 1995d, 77; and Kamenskaia 1995, 172). Thus, when Lotman describes Karamzin's final, post-Decembrist mood as one of "the most total, the most bitter disenchantment", in which "final illusions have been tossed aside" (1987, 312), one might compare these sentiments to those in one of Lotman's own letters to Egorov written as he was trying to get *Sotvorenie* to press [that is, after July 1985]: "I [...] am approaching my freedom. My freedom is the freedom from illusions. When all the soap bubbles have burst, there remains only freedom. [...] Having come to the conclusion that I have no followers [lit. 'pupils' — *ucheniki*], that my laboratory, for which I strove so hard and which seemed so important, is also a soap bubble, like so much else, having lived through a series of difficult disenchantments, I've suddenly felt a sense of cheerfulness, not despair, even a kind of sense

of beginning, not of ending. And of freedom. [...] Disenchantment frees one from pretence, from the fear of telling oneself the truth" (1995d, 77). Lotman's more upbeat public statements about the historical significance of the Moscow-Tartu School, particularly the summer seminars he hosted, are found in "Zimnie zametki o letnikh shkolakh" (1994c, 295–98) and "Zametki o tartuskikh semioticheskikh izdaniiakh" (1994b, 497–501).

20. Lotman's very first works as a demobilized student at Leningrad State University were on Karamzin — his 1947 *kursovaia rabota* on Karamzin's *Vestnik Evropy* (Messenger of Europe) for his beloved mentor N.I. Mordovchenko's seminar, and then in 1948 his first major piece of research, on "Karamzin and the Masons". At the time, of course, Karamzin was considered a reactionary figure.

21. See "Ne-memuary", Lotman's tales of his life as a front-line *telefonist* in World War II, in *Lotmanovskii sbornik 1* (1995c, 5–53).

22. As one former student recalled, "Iurii Mikhailovich, despite all his enlightenment pathos, was always ready to enter into play. His charm was irresistible" (Daniel´ 1995, 155).

23. As Uspenskii goes on, "I think that it was in this personal 'nobility' [*dvorianstvo*] that a large part of his charm consisted". Other of Lotman's traits that come up repeatedly in the emerging memoir literature include: empathy towards others (his "richness of the heart's imagination", in his sister's apt phrase); the "chivalrous traits" of "politeness, steadfastness, fortitude, and ardour"; and of course his "interest in personality" (L.M. Lotman 1995, 130, 139, 145). Likewise, in Egorov's necrology: "A great scholar/scientist has departed from life. But also no less a great man, a preserver of the best traditions of Petersburg culture, a man steadfast, chivalrous [*rytsartsvennyi*], always giving of himself to those nearby" (Egorov 1994, 485).

CONFORM NOT TO THIS AGE: AN INTERVIEW WITH OL´GA SEDAKOVA

Valentina Polukhina

Ol´ga Sedakova is one of Russia's most respected poets, heir to the tradition of Osip Mandel´shtam and Velimir Khlebnikov. Her period of growth was the sluggish and stagnant 1980s but she has swiftly developed her own accent and emphasis. A vast knowledge of European poetry and love of the classics have helped her to form the foundation of her own vision. Also influenced by modern philosophy, she has borrowed many motifs from it, whilst her knowledge of modern music allows her to take a delicious liberty with the rhythm which plays an important role in the general semantic conception of her verse. She has, with all, a keen sense of history and shares the belief that poets were the inventors of civilization.

Her name is regarded by many as being synonymous with religious poetry, but she herself avoids that term because Christianity for her is not only a cultural, generative principle; it is not just enlightened conservatism; it can also be radical, a rejection of the world and all its cultures. Nevertheless, she is one of the best confessional Christian poets writing in Russian today. Her poetry is metaphysically and theologically thought-provoking and is a demonstration of the beauty of faith. This may, perhaps, help Sedakova to realize her greatest ambition: to return poetry to the Russian Orthodox Church and to give the Church to poetry. It is also true that religious and secular motifs are inseparable in her poetry. Water, earth, air and fire appear with particular frequency on the pages of Sedakova's work. Those four elements bring with them a whole range of mythical, theological and symbolic allusions to the origins of our civilization. Like her beloved Mandel'shtam, she appropriates the whole of civilization, in a very unobtrusive way, by charging her poems with obvious, obscure and abeyant cultural references. But this *poeta doctus* has nothing in common with the players of postmodernistic games (a written poem can be memorized) and she is only too aware of the poet's duty to avoid polluting human memory with trivial and nonsensical images.

Two poets have been of paramount importance to her. Dante and Rilke are both synonymous with poetry itself for Sedakova. From them she has learnt how to convey the incurable longing of the partial and private for wholeness and holiness. This aspiration gives her poems inner energy. The acoustic splendour of her poems contributes greatly to *le plaisir du texte*: for instance, *raz* and *roz* in *razvernesh'sia* and in *mirozdan'e* announce in advance the appearance of a rose in *Dikii shipovnik* (The wild rose); love for Christ is expressed in the anagram: *i belyi belee liubogo*. The wild rose is a symbol of the truly poetic transformation which is taking place in this poem. It is a breathtaking spiritual expansion which takes us beyond the horizon of our vision; indeed, it extends our vision. The desire to go "beyond oneself" in search of some ultimate meaning is expressed in many of Sedakova's poems. Her main interest is the knowledge of the spirit buried deep within us; to restore the life of the spirit was Sedakova's prime concern during the eighties as it is during the nineties.

Sedakova talks about her work and life in Russia in an extended interview which took place during her stay at Keele University, as Poet in Residence, in 1993–94.

Ol´ga Sedakova was interviewed by Valentina Polukhina
21–27 May 1994
Keele University

Valentina Polukhina: *Now that time has put some distance between us and the 1980s how does the poetic landscape of that decade appear to you?*
Ol´ga Sedakova: Now, as it did then, the poetry of the eighties appears to me to be rather chaotic. The literary situation which in the seventies had acquired a certain clarity became muddled and complicated; and that predates any liberalization by the authorities. In the seventies the illegal "second" culture separated from the official culture in much the same way as oil separates from water; there was hardly any confusion. Towards the end of the seventies they began to shake things up again.

Official literature began to lose its aesthetic solidity, many discoveries of the "second" culture, at home and in emigration, were taken up (for example, there was a growing fashion for imitating Brodsky amongst already established writers). Transitional movements began to appear; I would number amongst those the "Metametaphorist" group which crystallized around the Literary Institute (Aleksandr Eremenko, Aleksei Parshchikov and others); they were writers of an avant-garde tendency but, socially, I would say, they were quite close to the Writers' Union. And at the same time the veterans of the "second" culture no longer placed such a high value on their isolation and would not have turned down official endorsement, if it had been offered them. That erosion of the boundaries between the two cultures I have described in my essay "On the lost generation" (Sedakova 1990b).

With the arrival of Gorbachev the picture became yet more confused. The generation of the sixties merged completely with the Establishment at about that time, whilst trying to fix themselves a second debut, as persecuted artists. As for new names making their appearance in books or journals, there were very few who really contributed anything new to poetics.

It seemed that the commanding positions were occupied by the Conceptualists and the more moderate "ironists"; they apparently were what were known as the "poets of perestroika". Another "loftier" line — "metarealist", M. Epshtein called it (Epshtein 1988) — was an independent poetry which remained in the shadows until the end of the eighties.

– *Who do you feel closest to among the poets who are getting published?*

Really it is not so much a matter of feeling close to someone, it is more a matter of whose work excites and attracts me. All of those poets went into the eighties already fully formed as writers; I did not come across anyone new to me during that whole decade.

First and foremost there is Elena Shvarts, a powerful poet with rare gifts. Ivan Zhdanov; his complex world, his images were a great novelty for the Russian tradition which is, in general, rather less sophisticated. Sergei Stratanovskii, who has created a sort of poetic equivalent of Platonov's prose. Viktor Krivulin about whom I have written (Sedakova 1991a). Petr Cheigin has not written very many poems, but they are of glacial purity recalling Khlebnikov. Aleksandr Velichanskii. Vladimir Lapin.

– *Has your estimate of their poetry changed since then?*

No, not a jot. Perhaps now I value their poetry even more highly.

– *Where do you find your refuge from the Imperial monster's senile decay?*

I do not think in terms of seeking refuge. I have no sympathy with escapism. Until the regime wrecked itself completely I wanted to go on writing, not in spite of it but against it; that does not mean I intended to write political tracts, though in the funereal atmosphere of the early eighties I did write "Elegiia" (Elegy) and "Puteshestvie v Briansk" (Journey to Briansk) (Sedakova 1992).[1]

But when the regime started to self-destruct, those things became muddled, the cards in the deck were reshuffled. I was not drawn to the ranks of the "reformers", those people were just too alien to me. An oppositional stance became anachronistic. But in thinking about a new responsible position, given the new situation, I never considered looking for a refuge. In the final analysis there is no position for me, except Pasternak's "to be oneself". During the years of Soviet rule the main obstacle to being oneself was fear, now it is cynicism; to be cynical has become, somehow, obligatory in our post-Soviet society — it is *bon ton*. It is, in a way, a rerun of the twenties: "Down with shame!".

 —   *Let us talk about your poetry. What interests me most of all is the way in which, to use your own idiom, your poetic world-text is "spun", on what cloth it is embroidered. An attentive reading of your poetry demonstrates that, to some extent, you are emulating God in His creation of the universe, taking as your base the four elements: water, earth, fire, air. How fundamental are those elements for you?*

I was not aware of that thematic thread in my work, not at the conscious level anyway; not until you told me about it a few days ago! But I do recall that from the very first I felt more attracted towards the non-human world or, more accurately, the non-social-human world. Remember Batiushkov's 'Ia blizhnego liubliu, no ty, priroda-mat´, / Dlia serdtsa ty vsego dorozhe!' (Batiushkov 1978, 349). ("I love my neighbour but thou, mother-nature, / are dearest of all in my my heart").[2] When I was fifteen I was writing about the same things, but not as well as, and much more abrasively than, "tender Batiushkov":

> Мне брата дороже лосиная поступь
> и клич вороний—только окликни!—
> и заячий страх, что русская осень
> борзой задыхающейся настигнет. (Unpublished).

("The elk tread and crow's call / are dearer to me than my brother — just call out! / and the hare's fear that the Russian autumn / will like a panting borzoi run her down...".) A non-human and, perhaps importantly, a non-verbal world; a world alien to our language. In some way or other it was more comprehensible to me. There is a poem dating from about that time: "I potomu mne blizhe slov / iazyk vetvei, iazyk stvolov..." ("And that is why I feel more intimate / with the language of the boughs, the language of the tree trunks...") or, differently put, it is a world where it is easier to lose one's consciousness of self; and people always force you to remember. At times it seems to me that society is like a large room where we are forced constantly to fill in a never-ending succession of forms asking every possible permutation of questions. It is not that I have some intimate secret, something shameful that I want to hide. It is just that the answers to those questions are, in the final analysis, unessential even though they are seen as being most essential.

Forget that you see yourself in the third person, in a mirror. Then your first person which is not social, not reflective, will begin to penetrate the essential: in particular the universal elements. It has nothing to do with that "love of nature" as it is known in our urban culture, a sort of trip to the country to get a breath of fresh air, to relax, "take things easy". Because an encounter with nature does not put one in the mood for taking it easy, "trampling upon the flowers or rolling about on the grass". Just the opposite: one wants to be like them; primed for action, alive. Amongst the thinkers of modern times I have encountered a kindred feeling for the natural world in Goethe. That sort of feeling can engender not just elegiac lyric poetry but also scientific theory building. It is a feeling for the elements as meaning, as structure. That found its expression with the so-called pre-Socratic philosophers, above all Heraclitus. Now, and even in Goethe's time, it was seen as symptomatic of an anachronistic, incurably classical-paganistic way of seeing things. I will not try to justify that, it is the way it was. However, even in our day, it seems to me that we all pass through that phase, in early childhood, in our own private Eden.

Everything that you have said about the elements, about the objective world, all of that is the fruit of my personal relation to them (mostly my childhood experience) not the result of any kind of philosophical teaching. I need to be precise about that because I am seen as a bookish person and people suppose that they can find the source of each and every one of my thoughts and images in books. That is to say, everything is quotation and allusion. But you can take my word for it that it is simply not the case. For a start, my learning has been much exaggerated. The "quotes" in my work I recognize *post factum*; it turns out that I quote things before I have read them! That has happened many times.

What is more, so far as I am concerned, culture is not the same thing as bookishness (that is how culture is seen in our *raznochinets* tradition). Certainly not. For me it has more to do with the development of an immediate, sensual perception of the world: improving one's sight, one's hearing and so on. And with what antiquity saw as the vocation of the poet — take the case of Orpheus — the softening of manners. For example, the mark of a well-educated person (the making, in our terms, of a cultured man) was in ancient Greece that one should not repeat mistakes twice. One can see the same landscape through cultured eyes or through uncultivated eyes. But the cultured view does not mean, as the father of postmodernism, Umberto Eco, would have it, that we must see it in terms of, say, a Bruegel landscape. What does it mean then? That we see it through the eyes of mankind, through the eyes, as Heidegger says, of "the shepherds of being". Incidentally the non-bookish sense of culture is very difficult to explain in Russia. But her old cultural tradition — that of the peasantry — is oral.

For me the most disturbing of the elements, the one I was least fond of, right from my childhood, was earth. I found it frightening. Earth when the snow has melted, out there beyond the garden fence... it is too alive, too like us, like us sensitive to pain. I remember I would be scared to tread on it, especially at the start of spring; I would only want to use an already beaten path. It was not as if at that age, three or four, I felt, to use erudite terminology, a chthonic element, one associated with death. The most frightening thing of all was its too obvious vitality, its corporeality; it breathes... There is plenty of material there for a psychoanalyst to investigate, is not there?

My favourite element was water: static or flowing, it drew me like a magnet. The sight, the sound, the touch, even the smell of it. There is an early poem of mine:

Но в плотности такой, в переплетеньях тесных
живые под корой им слышались ходы:
Там бормотанье шло в стожилиях древесных
И было чуть светлей от запаха воды... (Unpublished)

("But within such solidity, within the intertwined, close-knit / veins beneath the bark they hear the steps: / There is a mumbling in the hundred-veined timber / and it was just that little bit lighter thanks to the smell of water..."). Water gratifies all of the five nominated senses, the innominate ones as well. For example, the sense of spatial adaptation — what else would you call it? — when the body internally, as it were, echoes the outward form which confronts it. Later I came to love fire and finally, not without difficulty, earth.

Perhaps it is just my happenstance, then again maybe it is the contact with the extra-human world of nature — always one of the functions of art because forgetting about that contact is not only commonplace (it is something we suddenly remember about when catastrophe is already at the gates, as with the present Green Movement) it also has to do with our religious traditions, at least the Judaeo-Christian strain. Their demands on one's humanity almost always concern those closest to one; the constant theme is always People, People in history, People in society; not conversing with fire and water. That is why people of an artistic bent are so often drawn to those Far-Eastern traditions which have an intuitional world construct and do not worry themselves about history, or society. But then again I could just mention St Francis or the Eastern anchorites, such as Isaac Sirin, and you would see that it is not impossible to find the space for such intimacy with the created world within our own traditions.

– *In your work each one of the elements carries a plurality of meanings.*
 Water, for example, is on the one hand described in the following terms:
 as blessed by the Spirit of God (Sedakova 1994a, 20), and as our Lady
 water (44), or we have on pure water the divine light (47) and it is
 endowed with the following epithets: most beautiful (18), loving, healing
 (71), confused (27). On the other hand, it is "together cleaving sub-
 stance of the moment", terrifying (30), ponderous (36), unfamiliar
 water (73). Would it be reasonable to assume that water in your poetry
 sometimes serves as a metaphor of substitution for time? Such an
 interpretation is prompted by another metaphor: "As into the shell the
 ocean enters — / the heart's valve of time, a snare" (255).

Yes, of course. The two are even more directly associated in the poems dedicated to that marvellous singer Zara Dolukhanova. It is no accident: song (and music in general), water and time all speak of the same thing: "ragovory ognia / nad rekoi, unosiashchei podarki" ("the conversation of fire over the river, that carries away the gift") (Sedakova 1997, 62–63). That is, of course, the "river of Time", an all too traditional amalgam of time and water, so there is no mistaking it. But, by the way, thinking about the river of time, poets and people in general usually look exclusively at the water flowing away from them and so they only see what time is taking away. But, if you look at it from the other direction, the river of time, before it carries its presents away, brings them *to* you. That is obvious when one is a child, when the passage of time is still gentle, full of promises and growth. I do not think of the element of time as an exclusively regrettable thing, a succession of momentary deaths, as the stoics did. Time is, equally, a constant rebirth. Yesterday's me no longer exists, so many mournful elegies have been written on that theme. But today's me did not exist yesterday and, apparently, none of the poets managed to find that something to celebrate. With the exception of Goethe, perhaps, in his New Year poems.

Time is not the straightforward antithesis of eternity, it also belongs to being. It is a strange thought. People often remember with relief that, as it says in Revelation, time will be no more. But faith will no longer exist, nor will hope. And it does not follow that there is some other way, involving neither time nor faith, to get to where they will no longer exist.

But I have moved away from water. Its real significance in poetry is more obvious to the reader than to the writer: it is really engendered with those words, in those words. I never write about what is already known to me before I start writing and I do not have any kind of preconceived vision of the world. You can write about what you know, discursively, in prose, but poetry is the midwife that brings forth meanings new for the writer herself, otherwise there would not be much sense in doing it. And I am wary of thinking about my poems after I have written them. Collaborating with my translators forced me to do something along those lines for the first time. For all that, I really do like to analyse other people's poetry, especially the really great poems: take every analysable section — phonetics, syntax and so forth — and it augments the object of one's admiration, convinces one, as it were, that nothing like that could be the result of human endeavour.

—   *Earth is, perhaps even more complex and diverse in its symbolism, than water. But singling out its fundamental semantic nucleus is far from simple. Is it defined exclusively by the concrete context of a particular poem or does there exist a specific general function for that element?*

I could say, though at some risk, that to love the earth, the element of earth, and not earth, the habitat of humanity ("But I do love that poor earth"), is almost the same as loving a person. That is, love man in his entirety, in his bodily frame which "comes from the earth and returns to the earth". Such a perception of earth is linked not with the ancient concept of the elements but, seemingly, with the dualistic opposition of heaven and earth. To accept earth, to accept human beings, myself included, has never been easy for me. It is far easier to dream, like Plato, of the liberation of the winged, immortal soul from the "the grave of the body". The enlightened heathens accused the early Christians of being "lovers of the flesh" because they awaited the resurrection of that from which the heathens dreamed of freeing themselves.

In European culture, as everyone knows, spiritualism has held sway for centuries, not as a specific doctrine, but as an implicit hierarchy of values. It is imbibed along with the milk of one's education. And for anyone who loves "high culture", who is scornful of the flesh, it is more difficult to feel at one with earth, with humanity, harder than for those who are called "ordinary folk". In Russia, in any case, that is how it is. Some see in that the specific influence of Manichaeism; the fear of the flesh as something unclean, almost diabolical. But it is just as prevalent in the West as in Russia, and not just in the Middle Ages. But there is another and, strictly speaking, "correct" intuition of love of earth; Dostoevskii tried to portray it in the person of Father Zosima. It is to be found even in the very first fruit of Russian literature, *O zakone i blagodati* (On the law given by Moses and on benevolence and truth which proceed from Jesus Christ) written by the Metropolitan of Kiev, Hilarion: "And Adam was created of pure earth and Christ was born of the pure Virgin".

But again I am getting away from the elements. I love reading Heraclitus and I regret that the post-Socratic philosophers abandoned his themes, occupying themselves exclusively with human beings. A renewed attention to the world of creation, more properly an intimacy with it, appears in Heidegger and perhaps not for the last time, since his thought was inspired by such "*naturphilosophische*" poets as Hölderlin and Rilke.

− Is not that the provenance of your own particular commingling of the four diverse elements? "And water is the ashes of unknown fires" (Sedakova 1994a,177) "In the aerial water" (183) "on skyey earth" (300).

Your observations are eye-opening! Why do they change, one into the other? It is, I think, because that is the way it really is, and Heraclitus knew that. But, generally, I have no great liking for final judgements. One of the aspects of such finality is tautology: water is water, fire is fire and so on. It is a self-comparative impasse, like death. I would like (and I think that this is the case) every possibility to remain open, so that everything can be itself and something other and have the potential to transform itself into something else, as yet unknown.

−   As distinct from water, air has fundamentally positive attributes. It is, as a rule, gentle, delicate, luminous. The frequency with which air occurs in your poetic vocabulary is just one fifth of that of water. How significant is that? Is your relationship with air an easy one?

Yes, pleasant and easy. Air does not ask to be named or described. It is rhythm itself; the movement of a poem reproduces it. It seems to me that the rhythmic substance of my early poetry was more "watery"; it has slowly become more airy.

−   In your work the earthly and the heavenly often intersect in dream. The dream motif comes up so often in contexts where it produces the impression that the dream state is the chief means of communication

*with the other world; that it is in dreams that the meaning of many
things and events is revealed; as it says in Job, in dreams God "openeth
the ears of men, and sealeth their instruction" (33. 16). Your dreamer
is a sort of guide to the heavenly spirit on its visitations to earth: "but
choosing its dreamer, / The spirit returned to its former path" (95).*

Dreams, the state of dreaming, have, from childhood on, meant more
to me, perhaps, than reality. Often they simply outstripped it (prophetic
dreams). But it is not that anticipation that is important: they were obviously
more intelligent than me. I just did not possess sufficient intellectual power
to conceive of the things that I would see in dreams. So I become a sort
of hypnomaniac, living from one miraculous, instructive dream to the next,
I longed for them, I long for them now, because it has been a long time
since I have seen anything of that kind.

But Claudel, as I read not long ago in his diaries, noted — in connection
with the Romantic cult of the dream state — that in order to dream one
had to go to sleep. But vigilance and responsibility are only possible in
a waking state.

—   *The way in which you use dreams in your poetry suggests to the reader
    that that is one of your favourite means of translating the everyday
    to an aesthetic plane. What other means do you possess of transforming
    the real world into the poetic world? Something has first to be rescued
    from the ruins of existence in order to make of it a thing of aesthetic
    value.*

In everyday life there is a huge countervailing force which opposes what
you call the "aesthetic plane" and that opposition grows stronger the older
one gets. Being in another, non-routine, non-machine-like state of mind and
body means just as much to me as the creation of any text. The text itself
is just a trace of that experience, one which, evidently, is generally known
as inspiration. A state of a different intensity where other doors open. And,
really, a normal psychic state is vexing simply because those doors are not
there. In the midst of that Brownian movement there can be fleeting "beautiful
feelings" and "good ideas" but there is no co-ordination between them and,
for that reason, they vanish without leaving any visible traces. And where
do the doors open into that state of increased intensity in which everything
comes together? — in dreams of course. That is the simplest way to get
there. Music can also push those doors ajar. Visual images. But there is
an awful lot of things that can close them and even roll a great big boulder
in front of them; pointless socializing, political journalism... a whole host
of things.

– *Do you see it as being a part of your artistic mission to bring harmony where harmony seems almost impossible to achieve? The trivial daily round — stale, boorish and vulgar — how can you bring harmony to that through the use of the word?*

No, that is not my mission, not now, nor in the past. Perhaps that is precisely why I find myself in such a lonely position in the contemporary scene. Even those poets who are closest to me — Elena Shvarts, Ivan Zhdanov — that "extensive" movement has something that people find attractive (the apotheosis of "Pomoika" (The dump) by Elena Shvarts; the mythologization of technology by Ivan Zhdanov). For me, no. In Dublin recently I was asked by Carol Rumens what I felt about Sylvia Plath's idea that poetry should be all-inclusive. My answer was that it seemed to me to be so: it was a question of approach: did you look for extensivity or intensivity. Let us take Pushkin's "Skazka o mertvoi tsarevne" (Tale of the dead tsarevna): for me that is all-inclusive. And that is truer still of a Sapphic fragment, just a few words — even Ezra Pound's stylization of that sort of fragment in his "Papyrus" ("Spring... / Too long... / Gonghula...") manages to get everything in. You can "include everything" without even mentioning anything harsh, ugly or vulgar.

The inertia of downward movement is very apparent to me. That has been the vector which art has been pursuing for centuries now, "speculations on degradation". It seems that even in Renaissance times art felt drawn to extend the realm of aesthetics into the non-aesthetic. Transmute into a new, more complex, more spicy harmony things which are difficult to harmonize at all. That movement does have a kind of equity of its own about it, there is a pricking of the artistic conscience about things that are considered unattractive, unloved; someone has to take notice of them, describe them well. But that movement in one direction alone has become senseless inertia. It is time we admitted that it is not the "low" but the "high" that needs defending and there are very few defenders. The "high" has been seen as open to question, a beautiful notion, a gilded dream. The truth is to be found by thinking "low". Even someone who respects the "high" like Pushkin: "T´my nizkikh istin nam dorozhe / Nas vozvyshaiushchii obman..." ("One elevating deceit is dearer to us / than a host of lowly truths", Pushkin 1948, 253) always sees it as trickery, illusion. Pushkin does not speak of "elevating truth". It is as if there were some axiom, unthought out, lacking in proof: the truth is harsh, elementary and without hope. Maybe that conviction is not just confined to the realms of art but is a mark of our civilization as a whole, with its reductive theories such as Marxism and Freudianism. It seems to me that people just have not thought it through. It is weird and crazy to say that a whole civilization has not thought something through but that is precisely how I see it. Really, a negative concept of the "real truth" is not any more demonstrable or scientific than a positive one. Nobody has seen "the final things" — the sceptics like to keep telling us that, but for some reason they do not seem to think that "nobody" applies to them as well. And if enthusiasm affects one's vision, scepticism sees no better, and the universal doubt they see is, to boot, not the "last thing".

Everybody now knows that the Panglosses of this world are naive, but just look at how naive the Valmonts are! I have been foolish enough to say, just as they said in Antiquity, that "existence is blessed" that, deep down in his heart of hearts, man is not a mesh of aggressive, sexual and territorial instincts but made in the image of his Creator. The sceptical concept of things I find so unconvincing, just as mine is to the sceptics: we both have some fundamental reason for our respective concepts of the world. Moreover, I think that talk about our "abandonment" by God at the same time as Communion is being celebrated in our churches is somewhat premature. And that an artist can dedicate his talents to that and many other towering truths no less successfully than to the low, the harsh and the ugly.

In fact, incessantly moving in just one direction, downwards, towards the increasingly more trivial is wearisome and simply stops being interesting. When Baudelaire discovered the beauty of the trivial, of evil even, that grabbed his reader's attention as a widening of experience, in its own peculiar way an act of kenosis. It is no accident that in Rilke, that *poète maudit* is confronted by the image of St Julian who bestows a kiss upon a leper.

But it is a long time since we got excited by the latest non-aesthetic object to be transformed into a work of art; it is no longer a slap in the face of the bourgeoisie, the very opposite. It is simply conforming to some modern day norm. I am surely not alone in thinking that particular movement has had its day. There are a lot of things that reinforce the feeling I have that there has to be a radical change. For instance, the version of *Pericles* that, thanks to Marina Warner, I saw recently at the National Theatre. After the performance we were discussing the reasons why we found it so surprising. He speaks the language of the postmodernists but what is really unexpected is that it is a play of hope. Fate is denied — however crazy this might seem to a contemporary ear — because of the personal virtue of the main female character Marina. Contemporary art with an angel at centre stage. What daring avant-gardist would venture such a rash act!

You must understand that when I say that art is free not to seek its subject matter in the midst of chaos, monstrosities, the gutter and so forth, I do not mean that it should exclude them completely and that we should return to writing idylls about Chloe and anthology pieces about roses. That would be simply dishonest. No, I think that keeping that in mind, knowing about that, you can express new experience through the very intensity of language. The tensions of the age can be encapsulated in the description of a shrub, if you want them to be. I am not given to being all-inclusive. Practically nothing pertaining to what is in the headlines can be caught in the harmonious snares I set. I do not venture on to that ground. I allow myself the liberty of remaining within a very limited range of things — things traditionally considered "aesthetic" — and my vocabulary also is limited. I do not get very excited about "contemporary" language. What does excite me is the intensity of a word, its semantic, phonetic, grammatical strength, and it is there that I see new possibilities. Or — to put it another way — the iconic word, the word that resembles an image, that is one that will survive a lot of use. Ugliness, evil, chaos lack a well defined image and for that reason our consciousness is incapable of dealing with them. "I looked and went on", as Virgil advised Dante in the *Inferno*.

–   *Does a new poetic, a new form, a new composition always lead to new content?*

I think that the vector of those relationships is the other way round: communication seeks a form for itself or, as N. S. Trubetskoi wrote of medieval art, sense emanates its own form.

What I would call sense, however, might appear senseless, nonsensical: it is definitely not some sort of logically expressed content, just simply experience. It certainly emanates some sort of formal novelty, in the case where the artist is self demanding, if he pays heed to what it says to him and checks that against what he wants to say. Is that it? If not, why not? What is getting in the way? And he may discover that automatically making use of what lies immediately to hand, he has borrowed, unawares, something of his favourite writer's. Goethe said of some poet: "Our well developed German poetic tradition does his writing for him". But what he was writing did not stem from his own experience, it was something generalized, alien, lacklustre. What does my own work demand? That is the question. What have the others not yet talked about? That is what needs to be understood. For example, the regular rhythm may need to be broken; or in the middle of a regular rhyme scheme you might need to leave a line unrhymed; or you might suddenly introduce rhyme into an unrhymed poem. It may demand that you do not shy away from a particular, in the context, senseless word, from a stylistic catastrophe, and so on. For that active passivity one might find many comparisons: a dance where you have to guess what steps your partner is going to take; a ball game where it is not you who is in control of the ball (that is an image of Rilke's that Gadamer uses as an epigraph in his *Hermeneutics*). And so on. It's what is needed so that the discourse becomes your discourse and it is not, of necessity, a violent liberation from the norm, a shattering of the regular scheme of things. The sense can, on the contrary, seek an over harsh regularity, let us say a numeric coda. Take, for example, the formal theme of my "Puteshestvie volkhvov" (Journey of the Magi) (63–65), where it was three figures: 6, 7 and 8.

I do not believe in it when they start to search out new forms, new technology; in my opinion that is a gesture of despair. I do not believe in universal keys or, rather, structural passkeys which are accepted once and for all; for example, avoid epithets and similar advice. Maybe the next time you will need five epithets in a row! The main thing is, I repeat, to check: am I saying what I want to say? For example, rhythm often dictates to me the very first phrase, the one that sounds just right. Here is an example. In the very first line of "Neuzheli, Mariia, **tol´ko** ramy skripiat" ("Surely, Maria, it's not just the frames creaking", 6; translation in Smith 1993, 271) there was a superfluous unstressed syllable. To make the line regular was no trouble — and, evidently there was no loss of meaning. Like this: "Neuzheli, Mariia, **lish´** ramy skripiat" you see it becomes not just colourless but essentially false. That is how I find my new rhythms, by listening carefully: how natural the sentence sounds. If it sounds natural in classical metre all well and good.

But, of course, if every actual decision is *ad hoc* then, generally speaking, the attention one pays to questions of rhythm is conscious. I have always been interested in other systems of versification outside the Russian syllabo-tonic tradition: metres used in antiquity, folk poetry, prayers, things in which the rhythm of the poetic line is not yet separate from the *melos*. During my writing of "Tristan i Izol´da" (Tristan and Isolde) I was hearing the German of the *Nibelungenlied*, the old Italian of the *laudi*.

–   *How do you manage to follow tradition outwardly yet insensibly and, at the same time, consistently alter its vector?*

Continuing in a tradition always has its paradoxes; anything that is plainly foreshadowed in the work of one's predecessors is not tradition but epigonism. In my view one of the purest emanations of the Pushkin line is to be found in Mandel´shtam. But look at Pushkin and then try and foretell Mandel´shtam's: "I vcherashnee solntse na chernykh nosilkakh nesut..." ("the sun of yesterday is borne on a black stretcher", Mandel´shtam 1990, 126; translation in Mandelstam 1973a, 47). Or look at Nekrasov, and then

at Blok's continuation of that line: "Zla, dobra li? — Ty vsia — ne otsiuda..."
("Are you evil or good? You are altogether from another world", Blok 1955,
339; translation in Obolensky 1965, 279). Tradition, despite its common
use, remains a very personal matter; tradition (*traditio* : transferring) is a
handing on from one generation to the next and is not like sailing single-
handed through empty spaces. What becomes of what is handed over
depends upon the taker.

I loved poetry right from my early childhood and I always sensed how
much had been handed on — by Russian poets, and, later, by poets writing
in other languages. I do not feel afraid of leaving something that has been
handed on as it is, nor of changing it, sometimes quite abruptly, if that
cannot be avoided. I would not call my own position either conservative
or reformist.

In our relation to tradition, as with everything else, we are again confronted with the question: either, or? Either "traditionalism" (by which,
strictly speaking, we mean an uncritical, dilettante use of the **conventional**)
or idiosyncratic anti-traditionalism at any price. The ironic "all-embracing"
tradition in postmodernism is no third way; it is another aspect of anti-
traditionalism because within the tradition itself there is, inevitably, a certain
fastidiousness. I cannot say which of these two evidently polarized positions
is the more alien to me. (The same goes, incidentally, for that other notorious pair — the Apollonian and the Dionysian; I prefer Hermes, the
inventor of the lyre, to either of them.) Pasternak in *Okhrannaia gramota*
(Safe conduct) noted that all artists, unless they come into the world empty-
handed, are iconoclasts. That paradox is even stronger in the case of
Mandel'shtam; with him an image is an expression of image breaking: "S
ikonoborcheskoi doski..." ("From the iconoclastic board...", Mandel'shtam
1990, 150; translation in Mandelstam 1973b, 83).

It may be said that a great image (and that is the traditional image) is
painted on an iconoclastic ground: existing incarnations seem false simply
because they already exist, realized and available — what is needed is
something drawn from the realms of non-existence, from foam, like
Aphrodite. What demands that? The tradition itself, it seems to me. The
whole essence of the tradition is that it should be incessantly reborn: to
draw itself out, to maintain itself, is not its concern. Goethe's *stirb und
werde* is one of the best formulations of the tradition. And because, from
within, it gainsays itself much more imprudently than the most hysterical
anti-traditionalism.

And there is something else which, apparently, the anti-traditionalists
know nothing about; the love of that from which everything has arisen,
prior to being — at the very heart of that continuous discontinuity: *stirb
und werde.*

Und solang du das nicht hast,
dieses: stirb und werde,
bist du nur ein truber Gast
auf der dunklen Erde...

("And as long as you do not have it, / this thing: die and be! / You are
but a sorry guest / upon this dark earth.") (Goethe 1964, 240). And that
is just how I see those traditionalists and anti-traditionalists, "sorry guests
upon this dark earth".

– *Is there any one particular favourite poet you feel breathing down the
   back of your neck?*

Your question is, seemingly, prompted by Brodsky's famous image of
emulation as a stimulus to poetic growth. Poetic emulation is an ancient
tradition, as ancient as the legend of the duel between Homer and Hesiod.
But I can quite sincerely say that I only felt that spirit of emulation during
my schooldays, during my years in a literary workshop, where there were,
indeed, competitions held between us young poets and I, of course, always
wanted to win and, at the same time, outstrip those amongst us who were
generally held to be "geniuses". But it was not all that serious.

I got to know Elena Shvarts's poetry in 1975 or 1976 and it made me
extremely jealous. A great poet and she is alive? I sensed her poetic primacy,
the purity of her tone. But I knew it was another world and, though I felt
less pleasure in mine, I could not follow in her footsteps. I am deeply
grateful for having met her. She made me feel freer in my own world and
that was invaluable help and inducement. People usually teach each other
dependency. Various routines of dependency. My second memorable encounter with living poetry was the early work of Ivan Zhdanov. I read his
poems in samizdat in, I think, 1977. They astonished me with their unexpected intimacy with my own thoughts. It seemed as if we had been
dreaming some of the same dreams. Now you have heard about all of my
dramatic encounters with my contemporaries.

With other living poets my relationship is that of a reader (however
strange it may sound, that is a rare relationship among the poets and
scholars I know). The door remains open, our existence is far from
hermetic, a creative element visits our world — that is what the enriching
inspiration of others tells me. Yes, that was precisely the first impression
I got upon my first encounter with Brodsky's poetry in samizdat (at
university) in 1968. His themes, his music, were, I felt, far away from
me but you sensed the inspiration, possibly, at its most intense, in those
early poems of his.

But to return to rivalries and influences. The most powerful influence of my youth was Mandel'shtam. It was as if he were passing judgement. What could one write after that? It was not a matter of writing post-Auschwitz, as they say now, but of writing post-Mandel'shtam, writing in the wake of that new intensity and beauty, all that he achieved in his late poems. Now the sharpness of that relationship with Mandel'shtam has softened, though many of his things still seem to me to be landmarks.

The next of my idols was Rilke, in whom I saw the Poet *par excellence*. And in order to read him in the original I learned German. To read Dante I learned Italian. To read Baudelaire I mugged up on my French. *Les Fleurs du mal* was the biggest influence on me. It resulted in my book *Dikii shipovnik* (what a strange offspring!).[3] Of Russian poetry, Pushkin, who has always been more than a poet for all of us — he is, as it were, the *genius loci* or the Orpheus of Russian literature; Blok, towards whom I feel as though the Acmeist revolution had never taken place. I do not think it is worth going into detail.

Over the years you develop a subject matter that is particular to you (for all its lack of substance, its vagueness) and understand that it is something nobody else is dealing with and there is nothing else to compare it with. There is an inner theme in Mandel'shtam, as there is in Akhmatova, as there is in Pasternak. But it is difficult to analyse and define those inner themes, those poetic worlds; you recognize them by taste, by touch, as it were. And you come to realize that they are doing their thing and it is something different from what you want to do.

–   *Whose poetry do you wish you had written? Whose contexts do you need most often?*

There is a seven-year-old I know who composes music and he told me, "There is just one piece of music I would like to have written: Mozart's 40th symphony. But Mozart has already written it."

Whose poetry would I like to have written? Sappho's. Dante's *Divine Comedy*. Some of Goethe's poems. Pushkin's "Skazki" (Fairy tales) and his elegies. Almost everything of Rilke's. Up to this moment Rilke, for me, is the closest to being the poet who has set the limits, his poetry has the strength to enter Hades and return, like Orpheus, with a new word "more silent than silence", hymn-like and gentle. "Tol'ko iz bezdny dvoinoi / golos vernetsia / krotko zhivoi [*ewig und mild*]" (Rilke 1988, 14).

You said whose contexts? I would prefer to put it another way: the taking up of an interrupted conversation where it was left off. You have noticed that sometimes my first lines are direct quotations? It is a sign: this is where we continue the conversation. But quite often that sort of continuation is oblique and does not start with the first line. And the person I am talking to is not signalled through direct quotation but by, let us say, the rhythm. That sense of conversation (Zabolotskii on Pasternak, "interlocutor of the heart and poet" [Zabolotskii 1965, 131]) through the language, through time, is more important to me than any trial of strength.

– *Which possibilities, stylistic, thematic or formal do you consciously reject?*

First of all I can tell you what I have not rejected because it has not attracted me. It is, roughly speaking, expressionism (not the historical movement but all the sort of thing that in other epochs has been called Mannerism). An emphatic style with inflated lines, with wilfully deformed imagery, with an anticipated, if not obligatory, reaction on the part of the reader: a style which wants to lord it over the subject and the intended audience. It can be unusually impressive — that is what it wants to be. But that is not my type of poetry. I prefer communication to gesticulation. When something is communicated, passed on, especially when it is fragile or fluid (and that is the nature of artistic communication) then one should try to avoid staccato movements so that you do not break it, spill it, injure it.

But no less than by inflated expression, I am repulsed by its polar opposite, over smooth writing, what is generally called the academic style; "correct" writing, one that conforms to a standard that is somehow neither too laboured nor too fine. I find that style is really just as aggressive as the other. And what both of them exclude is the accidental, the unexpected ploy, air and open spaces — you cannot breathe there.

If I think about what I have had to reject... perhaps my own prejudices, They were fairly numerous. For example, until *Dikii shipovnik* having any sort of well-defined content seemed to me to be vulgar. It was not very easy for me to open up my writing more. After that I was afraid of anything lengthy, narrational. Short poems, things with a maximum of tension — there was a time when I could not imagine another kind of "contemporary" poetry. Then certain themes, certain words seemed to be unusable. A current political topic, street talk... When I read a book of Elena Shvarts's in samizdat, it was *Voisko, izgoniaiushchee besov* (The army that drives out demons), what struck me, amongst many other things, was her ability to raise street talk and everyday minutiae to the heights of poetry (usually prosaisms diminish the tension in poetry). But Shvarts gives those words and things a lift as if they were on crystal spears. I really love her satires. They are in the finest Horatian spirit.

At the same time I was afraid of being too elevated, having too hieratic a vocabulary, the sort of thing you find in Blok: blood, love, roses etc. That sort of decision, too, has to be made. Generally speaking I have had to "reject consciously" my own purism in various manifestations: to concur with what I considered a destruction of poetry's purity, that is, change the very concept of that purity.

And more instinctively than consciously, I try not to repeat my own "finds", write something again simply because it was obviously successful. I would have been ashamed to do that. It's something else again if a particular rhythm or set of images gets a hold over you and seeks another setting that is worthy of it. And it will seek that out not within the confines of an individual's opus but within the entire poetic tradition of the language. So, I think, rhythms that began in Nekrasov's work appear and realize their potential in Blok. And perhaps (this was noted by V.V. Bibikhin[4]) [Pushkin's] "Skazka o rybake i rybke" (The tale of the fisherman and the fish) found its continuation in my "Starye pesni" (Old songs) (Sedakova 1994a, 131–70).

–   *Do you have any stylistic preferences?*

I think that is obvious from what I have already said. Without going into great detail I would have said that my fundamental stylistic preference is for "transparency": an invisible, voided style. Barthes's "writing at degree zero"? Or, as Paul Valéry wrote, second nature? My first nature, the one I was born with, I do not put too high a value on. It's usually fouled with the accidental, the trivial, as a result of the inattentive picking up of this and that, here there and everywhere. From this natural acquisitiveness one has to develop a true spontaneity. Primal spontaneity is all right for school-children who have not got any further than the first class: after that the imbibing of the clichés begins. That first sincerity is certainly far from being freedom; it is a susceptibility to one's own complexes, habits, obsessions. Many artists value that psychic cash in hand and the only thing they want to do is to make it into actual legal tender by, as the popular phrase has it, "making silk purses out of sow's ears". And they even see it as a duty that they be true to themselves. In my opinion that is in no way being true to oneself. Our real self lies not in the past but in the future; you have to experience something to gain a self.

The style which definitely satisfies me is, in general terms, the self-effacing one. You can express yourself in the most varied ways: there is the genial negligence, the spontaneity which the old Chinese graphic artists used to mine, or the many-layered, sophisticated, highly imaged manner of writing of old Byzantium. There is another that you could call

the carefree style. As in the old English nursery rhyme about the lady
on the white horse:

> With rings on her fingers
> And bells on her toes
> She shall have music
> Wherever she goes...

Wherever she goes, even if the world turns topsy-turvy, she shall have
music.

From those stylistic preferences of mine you can see how little pleases
me in present-day art.

– *How do you manage to eliminate the first person singular in poetry?*

It's an illusion! I think that I use the first person singular as much as
anyone. I have never seen that as my mission, to eliminate the first person
singular. In the final analysis, it is only a narrative strategy: you can talk
about yourself in the third person. Nobody is really fooled as to the identity
of the "sick man" in Pasternak's "V bol´nitse" (In hospital): "On ponial,
chto iz peredelki / Edva li on vyidet zhivoi..." ("He suddenly knew this
adventure / Would hardly release him alive", Pasternak 1965, 468; translation in Paternak 1972, 80), nor as to the identity of the "lodger in the
raincoat, with a bottle of grappa in his pocket" (in Brodsky's "Laguna"
[Lagoon]) and the same goes for the hawk in his "Osennii krik iastreba"
(The hawk's cry in autumn). Ivan Zhdanov when he seeks that kind of mask
does not use the third person singular but the second: "Ty stsena i akter..."
("You are the stage and the actor..."). I am not very fond of that oblique
way of talking about oneself. The simple first person singular is more
honest.

I realize that your question has not so much to do with what pronoun
is used as with the general problem faced by poetry in this century, the
crisis of the "personal" lyric, with the obvious crisis of the traditional lyric,
of the character of the lyrical protagonist. I agree that Blok's monologues
like, for example, "Ia prigvozhden k traktirnoi stoike. / Ia p´ian davno. Mne
vse — ravno..." ("I'm nailed to the bar counter. / I'm long since drunk.
And I do not care", Blok 1955, 446) would sound strange coming from
a contemporary. Something has happened to the "hero" in our century and
to the lyrical hero as well. Is it the end of biography as a cultural value,
as Mandel´shtam supposed?

A long time before I became aware of that cultural situation, when I was
very young and inexperienced, it would never have entered my mind to

write something like Tsvetaeva's "Mal´chikom, begushchim rezvo, / Ia predstala Vam..." ("Like a boy, running playfully, / I appeared before you", Tsvetaeva 1965, 59; translation in Tsvetaeva 1988, 47) to describe oneself. Perhaps I have always felt myself to be more of a spectator or like the choir in Greek tragedy, but not the hero, not the protagonist of the drama. If there was anything that seemed to me to be a dream or phantom then it was my "I" rather than the external world: of **its** reality I was absolutely convinced and I could very easily imagine all those objects, all that space, existing without my being there, just as it had existed before my arrival and as it will exist after I am gone (that condition is the opposite of solipsism).

Most of the avoidances of the heroic "I" that have been made in our century and that are known to me lead down to a lower level. There has been, for example, the bursting of the bubble of the lyric hero, the portrayal of a poet not in the traditional mythic mould — the demi-god, herald of heaven-sent truth (Annenskii's "hero" — distastefully apathetic and lacking in self confidence; Khodasevich's — aggressive and misanthropic). It's the ironic and disparaging image of the self in Brodsky, bordering on the disgusting, that is the obverse of the traditional lyrical self-admiration. The parodic characters in the Oberiuty and Prigov are essentially that "I".

But there is some sort of limit to that downwards movement — the limits of the reader's interest. Hearing about a man's unpleasant traits sooner or later gets boring; what, given the traditional treatment, appears to be merciless and daring honesty becomes, in its turn, routine. It seems now to be much riskier to talk about the good rather than the bad — and that includes good about "oneself". "Funny", "outdated", "dishonest" — that is the probable response to anything that does not demonstrate an expertise in "alienation", irony, formal harshness, and aggressiveness.

But there are examples of an "upwards" escape route, away from the romantic "I". Rilke and his subjective lyrics (the subjective role is given to everyone and everything — apart from the poet: "things" talk, be it a panther in the zoo, a blue hydrangea or Saint Sebastian. This is in no way a mask for the lyrical "I", as it is in the examples I started with. The poet, as in the "Duino Elegies", shows these "things" to an angel ("Do not talk to him of heavenly things, show him the earthly"), serves as their mouths: "Wir sind nur mund" ("We are only mouth"). Both a guide and a translator of the language of silence — there you have the complete role of the Poet. And do we expect of our guide and translator stories about himself, confessions in the spirit of "Ia p´ian davno"? ("I'm long since drunk"). Or the "I" of Eliot, choral and representative, the "I" of the man of his time submitting to the court's verdict? The later Pasternak "I" finding himself in praise: "V slezakh ot schast'ia otstoiu" ("And weeping joyfully attend",

Pasternak 1965, 456; translation in Pasternak 1984, 147), and already freeing himself from his own particular fate, no longer preoccupied with it. Rilke's or Eliot's "I" is almost a "we": the poet speaks like a Greek chorus, often in the plural, for the singular is no longer appropriate, as in the section about Good Friday in *The Four Quartets*:

> The dripping blood our only drink,
> The bloody flesh our only food:
> In spite of which we like to think
> That we are sound, substantial flesh and blood... (East Coker, IV)

It is somehow different in Mandel´shtam's last poems. The "I" is transmuted but does not grow nearer to a "we". Still a young man, he said, "I forget the unnecessary 'I'". But, towards the end, that "I" sounds absolutely foursquare: "Vot ono — moe nebo nochnoe, / Pred kotorym kak mal´chik stoiu..." ("And that is my night, before me, / and I'm the child standing under it", Mandel´shtam 1990, 248; translation in Mandelstam 1973a, 127). In "Stikhi o neizvestnom soldate" (Verses on the unknown soldier) it coincides with the passport, the "worn" personality of official permit: "Ia rozhden v noch´ s vtorogo na tret´e / Ianvaria v devianosto odnom..." ("I was born in the night of the second and the third / Of January in the eighteen ninety-first...", Mandel´shtam 1990, 245; translation in Mandelstam 1977, 95). But, how shall I put it? It's somehow different, that last pre-mortem "I" when he almost does not care about self, but at the same time everything has to be answered for: "I za Lermontova Mikhaila / Ia otdam tebe strogii otchet..." ("And for the poet, Mikhail Lermontov, / I'll provide you the strictest account", Mandel´shtam 1990, 242; translation in Mandelstam 1977, 91). It seems to me that is the profoundest and truest break — with the ugly details of one's own life, with the individualistic obsession with self.

I do not know which of those "I"s is closest to what I am trying to express. It is not, I repeat, a matter of eliminating the first person singular and achieving some sort of impersonal point of view — that is a utopian task, even for a scholar. It is really a question of having something to look at from your own point of view in order to avoid thinking of yourself — either judgmentally or self-admiringly — like holding one's hand in front of one's eyes, an act which hides the whole world, as it says in one Hassidic parable. ("The world is so large", says one of the tzaddikim, "but a man can hide it with his own little hand".) The spectacle of oneself, looking at oneself from one side, in the mirror, that is what stands in our light. It is not so much "I", as "he" or "her": the imaginary, fabricated self-portrait in front of the mirror.

People accustomed to regular prayer know very well that the "I" of which we are all conscious is not the final reality. For instance in the prayer of St John Damascene there is a plea which goes like this: "Whether I will or no, save me." Is it not paradoxical, that plea from a person other than the willing or not willing "I"? What sort of an "I" is it which asks to be saved when that "I" does not want it and, what is more, I do not know whether that "I" within me wants it or not?

What do you call that second principle within oneself? Perhaps, as Pasternak said of Tsvetaeva, it is "like a face turned to God". Always turned. And that which stems from the first "I" is sometimes turned His way, sometimes away... No, one can not say that this is not serious, it is very serious, but not the whole "I" is involved. That first "I" is a question, a task, not an answer.

I am so accustomed to that dual psyche that I find it astonishing how many people believe in their own "feelings", how many see themselves as entirely coincident with their physical and mental condition — which changes like the weather within the constant landscape of the "inner man" — but that man is, perhaps, more distinguishable to others than he appears to be to ourselves.

It is, amongst other things, reflected involuntarily in form, and there, it seems, lies the most obvious thing of all. In Dante's lines you can even make out the physical leanness of the author, even his gait. But, really, is not that of about as much importance as how the mountain of Purgatory is structured or how the moon got its spots, when one thinks of one's own work?

– *Could you be more explicit about what you mean when you say "surpass yourself" in relation to poetry: to show the world a new vision of things, to achieve self betterment in the process of giving birth to the poem or to improve the language?*

We are accustomed to thinking that the poet at the moment of inspiration becomes greater than himself, another being altogether than his usual, everyday self — "the momentary personality". But another postulate was known to classical antiquity: "a work of art is no greater than its creator". That presupposes the essential unity of personality and, as it were, the impossibility of transcending that personality. It seems to me that antinomy does not require resolution, both poles are equally true. In reality an artist transmits through his work not only his talents but also his weaknesses; all that remains at his command when "silence falls upon the sacred lyre". And we, I mean the readers, are able to recognize those weaknesses; particularly in the idiosyncrasies of his form, which is where an author has least self-control.

And what does surpass oneself mean? I can, probably, only answer in a negative way and that by having recourse to someone else's, Eliot's, apt words. He talked of "the expurgation of intentions". You approach things unaware, perhaps, that your motives are not entirely pure; the best being, let us say, the perfectionist "to create something sublime", the worst, to make an impression, please those in the know, overwhelm the reader. However, any one of the deliberate motives for your action is bound to spoil your work. And then in the process of approaching the future text these ordinary motives disappear, "the goal grows less important as you progress along your way" and you find yourself like the hero of a fairy tale facing his mission: "Go thither — I do not know whither — fetch that — I do not know what". There you have pure intention or absence of intention; all that remains is intentness or, if you are not afraid of big words, service.

– *Service to whom or what: language, one's talents, the Lord?*

Oh, that is the question! If I could answer that: to whom, to what? But, it seems, nobody can, not the poets, not the philosophers, not the theologians who have been trying to define the status of art in the spiritual hierarchy. However strange it may seem, that old theme, the condemnation or justification of artistic creation from a spiritual standpoint, has now taken on a very particular actuality. Seemingly, it has to do with our return to the Orthodox fold. Some of our enthusiastic new Orthodox zealots have declared war on Apollo; free creation seems to them to be the devil's work; art is somehow at major odds with piety, obedience, humility, what have you. They are aware of the undoubted strength that art has at its disposal, and that strength, for them, has no connection whatsoever with anything good. Even the artists themselves have nothing clear to say about that — take Blok and his Muse, "Are you evil, or good? You are altogether from another world..." — and are inclined to combat her ethics and at the end of their lives repent of their service to the idols of Art and Beauty. That has happened from the very beginnings of secular art, take the cases of Michelangelo and Petrarch. Our own Gogol´ and Tolstoi are more recent recidivists to make such religious denials of Art. The most liberal of religious thinkers admit that art is a service, none the less, to God, "to the unknown God", not the God of Revelation; that the artist, involuntarily and unawares, serves Good even if he, consciously, combats ethics for the sake of aesthetics. Of course, I am unable to supply a simple answer to a question which has proved insoluble to the wisest and most ingenious of mankind.

It does seem to me though that when art is harshly repressed, it is religion that suffers a loss in breadth. It reduces itself to prescripts and morals and more or less closes itself off from the whole circumambient ocean of existence. It is left without the poetry of life, without the latter's play and openness. If it were really like that I cannot understand what its attractions would be. Why practise virtue if one does not know the why and wherefore? I, in any case, would not have even started. But, really, faith "enlivens life" as Ioann Zlatoust wrote in his pastoral letters. And surely art bears witness to that enlivening of life, makes one feel that enlivenment through the senses of taste, of hearing? And much more distinctly than ordinary everyday life, the realm of existential *Angst*.

– *Why is the appearance of one poem in the world inevitable but that of another accidental? Is that obvious to the author, or not?*

Mandel´shtam divided all poems into the categories of "authorized" and "unauthorized". It would seem that what he would call "unauthorized" I would call "necessary". That division between optional, arbitrary works and those arising out of some sort of necessity is possibly, for me at least, more important. But for whom is that necessary; for the language, for the literary world, for tradition, for the country, the reader, the poet himself or herself? I could not say. It seems to me that every author makes the distinction between what he writes arbitrarily, wilfully, and what he writes of necessity.

– *Do you consider that of importance for the fate of a poem?*

Undoubtedly, and in my view that is something that becomes clear while the poem is being written, or even before that, and not post factum: that is to say, it is not because a poem is successful, is loved, that it is consequently necessary. On the contrary, the poems succeed, they are loved, precisely because their creation was, in some way or other, necessary.

In my opinion that is one of the most serious tests for a poet: not to succumb to the temptation of creating something unnecessary. Because getting habituated to such "professional" writing, he can render himself incapable of that degree of concentration which a necessary piece of writing demands. Perhaps I am exaggerating. There are quite a few very fine poets (Fet, for example) who have written innumerable unnecessary poems, but in amongst all that babble he suddenly gives voice to "Oblakom volnistym" (In a wavy cloud) (Fet 1986, 236), or something comparable.

– *How would you define your role in the intellectual and spiritual recuperation of Russia?*

I was a complete outsider, a renegade, in Soviet society and I was used to that. I thought out and lived through that excommunication from the public realm, as my life, as the point of departure for everything else. What was hard was not that lack of a public life; at the close of the Brezhnev years the authorities and the population — or to use their terminology — the people and the Party, really did become as one; what that was like is described in my essay "Puteshestvie v Briansk" (Journey to Briansk) and, really, it was not just my poetry and prose that was not being published. Nor were the best translations (either these were translations of "unsuitable" authors including, for example, Claudel, or they took a form which deviated from the accepted norm) or my linguistic articles (except for those in the most specialized and marginal areas of interest for me, ethnolinguistics). And I did not expect things to change in my lifetime.

To make the journey from being a renegade within society to the public arena is no easier than returning from exile. I am not exaggerating. Exile within one's own country — I know the taste of that salt. There is no-one in public life that I could turn to as a helpmate. There is no movement, no group in which I could feel at home anyway, and no-one is asking me to join any either. They have changed the decor of literary life but the leading characters on stage remain the same.

I feel, no doubt, some sort of responsibility for what is happening. In the past the form that responsibility assumed was a radical non-collaboration. Nowadays, naturally, other forms are more appropriate. But I cannot say that I know which. Really, my most serious contribution is the texts, their existence. For me it has been a great and unexpected joy to meet members of the younger generation of readers. I had no expectations that poetry written in a different atmosphere, under quite different conditions, would say anything to them at all. But it turns out that I have more readers amongst that generation than I have in my own. But, of course, it is, roughly speaking, the same old university milieu.

But other things are possible. Now I can read my work in public, give lectures (which I have done at Moscow University), meet new faces, people who did not read samizdat literature, that is people who were not known to be "one of us". When I get that opportunity I do not turn it down. Whether it is beneficial to anyone is not for me to judge. But to participate in public debate on some controversial topic of current interest, I am afraid that I cannot do that now any more than I could previously.

— *But what stops you? Your temperament or the quality of the debate?*

Both. As a rule I do not like the way in which the questions are put, I do not like those vapid choices; for example you have the Westerners and the Slavophiles, the Humanists and the Nihilists, the Freemarketers and the Socialists. In many cases, in sociology, economics, law, I am simply not competent to discuss them.

Generally speaking our cultural situation in the last few years reminds me of Dostoevskii's *Bobok*: "Let us strip ourselves naked". Both physically and spiritually: what is there to be ashamed of? "We are all knaves, sir, and that is not such a bad thing; that is what they do in civilized countries." And whoever disagrees is a canting hypocrite, a Communist or a racist. A right-winger.

— *You were saying that the texts, the poems themselves, fulfil a definite social function. But now it has become much more difficult to get published and it is rarer for poets to read their works in public. What role would you assign poetry in Russia's present rebirth?*

Many people are talking about the end of Russian poetry as a significant social force. It does not seem wise to me to make judgments about such questions in the abstract. Poetry is to be found in poets, only there, and not in some other place; the appearance of one really great poet suffices for poetry to go on existing in its glory and in its necessity to the world. But whether such a poet appears or not we cannot foretell. To whom, if not to the inhabitants of our land, should the deficiencies of Marxist determinism as to existence defining consciousness, the basis and the superstructure and so forth, be evident?

As for the actual selling of books, the pessimism is exaggerated, in my opinion. Whether a book is published or not does not really signify; there are stacks of unsold books lying around Freidkind's shop. And those that are published are scarcely even mentioned in the papers. I have not found one single serious critical assessment of Elena Shvarts's, Viktor Krivulin's, Sergei Stratanovskii's, Leonid Aronzon's, Aleksandr Velinchanskii's books — the works of the most important poets of recent years. The most cogent reason for that is that our critics simply do not possess the necessary schooling in poetry to be able to discuss it intelligently. Which of the well-known critics of the sixties is capable of making a judgement on, for instance, Aronzon? The new, ironical, wave of critics are not up to it and they are not, in general, sufficiently adept at analysing the structure of poetry.

Poetry's role? In the dead years independent poetry was circulated in manuscript. Along with the living, Mandel´shtam, Tsvetaeva, Khodasevich,

Kuzmin and others were both cherished and vital as never before. They bore witness that our language was not dead yet, that man was not yet transformed into an Orwellian creature. Poetry foretold the end of that nightmare — and, in its daedalic way, led to it.

In post-Gorbachev times poetry of remark became noticeably rarer. But I would not advise any young poet to complain about the lack of attention to poetry in general; neither the publishers nor the readers are at fault just because the appearance of a book is no longer an event, as was the case when Brodsky's typewritten manuscripts first appeared. The silence of the poets and the degeneration of their public utterances are not auspicious signs. When I encounter some new strong poetic writing I sigh with relief. It means that the poetry's time of troubles is coming to an end.

The life of the Russian language, the life of rhythm, through that you can divine what is really happening, right now, down in the depths and how the past is continuing — and what the future holds in store. That divination, perhaps, reveals that what the future holds is a social role for poetry.

—   *Do you see any specific problems facing the Russian poets of the century's final years which did not trouble the poets of its beginning?*

No doubt. At times it seems to me that the potential of Russian poetry, for all its great achievements, has scarcely been touched. That there are many paths that have not yet been explored. That — and please forgive me for this anachronism — the soul of Russian culture has not said all it has to say about itself and there remains some unexpressed beauty which none of the poets has as yet expressed. Let us say there is some sort of a literary analogue to icon painting. Which of our poets of the eighteenth, nineteenth or twentieth centuries has tried anything like that?

And, as well as that, there are many things that, to me, seem to be exhausted. The personal lyric in the romantic sense, for example. Almost everyone senses that.

—   *How do you regard the words of St Peter in his Epistle to the Romans, "Be not conformed to this age"?*

Are you asking about those words because S.S. Averintsev took them as the epigraph for his postscript to my book? (Sedakova 1994a, 358–63). First of all I have to admit that I had never lingered over those words of St Peter's. As Metropolitan Antonii says, everyone hears their own words in the New Testament, the ones that particularly solicit their attention, and remembering those that have done that in my own life I notice that for some reason or other there are no imperatives and, especially, no prohibitions. For some reason (cowardice probably) words of encouragement and promises have more effect upon me.

Of course that call for renunciation is contradicted in the second half of the same verse, "but be ye transformed by the renewing of your mind, that ye may prove what is that good, and acceptable, and perfect, will of God" — that is an explanation as to what (or, rather, to Whom) one should conform one's will (more precisely, in what ways one should transform oneself). And that is the nub of it; without that it is impossible to make the distinction between what actually relates to "this age" and what is new.

Sergei Sergeevich [Averintsev] who knows the gospel extremely well, a thousand times better than I do (and most of what I know I learnt from him, as have so many who have read him or heard him speak), knows that age *(vek)* in the language of the gospels is a synonym for world. However in that article of his he concentrates on the temporal meaning of *vek*, deals with the opposition between "the spirit of the age" which is called, absurdly, "post-Christian" or "postmodern" or, and this is not absurd, the epoch following Auschwitz and the Gulag. That definition of our era is, for me, beyond dispute, that is the way it feels to me. The first two "posts" I, really, cannot consider with any seriousness. In the West you cannot avoid that way of thinking, but in the Soviet Union we did not live in a post-Christian world but an anti-Christian situation, not in a postmodernist world but in an anti- or super-modern world (depending upon your view of modernism). As for our recent, local, copy of postmodernism, it does not, at the moment, seem to me to be worthy of serious attention. In its Russian version it seems parodically similar to the long familiar world of Smerdiakov and other "low" heroes who have, seemingly, quit the pages of Russian literature and begun to write their own novels (like [Viktor Erofeev's] *Russkaia krasavitsa* (A Russian beauty) or [Eduard Limonov's] *Eto ia — Edichka* (It's me — Eddie) create their own philosophical systems (like Galkovskii 1992 and 1995), but have been especially successful in journalism. And it is about that *nichevochestvo* and *bezobraznichestvo* that Averintsev is apparently writing about when he alludes to "this age".

No doubt, what confronts us now, on the ruins of socialism, is simply a gala parade of all the obscenities, of all the slops of "this age". But that is not all one could say about it. "This age" can muster much more dignity than *Edichka*. It could be a very moral, hard-working, serious, modest, "good family man" but there is something that it cannot and does not want to be. Without the opposition between oneself and the time one lives in, without one's unworldliness, the Good News of the Gospels would be inconceivable. Though it is that same unworldliness of which, so often, they want to "purge" historic Christianity, and in its place put some sort of moral teaching: admittedly the loftiest of all moral teachings, but in accordance with this world, realized under its conditions. And that in place of what the Apostle calls senseless and enticing!

So as to give some sort of answer to your question I could call upon those biblical verses which express that same antithesis as in those cited by Averintsev but which struck me even at a time when I was still a child in school and, really, always. Perhaps it will then become clear what, for me personally, constitute the most repellent traits of "this age". In "Babochka ili dve ikh" (A butterfly or two) it says, "i dostroiat svoi cherdak..." ("and they will finish building their upper room", 299).

At the Last Supper (John 14. 27) Christ said "Peace I leave with you, my peace I give unto you: not as the world giveth, give I unto you". For some reason even at that early age I would imagine how "the world gives" and I would weep tears of rapture that Christ gives "not as the world giveth". How it, that world, takes, withholds, violates, all well and good. But when it gives it does not give. There lies the horror. It gives on credit or it gives in payment (measure for measure) stipulating the uses to which what is given may be put (thus and not otherwise), it gives for a term, it gives unwillingly, is not forgetful of itself, demanding, at best, gratitude (but that gratitude resembles subserviency). It does not give but exchanges, and what it takes in exchange for its gifts is your freedom. And that is because, in reality, it has nothing to give; it diminishes, if it gives; it does not augment, as in life by the law of miracle; giving, generosity is not in its nature. That is the divine nature, which like the sun shines alike upon the righteous and the wicked. But the world is not divine. And therein lies all its wrong. There, it seems to me, you have it, so niggardly and timorous — for it has no hope save in its laws and they, as everyone knows, are cheerless: the "age" which the Apostle does not counsel compliance with.

It seems to me that the gospel theme of total generosity, in antithesis to the world, was the principle inspiration behind Pasternak's late poems:

Жизнь ведь тоже только миг,
Только растворенье
Нас самих во всех других
Как бы им в даренье... (Pasternak 1965, 435)

("Life is just a moment's pulse, / Just a swift dissolving / of ourselves in everyone, / Like a wedding gift") (Pasternak 1984, 132). That, of course, is certainly not a theological exegesis, merely a personal account of what moves me in that resistance to the world. Others, no doubt, would quote something else when they turn their thoughts to what is "the victory which vanquishes the world".

By the way, in the eyes of the world that victory looks very like defeat — and poetry is extremely sensitive to the rapture of such a defeat: "Vse, vse, chto gibel´iu grozit..." ("Everything, everything that threatens ruin...").

–   I would like to hear what you have to say about the vatic element in poetry. We know of many poets who have foretold their own fates. To what extent does that gift go hand in hand with the literary vocation or is it something deeply individual?

Generally speaking the prophetic has nothing to do with predicting what is to happen, in one's own or in any one else's future. It is the actualization of vertical connections, the connections of our "world of effects" with "the kingdom of causes", as Dante would have put it. A reminder of the Absolute, of how earth looks through heavenly eyes, through the eyes of the Author of all things. I think that the primordial nature of poetry, the hierophantic and the *vatical* (in Latin *vates* meant poet and prophet) does not vanish till the end, even in its advanced form. When it is no longer a sacrament dedicated to a Muse — for a readership that does not believe in Muses or in other pagan gods — but, as you said, to *belles-lettres*. I think that prophecy is an indispensable element of the poetic gift (not in the everyday sense of a species of extra-sensory perception). But in the *belles-lettres* of our modern age authors of another kind are possible; poetry is wider-ranging than the ancients' *poesia sacra,* and includes the decorative, the comic and a multitude of other things.

Not all writers of verse experience creation as a special kind of sacrament when, as the young Brodsky wrote, "nesomnenna blizost´ Bozhestva..." ("None then can doubt God's presence or His power", Brodskii 1992, 431; translation in Brodsky 1973, 104). Can a person who has no dreams or visions, who is not beloved of the gods write poetry that is even halfway good? Apparently. But their work does not interest me overmuch.

On the other hand, the possession of the power of prophecy, of any sort of mystical aptitude does not guarantee the writing of successful poetry. Andrei Belyi, for instance, was known to have gifts of that nature, but they were unable to save his poetry. And it is not known if such faculties were in his possession, but in Rilke there are to be found images which, at times, resemble some ancient revelation (The "Duino Elegies").

I can recall one very interesting trichotomous division of poetry which was, once upon a time, in the fifteenth century, proposed by Pierre Ronsard (in his "Elegy to Jacques Grevin", which I happen to have translated). He speaks of two sorts of poetry: the divinely inspired, or the Corybantic, and well-constructed journeyman verse. But it is interesting that, in his opinion, poets of the first kind were very few, and that through the whole expanse

of recorded time: "Quatre ou cinq seulement sont apparus au monde"... All
the rest, including the Greek tragedians and epicists and Ronsard himself,
he assigns to a third order; the halfling poets, the masters of the middle
way, neither journeymen nor divinely inspired:

> Entre ces deux mestiers, un mestier s'est trouvé
> Qui tenant le milieu, pour bon est approuvé
> Et Dieu l'a concedé aux hommes pour les faire
> Apparoistre en renom par dessus le vulgaire...

I can only agree with Pierre Ronsard; the greater part of art and even its
most brilliant exemplifications are nothing more than half poetry. There
is just one thing that makes any dividing line more difficult to locate: many
of the halfling poets, if just for a moment, a line, or a poem, make their
way out into the immensity of truly divinely inspired poetry.

– *Your affinity with the culture of the ancients, how is that realized in
your poetry?*

Of the two ancient classical cultures — Greece and Rome — I wholeheartedly prefer Greece (though I can read Latin and scarcely decipher
Greek). What is more, all the poets of another age who excite me are
somehow connected with Greece. Hellenism is not what I love but the
Greece of early classical times; that of the early philosophers, of Plato, of
the first lyric poets, the ceramic artists, the masons and the sculptors... What
I love is the inexplicable, miraculous sense of measure which is, for me,
beauty itself. That is what Rome lacked. I love Greece. One almost feels
the breath of myth. But it is already pregnant with the ethereal, fluid,
transparent light of another, non-mythical sensibility which makes it different from the heavily hieratic cultures like the Egyptian.

How is that love reflected in what I write? I find that difficult to say.
Perhaps in the way I place importance on the whole, on proportion, on
symmetry (the word, in Russian, is etymologically related to our modern
"humility"). In the way that measure is dearer to me than the immeasurable
(the absolute opposite of Tsvetaeva). Or in the way I want the reader to
be able to catch glimpses, through my images, of the anti-types, of the
Platonic ideas. In the way that, like the Greeks, I love wisdom, the Higher
Wisdom even. My favourite Roman poet is Horace — the most Greek of
Romans.

– *How would you differentiate between the process of writing a poem
and that of working upon an essay?*

Unlike my poetry the stimulus for writing an essay may well be external. It may well be done to order; written on a subject that someone has asked me to tackle. That has happened fairly often over the years and I am glad of the stimulus.

I like to write prose in a prosaic way. The prose-poetic amalgam of many poets holds no attraction for me. Without rhythm, high-flown language and imagery confuse: as Pushkin said, "prose is humble". The essayists I have modelled myself on include Eliot and two quite different English essayists: C.S. Lewis and Chesterton. My little things in prose seem to me to be more like poetry. A compositional structure is much more of an imperative for small pieces. Often, when I start, just as with poetry, I do not know where things will end up; the text starts to lead. And that can produce the same surprise and delight; how did that come about? There is not the tension of poetry, the somehow unspoken certainty that this is the one and only form suitable for this particular job, there is nothing of that about the essay. It is a world where one is allowed to choose.

Of course, in the essay you cannot make as great a mess of it as you can in poetry; there is not much risk, and success does not signify very much either.

– *What was the stimulus behind your essay "Pokhvala poezii"* (In praise of poetry) (Sedakova 1991c, 135–64) *for which you received the Andrei Belyi Prize? The title itself is remarkable.*

Its title came from an early essay of Averintsev's, "Pokhvala filologii" (In praise of philology). The essay itself came about like this. It was a commission. I was asked, more precisely chided, to write it by Vladimir Arkadievich Saitanov, a Pushkin specialist, an authoritative figure in our "alternative culture" of the seventies. A critic, he was helpmate to many poets, a friend of Elena Shvarts and myself. Under the initials D. S. he wrote about Brodsky (D.S. 1986), and he is the author of the postscript to my Paris book (Sedakova 1986). Now he has abandoned Russian literature and vanished somewhere in the depths of Judaism.

He assisted with the publication — or the creation — of Elena Shvarts's samizdat books; collected, collated the poems and wrote an accompanying commentary. Once he had a brainwave: he made up a collection of my early poems and took them along to a publishing house. Because they were not as good as my later poems they stood a chance of being accepted. If the poems are not too good it means the author is still "looking"; if he is already found "it", and it is not the accepted thing, then there is nothing to be done. That is a secret I learnt at one publishing house while I was still at school. Well, Saitanov chose these juvenilia of mine, gave the book the unfortunate

title, *Ia zhizn´ v poryve zhit´´* (I am in a rush to live life), and took it along
to *Sovremennik*. The manuscript was returned, in a very short time, with
a refusal and critical comments (some of them are quoted in my Paris book).
But while we were putting together that pile of old poems Saitanov would
ask me about the circumstances in which I had come to write such and
such a piece. And he asked me to write down my stories, which he thought
were of interest. And so, in the form of a letter addressed to him — and
that is not just a rhetorical form, it really is a letter — out in the country,
in the summer, I started to write that whole account, about my childhood,
about poetry.

Of course, as usual, the external stimulus only helped to crystallize a
concept that had existed for a long while in my head. In this case it formed
this single entity out of two existing concepts. One of them was to write
the tale of my early childhood, something along the lines of Tolstoi's
Detstvo (Childhood). I really love that. In my opinion it is undervalued.
There are those giant works *Voina i mir* (War and Peace) and *Anna Karenina*
and they have pushed it into the shade. It is a marvellously composed work;
the subtlety of it both forestalls and outstrips Proust's cardiogram of feeling.
Thomas Mann compared it with the *Iliad* for the purity of its epic beginning.
The force which impelled its creation was explained by Tolstoi as the fact
that it seemed to him no-one had ever enjoyed such a happy childhood
as he had and he wanted to communicate that happiness. I also remembered
the happiness of my own childhood and wanted to display it, but I was
unable to find a way of doing so. I tried starting my narrative in the
traditional manner but nothing was right; the main character, the narrational
"I" that was where the difficulty lay. Perhaps it was that same difficulty
that made Tolstoi write not about his own childhood — in old age he
reproached himself for his fabrications and for taking not his own childhood
but that of someone he knew (the main character is called Nick and not
Leo). And he began to write about it all over again; the real truth about
his own this time. But, as everyone knows, he did not get much beyond
his memories of feeding at the breast, and bathtime. Fantastic realism!

So, the complexity of dealing with "myself", of telling about "myself"
got in my way. And another thing — the short story form. I understood
clearly the sort of revolution that had taken place in prose writing since
Tolstoi's day that made it quite impossible to gather this bouquet of stories
about my childhood as if I had been living in the middle of the nineteenth
century. But what other way there was, I just could not imagine. There was
another project, also long-standing, to write something in the way of an
ars poetica. And for that I could not find the form either.

And suddenly Saitanov's seemingly strange request formed this circle
around both of those themes and I understood that what I could do was

put them together and present a sort of two-handed play with my stories of childhood and my musings on the nature of poetry. In the course of "Pokhvala poezii" the second voice gets more and more voluble and squeezes out the first, my childhood, about which there is finally less than I would like. But, perhaps, everything I write in my poetry is really about my childhood.

So, in "Pokhvala poezii", two unresolved problems were resolved, only to be rolled into one.

– *What did you have in mind when you said in "Pokhvala poezii" that the hands on the face of the clock of art sometimes move as far as the 'Fourth Eclogue' only to stop there"*?

If only I could have had the opportunity to put that more clearly and in greater detail. But I will try now. "The Fourth Eclogue", as everyone knows, gave Virgil the reputation, in the Middle Ages, of being "the pagan prophet" and that is why it is he who leads Dante to the Terrestrial Paradise, to the summit of Mount Purgatory, that is why Statius says to him, *Per te poeta fui, per te cristiano...* (Canto XXII, *Purgatorio*).

That mysterious and triumphant "Eclogue" seems to foretell the Saviour's birth and the dawning of a new age on earth. Besides the language of Virgilian prophecy is quite unbiblical: his images come from Classical mythology that was in his blood — but he turns the age of myth upon its head and places it in the future. Classical mythology had its face firmly turned towards the past, and the age of justice, the Golden Age of myth, was always in the long vanished and distant past, after which had followed century after century of degradation. That about-face on Virgil's part has great significance! Incidentally, in the *Aeneid* the pagan myth of eternal return is broken; the centre of the action lies in the future, in the destiny of the hero and in the destiny of Rome: that is the magnet which draws about it the field of action and defines the psychological make-up of Aeneas himself. In that sense, in its apotheosis of faith in a higher will which guides his hero towards his future, the *Aeneid* is no less prophetic a work than the "Fourth Eclogue".

What I had in mind when speaking of the time of the "Fourth Eclogue" was that with the language which classical art has at its disposal to talk about the Saviour, it can only do so, dimly, under the cover of allegory or using images which are not even clear to the poet himself, as if he were guessing or crystal-gazing. He has not eyes for that, he is like an ancient statue.

It seems the great epoch of Christian (ecclesiastical) art refutes my assertion about the clock of culture which always stops when it reaches

the hour of dim presentiment. Church art was capable of expressing not
presentiment but sentiment and knowledge? But all of it, Byzantine icons,
Gregorian chant, church sculpture and architecture, liturgy, hymns, and
much else besides, cannot so easily be compared with secular art. Only
in recent times has it become possible to view all that in a purely aesthetic
light. But it was not simply aesthetic, it was functional, serviceable. But
secular art was, to all appearances, beholden to nothing outside itself; it
took any field of study or dogma and used it to spin out its own variations
on a theme. And that defined both the creative personality of the modern
artist and also the character of his creations, unserviceable things valued
for themselves.

What I have in mind, for example, is that the artist was not obliged to
create his works like an old icon painter in a state of prayer and fasting;
generally speaking he had no regard for his personal spiritual well-being
and in other epochs, such as the Romantic, he was simply obliged to be
immoral. Speaking of art, what I have in mind is this paradigm, the paradigm of secular art. But we have not changed it! Now we are scraping the
bottom of the barrel, as was obvious to many artists even in the first decade
of the present century.

The vicissitudes of pious or edifying art, the devotional as distinct from
the religious — Eliot's distinction — have not resolved the situation. It
remains marginal almost, one would say, amateurish in recent times. Usually those things, loyal and praiseworthy from a confessional point of view,
are, as a rule, in routine and simplified formats deriving from the individualistic tradition of art but adapted for a not very well schooled reader. It
is art that should not alarm, place the reader in a quandary or leave anything
at all unresolved. The authors are generally not very talented and are
insensible of even the most glaring contradictions between the forms in
which they work and their work's content (message). It is not a matter of
art but a matter of personal piety. But the art of the Middle Ages was very
different: it was working on the threshold of the possible in terms of
intellectual and spiritual effort. It was daring.

There are other attempts to return artistic inspiration to an art with a
Christian basis — and without rejecting the uneasiness and complexity of
modern individualistic art; I am thinking now of the poetry and drama of
Eliot and Claudel. Their experiments seem to me to have been undeniable
achievements though, apparently, most lovers of art do not take them
seriously. To them it is no longer art but something like poetic propaganda.

Today my views on the clock of art and the "Fourth Eclogue" are different
from what they were when I wrote "Pokhvala poezii". The exhaustion of
the resources of classical secular art is becoming more and more obvious:
it is degenerating into sheer negativity. It is as if it now feels that it is

impossible to deal with anything other than the ugly, the horrid: the gutter and the void. Plato compared that sort of thing to salty water; it is impossible to drink and you need to wash it off, as it says in *Phaedrus* "with words fit for drinking". Ones which will not take away from us what we have... could, possibly, have given us something. How can that come about?

Incidentally, it seems to me that the last example of classical art that is not doctrinaire and, what is more, is positive is the cinema of Fellini. *And the Boat Sails On* (E la nave va) may, possibly, be in its way a "Fourth Eclogue". It has the same problematical and powerful symbolism. I have not seen anything to equal it in literature these last years.

> – *How do you explain the fact that from your schooldays you have lived in the midst of Russia's best scholars and even been on the closest of terms with several of their number? Just a few names need be mentioned: Iu.M. Lotman, S.S. Averintsev, M.L. Gasparov, V.V. Ivanov, V.V. Bibikhin, M.M. Shvartsman.*[5]

My first acquaintance with those noted linguists and theoreticians of culture you mention was as a student. I saw them as my teachers. In that — I suppose one would call it semiotic — milieu was to be found the centre of our cultural life, especially in the seventies.

The academic avant-garde was then playing the role formerly played by Russian literature (and that, as everyone knows, was a lot more than literature). It was asking all the really important questions at the time — cultural, spiritual, even political. In comparison with the work of that group of academics the artistic products of that era seem somehow childish and makeshift. After a Lotman lecture or an article by Averintsev, Voznesenskii's poetry or Aksenov's prose was just impossible. It was not just the contrast of levels, they were, in a way, antithetical.

Now they have published Lotman (his death seems to have brought a whole era to an end) and I can define what it was... It was an attempt by Russian humanism at a *renovatio studium,* at something similar to the Florentine renaissance (incidentally one of the members of that circle, M. Batkin, made a brilliant study of Humanism, and in his analysis you can catch glimpses of the self-portraits of our own renaissance); in the same way V.V. Bibikhin was able to give an intimate portrayal of Petrarch, full of fellow-feeling and thought.

I can further reinforce my comparison, though really the subject deserves detailed historical study. As in any renaissance the humanist investigation into the workings of earlier epochs — from mythological societies to the Russian Silver Age — was not simply academic. It meant a kind of building a new life, a self-re-creation, a renewal of the image of *homo sapiens,* thinking and creative man, a confirmation of his dignity (*dignitas* is a renaissance word). Instead of a pure Latin, we used the metalanguage of structural description, *sui generis a nova lingua docta*. One could instantly gauge whether someone was one of us. Could they understand and express themselves in that "scientific" language? (Of course it was a kind of snobbery.) As in the first renaissance we were drawn towards the search for a universal philosophy, even a quasi-religious basis, but, in fact we did not find it. To return to one of the great historical faiths would have contradicted our aims, firstly our universality, the super- or post-historical position of our viewpoint and, secondly, our freedom of intellectual research untrammelled by any dogma whatsoever. Thus, behind the system of signs there was no discovery of any instance which these signs will give: culture with its signs lives within an enclosed circle (I dealt with that subject in my essay "Znak, smysl, vest'" (Sign, meaning, information) (Sedakova 1991b).

Like the Western renaissance, ours, in what it achieved, turned out to be not a restoration but an innovation. It might even be seen as avant-garde. Incidentally, about the part played by Antiquity without which the first renaissance would have been unimaginable: Lotman would recount that when he was absolutely fed up (with the endless feebleminded idiocy of Soviet working life, with the authorities and the general wretchedness of life under that regime) he would walk into the Tartu museum and contemplate the replicas of antique statues; in visiting them he would restore his spirits.

Like the original humanism, our cultural movement was composed not just of active humanists but of quite a wide circle of readers and lecture-goers in various cities. Over the years this circle grew. Here were the boundary lines of Soviet culture in the "dark Ages": on the other side of them, in my opinion, remained the people of the sixties, the generation of "Papa Hema" (Hemingway), of "Supermen" and juvenile individualism.

Those two cultures, pre- and post-renaissance, almost never met. Voznesenskii may well have been able to go abroad and visit Heidegger, Evtushenko, T.S. Eliot, but there was no way people like him could gain entry into the cultural élite at home. That circle (E. Meletinskii called it his cultural ghetto) set itself apart not just by its different (from that permitted officially) educational outlook and intellectual independence, but also by its demands for another type of behaviour, a different kind of personality altogether. It was an alternative to bohemian man (bohemianism was characteristic, really, of both official and unofficial artistic circles). Responsibility, hard work, the ability to debate, social decency and politeness (*inter alia*, a thing that was victimized in Soviet society at that time) were the norm. I have in mind the older generation: unfortunately, the Structuralists' pupils inherited very little of that, remaining simply specialists in their field. But I have no reason to go into that depressing story now.

I cannot imagine my life without that circle. It was, as I said, an exclusive and alien body within Soviet society (a ghetto!) But its existence was permitted — something that would not have happened in earlier Soviet times. We were able to meet at seminars in each other's homes, at conferences in Tartu and Moscow, at exhibitions and concerts. Of course, in a lot of things I am a product of that circle, that milieu.

My first experience of it as a participant was in February 1974 in Tartu, just after I graduated from university, at a conference where I presented an orthodox structuralist paper concerning the structure of ceremony. In the middle of the week of the conference, the day of Pasternak's birth, the day of Pushkin's death, there was an evening meeting at someone's home. Iurii Mikhailovich [Lotman] talked about the history of card games (in connection with *Pikovaia dama* [The Queen of Spades]). His improvised talks were in no way inferior to prepared lectures, as everyone knows who managed to hear him. We were drinking wine when suddenly N. I. Tolstoi, my university tutor, said to me: "I advised Iurii Mikhailovich to ask you to read some of your poetry. [Tolstoi was the only one there who knew I wrote poetry — OS] You won't refuse?" That was my debut. And, really, reading my poetry aloud was never again to be such an ordeal. My idols, my teachers, the most intelligent people in Russia, I had to do it in front of them! Just imagine that!

Tolstoi told me that after the reading Iurii Mikhailovich went up to him and said: "Do not turn Ol'ga into an academic. Let her remain a poet." The encouragement and attention of those people, no doubt, softened the ordeal of my literary ostracism (over a period of twenty years nothing of what I wrote was published). The opinions of each one of those people was more important to me than the judgements of the whole of the Union of Writers. For me their court was the court of the future.

There was one other person whose approval I very much wanted — and I never did get it. That was Venedikt Erofeev's. I first met him before his world-famous book *Moskva-Petushki* had been written and I ended up on the pages of that immortal work with the walk-on role of a "half-crazed poetess". I also regard Venedikt as my teacher. I tried to describe what he taught me when I was writing my recollections of him (Sedakova 1990a).[6] As for what he meant to me in my youth I can only compare that with the influence of Averintsev. Venedikt was liberating but could have become destructive, whilst Averintsev was constructive. What an enormous multilingual body of tradition he brought to those of us who read or listened to him. And he had not studied that tradition with the distant, and distancing, scrutiny the French analysts, for example, exhibit; he lived in it or, rather, it lived in him, with all its exigencies, all its promises. Sergei Sergeevich [Averintsev] laid bare our spiritual orphanhood: he exposed us to both fountainheads of Christian Europe, Athens and Jerusalem, their commingling and their passage through the Latin and Byzantine Middle Ages through Neo-Thomism and the latest German poetry, all of that with the penetration of the academic and the heartfelt feeling of the poet and, last but by no means least, with the conviction of a practising Christian. His thought is full of sobriety and good humour: those who really paid attention to what he said were hardly likely to be attracted to any sort of sectarianism, xenophobia or ideological fixation. In my opinion what Sergei Sergeevich does is best termed a new apologetics. With his work he answers the modern world in its own language, in one of that world's most authoritative languages: the language of scholarship. I cannot overestimate what I owe to him.

But besides the well-known figures from the academic world and Venedikt I could name many others who, to use an old-fashioned term, honoured me by their friendship; people whom it was a pleasure to meet. Elena Shvarts — I have already said something of the shattering effect her poetry had upon me when I first read it. M.M. Shvartsman, whose fame will grow and grow, I am convinced of that (I have been meaning to write about his extraordinary art for too long now). The astounding composer Aleksandr Vustin, the artist Iurii Iarin. I am also convinced that their art will be valued very highly indeed. The pianist Vladimir Ivanovich Khvostin who taught me to play: "Tristan" is dedicated to his memory.

But the people I am most fond of are scarcely known at all to the general public and, as you said, I have no doubt that they are amongst the best of them. Their names you can find amongst the dedicatees of my poems. It has become customary to come together on my birthday, generally at the studio of some artist friend, because you cannot fit sixty or seventy people into my flat and you should just see that crowd!

And there is the priceless, incomparable gift that life has given me in the person of my spiritual father. If not for him I would have the same idea of the Church that all outsiders have. And like them I would not have had, I do not suppose, the best experience of my life: my encounter with Divine Grace.

Besides my closest friends I have an amazingly wide circle of acquaintances, of various ages, in various cities, and I have known a lot of them for many years now. How did that happen? It astonishes me. I cannot begin to explain that generosity of fate. At the beginning of our conversation I was going on about how alone I was... But, it seems to me, that all my friends like to be alone, perhaps that is what unites us? Not the being alone but simply being with oneself. I have heard that there are a lot of people who go out of their way to avoid that.

– You have translated such greats as Dante, Rilke and Eliot. How do you see yourself, as the poet's ally, double, or rival?

First of all, at school, I was already attempting, whilst studying English, to translate poetry: a ballad of Yeats and a sonnet of Wordsworth. It was simply out of curiosity; how would it turn out? Our tradition of translation, as you know, unlike here [in Britain], demands the full reproduction of the original verse form. When Ezra Pound did that, the poem was published as his own original composition. Really, the need to preserve both meaning and form is over ambitious. But there are many people in our country who have mastered the art of doing that. What to translate is mostly a matter of reading something and thinking it is a pity that is not in Russian.

As for the authors, personal contact, I do not even think about it: the poem is the thing. I am choosy about what I translate, unlike the professional who has to do it all in one flood, thousands of lines at a time. Anyway, as with my own poems, it was not published. The one genre in demand was the essay or reports on linguistic studies abroad which would appear in learned journals.

– Did you enter into a spiritual relationship with your authors at a later stage as you began to change your estimation of their work?

It was Rilke who drew me above all, and there is no doubt I do feel he is there in his poetry — though it is well known that his intentions were to write impersonally. "Dinge! sag ich — Dinge! Dinge! Dinge!" How does a translator relate to that personality? Like any interpreter who spends his time in the company of some VIP, you must communicate what he has to say as accurately as possible. But the accuracy is a problem. In reproducing the form you are forced to deviate from the original. You have to change things selectively, but in which direction do you go? From what resources do you draw your changes? From a routine stock of poetic tropes, as our professional translators usually do? One of them attributed this line to Rilke: "Pesn´ - bytie. Bog mozhet pet´ bespechno...". That *bespechno* is just not possible from Rilke: what can you replace an unsuccessful image with? There is a line from the *Requiem for Count Wolf von Kalkreut*, the literal translation of which is, *Ty ne uznal sobstvennoi radosti. Kak zdes´ ona byla doma* (You did not recognize your own joy. How it was at home here) which I translated as an iamb: "Kak zdeshnemu ona byla k litsu...", because *at home* and *befitting* are very close in Rilke (translation in Sedakova 1988, 15). The inner connections between images can only be understood through a knowledge of his work as a whole: in translating one poem you really ought to keep in mind his whole poetic world. It is that whole Rilke that interested me. Besides the translations I also wrote a paper on him which is now lost. In the whole you will find the facial features of the author: "Litso ego i bylo tem prostorom, / Chto tianetsia k nemu..." (translation in Rilke 1965, 133). As Rilke himself wrote in "Death of a Poet", calling the human face of the poet "a timid mask doomed to decay". But it is even more difficult to translate someone who is not just a poet but a saint as well. I tried that with the poems of St Francis of Assisi. However in that instance the psychological and biographical personality of Francis did not interest me all that much. What did interest me was how to communicate the inseparable smile which lit up his face — so that the features disappear into it.

There is yet another side to translation. It satisfies the actor in one: to speak with the voice of a wise and masculine individual, like Rilke, or with the voice of a holy mendicant friar. An actor when he works uses his own body; the poet-translator, his state of mind. Of course the range of roles in my repertoire is limited. There are many styles and meanings I cannot play. But in choosing an author I seek in him not a reflection of myself (even an idealized, imaginary, reflection) but what I lack — the firmness of a Dante or a Rilke, let us say, or the dryness of Eliot, Claudel's sense of lofty comedy, St Francis's purity. Sometimes the changes one is forced to make are not lucky finds but real losses. One has to be, for example, harsher, cruder than I like to be.

—   *In as much as you translate, basically, authors whose work you admire,*
    what are the gains for you as a poet?

An outsider, perhaps, could see whether there was a gain or a loss. Loss is inevitable: loss of a certain spontaneity. Communicating a stranger's gestures, to a certain extent, makes your own seem strange to you; you can begin to see yourself from the outside. The question of lack of spontaneity... That is not a quality that I see as needing to be preserved at all cost. I value ripeness higher than spontaneity. There I agree with Brodsky when he quotes Lear, "ripeness is all" (*King Lear*, Act V, Scene 2).

What does a translation give you? In my opinion it extends your freedom. There are habits you acquire, habits of language, verse, style, and you find that they will no longer tug at you like *idées fixes*. Not that I want the opposite, I do not want to construct with a firm hand a thing that is not me. But I do want to be able to tell the difference: perhaps that stream pulls you along not because it is particularly deep or strong, but simply because you are weak and give in to your own lack of skill. For me it is that there is a certain distancing in translation, as there is in writing books for children or philological studies (I really do have the same fear of analysis of my work as Blok had. Remember how afraid he was of learning about any formal analysis of his work.) In essence, you see, I look at it as simultaneously a loss and a gain.

– *In which of your poems do you see yourself as reaching the heights of your powers, as a poet and as a Christian?*

That is difficult. Perhaps there is not a whole poem — but there are outbursts — individual images, lines, combinations of words. In "Tristan", in "Starye pesni" (Old songs), in "Kitaiskoě puteshestvie" (A Chinese journey). I do not know if the reader can make out those images but I distinguish them by their anti-gravitational force. With a few words, a combination of words to draw one's attention upwards — with the same naturalness as the earth draws falling objects downwards. I find many such words in Khlebnikov, or in Shvarts's "Solovei spasaiushchii" (Saving nightingale): "Khotia golosovoi almaznoiu igloi / On sshil Derevniu Novuiu i Kamennuiu dyshashchuiu mglu..." ('Though with the diamond needle of its voice / It stitched New Village to Stone Island's breathing haze...', Shvarts 1989, 60.[7] They, as it were, give us a glimpse, even though a very fleeting one, of our primordial heavenly dwelling place, the homeland for which humans, as in exile, pines. But you were asking not about Khlebnikov or Shvarts but about me? Perhaps if you were to take a whole poem, the second in "Babochka ili dve ikh" (Sedakova 1994a, 300) or "Elegiia smokovnitsy" (An elegy for a fig-tree) (306–08).

Translated by Chris Jones with Valentina Polukhina

REFERENCES

Batiushkov, K. N., 1978. *Opyty v stikhakh i proze* (Moscow: Nauka).
Bibikhin, V.V. 1993. *Iazyk filosofii* (Moscow: Progress).
Blok, A., 1955. *Stikhotvoreniia* (Leningrad: Sovetskii pisatel').
Brodskii, I., 1992. *Sochineniia* (St Petersburg: Pushkinskii Fond), I.
Brodsky, J., 1973. Selected Poems, tr. G. L. Kline (Harmondsworth: Penguin Books).
D. S., 1986. "Pushkin i Brodskii", in Lev Loseff (ed.), *Poetika Brodskogo*, (Tenafly: Hermitage), 207–18.
Epshtein, M., 1988. *Paradoksy novizny* (Moscow: Sovetskii pisatel'), 159–66.

Evtushenko, E., 1975. *Izbrannye proizvedeniia v dvukh tomakh* (Moscow: Khudozhestvennaia literatura), I.

Fet, A. A., 1986. *Stikhotvoreniia i poemy* (Leningrad: Sovetskii pisatel´).

Galkovskii, D., 1992. "Beskonechnyi tupik. Fragmenty knigi", *Novyi mir*, 1992, 9: 78-120 and 11: 228–83.

_____, 1995. "Beskonechnyi tupik. Iskhodnyi tekst", *Kontinent*, 81: 220–307.

Goethe, J. W. von, *Selected Verse* (Harmondsworth: Penguin Books).

Loseff, L., 1986. *Poetika Brodskogo* (Tenafly: Hermitage).

Mandelstam, O., 1973a. *Selected Poems*, tr. Clarence Brown and W.S. Merwin (Harmondsworth: Penguin Books).

_____, 1973b. *Selected Poems*, tr. D. McDuff (Cambridge: Rivers Press).

_____, 1977. *Fifty Poems*, tr. B. Mears (New York: Persea Books).

Mandel´shtam, O., 1990. *Sochineniia v dvukh tomakh* (Moscow: Khudozhestvennaia literatura), I.

Obolensky, D., 1965. *The Heritage of Russian Verse* (Bloomington: Indiana University Press).

Pasternak, B. L., 1965. *Stikhotvoreniia i poemy* (Moscow-Leningrad: Sovetskii pisatel´).

_____, 1972. *Fifty Poems*, tr. L.P. Slater (London: Unwin Books).

_____, 1984. *Selected Poems*, tr. J. Stallworthy and P. France (Harmondsworth: Penguin Books).

Pushkin, A. S., 1948. *Polnoe sobranie sochinenii* (Moscow: Academiia nauk SSSR), III.

Rilke, R. M., 1965 *Lirika*, tr. T. Serman (Moscow-Leningrad: Sovetskii pisatel´)

Sedakova, O., 1984. "Puteshestvie v Briansk", *Vybor*, 2.

_____, 1986. *Vrata, okna, arki* (Paris: YMCA-Press).

_____, 1988. "Stikhi Rilke", tr. O. Sedakova, *Rodnik*, 8: 13–17.

_____, 1990a. "Neskazannaia rech´ na vechere Venedikta Erofeeva", *Alma Mater*, 1 (3): 6–7.

_____, 1990b. "O pogibshem literaturnom pokolenii — pamiati Leni Gubanova", *Volga*, 6: 135-46.

_____, 1991a. "Ocherki drugoi poezii: ocherk pervyi — Viktor Krivulin", *Druzhba narodov*, 10: 258-66.

_____, 1991b. "Znak, smysl, vest´", *Nezamechennaia zemlia: Literaturno-khudozhestvennyi al´manakh* (Moscow-St Petersburg), 249–52.

_____, 1991c. "Zametki i vospominaniia o raznykh stikhotvoreniiakh, a takzhe POKHVALA POEZII", *Volga*, 6: 135-64.

_____, 1991d. "Neskazannaia rech´ na vechere Venedikta Erofeeva", *Teatr*, 9: 98–102.

_____, 1992. "Puteshestvie v Briansk", *Volga*, 5–6: 138–57.

_____, 1993. "Pri russkom imeni...", *Iskusstvo kino*, 10: 4–9.

_____, 1994a. *Stikhi* (Moscow: Gnozis).

————, 1994b. *The Silk of Time* (Keele: Keele University Press).

————, 1997. *The Wild Rose and Selected Poems*, tr. R. McKane (London: Approach Publishing).

Shvarts, E., 1989. *Storony sveta* (Leningrad: Sovetskii pisatel´).

Smith, G. S., 1993. *Contemporary Russian Poetry: A Bilingual Anthology* (Bloomington and Indianapolis: Indiana University Press).

Tsvetaeva, M. I., 1965. *Izbrannye proizvedeniia* (Moscow-Leningrad: Sovetskii pisatel´).

————, 1988. *A Life through Poetry: M. Tsvetaeva's Lyric Diary*, tr. J. A. Taubman (Columbus, OH: Slavica Publishers).

Zabolotskii, N. A., 1965. *Stikhotvoreniia i poemy* (Moscow-Leningrad: Sovetskii pisatel´).

NOTES

1. This work was first published in Sedakova 1984.
2. Unless otherwise noted, all poetry quotations are translated by Chris Jones.
3. Some of the poems from Sedakova's unpublished book *Dikii shipovnik* are in her 1994 collection.
4. V.V. Bibikhin is one of the most popular contemporary Russian philosophers; he teaches at MGU and is the author of, amongst other things, Bibikhin 1993.
5. M.M. Shvartsman is a very original artist who works in the tradition of the sacred art of temple painting which he calls *ieratika*. His first major exhibition took place in 1993 in the Tret´iakov Gallery.
6. A fuller version of this piece was printed in Sedakova 1991, 98–102.
7. Translated by Michael Molnar, unpublished.

ELENA SHVARTS AND THE DISTANCES OF SELF-DISCLOSURE

Stephanie Sandler

In the 1980s, a number of previously underground Russian poets came to new prominence, mostly Moscow poets from several different schools. They had shared their work with each other for years; the evidence of their collaboration and intense connections showed in mutual quotation and dedications, and in their preference for group publications (particularly in the case of the Moscow Conceptualists).[1] After the appearance of an astute essay about them by Mikhail Epshtein in 1987 — an important publication because he organized little-known poets into discernible trends and in several cases published their verse for the first time in a mainstream journal — a powerful awareness of avant-garde Russian poetry dawned on a wider reading public, including Slavic scholars and translators of Russian poetry, some of whom had followed these poets' work through samizdat and occasional émigré publications.[2] Anthologies and slim volumes of verse appeared in quick succession at the end of the decade, making available such differing poets as Dmitrii Prigov, Timur Kibirov, Sergei Gandlevskii, Ol´ga Sedakova, Mikhail Aizenberg, and Aleksandr Eremenko, among many others.[3]

All these poets lived and worked in Moscow, but poetry circles and prominent poets also continue to emerge in Russia's historic capital for poetry, Leningrad: some poets have drawn on that city's distinctive poetic tradition, whose stars included Pushkin, Blok, Akhmatova, Mandel´shtam, Kuzmin, and Brodsky.[4] For one contemporary Petersburg poet, Elena Shvarts, a different Petersburg literary tradition has been just as important: the alienated heroes, beginning with Gogol´'s clerks and Dostoevskii's poor folk, of nineteenth-century Russian fiction. Shvarts continues the habits of watchful self-revelation found in some of Russia's greatest novels. Her poems dramatize the processes of self-inspection and failed self-description, and the failure becomes an ironically enticing strategy for keeping curious readers at bay, rather than a refusal to burrow deeper into her own desires and contradictions. More than her contemporaries, she has churned out passionate lyrics driven by an energy for introspection.[5] Thus a paradox of self-expression defines Shvarts's lyric poems: she appears to know no limits in her relentless confrontation with her own desires, quests, fears, and failings, but she firmly establishes limits to what she believes any human interlocutor, including her readers, will ever understand about her. Shvarts's poems repeatedly and painfully ask the question whether the poet resembles other people, whether she can establish any human connections that are authentic and reliable.

The goal of this essay is to explore that paradox of self-disclosure, particularly to clarify its reliance on religious concepts and on the work of Russia's poets. I explore these questions through close examination of four short poems from the early 1980s. One cannot really argue for any texts being "typical" of Shvarts, for she is a poet of diverse and ever-changing talents, as we see vividly in her longer cycles of lyric poems on historical, religious, and fantastic themes.[6] The shorter poems treated here offer samples of Shvarts's flair for handling such material, and in a more compressed and compact way. In addition, these poems expose the paradoxes of comprehending the poet's psyche; their patterns for thematizing distances between self and other, poet and reader can help us recognize the patterns of self-disclosure that define her work.

Shvarts is perhaps not so well known in the West as to dispense with all further introduction. Her work has become much more readily available to readers, however, than was the case when she was largely a poet of underground Leningrad poetry circles and samizdat publications. Between 1985 and 1993, five volumes of her poetry appeared, and her long *Laviniia* cycle was published in 1987.[7] The 1990 Leningrad collection stands out among these as a kind of logical culmination, with poems grouped according to the six books of poetry she had composed by the close of the 1980s.[8] Shvarts's body of work is impressive, including over a hundred short lyric poems, more than a dozen poem cycles, plus the seventy-nine *Laviniia* poems. In recent years, helpful introductory essays about her work have appeared.[9] A picture of Shvarts's poems as a jangling mix of religious, violent, erotic, historical, and mythological themes comes into focus in these essays, although each tends to emphasize some aspects at the expense of others; she is roundly praised for the courage of these concepts, especially their strange and creative juxtapositions, and for the linguistic energy that keeps her poems lingering in the mind; and she is not infrequently subjected to some criticism, as well, for unevenness, or naiveté, or sheer excess. There is in Shvarts a depth of emotion and a wildness that eludes religious, psychological, or cultural explanation.[10]

It is this elusiveness that interests me. Shvarts has created a poetic persona of whom little can be known. This elusiveness co-exists with the many concrete references in her poetry: to her city, Leningrad, to neighbourhoods in which she has lived, to recognizable historical events. But these details are nearly always the distractions of Shvarts's poetry; they are the seductively casual facts that create the impression of a biography but hold in suspension the story of a writing, thinking self.[11] What Shvarts tries to do, head-on, is to make clear how much we are missing in every encounter, sometimes by claiming to know little herself.

In a striking poem of 1981, "Ia rodilas´ s ladon´iu gladkoi" (I was born with smooth palms), Shvarts writes a self-description that turns on the illusion of unknowability.

> Судьба плетет помельче сети,
> Чтоб в них позастревали дети,
> Но я... я вырвусь из сетей.

Я родилась с ладонью гладкой,
С ладонью ровной манекена—
Цыганка мне не нагадает
Казенный дом или измену.
Не нагадает мне любви,
Не напророчит мне разлуки—
В высоких складах синевы
Мне не хватило бечевы,
Когда ее вживляли в руки.
Ладоней мне не разрезали
И звезд на них не начертали,
Не рисовали линий в них,
Нет для меня любви и смерти,
И встречи нежданных роковых.
Ко мне ночами прилетает
Мой фатум с тяжкою сумой,
Набитой до краев нетраченной судьбой,
Царапает бессильно мне ладони
И, подвывая, в свете синем тонет
Мой рок невидимый, голодный, мой чужой. (47)

(Fate weaves its nets with tiny holes,
To catch children, hold them fast,
But I... I will burst through the nets.

I was born with smooth palms,
With the flat palms of a model.
No gypsy will tell me a fortune
Of jail or betrayal.
She will not predict love for me,
Nor prophesy separation —
In the lofty storehouses for blue pigment
They ran out of rope
When they were readying it for my hands.
They cut no design on my palms,
Sketched no stars on them,
Drew no lines into them,
For me there is no love, no death,
No sudden, fateful meetings.
Fate descends on me at night,
With its heavy sack
Stuffed to the top with unspent destinies;
It scratches weakly at my palms
And, with an echoing howl, drowns in the blue light
My future, unseen, hungry, my other.)[12]

As early as the epigraph to this poem (an epigraph that, as elsewhere, Shvarts herself seems to have written), the poet defines herself as someone who eludes all nets. She establishes her absolute difference, and in the epigraph, this elusiveness seems a form of freedom from the limitations of foreseen futures. As the poem begins the connotations of "smooth palms" seem vaguely welcome, especially since the lack of legible lines at first appears to prevent the prediction of dire fates. But the emotional content soon centres on loss, a loss that the poet increasingly feels as the poem continues, so that she herself seems to join in the echoing howl of the penultimate line. The poem adds up events as negations, listing eight experiences that the poet is denied before it is half over (rhetorically, the poem begins with a negation and stays within that register to the end).

There are stories that can be told, though: of birth, of night-time visitations from a representative of the fates who dangles possible futures before her only to sink them into engulfing blue light. The weight of that sack of fates feels heavy in the poem, a metrical effect of Shvarts's lengthening the iambic tetrameter line that has shaped lines 1–16 (plus the epigraph) in the four final lines, where iambic hexameter embraces iambic pentameter.[13] Paradoxically, the longer lines weigh in as absences, yielding a tattered plot of what cannot be: the poet *has* a fate, she will experience this lack of a knowable fate over and over. Not escaping the limitations of fate's repetitions or its certainty, she is instead denied the pleasure of guessing at its content, and she experiences that denial as self-shattering. Although this poem begins with the word "I" and syntactically proceeds as if certain of its subjectivity, the tale of a blank future is in fact a tale of alienated selfhood, and thus it ends with the words "my" and "other" (*moi chuzhoi*) in strange sequence.[14] These words refer to the possible futures held in fate's sack or floating off before the poet's eyes; they aptly describe the ambivalent way in which the stories of herself she can never know both belong to her and can never be hers. The poem's last line is perfectly balanced, the words "moi rok" and "moi chuzhoi" surrounding two adjectives, "nevidimyi" and "golodnyi", and this visual symmetry, despite its referring to something which cannot be seen, intensifies the ambivalence of the poem's ending. It could even be argued that the night-time visitations have something of a tender, cherished quality (and the final phrase, "moi chuzhoi", in that sense would be patterned on "moi milyi"). The guest comes to the poet almost in need: the diction makes him part beggar ("suma" can be a beggar's sack) and part dog ("tsarapat'") — both would appear in hunger, as the last line suggests — and his repeated entry into the poet's night-time life has the feel of a substitute for the erotic encounters her smooth palms deny her.[15] The final scene becomes small compensation for what takes place in the heavens: there, a lack of rope denied her a fate; here, an overabundance of fates spill from the visitor's sack, lost to view.

What readers take from this lyric is a richly emotional rendering of the poet's inaccessibility to herself, and to us. Written on her body from birth or, rather, *not* written on her body, this fate of being a person to whom nothing will happen can never be changed or overcome. The scene in the heavens is remarkable in its details: there is a kind of violence that the poet escapes, and unlike her often brutal verse, this poem nearly hides the violence. The rope that does not suffice is termed *becheva*, an alternate spelling of *bicheva* that in its change further hides the root of this word, meaning "to beat". And there are several verbs to name the act of putting lines into the poet's hands, the first of them (*razrezat'*) suggesting a deep cutting. This insufficiently violent scene, then, becomes the condition for the poet's having no fate of her own, and we might note what in particular her fate would have offered her: love, jail, death, and unanticipated encounters. These may seem the typical stuff of fortune-tellers' prophecies, but in this poem Shvarts stresses the loss of intimate connection to others, and thus one of her lost fates, love, is named twice. She has told us that some absence of original violence deprived her of this love; given the linkage of violence and strong emotion in her other poetry, along with the paucity of love lyrics in her verse (and the tortured nature of those that exist),[16] she may indirectly be telling us a great deal more of her "fate" than the poem itself reveals. She has recounted the origins of love's absence, the tale of her separateness and sad isolation.

Shvarts thus presents herself as the diametrical opposite of an earlier Leningrad poet, Anna Akhmatova. Two aspects of this poem suggest such a reading. The first is Shvarts's self-description as one who knows no future. Akhmatova, by comparison, readily took up the role of prophet, earning the nickname of Cassandra from Mandel´shtam. In one of Akhmatova's "Severnye elegii" (Northern elegies, 1940–55), for example, the poet describes the terror and pain she felt at knowing too much of her destiny ("Uzhe znala spisok prestuplenii,/ Kotorye dolzhna ia sovershit´") ("I already knew the list of crimes / Which I should commit"); in another poem in the same sequence, she writes that she knows beginnings and ends, and life without end ("Mne vedomy nachala i kontsy,/ I zhizn´ posle kontsa") ("The beginnings and ends are known to me, / And life after the end") (Akhmatova 1977, 333, 331).[17] This late Akhmatova cycle seems particularly relevant to "Ia rodilas´ s ladon´iu gladkoi", despite its starkly different format and tone: its first poem, "Predystoriia" (Prehistory), establishes a cosmogony and literary genealogy for Akhmatova, as Susan Amert has persuasively argued, and in its much simpler and less ambitious way, "Ia rodilas´ s ladon´iu gladkoi" takes up a similar task for Shvarts (Amert 1992, 60-92). She presents us with a mythic account of her origins, one that has special relevance for the kind of poet she has become. And that suggests the second way in which she establishes her distance from Akhmatova: the themes of love, betrayal, imprisonment, and death are central to Akhmatova's presentations of herself,[18] yet these are the very topics about which Shvarts professes to have nothing to say. Love poems, crucial to Akhmatova's achievements in her early work, are emphatically dispensed with in Shvarts's *oeuvre*.

In "Ia rodilas´ s ladon´iu gladkoi" it is not just love that is absent, but all sorts of intimate connections. The poem's images of nets and rope, textile derivations of the spinning mythologically associated with the Fates, are also instances of the kind of connecting threads or webs or networks that would link the poet to others: if caught in the tiny nets of the epigraph, she would be sharing her lot with all other children, and if the rope they tried to put into her hands in the heavens had not run out, it would link others to her, too. The word she chooses for this rope, *bicheva* (discussed above for its root) is more specifically a tow-rope, and thus a rope that would have tethered her to others, had it sufficed. Like the stigmata of Christ's passion, the palms of the poet ought to be lined with an emblem of these connections, an emblem that itself is weblike in appearance. But her fate is to escape such markings, and the poem tells us that the result of this fate is, paradoxically, to have no fate at all. The lines of our palms also individuate us, like fingerprints, so that the smoothness of the poet's hands represent a kenotic absence of individual identity.

The poem warrants these associations with Christ's suffering, but indirectly and almost reluctantly. In other poems we encounter more firmly religious foundations and plots. But even having visited the heavenly storehouses (note that Shvarts turns the loftier [and biblical-sounding] phrase "nebesnye zhitnitsy" into the more prosaic "vysokii sklad") makes the poet eligible for higher spiritual knowledge. She describes an experience in the heavens that has echoes in other Shvarts poems. Here, the trade-off is between spiritual knowledge or identity and earthly connections: because of this experience, the poet suggests, she is denied simpler human bonds. The exchange appears often in descriptions of religious vision or saintliness, and the sense of election recalls sectarians' and Old Believers' steadfast insistence on their closeness to divinity and renunciation of social pleasures. Shvarts, too, presents us with a statement of her difference, one that has been foreordained and can never be escaped, even in death.

In another untitled poem, Shvarts explores similar themes but in reverse: rather than a birth, this poem tells of near-death. Unlike "Ia rodilas′ s ladon′iu gladkoi", this poem begins with a statement of a distinctive mark on the self, indeed on the soul, but that mark is again an absence, a "gaping hole":

В моей душе сквозит пролом,
Туда, кружась, влетает вечность.
Я упаду горячим лбом
На скатерти большую млечность.
Так мужественно начала
Я было делать харакири,
Но позабыла, что была
Слабее всех я в этом мире.
Царапина—и нож отброшен,
Я зажимаю тряпкой рану,
И крови полные пригоршни
Мне видеть холодно в тумане.
Не помогай, не подходи,
Хотя бы я о том молила.
Ты только издали следи,
Как боль в глаза мне ужас влила.
Не помогай, не подходи,
Не то и ты скользнешь со склона.
Как корчусь—издали следи,
Как пальцы, локти в смерти тонут. (30)

(There is a gaping hole in my soul,
Eternity, swirling and dizzy, flies into it.
I will drop my hot forehead
Onto the great milkiness of the tablecloth.
So manly and brave, I was about to
Commit hara-kiri,
But I forgot that I was
The weakest person in the world.
One scratch, and I fling away the knife
And press a rag against the wound,
And I see whole handfuls of blood
In the darkness, and am cold.
Don't help, don't come near,
Even if I implore you.
You just watch from afar
The way the pain has poured horror into my eyes.
Don't help, don't come near,
Otherwise you, too, will slip off the edge.
The way I hunch into contortions, watch from afar,
The way fingers, elbows drown in death.)

Like the absence of connecting threads in the first poem, this poem, too, insists on an isolation of the speaking poet. In reacting to averted suicide, the poet pushes an interlocutor away, as if encroaching presence would rob her of this scene, its feelings, its losses. Her insistence that this person stay away is also a protective gesture: the third from the last line intimates that too near an approach might draw the other person into the scene of suicide, and thus be endangering. Shvarts suggests that danger by rewriting a line from Pushkin's *Pir vo vremia chumy* (Feast in time of plague, 1830), when Mary imagines the possibility of her own death and warns against too near an approach to her body for fear that the plague will spread (Pushkin 1975–79, V, 353). In Shvarts's repeated "izdali sledi" she suggests not that nearness can contaminate, but that she desperately wants her interlocutor not to abandon her. This watchful presence is entirely necessary to the poem, whose urgency comes from this bizarre dramatic scene where the speaking, suicidal poet addresses someone who is watching her hold rags to her wounds and contort her face with pain. The exhortation to watch is emphasized by repetition, as is the insistent instruction not to help, not to come closer. The poet seems able to edge closer to the scene of imagined suicide because there is someone on hand to watch, and a tense dance of invitation and repulsion ensues as she warns her observer to keep away. Her performance is one of pride, and thus it is no accident that Shvarts refers to the suicide as hara-kiri, an act which within Japanese culture carries powerful connotations of nobility, self-sacrifice, and pride.

At the back of one's mind on reading such a poem must certainly be Marina Tsvetaeva's "Vskryla zhily" (I've opened my veins, 1934), which contains a strong allegory of the poetic process (her short poem concludes with the word "verse", substituting poems for the blood pouring out of her veins); there, too, the poet speaks in imperatives to someone who watches the scene (Tsvetaeva 1990, 436).[19] But Tsvetaeva orders her observer to put cups and bowls in place to catch the blood, like rain through a leaking roof; her poem equates the pouring liquid with the outpouring of verse, so that she speaks to one who can come forward and collect the blood as if gathering poems. She draws that other person to her, in a way completely typical for Tsvetaeva, whereas Shvarts gathers strength from the possibility of pushing her viewer away. She insistently absorbs the observer's imagined horror into herself, and may seem to preserve a kind of privacy or mystery that recalls Akhmatova more than Tsvetaeva. She stops short of the violence described in the poem's final image of dripping blood, and earlier lines suggest a failure of will and thus an inability to carry out the horrible act of suicide not unlike the elided violence at the centre of the first poem.

Like "Ia rodilas´ s ladon´iu gladkoi", this poem stages an encounter with spiritual knowledge. The gaping hole in the poet's soul is large enough to hold "eternity", and the suicide scene that follows has the feel of a religious rite. The poet who describes herself as "the weakest person in the world" thinks on a cosmic scale, as if the watching presence were a god (or demon) with the ability to judge her spiritual fortitude. But in addition to the religious references of this scene, its details remind us that the speaker is a poet. Like Tsvetaeva, Shvarts has cultivated an image of the poet as suffering emotions and disappointments much larger than life, although her poetic presentations of these feelings tends to be cosmic and abstract, rather than the direct, apostrophic speech typical of Tsvetaeva.

The poem also calls to mind an early untitled Mandel´shtam poem, "Net, ne luna, a svetlyi tsiferblat" ("No, not the moon, but a bright clock-face", 1912), where we find a rhyme pair, *mlechnost´ / vechnost´*, that Shvarts repeats (she reverses Mandel´shtam's order brilliantly: whereas in his poem it is surprising for the answer to a question about the time of day to be "eternity", in her poem it is unexpected for her to describe the "milkiness" of a tablecloth).[20] Is Shvarts comparing herself to Mandel´shtam? More immediately, she has in mind Konstantin Batiushkov (1787–1855); he appears in Mandel´shtam's poem, and his insanity has long been thought to be its subject.[21] What emerges is a poetic genealogy in which Tsvetaeva, who killed herself in 1941 and whose passionate verse is exemplary for Shvarts, and Batiushkov, who spent his last decades so ill that he no longer wrote poetry, are terrifying antecedents. In this context, Mandel´shtam's experience of attempted suicide in Cherdyn and reported insanity in the transit camp in Vladivostok are also pertinent to Shvarts's poem. Shvarts may or may not be writing out of some "true" experience, and it is not my point to assert that she is. The mythologizing of these moments in the history of Russian poetry is what the poem takes up, and it contextualizes her recourse to Mandel´shtam's highly self-conscious, metapoetic early lyric. The self-mythologizing that emerges in Shvarts's poem once again focuses on an alienated, possibly even insane poet, one whose behaviour is enigmatic and extreme.

To whom, then, does the poet speak in "V moei dushe skvozit prolom"? If she were repeating Tsvetaeva's example, she might be addressing her readers. Her wish to warn off this watchful other would be an attempt to push her readers away, to make them wish to keep their distance by implying to them that they come closer at their own peril.[22] But this is not the only possible reading: the religious context also suggests a watchful divinity, as if the attempted suicide were a trial of faith the poet sets for herself; and more prosaically, the poem itself appears as an act of address to another (any other) human being who could intervene to stop the poet's pain. Like "Ia rodilas´ s ladon´iu gladkoi", this poem reiterates the distance that separates the poet from all other people. She gives us a scenario of her own pain in which someone else sits and watches — she even tells that other person to watch how "the pain has poured horror into my eyes". Her horror comes from the spectacle of her own pain, but also from the sad fact of her insistent helplessness. In this poem, "fingers, elbows drown in death" but there is no "net" or "rope" that can pull her out of her pain.

These two poems thus work as doubles or twinned poems.[23] Precisely the same length (twenty lines), they are built on iambic tetrameter (with no rhythmic deviations in the case of the second poem, which is also rhymed in regular four-line groupings). Both are untitled, which is not the norm in Shvarts's poems; the lack of a title might signal the importance of the poems to the larger project of her poetry (much as other poets signal key or emblematic poems by giving them titles like "Stanzas" or "Poem"). The scene of birth in its way has enabled the scene of near-death, and both poems establish an identity for the poet as nearly impossible to know and certainly impossible to get near. An aura of pain and violence surrounds her, an aspect of her work which is nearly inescapable. It can be seen as early as the titles of poems like "Zharenyi anglichanin v Moskve" (An Englishman roasted in Moscow) (Shvarts 1992b) and "Zarublennyi sviashchennik" (The hacked priest) (Shvarts 1993b), to take two stunning recent examples.[24] The violence is not confined to her titles, imaginative though they are: even a lyric innocently called "Podrazhanie Bualo" (Imitation of Boileau, 1970) and presented to the reader as harmless couplets, concludes with an image of the poet as a "Glaz vyrvannyi, na nitochke krovavoi,/ Na mig vmestivshii

mira bol´; i slavu" ("Gouged eye on a bloody thread, for a moment filled/
with all the pain and glory of the world").[25] The fibres of "Ia rodilas´ s
ladon´iu gladkoi", and the horror-filled eyes of "V moei dushe skvozit
prolom" come together in that image from "Podrazhanie Bualo", urging
us to consider how and why Shvarts requires such violent imagery in her
self-descriptions as a poet.

In the next poem I want to consider, Shvarts explores the role of shock-
value and physically horrifying descriptions in the generation of poetry.
Also untitled, the poem comes from 1982.[26] Here she explores the theme
of spirit possession, and, like Shvarts's other poems on this theme, it seems
a preparatory sketch for the *Laviniia* poems (1984).[27] In this lyric, demons
initially substitute for the poet's muse, but they are ingested, digested, and
transformed into poetic material.

Когда за мною демоны голодные помчались
Косматыми и синими волками,
Ах, что тогда мне, бедной, оставалось—
Как с неба снять луны холодный камень
И кинуть в пасть им—чтоб они взорвались.

От блеска взрыва вмиг преобразились,
Ягнятами ко мне они прижались
(Я рядом с ними теменью казалась)
И даже шерсть их снежная светилась,
И я их сожрала—какая жалость!

Я стала рядом с ними великаном—
Сторуким, торжествующим в печали,
По одному брала, рвала и ела,
Они же только жалобно пищали.

Но я им говорила—не вопите
И ничего не бойтесь. Вы
Так, в животе, немного полежите
И выпрыгнете вон из головы.

Но светом их набив свою утробу,
Сама я стала ясной и двурукой,
И новых демонов семья в голодной злобе
Учуяли меня. Все та же мука. (56)

    (When hungry demons hurtled after me
    In the form of mangy blue wolves,
    Oh, what was I to do, poor thing,
    But snatch the cold stone of the moon from the sky
    And hurl it into their jaws, exploding them.

From the flash of the blast they instantly took a new form,
Little lambs they cuddled up to me
(Next to them I seemed as darkness)
And even their snowy coats shone with light
And I ate them up. What a pity!

Next to them I seemed now a giant —
With hundreds of hands, triumphant in sadness,
One by one I took them, ripped them apart and ate them,
They just pitifully squealed.

But I said to them, don't wail
And don't be afraid. You
Just lie there in my stomach a little while
And then jump out of my head.

But when I had stuffed my womb full of their light,
I myself became clear, and two-handed,
And a family of new demons, hungry with spite,
Caught my scent. And again, the same torture.)[28]

This poem offers two tales of ingestion: first the poet force-feeds a stony moon to the devilish wolves that have descended on her, then she eats them after they have transformed themselves from wolves to lambs. Shvarts makes her story seem hagiographical here by choosing animals that appear frequently in saints' lives, and just as in the dog/demon image of "Ia rodilas´ s ladon´iu gladkoi", her presentation of these strange animals has an aura of tenderness as well as fear. Her act of consuming them is recast as a kind of impregnation when they turn up in her womb, and she subsequently gives birth to them through her forehead; the tale of generation continues in the poem's final lines, which wearily recount the same story, implying that this recurring process is a cycle which she has no power to end.

In describing the poet's act of ingestion, Shvarts rewrites the Old Testament story of Jonah in the belly of the whale. The poet's calming words to the lambs remind us of that story, as when Jonah rested for three days in the whale, and the lambs spring from her head as Jonah was spewed out of the whale's head in a burst of foam. Shvarts has written another, more explicit adaptation of this biblical story in one of her *Laviniia* poems, "Leviafan" (Leviathan), where it is the poet herself (in this case Laviniia) who spends three days in the belly of the whale, and the process by which she is thrust back into the world is figured as a form of birth.[29] In "Kogda za mnoiu demony golodnye pomchalis´", the religious context is tempered by mythological associations. The birth of a swallowed, feared thing through one's forehead recasts Zeus's hasty decision to swallow Metis, his first wife, lest she give birth to a second child who might usurp his power; Athena, goddess of arts, crafts, and war emerges from his forehead.[30] Shvarts's poem has the same gesture of eating a feared aggressor, but in her version this process gives rise to more than one cycle of ingestion and birth. Moreover, the poet has her own similarities to Athena, whose warlike characteristics she replicates when hurling projectiles in the first stanza (in general in Shvarts's poems, the association of aggressiveness with poetic composition is common). The consumed lambs/devils can be understood as metaphors for poems, so that the repetition of this process denotes the circular path through which devilish ideas insinuate themselves to the poet, take her over, and push out of her as poems, only to leave her evacuated and available for a new possession by spirits.

That evacuated state, which might be the condition that enables religious bliss and insight if the poet were more passively at peace, is for Shvarts a vulnerable and active way of being. It recurs in her poetry as hunger and greed (as in "Podrazhanie Bualo", where the poet is described as- ever greedy for praise ["do pokhvaly on zhaden"]), or it can be general and shared, as in this poem, where the wolves and demons come to the poet because they are hungry, producing as if in chain reaction her own desire for food.[31] We recall from "Ia rodilas´ s ladon´iu gladkoi" that the future that comes to the inaccessible poet in the final line was "hungry". Food, nourishment, and the process of ingestion and digestion are significant realms of meaning for Shvarts — unexpectedly so, because she is not in any simple way a poet of the material world. But, as all the following examples show, food is not a material substance in her poems; it is "transubstantiated", we might say, becoming a symbol of spiritual sustenance much as Christ's body and blood are imagined in the ritual of the eucharist.[32] These examples merit a brief digression, both to clarify Shvarts's use of religious motifs and to establish how the principles of distancing that emerge in her poetic presentations of human or animal others also apply to her descriptions of some objects, in this case food.

The poems typically establish equivalencies between food and verse: in the second line of "Mne snilos´ — my plyvem po risovym poliam" (I dreamed we were sailing through rice fields, c. 1983; p. 74), the poet observes that rice is used to make paper, a reminder of her preference for metapoetic descriptions. In another landscape poem, "Svalka" (The dump, c. 1983; pp. 76-77), the dump is invited to eat before it sings, as if food must precede verse; this turns out to be a sacred eucharistic act, tinged with Dionysian and mystical details (the poem ends "O rosa mystica, tebia uslyshat bogi") ("O rosa mystica, the gods will hear you"). Neither poem is pious, a possibility undone by the pagan allusions and irreverent site of a landfill in "Svalka". Her most famous poem on this theme, exemplary in its brazenness, is "Vospominanie o strannom ugoshchenii" (Memory of a strange refreshment, 1976; p. 33), which tells of the taste of a friend's breast milk. The poet explicitly says that the drink was taken not to quench thirst, but to satisfy the soul. The calmly ecstatic ending of the poem has time stopped, crowding into a corner as if hiding from the satisfactions the poet has declared for herself.[33] Even this more insistently optimistic poem is disrupted when the poet compares herself to a vampire, a comparison she wishes away. In general, these poems spurn the notion of food as a pleasure, or as a joyful creation of intimate connection with what is eaten. Food also produces no connection to those who happen to be in proximity to the poet (note her careful account of how she drank the breast milk from a cup, anxiously pushing from the reader's mind any mental picture of her at her friend's breast), or to the food itself.[34]

Spatial relationships thus undergo some transformation in "Kogda za mnoiu demony golodnye pomchalis˄". In addition to the two-dimensional measures of distance seen in the first two poems, this poem introduces the idea of engulfment, of things inside one another. It might appear that an act of envelopment would require a new intimacy and would break down the tense barriers to contact seen earlier. Thus the poet speaks tenderly to the lambs and twice invokes pity to describe her relationship to them. Yet the poem ends with a predicted and infinite repetition of this process of ingestion and ejection, redescribing the lambs as demons and the process as torture. The poet returns to a kind of powerlessness, and the other presence in her poem remains alien, frightening and entirely other. What is striking, then, is that a circular, spherical positioning of one thing inside another does not enable the poet's identification with what she has engulfed. In the final poem discussed here, that identification occurs, and we will want to consider how things are different in this case.

The following brief lyric, untitled, is from 1981: it is constructed almost entirely as an act of apostrophe, but Shvarts avoids the usually animating effects of this trope and writes a poem about death.

Земля, земля, ты ешь людей,
Рождая их взамен
Кастальский ключ, гвоздики луч
И камень и сирень.
Земля, ты чавкаешь во тьме,
Коснеешь и растешь,
И тихо вертишь на уме,
Что всех переживешь.
Ну что же—радуйся! Пои
Всех черным молоком.
Ты разлилась в моей крови.

Скрипишь под языком.
О древняя змея! Траву
Ты кормишь, куст в цвету,
А тем, кто ходит по тебе,
Втираешь тлен в пяту. (67)

> (Earth, earth, you eat people,
> In return for them, you give birth
> To the Castalian spring, a carnation's gleam,
> And stone, and lilac.
> Earth, you munch noisily in the darkness,
> Fall into inertness, and grow,
> And quietly turn around and around in your mind
> The thought that you will survive everyone.
> Well then, rejoice! Give everyone
> Black milk to drink.
> You have dissolved in my blood,
> Your grit is under my tongue.
> O ancient serpent! You feed
> The grass, the bush in bloom,
> But you smear decay into the heels
> Of the ones who walk upon you).[35]

Like "Kogda za mnoiu demony golodnye pomchalis´", this poem pursues a physical idea of contact as engulfing and absorbing. The process of movement from inside out (in this case, sinking into earth before rising out of it) again involves a transformation of substance: buried, decayed bodies re-emerge as springs or flowers or stone. This is a ruminative, vegetative poem, one that purports to speed up the slow process of plant growth but itself ambles along on verbs that seem as slow as a cow chewing cud in a field (there is something in this poem that calls an animal to mind, a nocturnal animal that has come out of the earth for its secret feeding; the image of decay in the last line also suggests mould or fungus that creepily grows in the dark).

This poem points to Shvarts's other poems about death and decay; its nearest double is the earlier "Zver´-tsvetok" (Animal-flower, 1978; p. 28), where the poet imagines the flowers that will sprout from her grave, fertilized by her dead body. In "Zemlia, zemlia, ty esh´ liudei", the action is similar — people buried in their graves participate in a process that makes things grow — but the imagistic emphasis is on food: the earth eats the corpses it receives, munching away at night, producing nourishment for (unseen) animals and people but also producing in living people the sure sense that they will return to the earth and thus to death. Death is clearest in the decay of the last line, but the poet seems, too, to have imbibed it into her own body, taken it in with her own food, felt it coursing through her blood.

This poem returns us to the terms of "Ia rodilas´ s ladon´iu gladkoi", but with an unexpected twist: we again have insights that can be interpreted by examining the body, yet without the assertion that this is a poet who has no "fate". In "Zemlia, zemlia, ty esh´ liudei", Shvarts confronts a universal fate, death, and she does so in ways that seem utterly unassuaged by the comfort of life after death, for example, something we might expect, given her apparently religious world view. When, in this bleak poem, there is the passing injunction to rejoice, it feels like an inappropriate reference to the faith that otherwise has abandoned this poem. That is what makes the poem so striking — for faith is surely one of the fates Shvarts repeatedly seeks. "Zemlia, zemlia, ty esh´ liudei" is also a powerfully physical poem, one in which we can feel the grit of dirt beneath the tongue, and heels sinking into decaying earth. The earth seems to have its own body, able to eat noisily, to turn over things in its mind, to rub its decay into the weak heels of wanderers, and to survive us all. It has the body, and the fate, that the poet envies.

Envy goes hand in hand with identification in this poem. The poet uses physical nearness but preserves the tone of irritability that kept others at a distance in earlier poems. This poem pictures proximity in about as close a way as we could imagine: people descend into the earth, but the earth is also inside the poet, poured into her blood and lying like Jonah in the cavern of her mouth. The metapoetic explosion found in other poems at first seems repressed here: there is no celebration of the growth that this natural process enables — indeed, the exhortation to the earth to celebrate its capacity to outlast everyone and everything is sardonic. But there is a suggestion that the earth's processes are like the generation of poetry. The "Castalian spring" of line 3 refers to the fountain of inspiration on Mount Parnassus, and thus figures as the source of poetry itself (*kliuch* means spring, source and key). The reference works in this case by an allusion to Pushkin, repeating even the line position of the words "Castalian spring" (*Kastal´skii kliuch*) from his poem "Tri kliucha" (Three springs, 1827); Shvarts, in her reliance on Pushkin, draws on the poet who is himself the "source" for Russian poetry (Pushkin 1977–79, III, 14). Nikolai Zabolotskii's poem "Proshchanie s druz´iami" (Farewell to my friends, 1952) is also an important subtext, a more clearly explicit source for the themes of death and burial, for the motifs of lilac, carnation, and grasses, and a further exploration of the links between these themes and poetry: his poem mourns Kharms, Vvedenskii and Oleinikov, and pictures them still clutching their notebooks of verse (Zabolotskii 1986, 257).[36]

In Pushkin's poem, the Castalian spring gives water to those banished to its deserts, but rather than identifying with the exiled wanderer or with the mourned poets in Zabolotskii's poem, Shvarts undertakes to incarnate the Castalian source. The poet, in her ingestion of the earth, becomes earth, and when she describes the chewing, thinking and food-producing earth she is also describing herself. She is Eve, tempted by the "ancient serpent", but not tempted into knowledge or disobedience: this serpent insinuates itself into her, seducing her into being all too like the snake and the earth. If earth produces plants, then she produces poems.[37] The rueful record of a poet's work as requiring the incorporation of dead others is fully in the spirit of self-descriptions we find elsewhere in Shvarts, including poems discussed here. The work of poetry is again presented as doing harm to others, and to oneself. Small wonder, then, that the "other" would be pushed away in Shvarts's poetry, if the very act of thinking like a poet is presented as a danger. The reciprocal identifications of Shvarts's poems, and the violence she describes so often, make this sense of poetry's harm almost a logical necessity: by casting the poet as the one who does violence and as the victim of pain, Shvarts repeatedly associates the process of creating poetry with some form of destruction.

The rhetorical substitution of earth for self is interesting in one other way. It is not unusual for poets to project images of themselves through the others who appear in their poems; indeed, it was this tendency that caused Bakhtin to interpret all poetry as monological (Bakhtin 1981, 275-300).[38] But in Shvarts's poems, we find a disposition to speak through others *as if that were not her own voice*, and thus to engage in forms of ventriloquism and impersonation. Strictly speaking, she does not make the earth speak in "Zemlia, zemlia, ty esh´ liudei", but elsewhere her readiness to throw her voice becomes the basis for whole poetic sequences.[39] In the *Laviniia* poems, for example, Shvarts explores the potential for impersonation as a strategy for extending the distances between self, text and audience. Here she writes in the first person but as if she were someone else: her poems are presented as the work of a noviciate nun, the self-doubting and easily tempted Laviniia.[40] The *Laviniia* poems are not unique — compare the two eight-poem cycles of Cynthia lyrics (1978), where Shvarts produces seemingly "lost" poems by an ancient Roman woman.[41] The much longer *Laviniia* cycle lets Shvarts work with a variety of characters (an Abbess, several other nuns, a seductively companionable lion, a hermit, various tempting devils), as in a novel. Unlike the solitary heroines of Shvarts's lyric poems, Laviniia emerges in a complex web of relationships, and she has the chance to reflect on her own experiences by seeing them enacted by the people around her.

One of the *Laviniia* poems expresses with remarkable lucidity the tense relations between self and other that this essay has traced in Shvarts's poetry of the early 1980s. It is entitled "Mezh 'ia' i 'ty'" (Between "I" and "you").

In its twelve lines, the poem describes a search for God, a wish on Laviniia's part that she could put behind her the dreams of worldliness that still come to her in the convent and give herself over more completely to contemplation of the divine. The poem ends with the acknowledgment of a different kind of search, however:

Vse iskala ia slova / rodnee, chem "ty",
I chut´/chut´ chuzhee, chem "ia". (Shvarts 1987b, 61)

(I kept looking for words that are more kindred than "you"
And just a little more alien than "I".)

Laviniia seeks words with which to address God here, not knowing how to make either "you" or "I" work for her. But through this impersonation of a nun speaking to and of God, Shvarts comes upon a pithy formulation for her own dilemma as a poet, indeed her own wish to speak in a voice that keeps some safe otherness from the self but also draws a listener closer than simple second-person address might allow. This poem thus turns the "moi chuzhoi" ending of "Ia rodilas´ s ladon´iu gladkoi" into a comment on the inadequacy of personal pronouns. Her desire is for terms of reference that extend the limits of first- and second-person denotations. For a brief moment, we might be seduced into believing that she seeks to bridge the distances between speaker and listener, between "I" and "you", that her poems have so elaborately set up. But that is no more than our fantasy that the poet is somehow curious about us. She is not. Her poetry shows us that she regards us with fear, suspicion, and occasional gentleness. In this intense scenario of performed subjectivity, we are allowed to watch, but only at a distance.

It remains to be seen how Shvarts's poetics may change in the 1990s, when curious audiences seek to encroach ever further (not least as scholars begin the intrusive process of writing about her poems), and when Russia itself is continuing to undergo such massive, unsettling social change. Will she still be able to capitalize on her marginality, one wonders, as underground poets generally did up to the end of the 1980s? One has been warned against predicting the future of a poet whose palms cannot be read even by fortune-tellers, but we can surely expect Shvarts to lose none of her skill in inventing scenarios that preserve zones of safety and solitude around her ever-changing poetic, not to say personal, self.[42] Embattled relationships with those within her poems, with readers, and with some of her poetic forebears will surely continue. Like the muse-demons who come to her again and again, her poems seem destined to retrace the paths between self and language, with results that range among ecstasy, mourning, frustration and obsession.

REFERENCES

Aizenberg, M., 1993. *Ukazatel´ imen* (Moscow: Gendal´f).

Akhmatova, A., 1977. *Stikhotvoreniia i poemy* (Leningrad: Sovetskii pisatel´).

Amert, S., 1992. *In a Shattered Mirror: The Later Poetry of Anna Akhmatova* (Stanford: Stanford University Press).

Bakhtin, M., 1981. "Discourse in the Novel" in C. Emerson and M. Holquist (eds), *The Dialogic Imagination* (Austin and London: University of Texas Press), 275–300.

Bynum, C. W., 1987. *Holy Fast, Holy Feast: The Religious Significance of Food to Medieval Women* (Berkeley: University of California Press).

Ciepiela, C., 1994. "Taking Monologism Seriously: Bakhtin and Tsvetaeva's 'The Pied Piper'", *Slavic Review* LIV, 4: 1010–24.

Epshtein, M., 1988. *Paradoksy novizny: O literaturnom razvitii XIX-XX vekov* (Moscow: Sovetskii pisatel´).

Eremenko, A., 1991. *Stikhi* (Moscow: IMA Press).

_____, 1994. *Gorizontal´naia strana* (Moscow: Izdatel´ SA).

Freidin, Iu., 1994. "Tema smerti v poeticheskom tvorchestve Mariny Tsvetaevoi", in Schweitzer, V. *et al.* (eds), *Marina Tsvetaeva: One Hundred Years/Stoletie Tsvetaevoi* (Berkeley: Berkeley Slavic Specialties).

Gandlevskii, S., 1989. *Rasskaz* (Moscow: Moskovskii rabochii).

_____, 1995. "Trepanatsiia cherepa: Istoriia bolezni", *Znamia* 1: 99–151.

Goldstein, D., 1993. "The Heartfelt Poetry of Elena Shvarts", in H. Goscilo (ed.), *The Fruits of Her Plume* (Armonk: M.E. Sharp), 239–50.

_____, 1994. "Shvarts, Elena Andreevna", in M. Ledkovsky, C. Rosenthal and M. Zirin (eds), *Dictionary of Russian Women Writers* (Westport: Greenwood Press), 598–600.

Golodnaia russkaia zima , 1991. (Moscow: N-Press).

Goricheva, T., 1981. "'Tkan´ serdtsa rassteliu Spasiteliu pod nogi...'", *Grani* 120: 198–214.

Goscilo, H. (ed.), 1995. *Lives in Transit* (Ann Arbor: Ardis).

Grazhdane nochi, 1990. (Moscow: SP "Vsia Moskva").

Heldt, B., 1989. "The Poetry of Elena Shvarts", *World Literature Today* (Spring): 381–83.

Kelly, C., 1994. *A History of Russian Women's Writing 1820–1992* (Oxford: Oxford University Press).

Kibirov, T., 1993. *Stikhi o liubvi* (Moscow: Izdatel´stvo "Tsikady").

Kruglova, Iu. G. (ed.) 1988. *Biblioteka russkogo fol´klora. Skazki* I (Moscow: Sovetskaia Rossiia).

Kuritsyn, V., 1990. "Prekrasnoe iazycheskoe bormotanie", *Oktiabr´* 2: 205–07.

Latinskii kvartal, 1991. (Moscow: Den´).

Lichnoe delo No.—-, 1991. (Moscow: V/O "Soizteatr").

Mandel´shtam, O. E., 1979. *Stikhotvoreniia* (Leningrad: Sovetskii pisatel´).

———, 1990. *Sochineniia v dvukh tomakh* (Moscow: Khudozhestvennaia literatura).

Molnar, M., 1993. Introduction to Shvarts 1993a: 9–13.

Nikoleva, O., 1991. "'... bez bytiia'", *Novyi mir* 10: 244–48.

Platt, K. M. F., (forthcoming). *Semiotic Catastrophes: Russian Literature and Revolutionary Social Change 1700–1994* (Stanford: Stanford University Press).

Poeziia novoi volny, 1990. (Novosibirsk: Izdatel´stvo Novosibirskogo universiteta).

Pollack, N., 1995. *Mandelstam the Reader* (Baltimore: Johns Hopkins Press).

Polukhina, V. (ed.), 1992. *Brodsky through the Eyes of his Contemporaries* (New York: St Martin's Press).

Ponedel´nik, 1990. (Moscow: Prometei).

Prigov, D., 1990. *Slezy general´skoi dushi* (Moscow: Tekst).

———, 1993. *Piat´desiat kapelek krovi* (Moscow: Tekst).

Pushkin, A.S., 1975–79. *Sobranie sochinenii v desiati tomakh* (Leningrad: Nauka).

Remnick, D., 1994. "Letter from Moscow: Exit the Saints", *The New Yorker* 18 July: 50–60.

Ronen, O., 1973. "Leksicheskii povtor, podtekst i smysl v poetike Osipa Mandel´shtama", in R. Jakobson, C. H. Schooneveld and D. S. Worth (eds), *Slavic Poetics: Essays in Honor of Kiril Taranovsky* (The Hague: Mouton), 367–87.

———, 1993. "Simvolika Mikhaila Kuzmina v sviazi s ego kontseptsiei zhizni", in R. Vroon and J.E. Malmstad (eds), *Readings in Russian Modernism / Kul´tura russkogo modernizma: To Honor V. F. Markov* (Moscow: Nauka), 291–98.

Shvarts, E., 1985. *Tantsuiushchii David* (New York: Russica).

———, 1987a. *Stikhi* (Leningrad-Paris-Munich: Beseda).

———, 1987b. *Trudy i dni Lavinii, monakhini iz ordena obrezaniia serdtsa* (Ann Arbor: Ardis).

———, 1989. *Storony sveta: Stikhi* (Leningrad: Sovetskii pisatel´).

———, 1990. *Stikhi* (Leningrad: Assotsiatsiia "Novaia literatura").

———, 1992a. "Coldness and Rationality: An Interview with Elena Shvarts" in Polukhina 1992: 215–36.

———, 1992b. "Zharenyi anglichanin", *Zvezda* 5–6: 3–4.

———, 1993a. *"Paradise": Selected Poems* (Newcastle-upon-Tyne: Bloodaxe Books).

———, 1993b. "Zarublennyi sviashchennik", *Vestnik novoi literatury* 5: 109–10.

———, 1994. *Lotsiia nochi* (Moscow: Sovetskii pisatel´).

Sedakova, O., 1990. *Kitaiskoe puteshestvie; Stely i nadpisi; Starye pesni* (Moscow: Carte Blanche).

———, 1994. *Stikhi* (Moscow: Gnozis/Carte Blanche).

Smith, G. S. 1993. *Contemporary Russian Poetry: A Bilingual Anthology* (Bloomington: Indiana University Press).

Tauler, J., 1910. *Die Predigten Taulers: Aus der Engelberger und der Freiburger Handschrift...* (Berlin: Weidmannsche Buchhandlung).

Tomei, C. (ed.), (1999). *Russian Women Writers* (New York: Garland Press).

Tsvetaeva, M., 1990. *Stikhotvoreniia i poemy* (Leningrad: Sovetskii pisatel´).

Zabolotskii, N., 1986. *Stikhotvoreniia i poemy* (Sverdlovsk: Sredne-Ural´skoe knizhnoe izdatel´stvo).

NOTES

Research for this essay was supported by a summer stipend from the National Endowment for the Humanities. Nancy Pollak, Laura Engelstein, Kevin Platt, Jehanne Gheith, Helena Goscilo, Alexander Zholkovsky, Dmitri Khanin, Sarah Pratt and Darra Goldstein extensively commented on earlier drafts of this essay, and their suggestions have been gratefully incorporated in many places.

1. See the collective publications of Moscow's Conceptualists and younger, like-minded poets: *Ponedel´nik* 1990; *Lichnoe delo No.—* 1991; *Latinskii kvartal* 1991; *Golodnaia russkaia zima* 1991. These group publications document closer connections than exist as the 1990s have progressed: compare the nostalgic tone of Kibirov 1993, an album-like volume of poems, photography, and kitschy decorations. For an astute discussion of Kibirov and of the cultural situation in contemporary Russia, see chapter 4 of Platt (forthcoming).

2. Epshtein's essay first appeared in *Voprosy literatury*, but an expanded version has been published in Epshtein 1988, 139–76.

3. In addition to the collections mentioned in note 1, see *Grazhdane nochi* 1990; *Poeziia novoi volny* 1991; Aizenberg, 1993; Gandlevskii 1989; Prigov 1990; Prigov 1993; Sedakova 1990; Sedakova 1994; Eremenko 1991; Eremenko 1994.

4. On poetic groupings and publications in Leningrad from 1950 to the early 1980s, see the essays, memoirs, bibliographies, and interview in *Novoe literaturnoe obozrenie*, 14 (1995), 167–264.

5. A possible exception is the frenetically productive Dmitrii Aleksandrovich Prigov. For an insightful characterization of Prigov, and of the contemporary literary scene in Moscow (and, a little bit, St Petersburg), see Remnick 1994, 50–60.

6. These include sixteen Cynthia lyrics (1978), where Shvarts sassily announces that she has translated into Russian otherwise lost classical poems, the novel-length impersonation that created the mad nun Laviniia (1987), and eighteen poems attributed to Arno Tsart (1984). See "Kinfiia. Kniga pervaia" (Cynthia.

Book 1) and "Kinfiia. Kniga vtoraia" (Cynthia. Book 2) in Shvarts 1985, 54-68; "Trudy i dni Lavinii, monakhini iz ordena Obrezaniia Serdtsa" (The labours and days of Laviniia, a nun of the order of the circumcized heart) in 1993c, 68–140; and "Arno Tsart: Povest´ o Lise" (Arno Tsart: A story about a fox), "Vtoroe puteshestvie" (Second journey), and "Eshche o Lise" (More about the fox) in Shvarts 1987a, poems 29, 30 and 31 (the pages in this volume are unnumbered). Shvarts 1985, assembled abroad without the poet's supervision, is unfortunately the only source for both parts of the Cynthia lyrics; for a more reliable text of the first half, see Shvarts 1989, 32–39. Excerpts from the Laviniia cycle and the first eight Cynthia lyrics are available in English in Shvarts 1993a, 53–66, 111-39.

7.   These volumes also moved her increasingly toward availability to her Russian audience, in that Shvarts 1985 came out in New York, and Shvarts 1987b in Ann Arbor, Shvarts 1987a gives Paris/Munich/Leningrad as its provenance, and Shvarts 1989 and Shvarts1990 are both Leningrad productions. Some of these volumes are mentioned in note 6, but repeated here so the reader can see the full sequence; they are: Shvarts 1985; Shvarts 1987a; Shvarts 1989; Shvarts, 1990; Shvarts 1993c; and Shvarts 1987b. For journal and almanac publications, see the bibliographies in essays about Shvarts cited below (note 9).

8.   I cite poems from Shvarts 1990 wherever possible, giving page numbers in the text; exceptions will be noted. All translations, unless otherwise indicated, are my own. It is also interesting to note that there has been a strange collapsing of all Shvarts's work into the decade of the 1980s: many of her best-known poems are from the 1970s and early 1980s but they were not published until the mid-1980s; towards the end of the 1980s she again began to be extremely productive, and although these poems largely appeared in the early 1990s, they are carefully dated to the 1980s; the *Laviniia* poems are from 1984.

9.   Molnar 1993, 9–13; Heldt 1989, 381–83; Kelly 1994, 411–22; and Goldstein 1994, 598–600. Several pieces have also appeared in Russian. Goricheva 1981, 198-214 stresses the religious aspect of Shvarts's worldview. See also two insightful but brief reviews: Kuritsyn 1990, 205–07; and Nikolaeva 1991, 244–48.

10. This high pitch of her verse is well captured by Molnar 1993 and Heldt 1989, in part because each finds a descriptive style commensurate with the qualities they see in Shvarts.

11. A remarkable exception to this pattern is "Detskii sad cherez tridtsat´ let" (undated, first published in Shvarts 1990, 107–08); for an English translation, see "Kindergarten Thirty Years On" in Shvarts 1993a,19-21.

12. This literal translation is mine; for a more lyrical version, from which I have borrowed several locutions, see the one by Catriona Kelly in Shvarts 1993a, 77.

13. The disruption of the rhythmic scheme is typical in Shvarts. Her rhymes are also typically arranged with irregularities, in this case a quatrain of alternating rhyme (ll. 1–4), two odd-numbered groups of lines (ll. 5–9, 16–20) where three lines have one rhyme, two have another, and five lines are interrupted by one that does not rhyme at all (ll. 10-14, where the unrhymed word, unsurprisingly, is "smerti"). Line 15 also has no rhyme (although it repeats the rhyme of l. 3). Shvarts has said that she likes to break up regular rhythmic patterns because the alternative is boring. See Shvarts 1992a, esp. 218.

14. An alternative translation of these words would be "mine, not mine." This version would better preserve one effect of Shvarts's syntax, in that her placement of the words at line's end makes them more important and, at least in terms of line position, more like a double predicate adjective than a mere sequence of modifiers. But such a translation disrupts the lovely symmetry of the line, discussed below.

15. The futile scratching to get in also suggests the tale of "Peryshko Finista iasna sokola" (The feather of Finist the bright falcon), although Shvarts typically takes only this image of failure to connect rather than the tale's happy ending of reunion and bliss. See Kruglova 1988, 342–47.

16. Shvarts does not write love lyrics in any conventional sense of the term, but love and anger can figure together in her poems. The striking poem "Liubov´ kak tret´e" (80), translated as "Love Eavesdrops" by Catriona Kelly in Shvarts 1993a, 97, presents a scenario of struggling lovers where love, like a third character in the scene, crouches to watch. The poet presents herself as watching, too.

17. The sequencing of the "Severnye elegii" has since been challenged, and subsequent editions have up to seven poems in the sequence, but the passages cited here remain unchanged (although the poems in which they appear have been moved around within the sequence).

18. Akhmatova's self-mythologizations have been re-examined by Alexander Zholkovsky in a series of recent essays. See, for example, his review of Roberta Reeder's biography of Akhmatova, *Slavic and East European Journal*, 40 (1996), 135–41, and his "Strakh, tiazhest´, mramor", in *Wiener Slawistischer Almanach*, 36 (1995), 119–54.

19. Shvarts's admiration for Tsvetaeva is profound, reducing her to near wordlessness. See her comments in Shvarts 1992a, 221–22. For a good discussion of themes of death and suicide in Tsvetaeva, although oddly without reference to this poem, see Freidin 1994, 249–61.

20. For the text of his poem, see Mandel´shtam, 1979, 71. His poem also includes the epithet "slabyi" (weak), which Shvarts repeats as a superlative; in his line, the stars shine weakly, but he connects that weakness to a protest about his own powers of perception ("chem ia vinovat, / Chto slabykh zvezd ia osiazaiu mlechnost´?") ("Am I to blame / If the feeble stars strike me as milky?"); in

Shvarts's line, the poet herself proclaims her weakness. Nancy Pollak, whose thoroughgoing critique of two versions of this essay was extremely helpful, remains unconvinced that "Net, ne luna" is a "true subtext", since the repeated rhyme is not that unusual and there are no other lexical correspondences (she was similarly sceptical about the Tsvetaeva connection involving "Vskryla zhily"). I have kept both comparisons, however, because I do not see Shvarts writing with the same kind of intricate subtextual repetitions characteristic of the Acmeists (and central to the scholarship about Acmeism by Omry Ronen, Kiril Taranovsky, Susan Amert, Nancy Pollak and others). Rather, Shvarts relies on more fleeting associations, and typically mixes sources very freely. My experience of having colleagues read drafts of this essay, and of presenting papers on her work, has strengthened this perception of Shvarts's way of drawing on other poets. Repeatedly, the reactions have included suggestions of verbal reminiscences, many of which now inform this essay. In other cases, the similarities have struck me, on closer examination, as more remote, but the fact that Shvarts has elicited this kind of response remains telling: she gets her readers to hear multiple echoes of earlier poets, often by using only a few words, a single image, or a lyrical situation that is barely sketched.

21. The anecdote may have been misattributed, however: see the notes in Mandel´shtam 1990, I, 460.

22. The topic of poetry causing harm is complex, and has been well studied in one of its aspects: poems whose apparent prophecies bring about doom. See, for example, Ronen 1993, esp. 296–97.

23. Shvarts has sometimes joined two poems, for example, "Solovei spasaiushchii" (The saving nightingale) and "Solovei spasaiushchii (stikhotvorenie dvoinik")" (The saving nightingale [a twin poem]), two poems that begin the 1990 collection (4–5); "Dva aspekta" (Two aspects), a short poem split into two mutually commenting pieces (46); "Dva stikhotvoreniia na osobyi raspev" (Two poems to a particular melody) (62–64). See also one of the *Laviniia* poems, "Dva stikhotvoreniia, konchaiushchiesia slovom 'slepoi'" (Two poems ending with the word "blind"), in Shvarts 1987b, 70–71. "Two Aspects" has been translated by Michael Molnar in Shvarts 1993a, 42, as has "Two Poems Ending with the Word 'Blind'" (131–33). Such doubles are another poetic device she has learned from a predecessor, in this case again Mandel´shtam. See, for example, his two poems on the theme of Persephone's descent into Hades, "Ia slovo pozabyl, chto ia khotel skazat´" (I have forgotten the word I wanted to stay) and "Kogda Psikheia-zhizn´ spuskaetsia k teniam" (When Psyche — life — descends among shades), both dated 1920; or the recontextualizing of lines and images within the two parts of "Solominka" (1916). A late and more complicated instance would be the first two poems of Mandel´shtam's "Vos´mistishiia" (Octets, 1933–1935), both of which begin "Liubliu poiavlenie tkani" ("I love the appearance of cloth"). I draw on the

ordering of the poems by Pavel Nerler in Mandel´shtam 1990, 200–01; in the commentary, Nerler observes that Mandel´shtam did not consider the second version a revision of the first, but rather saw the poems as two independent variants (531). For a subtle, compelling reading of "Vos´mistishiia", see Pollak 1995, 39–84.

24. Both poems have been translated into English by Sibelan Forrester in Tomei (1999). See also "Chernaia Paskha" (Black Easter) in Shvarts 1989, 40-47 (translated in Shvarts 1993a, 27–39), for a poem that juxtaposes Christ's passion with a scene of domestic violence.

25. English translation from Shvarts 1993a, 47. The poem opens Shvarts 1989, from which I cite the Russian original (6).

26. 1982 was an extremely productive year for Shvarts (twenty poems by my count, which is probably conservative, since a substantial number of her poems have appeared without dates).

27. Demons appear in a number of *Laviniia* poems, including "Soblaznitel´", "Vy lovites´ na to zhe, chto i vse", "Moia molel´nia" (My chapel), "Chudishche", "Teofil", and "Igra" (The game). Of these, several have been translated into English in Shvarts 1993a: "The Tempter", "You're Caught in the Same Trap as Everyone", "The Monster", and "Theophilus".

28. See also the translation in Smith 1993, 257.

29. "Leviathan" is among the *Laviniia* poems translated in Shvarts 1993a, 117. For the Russian original, see Shvarts 1987b, 22. In this poem, the time spent inside the whale is comforting and revelatory to Laviniia; memories of death and horror are wiped away, and her own identity seems washed aside as well.

30. Similarly, the myth of Ge's revenge on Uranus, for imprisoning his children in her body, and of their son Cronus's swallowing his children, offer pertinent sources for Shvarts, particularly since motifs of stone, lamb, and transformations between humans and animals appear in these tales.

31. The reversibility of actions and images appears elsewhere in her verse. See "Kniga na okne" (A book on the windowsill), where a line reads: "Noch´ — Iona v Kite, cherez noch´ — Kit v Ione" ("It is night and Jonah is in the whale, a night later and the whale is in Jonah") (69); this example is especially appropriate to the poems cited here, since it uses the same story from Jonah, but reversibility is not limited to that plot line for Shvarts. It is also the central idea of "Dzhokonda" (Giaconda): did the thief steal the Mona Lisa, or did she steal him, as the poet wonders slyly in line 2 (75). See also "Sonata temnoty" (Sonata of darkness), with its powerful meditation on the darkness within the poet, and the darkness outside.

32. Other instances of strangely spiritual food include the taking in and spitting out of earth in the end of "Solovei spasaiushchii (stikhotvorenie-dvoinik)" (5 — compare the way the same bit of earth is carried off toward the light in the first nightingale poem, 4); the pomegranate seed that ends "Elegii na

storony sveta" (Elegies on parts of the world) (45). Other examples are more complicated: food comes with the aura of Russian folk tales in the strange cycle of hunger and pointless violence, "Glukhonemoi i vzroslyi syn" (A grownup son who is deaf and dumb) (61); in "Dva stikhotvoreniia na osobyi raspev" (62–64), Shvarts writes a lament-ode to autumn, where crimson juices double for blood, fruits seem as flesh, and hunger can never be sated.

33. These poems have been translated as "The Dump" (26) and "Remembrance of a Strange Hospitality" (51) in Shvarts 1993a; and "I dreamed we were sailing through rice fields" (255) and "Memory of a Strange Refreshment" (249) in Smith 1993.

34. Compare the intimacy assumed in religious thinking about food, well articulated in a sermon by John Tauler earlier in this century: "There is no kind of matter which is so close to a man and becomes so much a part of him as the food and drink he puts into his mouth; and so God has found this wonderful way of uniting Himself with us as closely as possible and becoming part of us." Tauler 1910, 293; cited in Bynum, 1987, 4.

35. For an interesting rhymed translation, see Walter Arndt's version "You swallow people, earth, o earth", in Goscilo 1995, 292. Among poems mentioned here, he also offers "Imitation of Boileau", "I came into the world with palms unlined", and "Animal Flower" (titled "Beast of Blossom").

36. Zabolotskii wrote other poems that treat the motifs of burial and death in ways that clearly affected Shvarts. See in particular "Vchera, o smerti razmyshliaia" (Yesterday, reflecting on death,1936), for its images of water, stone, as well as the invocation of particular poets (Pushkin, Khlebnikov), and "Metamorfozy" (Metamorphoses,1937), whose wandering bull may be the reason one senses an apparition of chewing cattle in Shvarts's poem.

37. The poem's reference to feet also enables this metapoetic reading of the poem. Other texts considered here make repeated reference to hands, a part of the body also long used as a metonymy for the act of writing. Feet offer the association with poetic feet (and in this Shvarts has the example of Mandel´shtam's use of the metonymy). She takes up such metonymies with enthusiasm; compare the frequent appearance of birds in her work, associated through long tradition with the singing lyrical poet and with the god Apollo; on the cover of her 1990 volume, the plume in the bird's beak extends the metapoetic link, in that birds' singing resembles poets' songs, and birds' plumes yield poets' quills. On Mandel´shtam's usage of the same metapoetic link, see Ronen 1973, esp. 378.

38. Whether poetry is inherently monological is another issue, one others have spoken to well. See, in particular, Ciepiela 1994, 1010-24; and Ronen 1973, 384-85, where he gives as an example a Mandel´shtam poem mentioned earlier, "Net, ne luna, a svetlyi tsiferblat".

39. See also a cycle of gypsy verses from the 1970s, "Tsiganskie stikhi" (Gypsy verses), where she takes up the persona of the fortune-telling gypsy who knows others' fates — surprisingly, given the way she writes of herself as inaccessible to gypsy fortune tellers in "Ia rodilas´ s ladon´iu gladkoi". In the gypsy verses, the poem also records an inability to love, as in verse 6: "Ia kholodna, dusha pusta / Karaiut tak neliubiashchikh" ("I am cold, my soul is empty / Thus do they punish those who do not love) (Shvarts 1985, 45).
40. On the *Laviniia* poems, see Goldstein 1993, 239–50.
41. For references regarding the Cynthia poems, see note 6 above.
42. The very idea of the "personal" is much more contested in Russia in the 1990s than was the case under Communism. It will be especially interesting to see how formerly underground cultural figures present a "personal" self to their growing audiences. An intriguing example is the recent piece of autobiographical and perhaps fictional narrative published by the poet Sergei Gandlevskii: Gandlevskii 1995; see in particular the digression on literary culture in the late Communist period (119), where he writes, "I recount here the completely wild mores and habits of my native land. Literature was for us a personal affair. In our kitchens, courtyards, boiler rooms there was no abstract reader, people, or country. There was no one to startle wide-eyed or to teach. Everyone already knew everything."

AN ODD MAN OUT:
THE POETICS OF
MIKHAIL AIZENBERG

Zinovy Zinik

The beginning of my friendship with Mikhail Aizenberg dates back to the end of the sixties. We have now corresponded regularly for almost a quarter of a century — about three times the length of our acquaintance in Moscow. As became clear during the years of separation, we are of different temperaments, although in youth such differences are blurred by mutual enthusiasms. Enveloped in his own metaphysical conjectures, Aizenberg is ready to abandon everything, horrified by his conclusions, and to freeze in depressive hopelessness. In despair, I too abandon everything, in order to take some step, perform some action. I always place my hopes in the fact that, however hasty or inept, such a step will get me out of an ideological trap. In the seventies, after casting about for a long time, I emigrated. He remained. For many long years these different positions formed the subject of epistolary arguments. Such arguments have long since developed beyond the original theme of departure.

The theme of emigration, of leaving, or geographical separation and separating geography, is placed literally at the centre of his first (non-samizdat) verse collection, *Ukazatel´ imen* (An index of names).[1] The early verses from the beginning of the seventies, on the theme of departure, are placed not only at the centre but, symbolically, at the heart of the collection where they are framed by other, more recent, themes from the eighties and nineties. This, as it were, moves the theme of departure onto another plane: the poems are freed from their chronological and geographical entrapment.

There takes place a symbolic transfer, a metamorphosis of a concrete topic or theme into poetic speech. Just as emigration from Russia itself was not simply the geographical change of countries, peoples and passports, so Aizenberg's "poems of emigration" are not confined to themes of parting and farewell.

In Aizenberg's poems the subject matter itself can seem enigmatic, even to the majority of his faithful readers and admirers. They feel the hypnotic attraction of his enquiring, distraught, questing, doubting, stunned and, at the same time, stoic intonation, but they cannot understand what exactly the poems are about. In poetic terms, it is precisely this intonation of bewilderment which is the essence. The question of what is going on is in a way its own reply. Those few people who have written about Aizenberg (the opinions of fellow members of poetic groups, postscripts to volumes in which Aizenberg has participated, and critical reactions to *Ukazatel' imen*) all in one voice affirm the almost deliberate semantic obscurity, the muttering intonation, unclear inner speech, remote half-whispers, private prayers, latent melodies, hidden lyricism and so on. But all this is not said by the reviewers in the spirit of reproach to the author. As Pasternak said, "slozhnoe poniatnei im" (Pasternak 1965, 351) ("complexity is more understandable to them"), since, blinded by the clarity of party and ideology, the mind looks for the shadowy zones of sense, just as someone stupefied by the sun seeks the shade of tree-lined avenues. Apart from that, simplicity can be naively associated with ordinariness, whilst mysterious compexity elevates the reader in his own esteem.

There are poets of deceptive simplicity, like Pushkin. But there is also another category: poetry of deceptive mysteriousness. This deceptiveness hinders understanding of the complexity and harmony of the poetic design. It is not a question of deciphering some secret code. Poetry does not need this; poetry speaks, as it were, for itself, if not to itself. Poetry is something that, in Mandel´shtam's words, holds on "by its own eyelashes" ("na sobstvennykh resnitsakh") (Mandel´shtam 1967, 205). But eyelashes must have a face. And this face should be familiar to the reader. The word, particularly in anglophone culture, if public, is available to all, be it Prince Charles's telephone conversations with his lover or the fascistic grimaces of the émigré American poet T. S. Eliot in the small Faber publishing house: everyone knows where anyone has come from, whom they are married to, how much they earn, and therefore understand the background to a multitude of references. In a place where the word, despite its accessibility to the reader, is to this day divided into high literary style and the low language of the street, it is often forgotten to what degree high-brow literature in the civilized world was always essentially a journalistic chronicle.

In the European and anglophone tradition poetry reaches the reader propped up by prose, facts, biographical materials and legends. Just as in a novel, the hero's poetic voice is guaranteed in advance his own context — and the motivations of character and the logic of his reception by the reader — just as a refugee is guaranteed a passport and a roof over his head. In the Soviet tradition, on the other hand, the poetic hero used to be thought up anew every time and was as poor as a church mouse. He was without residence permit, without a place of abode, without the many-layered feather-bed of literary and everyday associations. Because the sources of such associations were periodically subjected to re-shaping by the censor's blunt scissors, garbling, destruction by prison, emigration or the simple settling of scores. It is in the nature of verses to turn personal relations into a poetic perspective; personal relations, in their turn, are distorted beyond recognition not only by Russian censorial "forgetfulness", but also by the poetical mirror of the verses which were originally connected with them. The result was a sense of farcical mysteriousness not only in the relations, but also in the verses which for decades were doomed to live without a proper address, lacking a clear meaning in the eyes of those readers who did not belong to the circle of the poet's personal acquaintances:

Те, кого жизнь как следует причесала
Тот, кто выскочил пулей, какой-то звонок услышав
Что им ответить?
      ведь летописи не будет.
Что нам сказать пришедшему в мир за справкой?
Каждый сражается в одиночку. (149)

(Those whom life has made properly docile
He who has lept forward like a bullet, hearing some bell
What should one reply to them?
      after all, there will be no chronicle.
What are we to say to someone who has come into the world
         for information?
Each of us fights in solitude.)

Let us try to provide the reader with this unthinkable, encyclopedic information. Talk of the loneliness of the fighter is significant in a discussion of Aizenberg's poetry precisely because thematically his poetry was always connected with his circle. Aizenberg is perhaps the only name known to me in contemporary poetry who is directly autobiographical (I have in mind, naturally, the autobiographicality of his poetic hero; like any hero, he is partly the author, but not all of him). This biography, however, is without named literary sources, without notes and references to that circle of friends which is the subject of his poetic account. References to this circle, or, more accurately, these circles, remain hidden, for various reasons, in the confines of the purely personal aspects of the poet's biography.

Many of these circles have long ago left only ripples in the water (or blood), and my aim here is to capture these disappearing ripples, which are themselves being absorbed in the dry sand of literature. These literary and biographical facts, for various complex reasons, remained outside semi-official and public Moscow conversations, literary or historical exchanges, allusions, references, recriminations and demolitions, quite simply, the chronicle of literature. And if representatives of these circles did appear on the Russian literary horizon, then it was without any connection with Aizenberg or, indeed, each other. But Aizenberg remained their invisible link, leader, messenger, ambassador, and even interpreter of their dreams. He conducted these ambassadorial services anonymously, and this very fact seemed suppressed and symbolic. "Ty gost´ i tam, otkuda net gostei. / Ty mechenyi, poka ia zdes´ stoiu" (50) ("You are also a guest there whence come no guests. / You are marked, while I stand here"). Even more frequently the poet found himself an odd man out: "zdes´ — mezhdu voilokom i faneroi, / tam — v pomrachenii i delakh" (37) ("here, between felt and plywood, / there, in madness and worries").

In an age of revolutions and emigrations literature is not much interested in the position of odd men out (perhaps just because they are in the centre and thus less conspicuous, unlike the extremes) and in personal relations (that is why they are personal). Using the title of Aizenberg's verse collection, I should like to consider this essay as an index of names: it is a biographical subtext to the poetry of Aizenberg — a naturally incomplete subtext, and like any subtext not exhausting of the poetry itself, but indicating what lies behind this or that line and the conceptual motif of any given poem. In Aizenberg's poetry, as will become clear, this motif is first of all the opposition of intimate, personal intentions to those of society, and, at the same time, the unthinkability of a lonely existence without the personal ties and bonds afforded by a circle; fear in the face of his own spiritual inadequacy, before dumbness, outside the word that circulates in any circle.

I am NOT talking here about the communal life of those years, the "kitchen" culture, the culture of discussion round a convivial kitchen table, although without such emotional priming it is possible that there would not have developed in Aizenberg such an intent, almost maniacally doomed attitude to the reactions of other people in conversation when every word was highly charged. His hope was at the same time to break free from the oppression and slavery of such an intimate relationship: "vyiti iz krovnykh, iz plotnykh, iz tesnykh. / Ostat´sia ulybkoi v gostiakh i v bolezniakh" (14) ("to leave the blood relations, the density of flesh, the family closeness. / To remain as a smile when visiting and in sickness").

The essence here perhaps lies not so much in convivial friendly conversations (they were often, in fact, far from friendly), but in the hope of a certain, as it were masonic, ritualized order of fellow-conversationalists who, consciously or not, were working out their own separate, alternative mode of speech, living speech, in contrast to the dead, clichéd language of the outside world. In the 1970s this outside world was identified by Aizenberg with ubiquitous officialdom and with it the polarization of personal relations. It must be made clear that officialdom was not only and not so much Soviet power itself as all those that engaged in discussion with this power: not only its representatives, but also the heretics and reformers. Russian culture, highly centralized in its hierarchy, with the incestuous nature of communal living, turns even dissidence into a distorted mirror reflection of itself. In this atmosphere of communal orthodoxy the search was on for a different timbre of speech, a search for bonds, not with heretics but with inveterate atheists.

Such a confrontation — of two ways of thinking, of bilingual identities — is not unique in itself, and it pertains to literary (and any other) orthodoxy at that time on either side of the Russian border. Correspondingly, manifestations of atheistic positions — those of the outsider — change from age to age, from country to country. That confrontation began, naturally, long before I met Mikhail Aizenberg. The circle of our mutual friend, my fellow-student, the poet Leonid Ioffe was a clear example of such opposition to the common language. In the mid-sixties this was a group of poets (including Evgenii Saburov, Anatolii Makovskii and Valerii Shlenov) linked not so much by their poetic manifestos as by their instinctive, aggressive rejection of the rituals and norms of both the official and the dissident literatures during Khrushchev's Thaw. Even their devotion to an alcoholic, ecstatic manner of day-to-day behaviour: was not that a kind of public gesture placing them once and for all outside that literature where, it seemed, two-faced (fault-finding) political correctness was the only criterion for poetical merit? The very notion of civic responsibility was instinctively perceived by this circle as morally bankrupt, which is not surprising in the atmosphere of overwhelming pessimism which seized the Russian intelligentsia when Khrushchev's political Thaw was coming to an end.

From a dead-end situation of clichéd language, when, in the words of Ioffe, "two kings (of prison and state) sat on the beam of fate's scales" ("u sud'by na koromysle dva kazennykh korolia") a way out is sought through the language of *zaum'*, of trans-sense. The "bureaucratic kings" here are also two extremes of the accepted norms of literature, which is no longer perceived as literature, but as a purely political phenomenon. In this apocalyptic atmosphere of a wake for poetry, given the complete political passivitiy of Ioffe and his circle, it was natural for them to turn to the poetic heritage of the Silver Age, to such figures as Innokentii Annenskii and Andrei Belyi, whose poetic language appealed to another tradition, unsullied, it seemed, by the deadly stains of ideological corpses. The poetry of the Silver Age was an antidote to the pitch black language of the antiworld of Soviet literary editors. In the same sense, the search for salvation had led inevitably to Khlebnikov and the experiments of OBERIU as the logical (anti-logical!) continuation of the same train of thought, or again in Mandel´shtam, particularly the late Mandel´shtam, where the ancient world turned inside out is sieved through the barbarity of Soviet newspeak, and where criminal jargon is woven into the melody of an ancient Greek flute.

The tendency of the poets of Ioffe's circle in those years was poetry "holding on by its own eyelashes", where only the style was ideological (and that only *post factum*), and logical connections gave way to phonetic play and decorative turns of phrases. Apart from everything else, it also represented nostalgia for lofty speech, high culture, heavenly beauty, in contrast to the poverty, "dark holes" and "shameful exposure" of Soviet banality. This was an attempt to smelt the low instincts and depressive aspects of the ordinary, everyday linguistic life of "outsiders" into a kind of neo-classicism.

Thus came about the birth of the poetic hero in the work of Leonid Ioffe: a renegade, a bastard, incapable of any human intercourse, but at the same time seeking a lofty meaning in his own prosaic worldliness. The main element in this romantic pose is the search for another language, "when what is dear to you is not dear, and you cannot love what is alien" ("kogda rodnoe — ne rodnoe, v chuzhogo ne liubit´") (Ioffe 1977, 24). This search in a paradoxical but expected way later acquired a socio-political meaning, when an alternative language for Ioffe became the language of the Bible, and the search for linguistic roots ended in the discovery of his own Jewishness. Aizenberg reacted to such a metaphorphosis of poetic theme in the following way:

О что наделал, человек,
Ты тарабарщиной пугливой:
Есть материк, и под оливой
—ни мертвых веток, ни калек. (Aizenberg 1978)

(Oh, what have you done, man,
With this timorous gibberish:
There is a continent, and under the olive tree
There are neither dead branches nor cripples.)

He also said, "How terrible to half-die / for bits of strawberry-like substitutes for native blood" ("Kak strashno umeret´ napolovinu / za krokhi zemlianichnogo rodstva") (Aizenberg 1973). Within the framework of this dichotomy of "rodnoe - ne rodnoe" Aizenberg was captivated not only by the poetics identified with Ioffe but also by a completely different poetic force, namely the unique kind of muscovite patriotism of Pasternak: a close lyrical attention to specific places, to the details of the local spiritual landscape. The propensity of the mature Pasternak to colloquial language, to prosaicisms, to "unthinkable simplicity" (Pasternak 1965, 351), his close involvement in the whirl of Moscow literary life, clashed, in an antagonism that was almost mythological for Ioffe's circle, with the poetics of Mandel´shtam, an outsider, whose ancient Greek *theta* and *iota* of the disintegrating classical world were glued together with the blood of Stalin's era.

In Aizenberg's poetry before the time of mass exodus to the West of his relatives, friends and acquaintances, there also seem to be two clashing principles, two motifs: the "seditious burden" ("kramol´naia nosha") of personal relations — in the "granite garden" ("kamennyi sad") where "tin feathers rattle" ("per´ia stuchat zhestianye") and "the cast iron tongue is in the deadly grip of jaws" ("namertvo szhat cheliustiami chugunnyi iazyk") (Aizenberg 1973). But the blueprint of Mandel´shtamian intonations is superimposed on a thin web of associations which are intimate by their nature, only partially deciphered, as if deliberately leaving a little logical gap open — like a door in the wall, to freedom, for Pasternakovian irresponsibility. Here the confrontation is not so much between a high and low order of poetic speech; rather it is a search for an intimate, individual language of personal relations, opposed to the harsh dogmatism of people who in "cast iron tongue" confidently proclaim what is right and what is not. As was to become clear later, doctrinairism is far from only arising from the leaders of totalitarian regimes: authoritarianism most usually manifests itself on a personal level, and not necessarily as the shadow of something socio-political; rather the contrary is the case. This is where another of Aizenberg's thematic spirals begins.

During the period of Aizenberg's friendship with Leonid Ioffe I myself was also closely linked to the company of the socratic journalist-philosopher Aleksandr Asarkan, the prose writer Pavel Ulitin, and the poet Iurii Aikhenval´d, people who were a generation older than us. In the typescripted word-collages of Ulitin, in the home-made postcards and essay writing of Asarkan I saw before my eyes the mythologization of the personal relationships between these "three musketeers" of Stalin's time. A word from a personal, almost casual conversation would become, as in an historical epic, the key to understanding the entire epoch, and, vice versa, the everyday epic of Soviet life from the newspapers would be ironically adopted for a dictionary of personal relationships. For me they were mentors and teachers, I was their attentive listener and obedient apprentice. I subconsciously imitated the colloquial manner of speech of Asarkan and Ulitin's prose style. In his turn, Aizenberg at one time looked up to me as his senior (there are only three years between us, but in youth these three years may sometimes feel like thirty), as his mentor and spiritual instructor. Is it not on account of these fevered relationships between the pupils of non-existant schools and their self-styled mentors that later in Aizenberg's poetry the insistent motif of an ironical double can periodically be heard?

где один, повторенный в едином движении,
и себя потерял, и почти не знаком
с непонятными теми, кто пляшет кругом
в бесконечно-далеком своем размножении. (79)

(where one, repeated in a single movement,
has both lost himself, and is almost unacquainted
with those incomprehensible people who are dancing around
in their unending-distant duplication.)

This ironical hierarchy, this masonic order co-existed in Moscow with the whirlpool of bohemian riff-raff from the "Artisticheskii" café, and thanks to such a bizarre mix of styles it was possible to experience at one's own personal expense the full dialectic of the intimate word and the social, ideologized slogan. In the context of their personal conversation you could detect an echo of your own word in an alien word imposed by others; in this round-dance of personal relationships it was possible to experience something akin to Stalin's terror, as well as Khrushchev's spring, and, finally, the period of Brezhnevite stagnation, resulting in emigration — for me and, for example, Asarkan.

After my departure Pavel Ulitin for a full fifteen years continued with his brilliant literary fireworks, in a domestic setting, outside literature, outside a circle, outside the history of his fatherland, daily proclaiming the "cult of the rough draft" (where the precision of a chance word was raised to cult status). It seems to me that this idea of heroic asceticism as personified by Ulitin could not fail to become part of the poetic temper of Aizenberg. But this tendency had a no less striking antithesis. I have in mind that motif in Aizenberg's poetry which is connected perhaps with the indirect but constant presence in his conversations of the figure of Aleksandr Melamid, the main opponent of such mythologization of personal relations as described above.

Melamid has been (and still is) one of my closest friends, but, unlike many others, he always revolted openly against the influence on me of

Asarkan and Ulitin. The "Sots-art" of Melamid and Komar is, in a certain sense, a manifesto asserting Soviet slogans in public squares as having the same significance and effect on our consciousness as lyrical confessions in intimate circles. This stance was a kind of challenge to the literary self-entanglement of Asarkan and Ulitin in a spider's web of personal relationships, as if that were the only possible path in art. Resistance to such ideological relativism as manifested in Sots-art can be felt in Aizenberg's entire poetic temper. Although Soviet (journalistic) language does creep into Aizenberg's own poetic vocabulary, this linguistic aspect of his poetic speech is not self-parody in its totality, as in Sots-art, but distorted by a grimace of personal horror: it is, rather, like the somewhat eerie pocket camera of his friend from student days, the hyper-realist Semion Faibisovich, and not the epic parodies of Komar and Melamid.

Another motif becomes resonant in his poetry: that of another life, a utopian idea of paradise, somewhere "over the rainbow", where a man is freed from slave-like drudgery and routine, from his own insignificance and spiritual poverty, as in Aizenberg's reference to Pushkin's *Tsygany* ("khodit lovkaia beda / kak tsygane za medvedem" (80) — "agile misfortune walks abroad / like the gypsies behind their bear"). All this gradually becomes "timorous gibberish", the motif of a hostile force, darkness, a moloch destroying the warmth of human bonds: "kto nas vodit za soboi / na tamozhennoi tsepochke" (80) ("who leads us behind them / on an excise chain?"). The epoch of emigration is the epoch that destroyed the everyday routine of personal ties. The unthinkability (for various reasons) of emigration for Aizenberg is sieved by his poetry into the idea of rejecting any ideological engagement, any moral absolutism. This rejection in its turn becomes an attempt at poetic survival in an environment of sensorial deprivation, with no companion or spiritual guide. Even the search for another language, escape into complexity of syntax or imagery, to symbolism, and to metaphorical thinking are all equalled in his poetic consciousness to a move into another geography. Such emigration from the exclusively present is for him a step leading to the ruin of what is personal and intimate, in other words, of what is truly living.

In being possessed by the idea of preserving at any price all that is dear, bright and warm in the memory, in this obsession, as in all Proustian things, there is also something of Pliushkin. Alongside this Pliushkin-like attitude there exists in Aizenberg the Tsvetaevan line "I live and it is a mortal sin" ("a ia zhivu i eto smertnyi grekh") (Tsvetaeva 1990, 376), in the sense that every gulp of air you take in is someone else's asphyxia. Any act, any decision is destructive, if not for yourself, then for someone else. The evil of earthly existence lies in the fact that in this world there are no absolutely just actions. But when even a word, a thought leads to departure, separation is murderous. (It should be mentioned that philosophically this is only true in so far as our words and actions depend on us alone.) As might be expected, Aizenberg's style was changing in the middle of the 1980s, becoming more neutral, conversational in tone and at the same time dryly aphoristic, as if he were trying to demonstrate an example of poetic survival on the pitiful rations of remaining in isolation:

> Ходасевич скрип уключин.
> Я его переиграю
> вовсе голос обеззвучу. (71)

(Khodasevich — the creak of rowlocks.
I shall outplay him:
I shall render my voice completely silent.)

He emigrates into himself, he is an internal émigré: the loneliness of one who has remained behind is an echo of the loneliness of the émigré, a silent one in a linguistically strange environment.

It was precisely in this period of cruellest emotional deprivation and isolationism that Aizenberg had become engaged with the most "promising" circle of literary friends, and in particular with the patriarch of poetic conceptualism, Vsevolod Nekrasov (a man who is a generation older, as were, to a greater or lesser extent, all the other literary men who exerted an influence on him). The ideas of Nekrasov about the poetic role of the repetitive mechanical intonation of the routine conversation, his turning to what seem to be chance disjointed werewolf clichés with transient sense, were for Aizenberg the development of earlier motifs connected with the classical dichotomy between what is his own and what alien, the intimate and the ideologized word. His instinctive early attempts to bring his own poetic speech closer to the intonational breathing of his own voice had acquired the consciousness of a poetic school, with its supporters and opponents. The geographical opposition of "here and there", "far and near" disappears. What remains here is the totality of what cannot be escaped, except into the secret closet of intimate whispering, of syncopated breathing against the background of loudspeakers: "na sebia nadeias´, / pro sebia gotovias´. // Rasstavaias´ to est´" (104) ("relying on yourself, / preparing yourself internally. // that is, parting").

The fact that this dialectical tendency is not accidental, and consciously employed by the poet is confirmed by his essays of the post-censorship period. These essays are the crystallization of those ideas which have been (and still are) discussed in a regular correspondence with friends over the last twenty years. This theme may be formulated as an attempt of the poet to survive beyond the prison-like verbal frames that have been imposed on him from outside. The classical motifs of the Romantics about the opposition between the poet and the crowd, word and deed, aesthetics and ethics here become the theme of spiritual survival beyond verbal falsity. The poet's task is now to create a language capable of conveying those aspects of personal relations which exist beyond party (in the broad sense of the word) directives, ethical clichés, and ideological dogmas.

It seems to me, however, that this line of thinking immediately encounters a paradox which has already been posed by the heroes of Samuel Beckett: to what extent is it possible to set oneself completely outside the hateful, numbing verbal frameworks imposed from outside? We speak words which have been imposed on us (by parents, nannies, teachers, leaders) and therefore all our rebellious thoughts are dictated precisely by those against whom our rebellion is directed. As Tiutchev reminds us, a thought once spoken is a lie. And for that reason hope of truth is to be found only in what is impossible to formulate. Realizing this, Aizenberg seems to avoid any kind of a reply, any kind of final verbalization of thought. What is more, he seeks just those moments of existence which do not lend themselves to formulation but manifest some tests of moral endurance. These are not declarations of truth, but the verification of a passing, barely noticeable falsity. In this fixity of gaze and the drooping of the edges of the poet's lips there is something frightening.

By now we have come right up against the philosophical problems inspired by the type of personal relationships outlined at the start of this essay. When and how does an alien word become one's own, and is there any word of one's own at all? To what extent are all our words dictated "from above"? In other words, is there an external source of verbal influence on our thinking, and does this influence have a single centre? To what extent are our words morally coloured, and if they are, to what extent is this moral universal? To what extent is the moral and ethical system of my individual "inner" world harnessed to the moral of the outside world, "abroad"? Are not these worlds ethically equal in value? To what extent are things independent of the names which we give them, and, as a consequence of such dependence, to what extent does the form of things acquire a moral colouring connected with its name? To what extent is form ethical?

Naturally, these questions are not new, but have existed from the time of the arguments between the positivists and the Kantians echoing the scepticism of Nietzsche as well as the moral sterility of Wittgenstein. These ideas are temperamentally dear to the thinking of all those who suspect that truth when publicly declared by too great a number of people ceases to be a truth. It is not surprising that these ideas found fertile soil in Russia where collective morality rules supreme. Equally unsurprising are the calls of the opposing camp for a compulsory re-introduction to the intellectual vocabulary of religious and moral absolutes. Let us note (although this is a theme for a separate essay) that neither the present-day defenders of moral absolutes in Russia, nor their opponents, realize that the argument between them is, in its essence, not a discussion about belief or lack of belief in the existence of these absolutes as ruling principles of our consciousness, but about the decrepitness of the moralistic lexicon, the verbal manifestation of these principles in everyday life. All these questions are linked, of course, with the type of relations in the Moscow circles referred to above, and with the question of emigration from Russian "civilization" (although all this too is a theme for a separate essay). All that comprises the basic sources and constituent elements of Aizenberg's poetry.

Poetry, however, is not exhausted either by its sources or by its constituent elements. Poetry does not give answers to philosophical questions; but if it does go in this direction, then it is to put questions, to indicate them (this is the "index of names"). The meaning in a line of poetry is an intersection of all possible interpretations of this line's meaning that are otherwise impossible to express verbally. This point of view, which no one had noticed before Aizenberg, is that of an odd man out; a new point of view, a fifth dimension. And Aizenberg's motifs themselves, as we have shown, are transformed in striking manner, as if crawling out of their own skin and looking into themselves from the other side of a looking glass; sometimes it is simply impossible to recognize this former motif, just as it is impossible to recognize a butterfly in a larva.

And yet these dilemmas, this insistent little ditty does not disappear, despite all the poet's attempts to escape from this dialectical trap, where, like Oscar Wilde, he experiences a clash between the temperament of the aesthete and the moralist, the man of words and the man of action, the teacher and pupil, the epigone and genius, the talkative and the taciturn, motifs of the dichotomy between the static and the changing, internal and external freedom, the far and the near, or, finally, faithfulness to personal connections and one's circle, on the one hand, and the sinister hypnosis of ideas and doctrines on the other.

I repeat, however, that all this is just the sources and constituent elements of a poem, of writing poetry. The content (that is to say, the poems themselves) begins precisely there where these motifs become entwined. It is precisely this inability of the verse to be reduced to any simple semantic sense that is a guarantee of its poetic power, just as a man's spiritual freedom lies in the fact that he cannot be reduced to his genealogical tree. The relations of Aizenberg with Leonid Ioffe, Evgenii Saburov or Zinovy Zinik, with Pavel Ulitin or Vsevolod Nekrasov are very easily (too easily!) arranged into the story of an eternal search for authority, for paternal words of guidance, for the solidarity of a clan; and, at the same time, a rebellion against it, a kind of emigration. This picture of Aizenberg's development is somewhat too neatly arranged to be entirely credible, as if he has left more clues than are necessary.

A striking example of a deceptively familiar theme is the poem "A, mozhet, ty poshel nazad" where everything, from the vocabulary to the intonation, seems to link this poem with poems of the period of departures, as may be seen from the last two stanzas:

А что ни строчки за сто лет,
так заблудился письмоносец.
Сменить просроченный билет
готов колониальный офис.

Ложится скатертью туман.
Не охраняется граница.
Я верю: вспомнит, возвратится
любимый сын из дальних стран. (138)

(And why no line for a hundred years,
because the postman has got lost.
The colonial office is prepared
to replace an overdue ticket.

Mist settles like a tablecloth.
The border is not guarded.
I believe that the beloved son will
remember and return from distant lands.)

Only the suspiciously radiant ending speaks of a new (thanks to perestroika? — the poem was written in 1991) attitude to those who have departed, seemingly for ever, from your life. But this is just the point: leaving life. I was amazed to learn from Aizenberg that the poem is in fact about the death of his father. He spoke of how in his last years his father had come to address him as if he, Mikhail Aizenberg, and not his father, were the senior member of the family; hence the almost unconscious — almost a slip of the tongue — metamorphosis of father and son in the last line. Poetically, it seems to me that this involuntary substitution of father by son in the poem is dictated or prompted by the words "return" and "distant lands", alluding to the parable of the prodigal son: there was, after all, no prodigal father. There is, however, another father: the Father, and, perhaps, it is precisely in the refusal to give a concrete decoding of this name that we can see the poetical and philosophical creed of Aizenberg.

Not by chance, in a recent essay, "Razdelenie deistvitel′nosti" (The division of reality) (Aizenberg 1989), Aizenberg quotes Mandel′shtam's comparison of art to children playing with the Father. In the last analysis it is possible to reformulate all that has been said about the poet hitherto, calling his main theme the search for an authority of equal significance to his father's. For twenty years he has tried on all possible uniforms of subordination to authority, only in order to feel in this the constriction[2] of the person who "has swapped his conscience for the off chance" ("smeniavshii sovest′ na avos′", 65). Only when he has trapped himself in a corner is this person able to realize his own unaccountability, the unique freedom of a certain poetical nature, "of sadness separated from the herd" ("toski, otbivsheisia ot stada", 67).

In Aizenberg's poetry there have always been heard notes of, if not resignation, then a doomed acceptance of everything that is foisted upon him. The strength of this deceptive submissiveness is in the firm belief that a man can only have taken from him what he did not own; what is more, he cannot have anything foisted on him which did not belong to him. This belief brings freedom from the omniscient, intimidating voice of the fatherland rather than of a true father, which quietly and persistently affirms that if you do not become "one of us" you will perish. This father is not from Aizenberg's family experience and not the figure of an authoritative mentor from the experience of his literary connections. This voice threatens with the loss of fatherland, one's circle, family: but the subject of these threats and attempts at persuasion is not the fatherland but the warm, stuffy, prison-like darkness of the "godfather", the chief gangster; not paternal support, but that horror which is colonized by humans ("liud′mi zaselennyi uzhas"). Here is Aizenberg's reply to these threats and attempts at persuasion:

Говорю вам: мне ничего не надо.
Позвоночник вынете—не обрушусь.
Распадаясь скажу: провались! исчезни!
Только зтот людьми заселенный ужас
не подхватит меня как отец солдата,
не заставит сердцем прижаться к бездне. (19)

(I tell you, I need nothing.
Take out my backbone, I shall not cave in.
Disintegrating, I shall say, vanish! disappear!
But this horror which is colonized by humans
shall not embrace me, as a father does his falling soldier son,
shall not force me to press my heart to the abyss.)

И, в океан братских ночей сжатый,
Я упаду тяжестью всей жатвы,
Сжатостью всей рвущейся вдаль клятвы,
И в глубине сторожевой ночи
Чернорабочей вспыхнут земли очи
И промелькнет пламенных лет стая.
(Mandel´shtam 1967, 254)

(and then, compressed in an ocean of brotherly nights,
I'll fall with the weight of an entire harvest,
with the exactness of that oath, ripping into the distance,
and deep in the dark sentry-night
the earth's unskilled-labourer's eyes will flare,
and a flock of flaming years will flash by. (Mandel´shtam 1973, 281)

The first stanza is Aizenberg's, the second Mandel´shtam's, and between them lies half a century. These terrifying Voronezh verses of Mandel´shtam's came to my mind through a rhythmical and intonational echo in Aizenberg's work. Mandel´shtam's poem is considered a weak one, written in a state of fear, panic, mental derangement, as a last hopeless attempt to justify himself to Stalin. But the Leninist-Stalinist ending of the poem ("Proshelestit speloi grozoi Lenin [...] budet budit´ razum i zhizn´ Stalin" — "Lenin will rustle by like a ripe thunderstorm [...] Stalin will arouse mind and life") seems to me just a postal address (the Kremlin, Moscow) written later, on the envelope; the letter itself has a quite different addressee. And it is not entirely about the poet's loyalty to the power of the people, although Mandel´shtam quite openly reckons the "people's judgment" amongst the things without which, it seems, he could not live: without "the right to breathe and unlock the doors / And insist that reality will remain real, / And that the people, like a judge, judges" ("prava dyshat´ i otkryvat´ dveri / I utverzhdat´, chto bytie budet, / I chto narod, kak sudiia, sudit") (Mandel´shtam 1967, 253).

This poem is not a signature affirming political loyalty, but, rather, a poetic manifesto, a declaration of Mandel´shtam's ideological stance as a poet: in the interests of preserving his poetic integrity, his full-blooded existence in the poetic consciousness of the nation, he is prepared to renounce his own self and fuse with anything on earth and above, with Lenin's thunderstorm and Stalin's night. This is the highest amorality of a poetic genius. And this pledge, camouflaged here in Leninist-Stalinist rhetoric, was first uttered by Mandel´shtam not in this poem but far earlier, long before the derangement of Voronezh: "Sokhrani moiu rech´ navsegda [...] za smolu *krugovogo* [my emphasis — ZZ] terpen´ia" (Mandel´shtam

1967, 235) ("Preserve my speech for ever [...] for the pitch of collective suffering"). In the same poem he he pledges:

И за зто отец мой, мой друг и помощник мой грубый,
Я—непризнанный брат, отщепенец в народной семье—
Обещаю построить такие дремучие срубы...
(Mandel´shtam 1967, 167)

(And in payment, father, friend, rough helper,
I — unacknowledged brother, renegade in the people-family —
I promise to build such thick log-walls)
(Mandel´shtam 1973, 195)

That same poetic pledge may be heard in the Voronezh lines, despite the hollow echo in them of Stalin's "paternal" jackboot; and with this pledge, given by the poet a long time ago, in his life before arrest, he also swears to leap into the sea of "fraternal" darkness, into the abyss of the "workers'" night.

Half a century later we know what lies hidden in this profoundly poetic longing for "fraternal nights". And in what is, so far as I know, an unconscious reply to Mandel´shtam, as part of their fated exchange, Mikhail Aizenberg, the odd man out, an inner émigré, again speaks of this "horror which is colonized by humans / [which] shall not embrace me from falling, as a father embraces his falling soldier son, / shall not force me to press my heart to the abyss", as it did to Mandel´shtam. But it is not the shout of a guard which pushes the poet towards the abyss, but the words of those close to him, his friends and fellow-poets — words which once were alive, but which grow numb and harden, like this very shout, along with a look which finds no response in one's companion's eyes.

Translated by Arnold McMillin

REFERENCES

Aizenberg, M. 1973. *Vtoroi sbornik* (Moscow: samizdat).
_____, 1978. "Dekabr´, pereplyv stolitsu", *Vremia i my* 35: 74.
_____, 1989. "Razdelenie deistvitel´nosti", in *Molodaia poeziia – 1989* (Moscow: Sovetskii pisatel´).
_____, 1995. *Ukazatel´ imen* (Moscow: Gendal´f).

Mandel´shtam, O. 1967. *Sobranie sochinenii v trekh tomakh* (Washington: Interlanguage Literary Associates), I.

_____, 1973. *Complete Poetry of Osip Emilevich Mandelstam*. Translated by Burton Raffel and Alla Burago. With an Introduction and Notes by Sidney Monas (Albany: State University of New York Press).

Pasternak, B. 1965. *Stikhotvoreniia i poemy* (Moscow-Leningrad: Sovetskii pisatel´).

Tsvetaeva, M. 1990-93. *Sobranie stikhotvorenii, poem i dramaticheskikh proizvedenii v 3-kh tomakh* (Moscow: Prometei), I.

NOTES

1. Aizenberg 1995. Page references to this collection in the text are given in brackets. All translations of quotations from Aizenberg are by the article's translator.
2. "Pokhozhe, nikogda nikak / ne lopnet obruch na grudi" (65) ("It seems that no way ever / the hoop around the chest will burst").

ZINOVY ZINIK'S GOTHIC SUBURBIA[1]

Robert Porter

"Cricket civilizes people and creates good gentlemen.
I want everyone to play cricket in Zimbabwe;
I want ours to be a nation of gentlemen."
Robert Mugabe

"Cricket — a game which the English, not being a spiritual people,
have invented in order to give themselves some conception of eternity."
Lord Mancroft

In many respects Zinovy Zinik (né Gluzberg) provides us with a special, even unique, view of Russian literature in the 1980s. A paradoxical way of putting this would be to say that he typifies through exception. He left Russia in 1975, just one more member of the Third Wave. His works neatly span the watershed of 1985–86 and thus reflect the Communist and post-Communist eras. (It would not be controversial to argue that the spiritual and cultural collapse of Communism coincided with the arrival of *glasnost´* its formal (political) demise lagging behind by some five years.) Consequently, the literary scene in the post-Communist era might be likened to a well-stocked, but not particularly well-managed, supermarket: there are some staple foods, well past their sell-by date, a lot of fast food, not particularly nutritious, and lots of foreign offerings which traditionalists are suspicious of or find unpalatable, all this to be washed down with a potent cocktail of *pornukha* and *chernukha*. The fastidious reader might discern elements of these last two qualities in Zinik if s/he tried hard enough. Now published in Russia, Zinik is part and parcel of the post-1985 literary scene. Yet he lives in London and is a British citizen.

125

At the same time, Zinik does not fit the pattern of the expatriate Russian writer for several reasons. Firstly, and most obviously, he has not gravitated to any of the more usual locations such as Paris, New York or Munich. After directing a Russian-language theatre group at Jerusalem's Hebrew University for a year, and after three months in Paris, he settled in London in late 1976, working for the BBC Russian Service, and continuing with his writing. Secondly, and more importantly from a literary point of view, his emigration — to judge by his fiction, articles and interviews — has been as much spiritual and intellectual as anything else. In this regard he might be compared to Nabokov, Conrad or, more recently, Kundera. He makes frequent allusions to Nabokov and even put together an "imaginary interview" with him, culled from published questions and answers, relating particularly to the subject of emigration (Zinik 1986a). These three writers, to varying degrees, mastered foreign languages to such an extent that they were able to write fiction in them (Kundera's *La Lenteur* [Paris: Gallimard, 1995] is his first novel to be written in French). To date, Zinik has not quite reached that stage, but these days his criticism and reviews are written in English, and the time may well come when he will not need the services of a translator at all. There is thus a world of difference between him and many of the leading representatives of the Third Wave (Siniavskii, Solzhenitsyn and Voinovich, for instance). Unlike many of the Third-Wave writers, he had not made much of a mark before emigration; his reputation rests on his achievements in the West. To that extent, and that only, he could be compared to Eduard Limonov. One notes that the latter also has fluent English and French, and before turning to full-time and extremist politics, repeatedly pleaded to be accepted just as a "writer". Zinik emigrated because, as he said in an interview, he "wanted to be a foreigner. A foreigner as regards my own past" (Zinik 1991a, 11). A fuller and more penetrating explanation is offered in an extensive article under the same title as the interview (see below).

This remark about "wanting to be a foreigner" leads us on to the third way in which Zinik is the exception rather than the rule. It also leads us to the essence of his creative writing. Despite the numerous Russian settings, Russian flashbacks and Russian reminiscences, and the fact that several of his works take place in Jerusalem, the centre of gravity of his fiction is the West, and more particularly the allegedly urbane, (sub)urban middle-class West, usually as found in London. Zinik specializes in heroes who are outsiders looking in, characters who, on one level, want to be accepted, but who, on another, delight in their foreignness. If one wanted to discern an ideology in this, it would be rootless cosmopolitanism, no bad thing in an age that has produced so many émigrés all over the world and witnessed nationalism leading to ethnic cleansing.

Moreover, it is difficult to pigeon-hole Zinik in terms of indigenous Russian literature, especially given the "mismanaged supermarket" situation that we have already referred to. In some ways he could be classed as a representative of Russia's "alternative prose" (the genre is broad, but some definition of it would include unbridled first-person narration, the use of uninhibited vernacular, parody, sexual explicitness and a rejection of simplistic didacticism and civic-mindedness). Yet his preoccupation with English mores and values militates against such a classification. Zinik, at bottom, is *sui generis*, and as such sums up all the incongruities of Russian literature in the 1980s, and beyond.

Zinik has apparently chosen a difficult furrow to plough. To some Russian intellectuals he may appear to have abandoned the most cherished traditions of Russian literature (though one notes that the same charge could be levelled at a good many writers currently operating in Russia); to other readers — no matter what their background — his special appeal might seem confined to those who possess the renowned English propensity to self-mockery coupled with a fairly developed reading knowledge of Russian. Zinik does lose something in translation, not least the bi-lingual punning. However, there is a broader perspective. As Mikhail Aizenberg wrote in his Preface to the publication in Russia of *Lord i eger´* (The lord and the gamekeeper, 1991):

> Here, writing in Russian, Zinik as it were does not need translators. More than that: for the Soviet (not the émigré) reader he himself is starting to perform this role. "Writing in Russian in England means describing with Russian words things that exist only in English", the author admits. With the passage of time Zinik is all the more palpably becoming a translator of Émigré into Russian. (3)[2]

So Zinik's concept of "emigration as a literary device", which we examine more closely below, can work both ways, East-to-West and West-to-East. Yet the author is only too aware of his anomalous position: Aizenberg calls the hero of *Lord i eger´* a "monster" (*Lie*, 5) and indeed several of Zinik's heroes, with their outlandish ideas and behaviour, seem something more than normal, especially to the sedate, civilized English men and women who beset them. Zinik, like any serious author, will not identify himself with any of his characters, but none the less he shares a good many of their dilemmas and incongruities:

> No matter who an author from Russia might consider himself to be, no matter what passport he may carry in his pocket, in his heart he does not want to part with the title of Russian writer. I wish to retain my martyr's status in belonging to Russian literature, without at the same time losing the privileges and liberties of a subject of the British crown. (Zinik 1991b, 13)

Emigration for Zinik is an adventure and an act of creation, not primarily a political act. In the Afterword (written by the author in English) to a recent collection of his stories (*One-way Ticket*, 1995), he once again goes into the question. After disclosing that he changed his name and talking about his duality and "dubious" nature, which contributed to his decision to leave his homeland, he writes:

> And there were as many other aspects of my Soviet past which might have prompted my decision to emigrate — the KGB, my Jewish origins, too many simultaneous love affairs [...] the unavailability of good beer and whisky, fear of the mob and harsh winters [...] On the other hand the reasons for *not* leaving were as numerous [...] No one in his right mind leaves his own country unless he is forced to do so. I wasn't forced to leave Russia: I must then either have not been in my right mind, or ceased to regard Russia as my own country. Or both. (Zinik 1995, 216–17)

Towards the close of this rather personal essay he tells us that "life is a permanent emigration, from past to present, from this world to another, from a wife to a lover, from life to death", and that "as an author I have been transformed into a vassal of the literary metropolis [...] For a writer there is, and always will be, only one way to liberate himself from this vicious circle of invisible confinement: to write a new work, to create a new style" (Zinik 1995, 224).

We should consider in some detail the author's notion of emigration as a literary device (Zinik 1983). He tells us that as a child he was very Soviet, and he joyfully recalls the public holidays when Gor'kii Street was festooned with party slogans, and he and a friend tried to pierce the police cordons in order to mingle with the official demonstration. With de-Stalinization, Zinik then discovered that there was a different side to Russia and the Soviet Union, as returnees from the GULag told their stories: hitherto the only camps he had known about were young pioneer camps. For him Russia and the Soviet Union disappeared, or rather "disintegrated into a heap of persecuted friends and a stoney, faceless crowd [...] That's what emigration begins with" (Zinik 1983, 174).

He goes on to cite the story of Oscar Wilde encountering André Gide and relating to him the following parable. When Narcissus was dying he told the woodland pool he was sad because he would never again see his own reflection in its waters. The pool retorts that that she is sad because she thought that Narcissus sat on the river bank so that "I might observe my own reflection in your eyes" (Wilde's original text has " in the mirror of his eyes I saw ever my own beauty mirrored" [Wilde 1990, 844]). Zinik tells us that Wilde then added the word *Uchenik*, which is the title of the story (Wilde's original is, of course, "The Disciple"). Here we come close to one of the major building blocks in Zinik's fiction. He writes:

> For me the moral of this parable resides in the fact that in similar relationships between the disciple and the teacher, that is between the youth and the mentor, there is no hero. Or rather, there is no main hero, that is, no author's point of view — no view from above. There are two views seeking their reflection in each other. [...] there is no novel, because both have forgotten about the existence of a third point of view: from above. [...] For both of them the sky does not exist because they cannot see their own reflection in it, they only look into each other. For them only the historical process of contemplating their own place in the eyes of the other exists — it is a moral-epic relationship to reality. They have "become entangled (*vputalis´*) in history". For me the novel starts with the transformation of the hero, with the plot (*siuzhet*) as an external angle on what is taking place, from the side, from above as it were. (Zinik 1983, 176)

Later on in his essay Zinik tells us pointedly that "Freedom is the right to drop out of the historical process", that emigration was for him a "literary device", that it is also "alienation from one's own past" , that "your words cease to be intimate" (Zinik 1983, 178). For Zinik, emigration is also revolution, a personal revolution. He argues that in the 1920s the literary achievements were not due simply to the abolition of censorship, but to the fact that hitherto private conversations were now "epochal", "phenomenal", "unique", since there was now a "dynamic" in them — a before and after. People now saw themselves, and other things, "from the other side of the mirror" (Zinik 1983, 179).

Zinik's fiction is the embodiment of these considerations; it is a fiction of comic contradictions and improbable, but by no means impossible, individuals, of interlocking misperceptions and misinterpretations. The three key works examined below have been selected as good examples of this embodiment, and because they fit neatly in a volume devoted to the literature of the 1980s. *Russkaia sluzhba* (Russian service) was completed in London in 1981; *Russofobka i fungofil* (The russophobe and the mushroom-lover, translated as "The Mushroom Picker"), Zinik's best-known novel, was finished in London in 1984, and "Kriket" (Cricket) in London in 1990. The first two are set against the old world order, the last in an era when Communist ideology, but not international political problems, has collapsed.

There are two especially salient motifs in Zinik's fiction: the Gothic element, and what can be loosely termed the "set-piece of English life". The story "Nezvanaia gost´ia" (An uninvited guest, completed 1990) has the narrator on holiday in Portugal:

I was inclined to turn sundry philosophical conclusions and syllogisms over in my mind — that year they revolved around a comparison between the English eighteenth-century Gothic novel and the phenomenon of the third wave of Russian emigration. This metaphysical conundrum, pleasantly fuddled with alcohol, found an illustration in the never-ending arabesques which the semi-wild cats would perform in front of me with the zeal of harem women. (Zinik 1995, 149)

In his 1991 interview "Emigratsiia kak literaturnyi priem" Zinik offers a few "speculative historical parallels":

Moscow in the 70s and 80s in many respects is similar to London at the start of the eighteenth century, when literary and religious-ideological thinking were indissoluble and led to denunciations, conspiracies, prison and emigration. This was the epoch of the blossoming in England of the genre of the Gothic horror novel. That's why one of my essays about émigré thinking I actually entitled "The Gothic Horror Novel of Emigration" [...] Similar stylistics were appropriate in both the age of Wordsworth and Stalin when everyone lived in the unshakeable certainty that there would be no changes expected for the next thousand years. (Zinik 1991a, 3)

One might quibble that there is something of a sleight of hand in the first two sentences quoted here, given that the English Gothic novel is generally dated from Horace Walpole's *The Castle of Otranto* of 1765. However, Zinik's lengthy article on the Gothic to which he refers in the interview (Zinik 1986b) cuts no such corners. Moreover, it is entertaining and perceptive. The Gothic novel, he argues uncontentiously, arose in the mid-eighteenth century as a reaction to the age of Enlightenment with its ideas of progress and rationalism (Zinik 1986b, 41). This was a time of papal conspiracies, religious persecutions of Catholics, and of emigration of intellectuals. The Gothic novel sought out a mythical world of medieval castles and folklore, of pagan sects, of the supernatural, of ghosts and vampires. Zinik also points out that one of the key themes in the Gothic novel was that of usurpation of power. What should all this have to do with the Soviet Union in the 1970s and 80s? In Zinik's view the émigré is a ghost or vampire possessed by devils, a ghost who cannot escape the Soviet jargon he was reared on, but one who has to acquire a foreign language; hence, for example, he will asssociate the English word "cash" with the Russian word for porridge *kasha* (Zinik 1986b, 43). The émigré has a linguistic duality, and thus we find Zinik's prose peppered with the most ingenious bi-lingual puns. In private correspondence, Zinik says that in his later novel *Lord i eger´* "the whole dramatic collison is triggered off by a different perception of the word 'asylum'": England, for a Russian, means "political asylum", but for an Englishman, a victim of ancestral intrigue, "asylum" means a prison-style mental institution (with, it goes without saying, Gothic connotations).

Zinik cites several examples in Soviet public life of phenomena that we might associate with the Gothic novel. The huge official portraits of Marx and Engels always seemed to Zinik to have blue rather, than black, beards, owing possibly to the quality of the printer's ink: they were "Blue Beards". These gave way to Lenin's goatee, which in turn made way for Stalin's moustache, which became transmogrified into Brezhnev's eyebrows. The exception (until Gorbachev) was Khrushchev, so no wonder they got rid of him (Zinik 1986b, 47). Incidentally, this observation is reminiscent of another delightfully irreverent analysis of the Soviet leadership: that it alternated between bald, reforming idealists, and hairy reactionary cynics. Both analyses have an element of truth in them and, if nothing else, illustrate the alchemic, Gothic aspect of what was Sovietology or Kremlinology. Zinik goes on to remind us that Brezhnev's coffin was dropped at his funeral, and that in 1978 a Bulgarian defector was murdered on a London street with a poisoned umbrella.

Zinik's best example comes in a supplement called "The Soviet Frankenstein". Mary Shelley worked on her novel primarily throughout 1817 (it was published in 1818). Just one hundred years later we see the introduction of the New Soviet Man. Now Lenin lies embalmed in the Mausoleum, and rumours circulate constantly, as to how authentic the corpse is. One rumour, Zinik tells us, even involves a tank of embalmed "spare parts" (Zinik 1986b, 67).

The stance of the émigré writer in this modern Gothic situation is clear:

As long as (*poka ne*) the émigré hero does not recognize the new citizenship of the birch trees that look so near and dear to him (*rodnykh na vid berezok*), as long as he does not cease usurping the Russian present which is inaccessible to him, while passing it off as his own past, as long as he does not cease calling himself in his soul a Russian, without understanding that his "Russianness" has long ago become a part of that country in which he has now settled; as long as the émigré does not realize that the past is not a unified whole, but looms up as isolated islands while the pilot navigates his way through the fog of the present; as long as he does not accept as a defence mechanism the neat Stalinist relativity in respect of his personal history; as long as he does not recall that the Russian word *poka* [one should note the pun here — RP] also means *do svidaniia* — the émigré will remain a character in a Gothic novel, he will be in need of a miracle and of armed revolts to rid him of his ghostly state; he will be a slave and idol-worshipper of the other world and of all sorts of devilry, of settling accounts and searching for the guilty... (Zinik 1986b, 66)

Hence Zinik's predilection in his fiction for the macabre, his fondness for the word "monster" (frequently *monstr*, but also *urod, chudovishche* and their cognates), and his occasional forays into violent, bloody scenes. His depiction of these hovers curiously between the humorous (*à la* Tom Sharpe) and the macabre. Near the beginning of the novel *Nisha v panteone* (A niche in the pantheon, completed 1979) he describes a re-encounter in Israel with a former acquaintance from Russia (such meetings in themselves constitute a recurrent theme in Zinik): a trick of the light makes him appear to the narrator like a King Kong figure ("gigant i monstr iz fil´ma po-obez´ian´i" — "a giant and monkey-like film monster") (Zinik 1985, 23), like a giant towering over tower blocks, when in fact he is just a down-at-heel mortal in a cemetery, whom the narrator has been talking to not a minute before.

In *Russkaia sluzhba* the chief Gothic element is grounded very much in fact. Just under two years after Zinik began to work for the BBC Russian Service in late 1976, the Bulgarian defector, Georgi Markov, who also worked there, was murdered by the Bulgarian secret service in a manner that was more redolent of a James Bond story than of Zinik's world of bathos and banal misconceptions (one notes in passing that Ian Fleming's stories are an excellent example of the way that the Gothic has survived into the present era: power-crazed villains living in palatial hide-aways, naive, vulnerable heroines, scientific wizardry, clear-cut morality): *The Times* reported that Markov, who had defected in 1969 and was a staunch anti-Communist, died on 11 September, having been stabbed a week before with a poisoned umbrella, in what at first was thought to be an innocent accident. It soon transpired that another Bulgarian dissident, Vladimir Kostov, had suffered, but survived, an identical attack in Paris earlier.[3]

Russkaia sluzhba tells the story of Narator, employee of a Soviet Ministry, who comes to England to make contact with the man behind the voice he listens to on the mysterious External Broadcasting Corporation (*Inoveshchanie*). The External Broadcasting Corporation is a somewhat Gothic amalgamation of all the foreign stations that the hero tunes in to: The Voice of America, Radio Liberty and the BBC. Narator is something of a parody of Gogol´'s Akakii Akakievich: forty-years-old, balding, sexually inexperienced and engrossed in his work as a corrector of misprints. Inept and monolingual (one might detect a parody in this of Vladimir Korolenko's story "Bez iazyka" [Without a language, 1895]), he finds himself defecting, and eventually working for the External Broadcasting Corporation. The man he wanted to meet, Naum Gerundi, has died; on his first day he hears that it was of some mysterious ailment involving something about an umbrella. Narator has lost the umbrella that his erstwhile colleagues in Moscow gave him, and it has become, in a curious way, his only hope of getting back to Russia. The older generation of Russian émigrés, in the figure of Tsilia Kharonovna Bliafer, see a Muscovite conspiracy in everything, and consequently, through the mediation of Doctor Ierarkh Lidin, Scotland Yard is called in. Near the end of the story, the hero is jabbed with an umbrella and his soul flies off to heaven.

Other Gothic motifs can be glimpsed in his being told by Tsilia to chew garlic to ward off revolutionary infections when he is participating in a film version of John Reed's *Ten Days that Shook the World*;[4] or the fact that he becomes unsure as to when his birthday is, given that he was reared by his grandmother who did not recognize New Style dating (*Rs*,16). After the filming he discovers his clothes have been stolen and he leaves wearing his costume of a revolutionary sailor. Tsilia left revolutionary Petrograd as a small child, learning in later life that her family suffered at the hands of revolutionary matelots. So she can be forgiven for fainting when she sees him.

Then we have his routine struggle to come to terms with English life. One of the most humorous episodes concerns his attempts to keep warm. Russian houses being usually over- and centrally-heated, Narator is perplexed that in England he has to buy an electric fire. When he gets it home, he discovers he has to buy a plug for it. Then he has to feed his electricity meter. He cannot cope with Moscow Time, Greenwich Mean Time and British Summer Time, finally resorting to three alarm clocks set at different times, but still cannot remember which one is which.

Yet it is what is going on in Narator's mind that is of the greatest interest. His values are confused and contradictory. While acting as an extra in the film he is keen to be the standard bearer of the Revolution, recalling his own father's real participation in the stirring events. Yet he is at the same time a Soviet defector and works for an organization that broadcasts anti-Soviet material.

Like a good many of Zinik's heroes, Narator has difficulty perceiving and then coming to terms with the realia around him. Back in Moscow he was very slow even to learn of the existence of foreign broadcast stations; and when he started listening to them, suddenly there were two "truths" (*pravdy*). In England his limited English does not so much present a barrier as generate all manner of strange associations. Thus we are treated to a series of puns and neologisms: Waterloo Station as *Vaterklozet* is one of the chastest; saltier examples include *disrachi* and *pizderachi* (*Rs*, 42); the pun on a certain ayatollah's name is so obscene that the reader might be left worrying that the author could be running the risk of a *fatwa* (*Rs*, 50), while a German philosopher springs to the hero's mind when he sights some demotic graffiti referring to the female genitalia (*Rs*, 52).

Moreover, the Russian language in emigration takes a pounding. Narator is keen to correct the stresses in his colleagues' pronunciation, while Tsilia can even tangle up various Russian proverbs, telling Doctor Lidin that he wants the sheep to be well-fed and two hares to be safe (*Rs*, 75). The originals are, of course: *ovtsy tsely i volki syty* (the sheep are safe and the wolves well-fed), that is, everyone is happy, that suits everyone; and *za dvumia zaitsami pogonish'sia nichego ne poimesh'* (if you chase two hares you will catch nothing), that is, don't fall between two stools, or a bird in the hand is worth two in the bush. Almost in retaliation for this sort of improprieties, we have Narator and others making heavy weather of the English tense system, the comedy here depending largely on the Russian original:

> "A zachem? - udivilsia Narator. - Mne ved´ i tak ne moglo by byt´ bylo luchshe. Ia schastliv i bez."
> "No esli bez, vse bylo by byt´ kak i bylo." (*Rs*, 117)

> ("But why — Narator was amazed — After all, for me it couldn't be was better. I'm quite happy without."
> "But if without, everything would be to be as it was...")

We should bear in mind that the hero of course never meets Naum Gerundi; there is enough of him on tape to last four generations ahead, we are told. Neither does the hero altogether sort out the mix-up over the various umbrellas and what has happened to his own. This inability to grasp reality and the linguistic games that accompany it underscore the serious question of identity. The exchanges recorded above between the hero and the journalist Val, who wants a story from him and with whom he co-habitates for a time, continue in an excruciating form of what, analogous with "Franglais", we might term "Rangliiskii". Narator argues that he will no longer be what he used to be, while his interlocutor, always the sensation-seeking journalist, says he will be a victim or nobody.

Emigration then forces the individual to confront his own self, and, in this respect, Zinik is fully justified in calling it a literary device. In an Epilogue to *Russkaia sluzhba*, which was not included in the 1983 Paris edition, but appeared in the 1993 Moscow collection, emigration is given other billings too. A conversation takes place between old Doctor Lidin and a Scotland Yard acquaintance at the "Refrain Club" (*Rs*, 128). (Would a Muscovite reader register this reference, or for that matter the later one to the "Kurbsky Club"[*Rs*, 132]?) Since the conversation is reported by the author, it is not entirely clear whose views are offered. However, we are given the following interpretation of Narator: that he was one of those advocates of the freedom of the word, who literally have lost that freedom because they cannot express in the local language their penetrating and super-original thought concerning the absence of freedom of the word in their own homeland. There then follows a predictable metamorphosis in the likes of Narator: at first confused articulation (*kosnoiazychie*), then getting locked within oneself, and lastly, hostility towards and suspicion of all those around you. "And the main thing is that they justify their ignorance of foreign languages as alleged love for Russia and the common Russian people" (*Rs*, 132). Lidin's friend, Nabokov - so this argument goes - thus discovered in Lolita all the anguish (*nadryvnost'*) of his inability really to fuse with Russia. At this point the author breaks into English: "Emigration as a soft pornography, indeed" (*Rs*, 132).

Later Lidin reflects that there is hypocrisy in both the Soviet and British (perhaps more particularly, it is implied, the Victorian) systems. Emigration can cure one of the feeling of the totalness (*total'nost'*) of the Soviet system: "Emigration as a medicinal device" (*Rs*, 134). He then goes on to meditate on English pubs, French cafés and other culinary matters, reflecting that the Russian émigré refuses to adapt his diet and suffers accordingly: "Emigration as a culinary recipe" (*Rs*,136).

There is a strong hint in this Epilogue that Lidin instigated Narator's death: "All Lidin did was quickly and effectively to transform into real life everything that kept nagging at Tsilia Kharonovna Bliafer's tormented soul. He picked up the telephone, had a word in the necessary quarter, and the fate of the man was settled in a trice" (Rs, 133). At the same time, Lidin delights in the English way of life — with all its incongruities and short-comings — and to an extent gets his comeuppance. The novel closes with him seeing the film in which Narator played a bit part, and seeing a vaguely familiar figure shot down. Lidin decides that he was right when as a young man, he cleared off from the "barbaric, pretentious and pitiless country called Russia", and then he nervously reaches for his heart tablets (*Rs*, 138).

At the beginning of the Epilogue the "Refrain Club" is decribed at some length, and it has all the hallmarks of a Gothic, or more precisely, a mock-Gothic setting: panelled walls, a menu reminiscent of school dinners, more especially its "feudal guarantee of protection", which a Russian, used only to "totalitarian autocracy", finds difficult to fathom (Rs, 128-29). Thus the Gothic — which proved so resilient throughout the nineteenth century and is still with us in the form of popular horror, spy films and the like — is not going to go away in Zinik's fiction. Similarly, emigration is not simply an irreversible act, but a way of life, an attitude of mind, a challenge, at times painful, at times inspirational.

There are hints of key elements in *Russofobka i fungofil*[5] of *Russkaia sluzhba*: firstly, the throw-away line of "emigration as a culinary recipe", and secondly, what might be termed the "set-piece" of English life, whether it be the pub, with, in the days *Russkaia sluzhba* was written, its quaint opening hours, or the smoke-choked top-deck of a London bus. In *Russofobka i fungofil* Zinik expands on these, while at the same time retaining prominent traits of the Gothic.

He tells us that the starting point, as with all his novels, is some quite absurd idea, in the case of this novel, the longing that an émigré will get for, say, Russian black bread, to such an extent that he will be prepared to return to his homeland (Zinik 1991a, 11). One of the more literary inspirations for the book was a work by V. Pokhlebkin called simply *Chai* (Tea), which enjoyed some popularity in Russia in the 1970s and 80s:

> We were awfully entertained by this book: in a world in which everything was subordinate to ideology, it was finding something that did not have any relationship to Soviet power; or rather established its own hierarchy - infernal (*kromeshnyi*), farcical (*farsovyi*), parodic (*parodiinyi*): not through Party slogans, but through one's attitude to brewing tea. That is how the image of the hero, a cooking specialist and fungophile, arose. (Zinik 1991a, 11)

Indeed, Zinik pays open and good-natured homage to this author when, at the end of *Russofobka i fungofil*, he introduces a Soviet professor named Pokhlebkin, who appears in Kostia's rambling unpublished tract (*Rif*, 231–32).

Another major aspect of *Russofobka i fungofil*, not so much in evidence in *Russkaia sluzhba*, relates to Wilde's "The Disciple" mentioned above. In *Russofobka i fungofil* there is very much the sense that two mirrors are facing each other — East and West — yet they are distorting mirrors. Zinik is at pains to turn the mutual misunderstandings into a novel, in his words, to offer an "author's view - a view from above". At the same time Zinik is too sophisticated a writer to fall into the trap of didacticism. He is an accomplished juggler of characters, never hanging on to any one of them for too long; and the reader remains perplexed as to which of them, if any, to reach out to and catch.

On the surface we have a routine love story of an English girl, not very street-wise, marrying an exciting, if somewhat unstable, Russian. After a period of residence in Moscow, the couple move to England. The story unfolds through a series of flashbacks stemming from the English set-piece of a small lunch party, held in the garden. Personalities and the weather conspire to turn the whole occasion into one of outrage and conflict, the process being akin to a Dostoevskian *skandal* scene, but heavily laced with farce. As in Dostoevskii, the essential quality of such a scene resides in the attempt on the part of some of the participants to behave with good manners and decorum being undermined by subversive elements intent on insulting and injuring the would-be upholders of propriety. "Insulted and injured" is one of the more common phrases, among many parodic features, in Zinik's novel. *Skandal* in Dostoevskii frequently involves the activity of clowning and inappropriateness, of dress, behaviour, speech or anything else. Malcolm Jones writes: "It may be said that there are three types of buffoon in Dostoyevsky: the pathological liar, the passive clown and the destructive clown. The last category can be subdivided into amateurs and professionals. General Ivolgin belongs to the first category, Marmeladov to the second" (Jones 1976, 24). Zinik's "hero" would seem to be all of these. The conventions of English life are an irresisitible target for his disruptiveness. Yet it is not only the Russian who is to blame for the sequence of events; the English weather can be just as subversive.

Another set-piece which is turned on its head is the office Christmas party. Beneath the pleasantries expressed in this season of good will, we discover a broken family (Colin's father unable to approach either his son or ex-wife, even to pass on a gift to the former), and Clea to be the apparent victim of Colin's apparent attempt at rape. There is the pretence of togetherness and even equality for staff of all ranks, but the author leaves us in no doubt as to the hypocrisy of it all, given the differences in income and life-style. He even hints at the almost Soviet nature of it all. Note Anthony's speech: "How many of us were there just four years ago? And how many are there of us now? But the atmosphere in the firm is just the same — the atmosphere of a family and a collective, of a family collective, of a collective family" (Rif, 55). Other set-pieces might include the legal proceedings against Kostia and Colin's funeral. There is all manner of other specifically English features that the author presents with good-natured satire.

This entire picture of the English way of life is counter-balanced by the scenes set in Russia, the cramped communal flat that Clea and Kostia share after their wedding, the queuing for food, the rambling drunken conversations about literature, politics, art and history. Clea is never sure what is going on around her in Russia, just as Kostia never adjusts to the English way of life. Both are regarded, often hostilely, as curiosities by the natives.

The duality is maintained throughout the text. However, the novel is not a simple comedy of contrasting manners, a satire on the English and Russian ways of life; it is rather a satire on the *stereotyped views* that each society has of the other, views that have been formed by the media first and by first-hand experience second. Kostia's passion for birch trees and mushrooms is as reprehensible as Clea's plaster-cast gnome in her garden. Each side is incapable of explaining a situation or justifying itself except in terms of the established clichés: in Russia Clea tears up her husband's treatise on cuisine out of anger and frustration, the straw that broke the camel's back being her futile attempts to buy some sour cream. Meanwhile, at work, Kostia and others are obliged to listen to a Party activist preaching to them about Zionism and the plight of Palestine. The diatribe is of course generalized and sententious, but because of its gustatory imagery it prompts a verbal response from Kostia (as opposed to the universal yawns that such political speeches usually provoke). Kostia's contribution to the debate is wholly culinary and even more dubious in content, as a result of which he gets beaten up by anti-Semites. Kostia leaps to the conclusion that the authorities are to blame for what he takes to be the ransacking of his flat (Clea's damaging his book) and the "pogrom" he has been subjected to (*Rif*, 113–15). Elsewhere, Kostia happily contends that the world should really be viewed in terms of coffee and tea zones, rather than in terms of democracy and totalitarianism, and that there will never be a war between Russia and America because they are both tea zones (*Rif*, 120).

In Russia Clea has been forced to compromise her own spiritual values, such as they are, for the sake of her stomach. Kostia can only obtain food by sexually satisfying Tonia, who shares their communal flat and works in a grocery store. Clea goes along with the arrangement. Tonia's drunken husband castigates Clea, calling her *inosranka* at one point (*Rif*, 105), and beats his wife to death. Later, in England, Clea overhears Kostia blaming her for the murder, for she "denounced Tonia" (*Rif*, 153–55). In Kostia's view it was Western interference that led to her death, as in his drunken conversation with the Polish delicatessen owner and Anthony, he pours out his affection for Russia. The episode is a delightful illustration of Zinik's contention that the émigré must emigrate from his past as much as from anything else if he is to survive.

> "Tonechka was", said Kostia swaying, "all power: Soviet power, and she was anti-Soviet activity as well, she was ham, she was a joint of beef and the people's gibblets, she was springtime in the winter frosts, in the form of a fresh green cucumber, she was my grocery shop and my house management committee, the church and the state, the unity of spirit and body — and the way she used to perform in bed: she was a real samovar! Hissing, roaring, gurgling! Tonechka, in short, for me was Russia!" (*Rif*, 152)

This kind of rambling, dependent to an extent on puns in the original (for example, *sovetchina / vetchina*), as well as on drink and unbridled nostalgia, is to be paralleled with Anthony's left-wing "reasoning" that slips easily from his experiences of mutual masturbation in his public school to Marxism, and on to his rejection of Stalinism, his admiration for the Soviet Health Service and the generosity, cordiality and breadth of the Russian character, so devoid of affectation and snobbery (*Rif*, 157). Anthony is scarcely less glib when sober: he cannot accept Clea's complaints about the everyday hardships in Russia, but talks fluently about Soviet patriotism, dissidence, of how the Orthodox Church offers the only real alternative to the unsavoury ideas of the dissidents, who "blacken the past" of their own country and are "blind to the ulcers of capitalism" (*Rif*, 68–69). The stereotyped views of the main characters are present elsewhere: Colin's mother calls Clea a Communist at her son's funeral. English liberal *apologia* or extreme Russian polemic, both caricatured here by Zinik, remain in place to the end. A middle road is suggested, but at a cost.

Cerebral interpretations of the world turn out to be no less reliable than simple perceptions: so many incidents in the book are presented in one way and are then explained as something else, with the possibility of further interpretations. Colin tries to rape Clea, but it turns out that he has been led on by Anthony, who is gay. Kostia's nocturnal expeditions have nothing to do with cannibalism as Clea thinks, but are merely to gather mushrooms. At her first party in Moscow Clea is called a *kominternovskaia mandavoshka* (a comintern cunt louse) by a "poet" whom she refuses to help, but it is clear that Margot, Anthony's wife and Clea's erstwhile over-intimate schoolfriend, is the really promiscuous one. The chapter entitled "Beauty and the Beast" (Deva i monstr) depicts Margot as the beast manipulating the naive Clea, telling her that her marriage to Kostia is an inversion of the fairy story: Clea has kissed the beast and turned into a toad. At the end of the novel it transpires, if we are to believe Kostia, that the marriage was engineered by Margot so that she could continue her affair with Kostia. Clea's attempts to adapt to Soviet life were, in Kostia's view, pathetic and ridiculous. This is an acceptable *coup de théâtre* but given all the other bluffs and self-deluding that has gone on, should the reader accept it at face value?

The author is brought in at the end of the story as a literary expert with knowledge of both Russia and England who will help with an assessment of Kostia and his writing; the author is there to try and strip away some of the clichés. Kostia's defence solicitor has managed to gain him some sympathy with the court by airing every English stereotyped notion of Russia and the Soviet Union that exists. Kostia is presented as "a brother Karamazov, who had lived through Tolstoi's war and peace, while dreaming of getting married to one of Chekhov's three sisters" (Rif, 225–26).

The dénouement has Kostia fleeing back to Russia, and the complacent English bourgeoisie, in the form of Anthony and Margot, continuing in their hypocrisy and material comfort. If we leave aside Colin, whose death was largely accidental, there are two victims: Clea and the author.

Clea may have flirted with left-wing ideas, feminism, pacifism and so on, mainly at the instigation of her self-confident and well-heeled associates, but she does little to verbalize any real values; she is far too busy coping with Russian or English *byt*: at the survival level in Moscow; in vain efforts to keep up with the Joneses in London. Her attempt at suicide — she brews some soup from poisonous mushrooms — her violent vomiting and her calling the ambulance, show her exhibiting the notorious English talent for squalid compromise. She will suffer and survive.

Similarly, as he interviews Kostia at length, the author is confronted with his own hypocrisy, to be more precise his own "double-dealing" (*dvurushnichestvo*):

> The bastard was right, and I was wrong. The bastard possessed spiritual wholeness. I was a double-dealer. But I preferred this double-dealing, this drawn-out flight of a suicide, trying to collect his thoughts in that short space between birth and death. (*Rif*, 249)

The author is then promptly knocked over by a motorcycle, having, in his abstract reflections on Russia and England, forgotten about traffic keeping to the left.

Although trying to avoid polarity has its dangers (but not too many — the author is not seriously injured) the alternatives are even less attractive. At the back of the duality in *Russofobka i fungofil* lie the two poles of the eighteenth century: Rousseau and the Gothic. The *russofobka* of the Russian title is another pun of course: in the end Clea fears not just Russians, but *some* aspects of the French philosopher's ideas. She has a degree of affection for the *Confession* which she is meant to pass on to Colin, and she resents the way Margot leafs through it (*Rif*, 64–65), but one notes in passing that, in her attempts at petty bourgeois respectability, she is certainly rejecting any notion of "back to nature". Without going deeply into Rousseau's thought, one can say simply that he stands for the Enlightenment, rationalism, doubt, self-doubt and personal honesty; in short, qualities which do not loom large in characters like Anthony, Margot and Kostia. Of course, other interpretations of Rousseau's significance in the novel are possible, not least, as we note below, those to do with the noble savage and bodily functions performed in the forest.

The other pole, the Gothic, Clea encounters at every turn, but it is largely a matter of her own misconstruings. True, there are Kostia's lurid stories of cannibalism and infanticide. And these she uses to explain his nocturnal outings. Yet, after what she thinks is her attempted rape, she sees two tramps, and the sight of them, rather than her ordeal at Colin's hands, makes her faint (Rif, 60); the volume of Rousseau remains dear to her mainly because it was the only witness to the attempt on her honour. In Clea's view Colin was trying to save her and "Jean-Jacques Rousseau" when he fell under Kostia's knife (*Rif*, 214–15). Thus, Clea is the bone over which Gothic and Enlightenment forces contend.

Clea's qualities, and perhaps at bottom the author's, are worth suffering for, even though they have nothing to do with ideas, politics or language. The climax of the novel occurs at the military base (reminiscent of Greenham Common), where Kostia has gone to collect mushrooms, with Clea, Tadeusz, the delicatessen owner, and Colin in hot pursuit, and where Anthony and Margot assemble for an anti-nuclear rally. When Kostia defecates in the trees on the base, the detailed and lengthy description is not simply a revelling in the bawdy: there is the rhetorical question that, if we could all do the same, "how peacefully and amicably humanity's days would flow by! Without conceit and pretensions, tyranny and social climbing" (Rif, 196). The episode could be compared with Clea's vomiting after poisoning herself: she brings up not just the things she has physically swallowed but also "Slavophilism, vegetarian ideas, radioactive waste from tea, pacifism and Margot's condescension, fly agaric mushrooms and Soviet power, East and West, the 'third world' and English mediocrity (*ubozhestvo*)" (*Rif*, 221). She has just been struggling in vain to understand passages from the Rousseau volume.

Earlier Clea has come to the conclusion that the real culprits are words:

> The formulations, which did not permit the racing mind to take a single step back, which turned gloomy thought into lofty principle and you yourself into a destroyer of your own principles — into an apostate, were to blame for it all. These damned convictions were to blame for it all. Philosophers, religious thinkers, all those who appoint themselves as prophets were to blame for it all. If all these words which pronounced the final sentence on our actions just didn't exist, she would survive somehow in this wretched life, without feeling either false guilt, or false shame: unconsciously, just like a lawn when the time comes for it to be mown. (Rif, 171–72)

One detects in this a certain admiration not just for a Rousseauesque return to unthinking natural states — utopian in the extreme, especially given Clea's petty bourgeois orientation — but also a muted admiration for the well-attested English attribute of anti-intellectualism. The Russians and most other nations have an intelligentsia, but the English (curiously, not so much the British) have tended to shun the term; and indeed, since the early 1980s the word has been more or less replaced by a phrase more chillingly illustrative of the philistinism of those who use it in denigration than of those whom it is supposed to denote: "the chattering classes". A less derogatory term than anti-intellectualism, and a quality that Clea and her creator would doubtlessly advocate, would be simply "common sense".

The fact remains that Clea, despite her naivity, unsubtle taste and limited cultural horizons (the Russian word *poshlost'* seems to suit her well, though it does not figure in the text), is the most attractive character in the novel. Caught between the values of East and West, she learns to identify real "foreignness" in other ways: Margot, ostensibly her best friend, has "long since become for Clea a 'foreigner', speaking another language and living with other people in another world, where people even ate and dressed differently" (*Rif*, 176). Similarly, one feels some attraction to Tadeusz, the Polish delicatessen owner, who seems to provide a spiritual as well as linguistic bridge between East and West, though his own interests do not really extend beyond his catering establishment.

If Clea is right when she identifies "words" as the true culprits in this world, then we have a *raison d'être* for the ubiquitous puns in Zinik's text. *Khamstyd* for Hampstead (*Rif*, 25), *S novym gadom* [*sic*] for Happy New Year, as well as the other puns noted previously, can be enjoyed for the unfortunate associations they generate; yet the exercise extends to people's names: there is a *mandel'shtiukovskii* (Mandel'shtam?) jar of caviare (*Rif*, 74); a poet called Evtusenskii is rumoured to own a luxury dacha in southern Russia called *Babii iar* (scene of a terrible massacre of Jews during the War and the title of Evtushenko's most famous poem), and he has built himself an ivory tower in Moscow (*Rif*, 89); and there is an artist called Glazoment, clearly a reference to Glazunov (*Rif*, 89). In addition, factual accuracy goes by the board: Clea is told that Mandel'shtam was shot by firing squad (*Rif*, 33). Such ineptitudes point up the dangers of stereotyped views and generalizations. Indeed, the subtlest way in which the author underscores, as does Clea, the treacherous nature of language is in his parodying of English urbanity, with its verbose, bland, unassailable, but essentially meaningless generalizations, particularly as they roll off Anthony's tongue. For him, as for so many English sophisticates, as they figure in Zinik, it is form rather than content that is all important.

Which brings us to "Kriket", a work, unlike *Russkaia sluzhba* and *Russofobka i fungofil*, that is almost entirely liberated from the stereotypes thrown up during the Cold War era, yet a work that illustrates some traditional English vices, such as xenophobia, superficiality, and the pre-eminence of form over content. Taking this story in the context of all Zinik's works, one might be tempted to ask if the notions on display in it contributed as much to the Cold War as did the surface political debates and actions of that era. In what purports to be a civilized and educated stratum of English society, the mutual misreadings and hostilities are almost endless. And beneath the social veneer there lurks a Gothic strain.

The first-person narrator is a Russian expatriate of fifteen years' standing, who is still referred to by a female friend, Joanna, as "my Russian", and who always introduces him as coming from Moscow. For her he will always be a foreigner. The game of cricket, notoriously difficult for foreigners to comprehend, is something quintessentially English for which he acquires some understanding and empathy initially. These are blasted away by an encounter with a man called Ricketts at the match, who abuses him in anti-Semitic tones. The narrator feels like a monster from outer space. However, he is later to regain a sense of belonging.

This he does because it turns out that human relations and human perceptions of one another are infinitely more complex than the rules of cricket, and can make foreigners of us all. The narrator has a girlfriend Sil´va, an expatriate Russian like himself. As his relationship with her crumbles, he meets Joanna, but is unable to take the relationship with her as far as he would like to, sexually at least. She has a lover, a married man with a wife and two children, whom the narrator identifies as Ricketts. The narrator's friend, Arthur Simmons, offers him a wholly new version of events: Ricketts is not really an anti-Semite, given his own Jewish origins. Ricketts was not jealous of the narrator because of Joanna, but because of Arthur, since Ricketts is gay; Arthur himself had had a fling with Joanna at one time — in the same breath intimating that he is in fact gay himself — and, as it happens, has a wife and two daughters. Moreover, Joanna is French, not English, hence her rather exotic dress (bowler hat and black umbrella at the cricket match) appears as a rather pathetic attempt to look English, when in fact to many she looks slightly ridiculous. Heartened by all these tales of alienation ("I was not, after all, a solitary monster in this world. I was not alone" ["K", 207]), the narrator goes to see Joanna again, only to discover her covered in blood after a fracas with Sil'va — over him. Sil'va is released on bail and she and the narrator go home. He can now score as many runs as he likes with her...

The story has some engaging comments on the rifts between Russians — émigré or otherwise — since the collapse of Communism, but its real centre of interest is in the interplay of appearances and reality, and with the interaction of thought, word and deed. Arthur tells the narrator that Ricketts's anti-Semitic outbursts are just a "linguistic exercise" ("K", 204). After hearing all Arthur's revelations the narrator is invited to join the company from which he felt so alienated before, but is happy to refuse: "For a moment it seemed to me that I was one of them. And therefore I could calmly refuse this invitation, and this exclusivity (*izbrannost´*). I could exist in my own right. This was the important thing for me in principle. That is, it was more important than the word or the deed. The thought was more important than the word" ("K", 208).

Here one is drawn back to the sentiments expressed by Clea, that words are to blame. Joanna's and Sil'va's words — the words of two people who

have not succeeded in emigrating in Zinik's definition of the term — lead
to a Gothic outcome (a blood-stained head, a torn dress). Zinik's continuing
endeavours to find the right words, words that are not to blame, have led
to a broadening of the term "foreign", which anyone can become in any
circumstances. They have also led to a narrowing of the term "emigration",
which, in Russian at least, has always sounded politically loaded, and, in
the post-Communist era, is beginning to feel faintly obsolete. Moreover,
Zinik's fiction may, in the long run, help to keep the Gothic, with its
embalmed megalomaniacs, murderous gadgetery and the like, where it
properly and safely belongs: within the covers of a book.

REFERENCES

Jones, M. V., 1976. *Dostoevsky: The Novel of Discord* (London: Paul Elek).

Pülsch, A., 1995. *Emigration als literarisches Verfahren bei Zinovij Zinik* (Munich: Otto Sagner).

Simpson, M., 1986. *The Russian Gothic Novel and Its British Antecedents* (Columbus, OH: Slavica).

Wilde, O., 1990. *The Complete Works of Oscar Wilde* (London: Blitz Editions).

Zinik, Z., 1983. "Emigratsiia kak literaturnyi priem", *Sintaksis* 11: 167–87.

———, 1985. *Nisha v panteone* (Paris: Sintaksis).

———, 1986a. "Voobrazhaemoe interv´iu s Vladimirom Nabokovym", *Sintaksis* 15: 178–87.

———, 1986b. "Goticheskii roman uzhasov emigratsii", *Sintaksis* 16: 34–70.

———, 1986c. *Russofobka i fungofil* (London: Russian Roulette Press).

———, 1987. *The Mushroom Picker*, tr. Michael Glenny (London: Heinemann).

———, 1991a. "Emigratsiia kak literaturnyi priem", *Literaturnaia gazeta* 20 March: 11.

———, 1991b. "The Hero in Search of an Author", in Arnold McMillin (ed.), *Under Eastern Eyes: The West as Reflected in Recent Russian Emigré Writing* (London: Macmillan), 12–16.

———, 1991c. *Lord i eger´* (Moscow: Slovo).

———, 1991d. *The Lord and the Gamekeeper*, tr. Alex de Jongh (London: Heinemann).

———, 1993. *Russkaia sluzhba i drugie istorii* (Moscow: Slovo).

———, 1995. *One-way Ticket* (London: Harboard).

NOTES

1. The first monograph on Zinik appeared shortly after the writing of the present article. See Pülsch 1995.
2. Zinik 1991c and Zinik 1991d. Page references are to the Russian text as *Lie*. All translations from this and other texts by Zinik (except for that from "Nezvanaia gost´ia" [Zinik 1995, 145–66]) are my own.
3. For a scholarly examination of the Gothic in nineteenth-century Russian literature see Simpson 1986.
4. On the Markov case see *The Times* , 12 September 1978: 4; ibid., 16 September 1978: 2; ibid., 30 September 1978: 15; *The Sunday Times* , 17 September 1978: 17.
5. Zinik 1993, 5–138 (15). All subsequent page references in the text are to this edition as *Rs*.
6. Zinik 1986c and Zinik 1987. Page references are to the Russian text as *Rif*.
7. "Kriket", in Zinik 1993, 177–212. Page references are to this edition as "K". The "other stories" here are amongst those translated in *One-way Ticket* (Zinik 1995).

BACK TO THE FUTURE:
ANDREI SINIAVSKII AND
KAPITANSKAIA DOCHKA

Jane Grayson

At roughly mid-point in his critical appreciation of Pushkin's *Kapitanskaia dochka* (The Captain's daughter), "Puteshestvie na Chernuiu rechku" (Journey to Chernaia rechka), Siniavskii breaks off in an outburst of frustration at misinterpretation of his own work: "'Russophobe!' — they shout — 'Russophobe!'". His lot, he reflects, was not unlike Pushkin's own. Pushkin, too, was dogged in the last years of his life by misunderstanding and malicious slander, and by the solicitous enquiries of literary ladies anxious to know when he would again produce something really good: "Pushkin reflected gloomily: 'Will this all soon be over?' In his writing desk, instead of a reed pipe, lay *Kapitanskaia dochka*" (Tertz 1994, 27–28).[1]

This aside gives both a statement of Siniavskii's intention in this essay and an indication of his approach. It is a "Reply to My Critics", but, like Pushkin with *Kapitanskaia dochka*, he has chosen the weapon not of the political pamphlet nor of scholarly literary criticism, but the realized imagery of art. He writes in the persona not of the academic literary critic, Andrei Siniavskii, but using the literary mask of his *alter ego* Abram Tertz. His "Journey" is his artistic response to the critical furore provoked by his earlier essay on Pushkin, *Progulki s Pushkinym* (Strolls with Pushkin), also written under the name of Tertz, which had shaken Russian émigré circles when it was first published in 1975 but which had aroused a far wider and even more virulent response when an extract from it was published in the Soviet Union in 1989. The excerpt, chosen by the author himself, and

147

constituting a substantial central section of his essay, appeared in the April
number of the journal *Oktiabr'*.[2] It exploded with the full force of a stra-
tegically placed time-bomb. Indeed, one commentator, Viktor Likhonosov,
actually used this image: "It was like a bomb exploding" (Nepomnyashchy
1991b, 36). Another, Sergei Bocharov, compared the scandal to that which
had surrounded Akhmatova and Zoshchenko in 1946 (Bocharov 1990, 78).
The appearance of the works of Siniavskii-Tertz in the Soviet Union belongs
to the later stages of the relaxation of censorship controls under Gorbachev.
From 1986 onwards great quantities of so-called "delayed literature" began
to reach the Russian reading public. After the publication of deceased
writers who had previously been printed only selectively, if at all, came
the more controversial publication of works by recent living émigrés, many
of whom had been branded as anti-Soviet or exiled as enemies of the
régime. Joseph Brodsky had the distinction of being the first of the living
Russians resident in the West to appear in print, when at the very end of
1987 six of his poems were published in *Novyi mir* (Brodsky 1987). And
by the end of the decade observers were entitled to conclude that all taboos
had been lifted, that "all was permitted". Symptomatic was the removal
in 1989 of the final restriction on Nabokov's works, when *Lolita*, the novel
condemned as pornographic, was published in a supplement to the journal
Inostrannaia literatura. But far more importantly, the year 1989 saw the
"return" in print of the two live cold-war warriors, Aleksandr Solzhenitsyn
and Andrei Siniavskii. The publication of Solzhenitsyn's monumental
documentary history, *Arkhipelag GULag* (The Gulag archipelago), was
undoubtedly the single most significant event of *glasnost'*, but Siniavskii-
Tertz with his slight excursion into early nineteenth-century literary history
undoubtedly caused the greatest sensation. The editorial notes which accompanied these publications in retrospect acquired a touch of irony. Sergei
Zalygin's announcement of the first chapters of *Arkhipelag GULag* in the
August edition of *Novyi mir* welcomed the arrival of the "long awaited
freedom — the freedom to publish and to read — without which there can
be no genuinely active and socially useful literary life" (Zalygin 1989, 7).
The unsigned prefatory note accompanying the extract from *Progulki s
Pushkinym* set out to remind readers of the circumstances which had led
Siniavskii to adopt the pseudonym Tertz in the late 1950s and referred to
his trial together with Iulii Daniel' in 1966 as "a landmark in our social
history which marked the end of the Khrushchev 'Thaw' of the 60s" (Tertz
1989, 192). Both these professions of tolerance were to be sadly belied
by events later that year. However, the year began quietly enough when
in early January Siniavskii revisited the Soviet Union, sixteen years after
his departure for Paris and eighteen years after his release from labour camp.
He had obtained a visa to attend the funeral of his old friend Daniel' who

died on 30 December 1988, but received it just too late to be present. The following month, February, saw the first publication of his work. It was a short article on Zoshchenko written under the name of Andrei Siniavskii (Siniavskii 1989). The extract from *Progulki s Pushkinym* was the first Tertz work to appear and it was this that made the impact, completely overshadowing the successive republications of his work in periodicals throughout the remainder of the year as well as the appearance of a book, *Tsena metafory* (The price of metaphor), which included materials relating to the trial and all of Arzhak and Tertz's "fantastic stories" as well as Tertz's essay "Chto takoe sotsialisticheskii realizm" (On socialist realism) and an extract from his autobiographical novel *Spokoinoi nochi* (Goodnight!). In September *Literaturnaia Rossiia* published an article by the extreme nationalist conservative Igor´ Shafarevich in which he compared *Progulki s Pushkinym* with Salman Rushdie's *Satanic Verses* and, whilst not going so far as to repeat the Ayatollah's call for the death penalty, appealed to Russian readers to emulate the example of Muslim protesters against this sacrilege (Shafarevich 1989b, 5). The culmination of this campaign of vilification waged in the press was the Sixth Plenary meeting of the Administration of the Writers' Union in November at which the majority of speakers arraigned Siniavskii as a "russophobe".

The ironic sense of *déjà vu*, of history repeating itself, was not lost on Siniavskii's supporters. Here was yet another trial in the unquiet life of the Soviet literary scholar. Mariia Rozanova, his wife, in her commentary of the affair, "K istorii i geografii etoi knigi" (On the history and geography of this book), identifies two phases of the attack and terms them Siniavskii's second and third trials (Rozanova 1990, 157-58). Revealingly, though, she locates these two phases of reaction not in an émigré response (trial 2) followed by a Soviet (trial 3), but as first a literary and then a political reaction. (The first trial was, of course, the judicial trial of 1966, when Siniavskii, together with Daniel´, were convicted of slander against the Soviet State and sentenced respectively to seven and five years hard labour.) Rozanova recognizes the same strains of conservative nationalism cultivated in emigration transplanted to Gorbachev's Russia of the 1980s. It is a point echoed by Siniavskii himself in interview: "As Mariya, my wife, says, 'the emigration is a drop of the nation's blood that has been taken for analysis'. The emigration has something in common with the mother country. If a wave of nationalism appears in the emigration then there will be a corresponding one in the mother country" (Nepomnyashchy 1991a, 21). The so-called "second trial", therefore, was for the writing of what was considered to be an improper, grotesque lampoon of Russia's most cherished poet, in a grossly offensive vulgar style. This attack was initiated by the "Old Guard" of the emigration and led by Roman Gul´, in an article entitled "Progulki khama s Pushkinym" (A boor's strolls with Pushkin) which he published in 1976 in the American journal of which he was editor, *Novyi zhurnal*. It was Tertz's talent for hyperbole and *épatage* which touched a nerve and some of his images were quoted, requoted and misquoted again and again in the controversy which ensued: his likening Pushkin to a vampire, for example, and the fatal duel to folk theatre and carnival; and this, the image that caused the greatest offence of all: "Pushkin ran into great poetry on thin erotic legs" (Tertz 1993, 55).[3] Passions certainly ran high in the émigré community on both sides of the Atlantic. Rozanova recalls an elderly lady (*intelligentnaia starushka*) demonstrating outside a lecture hall at the University of Columbia with a placard bearing the words: "Styd i sram, tovarishch Abram!" (Shame and disgrace, comrade Abram!). She relishes the piquant irony that the subject of the lecture which Siniavskii was due to give on that occasion was that intransigent dissenter, Archpriest Avvakum. In Paris she recalls another Russian lady calling the French translator of *Progulki s Pushkinym* a "d'Anthès" and thereupon cutting him dead (Rozanova 1990, 157). This last is a detail worth remembering for the role d'Anthès comes to play in "The Journey". However, this first stage of the book's reception remained, Rozanova emphasizes, a purely literary scandal. It was when Solzhenitsyn entered the fray in 1984 with a critique of *Progulki s Pushkinym*, entitled, in allusion to Pushkin's famous 1830 lyric "Poetu" (To the poet), " ... Koleblet tvoi trenozhnik" (Shakes your sacrifical altar), that she dates the beginning of the "third trial of Siniavskii", when the arena of disputation about the book shifted from literature to politics.

The ideological split between Solzhenitsyn and Siniavskii had developed in the late 1970s in emigration, with Solzhenitsyn emerging as the leader of the conservative national wing and Siniavskii defending the liberal democratic position. In 1983 Solzhenitsyn had published an attack on the liberal position, "Nashi pliuralisty" (Our pluralists), in which he divided thinking Russia into patriots and russophobes. Siniavskii had counter-attacked with an article entitled "Solzhenitsyn kak ustroitel´ novogo edinomysliia" (Solzhenitsyn as the organizer of a new uniformity of thinking), published in *Sintaksis*. Solzhenitsyn's critique of Siniavskii's Pushkin book followed directly upon this. And Siniavskii retaliated with another piece of polemic, "Chtenie v serdtsakh" (Reading in anger), again published in *Sintaksis*. When in the late 1980s Siniavskii and Solzhenitsyn "returned" to Russia, the "second" and "third" trials were simply re-enacted on Russian soil. In June a shortened version of Gul´'s accusation of boorishness was republished in *Literaturnaia Rossiia* while, in the same month, *Nash sovremennik* published a shortened version of Shafarevich's reactionary article "Russophobia" which had appeared a few months earlier in the West

German émigré journal *Veche*. Battle was joined between liberals and nationalists, and *Progulki s Pushkinym* became the symbolic focus for the anxieties unleashed by the collapse of the Soviet system. Siniavskii thus again, as he had in the 1960s during the Thaw, found himself accused of being a traitor to his country, and a traitor to its national heritage.

The scandal can be seen to have peaked in late 1989 with the November plenum of the Writers' Union, but it was by no means over. Following the debate in the national press, the book was submitted to the "dispassionate", "objective" scrutiny of the Russian academic community. The editorial board of *Voprosy literatury* organized a forum to which it invited eminent critics, writers and recognized Pushkin specialists. The record of this debate appeared in the October number of the journal, directly following the first complete publication of the text of *Progulki s Pushkinym* in numbers 7,8 and 9.[4]

There is no disputing the editorial intention to give a fair representation of the *pro et contra* of the debate. A staunch defence both of Siniavskii's critical insight and integrity was mounted by, among others, Sergei Bocharov, Iurii Mann, Petr Vail´ and Aleksandr Genis, while Mariia Rozanova's critical commentary was included in the same issue of the journal. There she was able to set the debate in its context and correct some of the crassest errors of fact and interpretation. She contradicted Dmitrii Urnov's assertion that Siniavskii did not actually write *Progulki s Pushkinym* in the camps, but only presented it as though that had been the case (Urnov 1990, 142; Rozanova 1990, 156). She also drew attention to the persistence by even the most sophisticated readers in taking everything that Tertz wrote literally. The "price of metaphor" in the 1960s had been a sentence of seven years hard labour, but still its lessons had not been learned today, when even a writer such as Georgii Vladimov who had himself written an entire "novel-metaphor", *Vernyi Ruslan* (Faithful Ruslan, 1975), could trip up over Pushkin's "thin erotic legs": "'Andrei Donatovich, where did you get the idea that Pushkin had thin legs when everyone knows that he was a very fit and active man?'" (Rozanova 1990, 160). But if some of the criticism could be laughed off, much cut too deep to be lightly brushed aside. Valentin Nepomniashchii, in what purported to be a summing-up, in fact brought home the case for the prosecution. This was that the book was deeply dishonourable; that, far from constituting the restoration of links with the Russian literary tradition lost during the Soviet period, it was in fact but a product of that very Soviet heresy; finally, that the book and the storm of controversy which had surrounded it, were an offence against the sacred Russian Word. The key words in this condemnation deserve emphasis: *pravda* (truth), *chest´* (honour), *Slovo* (The Word). To this can be added the reference to *buria* (storm) in Nepomniashchii's introductory remarks:

"reaktsiia [...] ves´ma burnaia" (an extremely stormy reaction).[5] Here we have the key words which serve as milestones, or rather verst-markers in the "Journey to Chernaia rechka", because, however many honours have been bestowed on Siniavskii in recent years by the international academic community, the only recognition that really mattered to him was recognition in Russia by the Russian intelligentsia. Viewed in this local context "Journey to Chernaia rechka" can be seen as constituting his reply to this critics' forum, his reply to Valentin Nepomniashchii, and perhaps, too, a response to Bocharov's prompting that he had not explored in sufficient depth Pushkin's writings on the workings of Providence in *Pikovaia dama* (The Queen of Spades) and *Kapitanskaia dochka*.[6] The essay does, however, have a considerably wider frame of reference, as will be seen below.

Taken together, the three essays, "Chto takoe sotsialisticheskii realizm", *Progulki s Pushkinym* and "Puteshestvie na Chernuiu rechku", form something of a critical trilogy; they tell the story of the evolution of Tertz's distinctive method of "fantastic literary criticism" (*fantasticheskoe literaturovedenie*) from the late 1950s to the present, his response to changing literary processes in Russia and his unswerving defence of the artistic values of "pure art".

In "Chto takoe sotsialisticheskii realizm" Tertz affects for most of the essay to speak as one of the Communist "we", as a voice from the chorus of believers in the Purpose of Communism and the Purpose of Soviet art. The capital letter is used throughout to highlight his mockery of the Soviet worship of the false god of teleology. But behind this mask of irony he constructs a covert defence for the humanist literary tradition by insisting on viewing socialist realism, with its cult of the positive hero, as a complete break with Russian literature of the nineteenth century, not its natural continuation. As he puts it, nineteenth-century literature and Soviet literature are "two hostile and mutually exclusive cultures" (Tertz 1982, 188). And in his historical reading it is Pushkin who stands at the opposite pole from Soviet art, for it is he who "was the first to taste the bitter joys of self-negation" (Tertz 1982, 199), who was the first master of irony, and the creator in Onegin of the first "superfluous man".

Having in his first samizdat essay concentrated on exposing what was *not* art, Siniavskii proceeded in the labour camp to reflect on what *was* art. There he found the existential freedom within unfreedom to set down on paper what art meant for him and what he stood for as a writer: "*Progulki s Pushkinym* was for me to a certain extent a continuation of my closing speech at the trial" (Nepomniashchy 1991a, 11). It is his artistic credo, a defence of "pure art", but pure art conceived not in the narrow, purely decorative sense, but as a free play of the imagination which is at one and the same time a powerful instrument of intellectual and spiritual enquiry.

In Pushkin's poetry he found the best illustration of art's paradox, being at once frivolous yet serious, empty yet profound, fragile and ephemeral yet indestructible. In Pushkin's biography and the history of the reception of his work in his lifetime and after his death he found a paradigm of an artist's embattled relationship with readers, critics and with authority. Given Siniavskii's close identification with his subject and subject matter it is not surprising to find him combining the light-hearted and the serious in his own essay, nor is it really surprising even to find him adopting such a playful manner *in extremis*, writing from a labour camp. He sent the essay out, as is known, in the guise of letters to his wife. On Mariia Rozanova's testimony it was a response to her request before his arrest to write something "joyous, angelic", to write something about Mozart.[7] More than that, it was an indication that he was drawing on his deepest reserves of character; it is his spiritual strength that gives the work its sense of space and effortless ease. [8]

The Tertzian method is disconcertingly, exhilaratingly perverse, and the reader is constantly brought up short against apparent contradictions, seeming dead-ends, a succession of peremptory provocative "NOT"s. Yet what is irritatingly reminiscent of a negation and a deflation turns into something positive and enriching. A structure which affects to be loose and meandering turns out to be tight-knit and targeted. An argument which is flippantly carefree turns into an impassioned defence of art's responsibility.

Thus, for example, Siniavskii undermines the reverential view of Pushkin's "benevolence" and "universality", exposing him as "empty", "indifferent", "trivial" and "superficial". He points out that this master of order and harmony thought mainly in fragments: "his works resemble a collection of antiques: mostly torsos and busts, this one without a head, that one without a nose" (Tertz 1993, 101). But he then proceeds to inject the self-same clichés with new life and meaning. Pushkin *is* benevolent, deep, universal; his very fragmentariness is boundless like the sea: "And instead of a rudder, there's a half page, a whole ocean — of nothing but dots" (Tertz 1993, 108). Siniavskii here, in sympathy with his subject, concludes this section with three and a half lines of dots.

Similarly with the structure. He flamboyantly refuses to follow the accepted academic critical conventions and present a logically developed argument. In its stead he offers a construction which appeals first and foremost to the imagination. He enjoys playing with time and reshuffling past and present, as when, for instance, he here is reflecting on Pushkin's boyhood: "In those days children probably didn't read Mayne Reid and Jules Verne..."(Tertz 1993, 120). But the reader soon sees that this is just a way of animating a comparison, and elsewhere recognizes that these shifts, these *sdvigi*, are there to make a serious point about Pushkin's unique place in Russian literature:

> Pushkin is the golden mean of Russian literature. Having given it a swift kick
> into the future, he himself swung backwards and came to play in it more the
> role of an eternally flowering past to which it returns in order to be rejuvenated.
> Every time a new talent appears, Pushkin is right there prompting and sup-
> plying crib notes, and successive generations, decades later, will again discover
> Pushkin standing behind their backs. If we transport ourselves back in thought
> to days long past, to the sources of our native language, he'll turn up behind
> us even there — before and on the eve of the first chronicles and songs. An
> archaic smile plays on his lips. (Tertz 1993, 97)

Siniavskii also enjoys demonstrating his skill in fashioning a seamless robe,
a narrative sewn together by gossamer threads of associations and word
pictures. None the less, there is a tight logical thread which is drawn towards
a precisely calculated conclusion. In actual fact his analysis of Pushkin's
life and works traces a chronological line from his childhood and poetic
début to his last works, the duel and his death. And, as the poet's life and
destiny plays itself out, so the apparently inconsequential associations of
imagery and anecdote come together to form a clear pattern. The theme
of statues, for example, which is initiated in the opening paragraph in the
reference to busts and wreaths, and taken up again, via the image of the
antique torsos, in the discussion of Pushkin's fragmentariness, is subsequently realized as the actual statue of the Bronze Horseman and then,
lastly, as the two statues in the park at Tsarskoe Selo which had so impressed
themselves on Pushkin's imagination as a schoolboy: Apollo and perhaps,
Siniavskii speculates, Dionysus.[9] The circle is joined, the end reaches back
to the beginning, the narrative has gently taken the reader back to the point
of departure and thus the title and aim of the book, "Progulki s Pushkinym",
is affirmed. This is literary criticism which has no goal or Purpose other
than literature itself. Not only has Tertz through this "realized metaphor"[10]
made his point about the compact meaningfulness of anecdote, but he has
given a masterly demonstration of a criticism which works by mimicking,
by "echoing" the method of its subject. More than once in the course of
the essay Siniavskii has repeated Pushkin's observation that the poet is an
echo (Tertz 1993, 107). He sums up his analysis of Pushkin's poem "Mednyi
vsadnik" (The bronze horseman, 1837) by observing that the title turns into
an exhaustive definition of the poem: "If we were to draw an outline around
the poem with a pencil, we would get the Bronze Horseman" (Tertz 1993,
129). Finally, he succeeds in doing exactly the same. His title sums up,
encapsulates his argument. Just as a person who sets out on an afternoon
stroll will arrive naturally back at his starting point, so too does art. It has
no end outside itself, no Purpose. But in denying the teleological principle

for art Siniavskii is only affirming its ethical importance. The tendentious-
ness of this essay and its fundamental seriousness become apparent towards
the end when the figure of Pasternak which has been glimpsed earlier
between the lines of the narrative comes out centre stage and speaks the
opening words of Zhivago's poem "Gamlet" (Hamlet):

> There may come a time when an author who his whole life long has remained
> out of sight, who has avoided speaking in his own name [...] is in the end
> forced to take part in a spectacle not even of his own conception... "The noise
> died down. I stepped out onto the stage." (Tertz 1993, 139–40)[11]

The date and place of composition appended silently at the end of the essay
are all that are needed to complete this line of thought: "1966-1968,
Dubrovlag".

"Puteshestvie na Chernuiu rechku" can very obviously be viewed as a
continuation and development of *Progulki s Pushkinym*. It is cut from the
same cloth, using the same characters, the same props and narrative devices:
Khlestakov and Pugachev, imposters and Pretenders both; statues, vampires
and werewolves; anecdotes, memory, time shifts. In a couple of places the
cross-reference is quite explicit when Pushkin is glimpsed, as though he had
walked straight on out of the pages of *Progulki s Pushkinym*, swishing his
cane, now crossing the border, now crossing the road. This conceit carries
right through to the small line drawing appended at the end, depicting Pushkin
in top hat and coat, sitting soaking his no doubt weary feet in a basin of
water (Tertz 1994, 21, 23, 51). Furthermore, since this essay discusses
Kapitanskaia dochka, the last major work which Pushkin completed before
his death, it might justifiably be approached as a coda to the earlier work.
But it is more than that. It is more complex and, though less cheeky and
considerably less irreverent, is in its way more audacious and plays for higher
stakes. The tone is altogether more serious. This is not, after all, a message
of hope from the camps sent out to a loved one, like a message in a bottle.
It is Siniavskii's defence of his integrity as an artist and a citizen, conducted
through the account of Pushkin's own last defence of his honour. Here
Siniavskii follows Pasternak's Hamlet out onto the stage:

> Ia, odin, vse tonet v fariseistve.
> Zhizn′ prozhit′ — ne pole pereiti. (Pasternak 1957, 532)

> (I am alone; all drowns in the Pharisees' hypocrisy.
> To live your life is not as simple as to cross a field.) (Pasternak 1958, 467)

Siniavskii's earlier critics, some with indulgence, some with distaste, depending on the *parti pris*, had classified his writing on literature as "writer's

criticism". The round table gathering in 1990 had yielded a typical range
of comments which can be summarized as "idiosyncratic and insightful"
(Bocharov), "self-indulgent and offensive" (Nepomniashchii). Bocharov,
albeit sympathetically, described the Pushkin of *Progulki s Pushkinym* as
"Tertzified Pushkin". And, indeed, the eye and ear of Tertz are plainly
visible and audible in the work. So many of the observations reflect
Siniavskii's own preoccupations and recur elsewhere in his writings. He
clearly identifies with Pushkin, as when he mimics critics' reactions to his
love of dressing in foreign costumes: "Just look [...] Pushkin is a Turk,
Pushkin is a Jew, he talks just like a Jew" (Tertz 1993, 75). This recalls
comments made back in the 1960s at the time of the trial. Another instance
where it is not difficult to recognize a degree of self-identification is when
he speaks of the way Pushkin combined aristocratic manners with the ability
to find a common language with the humblest of men (Tertz 1993, 99).
But the most obvious example is the way he sees Pushkin as having split
the "single whole of man-poet in two, into Poet and man [...] turned them
into his right and left hands [...] worked them together and separately, like
a juggler" (Tertz 1993, 115).

   With all this evidence of subjectivity the approach in *Progulki s Pushkinym*
remains, however, far removed from the coy possessiveness of a "My
Pushkin", nor is this a revival of the old-style biographical criticism. Siniavskii
is firmly insistent on the autonomy of a work of art, existing independently
of its author. With the passing of time it is the writers who can "slumber"
and lie forgotten while their works and their characters continue to live.[12]
Yet with Pushkin Siniavskii was fascinated by the phenomenon of the first
Russian poet to have a biography: "Pushkin was the first civilian to attract
attention to himself in Russian literature. [...] He was the first poet who
had a biography instead of a service record" (Tertz 1993, 109). He sensed,
moreover, that Pushkin was drawn to seek out in life artistic, fantastic
solutions: "Pushkin was drawn to a fantastic dénouement. His biography
is a tree-trunk, blossoming with legends. New every time" (Tertz 1994, 26).
In *Progulki s Pushkinym* he, as a consequence, made great play of the
interconnection of one work with another and of the life with the art, even
going as far as to suggest that Tat´iana was never truly in love with Onegin
since in reality it was Pushkin whom she loved.

   In "Puteshestvie na Chernuiu rechku", however, Siniavskii puts two more
balls into the juggler's hands. As well as juggling with Pushkin's art and
his life, he adds his own biography and his own art. He weaves into the
story of *Kapitanskaia dochka* the return of Siniavskii and Tertz to Russia:
Siniavskii in person, Tertz in print. If in *Progulki s Pushkinym* it was
Pushkin whom he described as a vampire, here it is Tertz; it is all writers
engaged in the act of creation. If there Pushkin was seen as able to transform

himself now into Grinev, now into Pugachev, here in the "Journey" it is Tertz as well. It is an enterprise which presents both a challenge and a risk. The challenge is that the mesh of past and present, of two men's biographies and their writings will interact dynamically and realize more effectively than any plain discourse the ossified metaphor that "literature lives" and serves as the carrier of a culture's most cherished, vulnerable, but ultimately indestructible values. But the danger is obvious. It is the danger of the exercise in literary criticism being overloaded and distorted by extraneous information and becoming both too personal and too polemical. Russian literature has plenty of precedents for this: Dobroliubov, for one. The political beliefs may differ, but Dobroliubov's articles, "Chto takoe oblomovshchina?" (What is Oblomovshchina?, 1859) and "Kogda zhe priidet nastoiashchii den´?" ("When will the real day come?", 1860), in their day blatantly exploited literature for political ends and sought to enlist the work of Goncharov and Turgenev in the cause of radicalism. Is Siniavskii doing something not dissimilar and, for all his parade of "art for art's sake", using *Kapitanskaia dochka* to plead the cause of liberal democracy? Is he doing something even more reprehensible and using Pushkin, the one untarnishable icon of Russian culture, as a cover, to lend legitimacy to his defence of his own conduct? But to Russia's new generation of pharisees and philistines the answer from "Puteshestvie na Chernuiu rechku" comes loud and clear; as Maiakovskii earlier had it: "Nate!" (Take that!).

Separating "Puteshestvie na Chernuiu rechku" out into its main compositional elements (first, the text of *Kapitanskaia dochka*; second, *Kapitanskaia dochka* and Pushkin; third, *Kapitanskaia dochka* and Tertz), it is appropriate to begin by considering the way Siniavskii analyses the primary text.

Siniavskii is interested, first of all, in the source of the work, in the way a work of fiction sprang from a work of fact, Pushkin's *Istoriia Pugacheva* (History of the Pugachev rebellion, 1834). Pushkin presents *Kapitanskaia dochka*, in a draft of a "sketch of a preface", as an anecdote which circulated in the locality of Orenburg: "The anecdote which serves as the basis of the story published here is known in the Orenburg region" (Tertz 1994, 21). The "realism", of course, is illusory, a mere fictional device like Belkin, but it carries over into the narrative framework and the way the story is presented as an eye-witness account set down as a family memoir for the entertainment and edification of future generations by Grinev, a semi-educated ex-army officer with some modest literary pretensions.

Beyond consideration of sources Siniavskii's interest extends to the novel's genre and what it owes to the tradition of the adventure story, the tale of chivalry, the didactic novel, as well as the historical memoir. He looks, too, at literary antecedents of the characters. Whilst noting Shvabrin's

sneering reference (in the omitted chapter) to Grinev as "the Belogorskii
Don Quixote", he recognizes no real similarity with Cervantes's forlorn
knight, though he allows that Savel´ich, complete with lame and skinny
nag, makes an excellent Sancho Panza. He finds a model for Grinev not
in Cervantes, but, rather, in Fonvizin's comedy *Nedorosl´* (The minor,
1782), seeing him as a positive version of the young Mitrofan Prostakov.
Grinev grows enormously in stature through the tale in response to the
pressure of events, as do the other positive characters: Masha, her parents,
even the carefree billiard-playing Zurin. It is Pugachev who triggers these
events, and it is he who holds most fascination for Siniavskii, as he senses
it did for Pushkin when he made him into a more attractive character in
his fiction than in his history. He describes Pugachev's dual role as brutal
butcher and fairy-godmother first by analogy with the faithful wolf from
Pushkin's poetic fairy tale *Ruslan i Liudmila* (Ruslan and Liudmila, 1820):
"A buryi volk ei verno sluzhit" (And the brown wolf serves her faithfully),
and then by comparison with that mythical being, the werewolf (Tertz 1994,
28–31). The moment which Siniavskii sees as encapsulating the irrational
ambivalence of Pugachev's characterization is when Grinev and he find
themselves alone in the Belogorskii fortress, following the killing of both
Masha's parents; they look at each other in silence and then both burst out
laughing (Tertz 1994, 33). Although he eschews the use of anything which
might smack of critical jargon, Siniavskii can be seen here to be uncovering
Pushkin's use of archetypes: the knight, the servant, the werewolf and, in
Masha, the Captain's daughter, the fair maiden ("krasnaia devitsa", 29) the
"eternal bride" ("vechnaia nevesta", 19).

Perhaps the most effective aspect of Siniavskii's analysis is his uncovering of the devices that set the story in motion. He notes especially the
multiplicity of balanced pairings at every level of the work's construction:
event, character, motif, detail (44–45). These correspond in his view to the
sense of balance and harmony which is the foundation of Pushkin's world
view. The main dynamic of the book he sees as provided by honour, the
public code which binds Grinev to loyal service of the State, and the private
code which makes him honour his parents and honour his love as Masha's
true knight. When the two codes come into conflict with each other Siniavskii
is in no doubt that it is the latter which weighs more heavily in the balance
(50). The pursuit of honour motivates the main structural device of the story:
the journey. It is foreshadowed in the image of the kite which the young
Grinev fashions out of the geography map in his school-room and the tail
which he attaches to the Cape of Good Hope. Siniavskii charts Grinev's
passage ("not for nothing does Grinev's carriage [in the snowstorm] resemble a ship" [14]) through the stormy seas of rebellion, pursuit,
incarceration until, finally, he returns to the point of departure and the safe

haven of his parents' home and reunion with his bride. Siniavskii, who is fond, as we have seen, of a circular construction, takes up towards the end the nautical imagery with which the story began. He refers to the structure of balanced pairings as the "rigging of Pushkin's boat" (44). If it is compliance with his father's wishes which motivates the first stage of his journey out to the Belogorskii fortress, it is Grinev's love for Masha which motivates all the rest, and it is she who makes the final decisive journey to Tsarskoe Selo to see the Empress and secure his pardon. The role of the Captain's daughter is pivotal.. She is not, Siniavskii emphasizes, the colourless nonentity recalled by Marina Tsvetaeva (Tertz 1994, 12), and it is this which explains and justifies the novel's title. As he had observed earlier of "Mednyi vsadnik", the title sums up the whole work.

This is an exercise in textual criticism which is both accessible and demanding. It requires no prior knowledge of the critical literature nor of the language of literary theory, but it is exacting in its requirements of close knowledge of the text and of Pushkin's other writings, as well as familiarity with the literary context, both Russian and West European. A reader who is equipped with this knowledge and who entrusts himself to Siniavskii's guidance finds a delightful, informative companion with a keen eye, a lively imagination and, most importantly, with an understanding of the work's driving force, its spiritual centre.

Into the account of Grinev's journey Siniavskii weaves two journeys by his creator Pushkin. The first is the journey which he undertook in August and September 1833 to the Orenburg region in search of background materials for his History, in particular to hear accounts by surviving witnesses of the Pugachev rebellion. He set out from his dacha in Chernaia rechka, in the outskirts of Petersburg, in a violent storm, totally unseasonal for August. He describes it vividly in a letter to his wife later that month, writing that he nearly turned back at the Troitskii Bridge where his carriage was held up. This freak storm, Siniavskii suggests, gave Pushkin the idea for the storm which waylays Grinev's carriage and which heralds the arrival of Pugachev. Siniavskii's interest here is to show the workings of the writing process, how the "raw material" of chance incidents becomes shaped into an artistic design. To show this he draws on Pushkin's letters and contemporary memoirs, for which a favoured source, it seems reasonable to assume, is still, as it was in Dubrovlag when he wrote his first Pushkin essay, Veresaev's *Pushkin v zhizni* (Pushkin in life).[13] In Paris he evidently has access to a fuller edition of Pushkin's letters, yet all but one of the quotations from documents in his text are located in Veresaev. A reader can also find confirmation there of several of his suggestions concerning Pushkin's treatment of his material: for example, the ambivalence of the characterization of Pugachev, and the transference of Pushkin's experience as a "field-worker" to Grinev's role as eye-witness and recorder. Consultation of Veresaev yields the added bonus of showing where Siniavskii himself may have come by some of his ideas. The images of vampire and werewolf, for instance, may derive from the superstitious distrust with which Pushkin was met by some of the old people he interviewed. They saw him as the stranger with the long fingernails who went round offering "devil's money" for talk; in a word, they saw him as the Antichrist (Veresaev 1990, vol. 3, 18–20; Tertz 1994, 33). An interested reader finds that Veresaev also inadvertently suggests a source for Grinev's constant grouses about Savel´ich in Pushkin's comment about his man-servant: "The one thing that really distresses me is my valet" (letter to N. N. Pushkin, 19 September 1833: Veresaev 1990, vol. 3, 14). And might not the providential hareskin coat (*zaiachii tulup*), the gift of which ensures Grinev's safe passage through the novel, be an artistic inversion of the ill-omen of the hare which crosses Pushkin's path at his first attempt to leave Simbirsk for Orenburg? (letters to N. N. Pushkin, 14 September 1833, 2 October 1833: Veresaev 1990, vol. 3, 13–14, 23). Siniavskii does himself refer at one point to "Pushkin's hare", but without Veresaev's documentation of the Orenburg journey a reader would take this as a reference to the better-known — and this time providential — hare which persuaded Pushkin not to continue his journey to St Petersburg in December 1825.

   The second journey which Siniavskii weaves into his story is both actual and metaphorical: Pushkin's journey to his death. He sets the clock ticking in 1833 when he interprets the freak August storm which accompanies Pushkin's departure for Orenburg as a grim portent of the arrival in St Petersburg of d'Anthès just a month later (Tertz 1994, 10). The love of Grinev and Masha, their separation, trials and ultimate happy reunion are set, firstly, against the background of Pushkin's recollection of the agonies of jealousy that he suffered before his marriage in 1830 when his betrothed was being fêted in St Petersburg while he was marooned in Boldino by the cholera epidemic. Siniavskii lets a comment by Pushkin make the connection, quoting from a letter that he wrote home to his wife dated 2 October 1833: "In the village of Berda where Pugachev stayed for six months, I had 'une bonne fortune' — I found a seventy-five-year-old Cossack woman who remembers that time just like we remember 1830" (Tertz 1994, 11).[14] He then glosses the comparison, emphasizing Pushkin's awareness of the parallels between public and private conflict and of the way the past carries into the present. This leads him to point the connection between Pushkin's personal situation during the years that he was planning and writing *Kapitanskaia dochka* and the accumulation of humiliation and frustration which culminated in the fatal duel. Grinev's rival, Shvabrin, Siniavskii observes, is unique in Pushkin's gallery of characters. He alone is depicted as totally, unrelievedly, wicked. This was because, he suggests, Pushkin put into his characterization all that he saw as despicable and dishonourable in d'Anthès (Tertz 1994, 42). And the ideas of honour which govern all Grinev's actions are also to be seen as Pushkin's own. There is the essentially aristocratic code which Pushkin idealistically, like the Decembrists, believed might ultimately be shared by the common people. Thus Pugachev and his band of illiterate cut-throats are shown to be not without honour. Thus Grinev comes to scorn "service" (*sluzhba*) as did Pushkin himself. Then there is the even stronger sense of personal honour which spurs Grinev on in defence of the reputation of his betrothed. The catch is, though, in Siniavskii's telling of the tale, that to defend Masha's reputation Grinev needs to stay alive, and to stay alive he compromises his honour as a serving Russian officer by "dealing" with the rebels. It is the intervention of his proxy father Pugachev which keeps him alive for most of the book. It is the intervention of the Captain's daughter which finally secures his release and removes the stain on his honour. There is no need to labour the contrast with Pushkin's fate. He had neither a Pugachev to save his life, nor a Masha to safeguard his honour. Pushkin's journey ended in 1837 where it began in 1833, at Chernaia rechka.

Tertz's narrative again describes two journeys. One February day in the late 1980s a freak storm hits Paris. Siniavskii has a nightmarish journey back home to the suburbs. Coincidentally, it is the very day that his wife, "Masha", has set off for Leningrad by plane in connection with the planned publication of his works there. He describes how he had to crawl to the metro on all fours. In the train a young well-dressed woman became hysterical and stood up letting out a stream of unprintable obscenities "like a Bacchante" (Tertz 1994, 9). All night cats howled, actually howled.

Tertz's second journey takes place in what has been identified by external evidence as early summer 1991. Siniavskii and his wife have this time travelled together to Leningrad. He has arrived "armed" with his spectacles ("Spectacles are for me what a pistol is for other people" [Tertz 1994, 34]), with his foreign passport, and with his other constant travelling companion, a copy of *Kapitanskaia dochka*. They decide to go to Chernaia rechka and take a look at the scene of Pushkin's duel. It is thirty and more years since he has been in Leningrad and, rather like Rip van Winkle, he has woken up to find himself in a strange new world. The disorientation is compounded when they find themselves caught up in what appears to be a crowd scene for some film. Here a historical reminiscence of the crowd clamouring outside Pushkin's flat after his death combines with a vivid personal reminiscence of a scene witnessed by Siniavskii and his wife in the Prado, Madrid. A group of Soviet tourists, an outlandish cohort of the descendants of Tamburlaine, trouped after their guide through the rooms of the gallery and finally came face to face with the nightmarish canvasses painted by the deranged Goya. At that moment East met West, the present clashed with the past in a silent symbolic act of violence. Siniavskii's narrative at this point shifts back to Pushkin's death and the outcry against d'Anthès, the foreigner who had murdered the Russian people's national poet. He quotes from the memoirs of a Polish doctor who attended Pushkin after the duel, Stanisław Morawski:

> The whole population of Petersburg, especially the common people and the peasants [...] passionately longed to revenge themselves on d'Anthès [...] They even wanted to settle scores with the surgeons who treated Pushkin, claiming conspiracy and betrayal, claiming that one foreigner had wounded Pushkin and other foreigners had been entrusted with his medical care. (Tertz 1994, 40; Veresaev 1990, vol. 3, 265)

Here Siniavskii jumps abruptly forward in time to the early 1950s to recall another episode of nationalist hysteria, the Doctors' Plot, when, at the height of the anti-cosmopolitan campaign, Jewish doctors were accused of conspiring to murder Stalin. The parallel with Siniavskii's own position at this point becomes obvious. The reader recalls the incident of the Russian lady calling his French translator "d'Anthès", recalls the whole witchhunt mounted against him by the nationalists for defiling their national hero. "'Russophobe!' they cry, 'Russophobe!' He showed Pushkin no respect !...'" (Tertz 1994, 27). Siniavskii and his wife move off, away from the crowd: "Time to push off, Masha!" (Tertz 1994, 40).

From there it is but a step, literally and metaphorically, to Chernaia rechka. There stands a monument, an obelisk, which may or may not mark the actual spot where Pushkin fell. A passer-by, perhaps a seaman, walks by, muttering drunkenly to himself: "Don't lose your nerve in a fog and don't hoot!" (Tertz 1994, 51). With this nautical echo Siniavskii's personal narrative rejoins *Kapitanskaia dochka*. As he walks away from the scene of the duel Siniavskii takes a last look behind him, and there she is, the Captain's daughter, sitting weeping on the park bench.

Towards the start of his essay Siniavskii observed that Pushkin does not retreat into history, but "recalls it like a fact of his own biography and sits it down on a bench surrounded by its close family" (Tertz 1994, 11). He does the same with the story of his own life and with his treatment of literary history. In a central extended digression on literary classics and the obligations of the literary critic (sections 5–9) he accuses academic literary historians of behaving like undertakers, of embalming the classics, instead of letting them live. He accuses them of parasitism, of cowardice and dares them to take risks, to engage with literature boldly, creatively, as equals: "Put yourselves on equal terms. Yes, on equal terms with the literature you are writing about. Be bold, like Pushkin. Don't be afraid to take risks!" (Tertz 1994, 20). Siniavskii's essay is itself a bold demonstration of these beliefs in the accessibility of the past and the obligation of the critic not to bury his talent in the ground, but use it to the full in the service of his art. Just as Pushkin was a writer with a biography, so Tertz is a literary critic with a face. He does not shrink from drawing attention to points of contact between his own life and Pushkin's and using his instrument of creative criticism to journey to Chernaia rechka and enter the fictional world of *Kapitanskaia dochka* and there "reflect upon the strange ways of love, upon Pushkin, upon the nature of art" (Tertz 1994, 25).

Pushkin created *Kapitanskaia dochka* out of the pressures of his own life, the stain on his honour, his hopeless love for his wife, his growing awareness that only in fairy tales was it possible to have a happy ending. A hundred and fifty years after Pushkin's death his creation was still open and accessible to a contemporary writer's musings on some of the same themes. Siniavskii's point of view and his circumstances are, self-evidently, very different from Pushkin's and he interacts with the fiction in his own individual way, entering into counterpoint with Pushkin's biography and developing a new set of variations. The fiction can amply accommodate them, and, far from being distorted and disfigured by its new occupant, it gains life from the fresh air that blows through it. Siniavskii, like Grinev and like Pushkin, is preoccupied by the defence of his honour and by the conflicting claims of public and private loyalty and duty. The personal accent of his reading is easily recognizable in the details he remarks upon and where he chooses to place his emphasis. The reader will note that in the above-quoted description of the purpose of his "Journey" the first subject Siniavskii names is not Pushkin, not art, but love. Certainly, this constitutes a bold reply to his critics and a defence of his political and artistic beliefs, but, as well as that, it is a token of gratitude, homage and love to his wife.

This is a reading which gains much of its emphasis by contrast with Pushkin's situation. Pushkin created in Masha Mironova the ideal of the devoted woman which was so glaringly absent in his own married situation. Siniavskii does not have to imagine; he has his own Mariia, Mariia Rozanova. When Grinev stands accused of treason and Masha goes to St Petersburg to plead his cause with the Empress she cries out: "Everything he has done and been through, he did for me" (Tertz 1994, 50). When Siniavskii stood accused of treason for writing *Progulki s Pushkinym* and Mariia Rozanova went to plead his cause in the pages of *Voprosy literatury*, she cried out: "It is all my fault! Because it is my book, I begged him to write it, it was written for me..." (Rozanova 1990, 154). In his essay Siniavskii does not himself make this juxtaposition. Nor does he respond with a catalogue of all that his wife has done to safeguard his person and his works: "But look how much she has done for me!" His touch is not so heavy or so crude. It is enough that he highlights the significance of the Captain's daughter's words to the Empress. And that he makes her the central character of his reading, its real heroine. It is she, he points out, who receives all the honour and praise from the Empress, not Grinev. All that Grinev's bravery and heroism earns him finally is "opravdanie", the acknowledgment that his conduct was "justified" (Tertz 1994, 50). This is because, when a conflict arose between his public and private code of honour, he put personal and private loyalties above his public duty to his country and his Sovereign.

*

It is the conclusion of this reading of Siniavskii's essay that the authorial subtext does not detract from the exercise in literary criticism that he is performing. Of course it interferes and complicates — Siniavskii always demands attention and re-reading — but, finally, subtext returns to primary text and illuminates it. It is important to make this point here and now, having only Siniavskii's text in view, before looking at the new context which it acquires by its placement in *Sintaksis*. *Sintaksis* is a polemical and literary journal, based in the Siniavskii Paris home, and produced and edited since 1978 by Mariia Rozanova. Initially, she edited the journal jointly with Siniavskii, but for many years now has run the enterprise single-handed. Siniavskii's is the first article in the volume, heading the "Literature and Art" section. A third section of the volume, forty-four pages long, entitled "Obratnaia perspektiva" (Retrospective), is a presentation by Mariia Rozanova of articles and documents which describe the resolution of the cloud that had hung over the Siniavskiis ever since they left Russia in 1973, namely the accusation of collaboration with the KGB.[15] The rumours that Siniavskii had been given permission to leave Russia with the specific purpose of subverting émigré activities, in particular those of Solzhenitsyn, had persisted in émigré circles ever since he and Rozanova arrived in Paris. The history of his involvement with the KGB is a long one, dating back to the late 1940s, and does have a real source in the KGB's attempt at that time to recruit him as an agent to entrap a friend of his, Hélène Pelletier (Zamoiska), daughter of the French naval attaché in Moscow. Siniavskii gave an account of this episode, of how he used his involvement with the KGB to save Hélène, in his autobiographical novel *Spokoinoi nochi* (1984). In the same novel he also described how a schoolfriend of his, whom he calls there simply Serezha, did become a genuine traitor, leading to the arrest and imprisonment of two other friends. It was this latter account that stung Sergei Khmel´nitskii, the real "Serezha", into flinging the accusation of "traitor" back at Siniavskii in the pages of the Israeli journal *Dvadtsat´ dva* in 1986 and thus brought the issue into the open for the first time. The accusation was taken up by the conservative camp of émigrés and fuelled by Vladimir Maksimov, the editor of *Kontinent*. Though not overtly stated, it lay behind many of the accusations of "russophobia" in the polemics of the late 1980s. This constituted the real "third trial" of Siniavskii which was quietly in session during the entire period of his life in emigration. However, the issue resurfaced in print a second time in 1992, when the Israeli newspaper *Vesti* published a copy of a letter sent by Andropov to the Central Committee in 1973, presenting the case for allowing Siniavskii to leave Russia for Paris. The implication of the letter was clearly that Siniavskii would be going to serve the KGB interests among the émigré community (Rozanova 1994, 150). It was Mariia Rozanova who, using every channel at her disposal, worked to refute this second open assault on her husband's honour and succeeded finally in obtaining evidence which, it would appear, has at last "acquitted" her husband. She, firstly, secured proof that the document published in *Vesti* was a forgery, a collage made by judicious cutting of the original letter. Second, she succeeded in obtaining from secret KGB archives a document, dated 1976, which stated clearly the KGB intention to compromise the Siniavskiis by leading the émigré community to believe that they were KGB agents. For anyone with a curiosity for the cloak-and-dagger skulduggery of secret service operations this document, authorized by a certain comrade Ivanov E. F., is compulsive reading, a sinister miniature masterpiece of bureaucratic euphemism, in which Siniavskii and Daniel´ are alluded to just by operational code names, the comically alliterative "Diktor" and "Don" (Rozanova 1994, 161). These discoveries would seem to have laid the ghost of treachery once and for all. Maksimov himself, who had spearheaded the campaign, retracted his accusations and issued a press declaration in which he published the KGB document together with a full apology. He also presented his apology in private to the Siniavskiis at their home. His declaration is reproduced in this section of the *Sintaksis* volume, together with a collation of other key "documents" in the case. The section ends with Rozanova's drawing of a handshake: a hand in a suit clasping the hand of a woman in a frilled cuff (Rozanova 1994, 163).

With the death of Maksimov in March 1995, a chapter of émigré history came to an end. But Solzhenitsyn and Siniavskii were still left as embattled opponents, both deeply entrenched in their diametrically opposed aesthetic positions, Solzhenitsyn maintaining the position of the politically committed artist and Siniavskii insistent that art has no end but itself. Siniavskii's beliefs remained unchanged from the 1960s when, at his trial, he made his now well-known statement about the incompatibility of art and politics:

> I am not a political writer. No writer expresses his political views through
> his writings. An artistic work does not express political views. You wouldn't
> ask Pushkin or Gogol about their politics. My works reflect my feelings about
> the world, not politics. (Labedz and Hayward, 195)

It was not my original intention in examining Siniavskii's literary article
to enter into any discussion of émigré polemics, but it has been impossible
to ignore these issues when Siniavskii's essay sits cheek by jowl with
Rozanova's collation. Her account of the "third trial" compels attention as
an adjunct to Siniavskii's text. It prompts a return to Siniavskii's essay and
a little reflection on Siniavskii's aesthetic stance.

After reading Rozanova's section it becomes a great deal clearer why
Siniavskii picked out certain features of Pushkin's text. What is also highlighted is the uncanny degree to which Pushkin's story seems to foreshadow
Siniavskii's own. One is reminded of the passage from *Progulki s Pushkinym*
quoted earlier where Siniavskii imagines successive generations of writers
discovering Pushkin standing behind their backs. The foreshadowing extends beyond the large patterns of destiny to very particular correspondences,
the most striking example being the prominent part played by documents.
Documents figure large in *Kapitanskaia dochka*, but two are given especial
prominence. They are the two documents which enshrine the key concept
of honour: Captain Mironov's officer's diploma and Catherine II's letter
exonerating Grinev. Both hang "framed and behind glass". Siniavskii points
out this feature of Pushkin's novel in his reading and it is in obvious
intentional counterpoint that Rozanova reproduces so many newspaper
headings, as well as the two key documents which first accused and then
exonerated her husband.

The relationship between Siniavskii's and Rozanova's texts invites further exploration. Besides the interplay with *Kapitanskaia dochka* offered
here in the pages of *Sintaksis*, there are, now that Rozanova has published
"Abram da Mar´ia" (Abram and Mar´ia), two sets of memoirs, hers cast
as plain narrative, his, *Spokoinoi nochi*, cast as fiction, which offer reflections and refractions of experience (Rozanova 1993 and 1994, 125-51).
However, the aim here was simply to point out a new departure in the
redoublement of Siniavskii's artistic persona. Siniavskii's *alter ego* Tertz
was born out of the restrictions and unlawfulness of late Stalinist Russia:
a bold fantastical free spirit, safe-guarding the inner freedom of Siniavskii,
the quiet academic. The appearance of the redoubtable Rozanova at her
husband's shoulder has been summoned by the calumnies that have dogged
their life in emigration. She stepped forward in the role of "warrior queen",

fully armed and ready to do battle with the adversary. Siniavskii was a complex personality and complex writer, and the motivations for any sort of division or doubling are always many-sided, but, viewed from just the socio-political perspective, the fact that Siniavskii needed to subdivide himself, or divide roles with his wife in order to maintain equilibrium makes an eloquent statement about the nature of the pressures attending Russian writers both within Russia and in emigration. The interaction that we have here between Siniavskii and Rozanova constitutes, in human terms, an admirable model of a husband-and-wife partnership, pulling together in adversity. But beyond that, in literary terms, it offers an illuminating division of forces between art (Siniavskii's essay) and politics (Rozanova's polemical materials). This makes a reader pause and consider the paradox of Siniavskii's artistic position. On the one hand, the very separation of the activities in this volume of *Sintaksis* patently reaffirms his claim that art and politics are two entirely separate activities. At the same time, we are forcefully reminded by the interplay between the two sets of materials of just how vital politics was to Siniavskii's art. Enmeshed as he was in political intrigue, far from aspiring to escape from the net and write about "butterflies in a meadow",[16] he drew his artistic inspiration from it. Politics was the very life-blood on which he the vampire-artist feeds. In his reading of Pushkin and the considerable use he makes of Pushkin's letters and contemporary testimonies we observed earlier just how interested Siniavskii was in looking at the way Pushkin fashioned the raw material of life into art. Here in the *Sintaksis* volume the device is laid bare and readers have a chance to do the same.

REFERENCES

Andreev, D. L., Parin, V. V., Rakov, L.L., 1991. *Noveishii Plutarkh: illiustrirovannyi biografichiskii slovar´ voobrazhaemykh znamenitykh deiatelei vsekh stran i vremen ot A do Ia* (Moscow: Moskovskii rabochii).

Bocharov, S., 1990. "Obsuzhdenie knigi Abrama Tertsa 'Progulki s Pushkinym'", *Voprosy literatury* 10: 77-153 (78-83).

Brodskii, I., 1987. "Niotkuda s liubov´iu", *Novyi mir* 12: 160–68.

Gul´, R., 1976. "Progulki khama s Pushkinym", *Novyi zhurnal* 124: 117–29.

____, 1989. "Progulki khama s Pushkinym". Abridged version, *Literaturnaia Rossiia* 26 (30 June): 18–19.

Khmel´nitskii, S., 1986. "Iz chreva kitova", *Dvadtsat´ dva* 48: 151–80.

Labedz, L. and M. Hayward (eds), 1967. *On Trial: The Case of Sinyavsky (Tertz) and Daniel (Arzhak)* (London: Collins and Harvill).

Nepomniashchii, V., 1990. "Obsuzhdenie knigi Abrama Tertsa 'Progulki s Pushkinym'", *Voprosy literatury* 10: 77–153 (77–78; 143–53).

Nepomnyashchy, C. T., 1991a. "An Interview with Andrei Sinyavsky", *Formations* 6.1: 6–23.

_____, 1991b. "Andrei Sinyavsky's 'Return' to the Soviet Union", *Formations* 6.1: 24–44.

"Obsuzhdenie knigi Abrama Tertsa 'Progulki s Pushkinym'", 1990. *Voprosy literatury* 10: 77–153.

"Ot redaktsii i pushkinsoi komissii IMLI AN SSR", 1990. *Voprosy literatury* 7: 155

Pasternak, B., 1957. *Doktor Zhivago* (Milan: Feltrinelli).

_____, 1958. *Doctor Zhivago* trans. Max Hayward and Manya Harari (London: Collins).

Pushkin, A. S., 1836. *Kapitanskaia dochka*, *Sovremennik* 4.

Rozanova, M., 1990. "K istorii i geografii etoi knigi", *Voprosy literatury* 10: 154–61.

_____, 1993. "Abram da Mar´ia: memuary M. V. Rozanovoi", *Nezavisimaia gazeta* 12 January: 5, 13 January: 5.

_____, 1994. "Obratnaia perspektiva", *Sintaksis* 34: 120–63.

Sandler, S., 1992. "Sex, Death and Nation in the *Progulki s Pushkinym* Controversy", *Slavic Review* 51.2: 294-308.

Shafarevich, I., 1989a. "Russofobiia", *Nash sovremennik* 6: 167–92.

_____,1989b. "Fenomen emigratsii", *Literaturnaia Rossiia* 36 (8 September): 5.

Siniavskii, A., 1985. "Solzhenitsyn kak ustroitel´ novogo edinomysliia", *Sintaksis* 14: 16–32.

_____, 1987. "Chtenie v serdtsakh", *Sintaksis* 17: 191-205.

_____, 1989. "Mify Mikhaila Zoshchenko", *Voprosy literatury* 2: 50–67.

_____, 1990. "Vek Pasternaka". Supplement to *Literaturniaia gazeta*. February: 22.

Solzhenitsyn, A., 1983. "Nashi pliuralisty", *Vestnik Russkogo khristianskogo dvizheniia* 139: 133–60.

_____, 1984. "...'Koleblet tvoi trenozhnik'", *Vestnik Russkogo khristianskogo dvizheniia* 142: 133–52.

_____, 1989. *Arkhipelag GULag 1918-1956. Opyt khudozhestvennogo issledovaniia*, *Novyi mir* 8-11. Book edition, 3 vols (Moscow: Sovetskii pisatel´; Novyi mir).

Tertz, A., 1975. *Progulki s Pushkinym* (London: Overseas Publications Interchange).

_____, 1982. "On Socialist Realism" tr. G. Dennis (Berkeley and Los Angeles: University of California Press).

_____, 1984. *Spokoinoi nochi* (Paris: Sintaksis).

_____, 1989. "*Progulki s Pushkinym*: fragment", *Oktiabr´* 4: 191–99.

_____, 1990. "Progulki s Pushkinym", *Voprosy literatury* 7: 155–75; 8: 81–111; 9: 146–78.

_____ 1992. "Progulki s Pushkinym", in *Sobranie sochinenii v dvukh tomakh*, vol. 1 (Moscow: Start): 339–436.

_____, 1993. *Strolls with Pushkin* tr. C. Theimer Nepomnyashchy and S. I. Yastremski (New Haven and London: Yale University Press).

_____, 1994. "Puteshestvie na Chernuiu rechku", *Sintaksis* 34: 3–51.

Tsena metafory ili Prestuplenie i nakazanie Siniavskogo i Danielia 1989. Comp. E. M. Velikanova (Moscow: Kniga).

Urnov, D., 1990. "Obsuzhdenie knigi Abrama Tertsa 'Progulki s Pushkinym'", *Voprosy literatury* 10: 77–153 (137–43).

Vail′, P. and A. Genis, 1990. "Obsuzhdenie knigi Abrama Tertsa 'Progulki s Pushkinym'", *Voprosy literatury* 10: 77–153 (122–28).

Veresaev, V., 1990. *Pushkin v zhizni*. Vols 2 and 3 of *Sochineniia v chetyrekh tomakh* (Moscow: Pravda).

Zalygin, S., 1989. Introduction to "Aleksandr Solzhenitsyn, *Arkhipelag GULag*", *Novyi mir* 8: 7–94.

NOTES

1. All translations from the Russian are my own unless otherwise stated.
2. Tertz 1989. The sub-title "fragment" is misleading; the journal excerpt constitutes, in fact, one-fifth of the whole work. In the book edition it already appears as a separable section marked off by asterisks. It begins, appropriately, with a reminiscence from the camps and the anecdote told to the author by a fellow prisoner about Pushkin always carrying two revolvers with him; it ends with the discussion of Pushkin's mystery play, *Pir vo vremia chumy* (The feast in time of plague, 1832) (Tertz 1975, 48–76).
3. All quotations are from Tertz 1993, with page references in the text.
4. These three "1990" numbers actually appeared only late in 1991. The editors included the following announcement of the "round table" in the July number which began serialization of Siniavskii's work:

    > As is well-known, the reaction to the appearance in our press of an extract from Abram Tertz (A. D. Siniavskii)'s book *Progulki s Pushkinym* has turned into a socio-political event. For an academic literary journal to leave such a situation without comment would show unpardonable indifference to issues of contemporary literary life, problems of national culture and civic morality, in sum, to our professional obligations.

    "Ot redakstsii i pushkinskoi komissii IMLI AN SSR" 1990.

    The participants in the discussion, "Obsuzhdenie knigi Abrama Tertsa 'Progulki s Pushkinym'", were listed as follows: V. Nepomniashchii, S. Bocharov, S. Sergeev, I. Rodnianskaia, A. Kazintsev, A. Marchenko, Iu. Mann, S. Kuniaev, A. Arkhangel′skii, I. Zolotusskii, V. Skvoznikov, S. Lominadze, S. Nebol′sin, P. Vail′, A. Genis, Iu. Davydov, D. Urnov.

Progulki s Pushkinym first appeared in book form in Russia in vol. 1 of Abram Tertz, *Sobranie sochinenii*, 1992.

5.   V. Nepomniashchii. "Obsuzhdenie" 1990, 77–78, 143–53. See especially his final remarks:

>   I am disturbed by the calm attitude of some of my colleagues to the powerful layer of untruth (which they now term freshness, now originality, now *épatage*, now heresy — but call it what you like, untruth is untruth) which there is in this book and which, not merely carries false information, but teaches people to think **dishonestly**. [...] Russian literature — that literature which brings honour to Russia — knew that **the word was sacred**, that in the word is contained all the fullness of the world and all the fullness of truth, the one truth of the whole world. Over the last seventy years [...] the word lost its sacredness in people's eyes, its link with truth [...] people treat the word not, as they ought, as something sacred, linked with the Word which was "in the beginning". [...] This [*Progulki s Pushkinym*] is **our** book, it is not at all "anti-Soviet", it is Soviet literature through and through, that literature which has severed or severely strained the links with Russian literature of the relatively recent past... (152–53).

6.   "Pushkin's idea of chance [...] is also too weighty for the conception of this essay, and the author is not interested in analysing just how meaningfully chance (the hareskin coat) operates in the plots of *Pikovaia dama* and *Kapitanskaia dochka"* (Bocharov 1990, 83).

7.   "...write something for me about Mozart [...] And he did — in the camp. Because Pushkin is Mozart" (Rozanova 1990, 155).

8.   Other writing from the camps exhibits a comparable sense of imaginative freedom. A reader is reminded of some of the story-telling of the inmates of the *sharashka* in Solzhenitsyn's *V kruge pervom* (First circle). Another example is the delightful invention, *Noveishii Plutarkh* (The latest Plutarch), composed in the Vladimir prison in the late 1940s by three prisoners who found themselves sharing the same cell: the poet and philosopher L. L. Andreev, the biologist V. V. Parin and the art historian L. L. Rakov. It is noteworthy, too, that Siniavskii, in his centennial essay, "Vek Pasternaka" (A century [the age] of Pasternak), elects to highlight just this same quality of Pasternak to transcend tragic events. In a paraphrase of Pasternak's own poem "Dusha" (The soul, 1956), he writes: "In this sense Pasternak's poetry was a living plant which, using history like soil, served as an accumulator of goodness and humanity, drawing vital juices out of death itself" (1990, 22).

9.   The poem being referred to here is "V nachale zhizni shkolu pomniu ia" (At the beginning of life I remember school, 1830).

10.   The expression figures prominently at Siniavskii's trial when the Prosecutor confronts Siniavskii with his own statement that "Stalin made Lenin's metaphors come true" (Labedz and Hayward 1967, 208).

11. The quotation is recognizable as the first two lines of Pasternak's poem "Gamlet" (Pasternak 1957, 532). Earlier Siniavskii quotes the first two lines of Pasternak's poem on Pushkin, "Podrazhatel´naia" (Imitation), from the cycle *Temy i variatsii* (Themes and variations, 1923): "Pasternak sensed this when he wrote so brilliantly of Pushkin:

    On the bank by deserted waves
    He stood, full of great thoughts..." (Tertz 1993: 122).

    Siniavskii is being playful here. These lines are recognizable first and foremost not in Pasternak's "imitation", but as the opening of "Mednyi vsadnik" (Tertz 1993, 122). Earlier still, Siniavskii echoes a central theme of *Doktor Zhivago* when he speaks of the proximity of art and death in Pushkin's outlook. The phrase "art clings to life through death, sin, lawlessness" recalls Iurii Zhivago's realization that "art [...] is always meditating upon death and is always thereby creating life" (Tertz 1993, 89; Pasternak 1958, 89).

12. "Like Tatyana, Pushkin believed in dreams and portents. They say he had his reasons for that. We needn't go into them. It's enough to refer to his works" (Tertz 1993, 64).
    "We don't even remember, it has still not been finally established, whether there was such a writer as Shakespeare or whether there wasn't. Yet Hamlet still goes on arguing. And we have no means of knowing when he was younger or more eloquent, now or in Shakespeare's day" (Tertz 1994, 20).

13. The work first appeared in 1926–27. It proved hugely popular and went through six editions before 1936, but thereafter was not republished until 1990. Siniavskii has said in interview that Veresaev was his reference book for *Progulki s Pushkinym* and that he read him in prison camp (personal interview, January 1993). Mariia Rozanova also describes how fond she always was of the book since her schooldays and of how she kept trying to persuade Siniavskii to read it before his arrest (Rozanova 1990, 155).

14. This quotation is not to be found in Veresaev. He quotes from the same letter, but does not include this extract.

15. The contents of the "Obratnaia perspektiva" section are as follows: M. Rozanova, "Aprel´skie tezisy Ed. Iodkovskogo": 120–24; M. Rozanova, "Abram da Mar´ia": 125–52; Iu. Vishnevskaia, "Misha Kheifets v strane durakov": 152–60; V. Maksimov, "Zaiavlenie dlia pechati": 161–63; M. Rozanova, "Konets prekrasnoi epokhi": 163. The publication is accompanied by collages of headlines and extracts from the Russian and émigré press.

16. The phrase is taken from Siniavskii's concluding speech at his trial, where he took up Z. Kedrina's assertion that "nobody would read political significance into butterflies in a meadow" (Labedz and Hayward, 266).

SYSTEM AND STRUCTURE
IN THE WORK OF
ALEKSANDR ZINOV´EV

Michael Kirkwood

In the 1970s Aleksandr Zinov´ev wrote mainly long books: *Ziiaiushchie vysoty* (The yawning heights, 1976), *V preddverii raia* (The antichamber to paradise, 1979), *Zheltyi dom* (The yellow house 1980). In the 1980s (and 1990s), with the exception of his autobiographical *Les confessions d'un homme en trop*, his books have been relatively short. Why? Zinov´ev himself offers one explanation: publishers do not like long books.[1] Since that is apparently the case, he will write short ones. This rather pragmatic attitude to his creative work ("never mind the quality, feel the length", as it were) sits oddly with the high regard which he has for his own writing. He is quick to point out that the appearance of *Ziiaiushchie vysoty* led to his being compared with writers of the calibre of Apuleius, Rabelais, Sterne, Swift, Defoe and Saltykov-Shchedrin. His views on literature and literary theory serve almost entirely the purpose of justifying his own approach to writing and he has gone so far as to claim that he is a "literary descendant" of Anton Chekhov (Zinov´ev 1989b, 181; see also 100–01). Modest about his achievements Zinov´ev is not.

On the other hand, Zinov´ev's preferred mode of writing is such that he has no difficulty in determining the length of any book that he sets out to write, or as he puts it, "make". (Zinov´ev, in a conversation with the present author, used the interesting phrase "kogda ia delaiu knigu...".) The reason is simple: his books are concatenations of very short texts, the average length of each text tending to be less than a page. Each text carries

173

its own individual title. Moreover, each text seems to be self-contained, leading some observers to conclude that the order in which the texts are presented in a Zinov´ev work is unimportant (see, for instance, Brown 1987, 308). Others conclude that his texts are actually interchangeable (McMillin 1988, 63), and that they could occur in more than one book.[2] Whilst, however, evidence can be found to support these impressions, there are also grounds to support another view, namely that Zinov´ev's works are partially structured, and that the partial structure can be exceedingly intricate. We shall return to this question later.

Zinov´ev's "generative device" for the production of his texts is simple and offers support for Michel Foucault's contention that any writer is at the mercy of the "juridical and institutional system that encompasses, determines, and articulates the universe of discourse" (Foucault 1988, 198). In Zinov´ev's case, the "juridical and institutional system" of the Soviet Union happened to be deeply inimical to the type of discourse which he favoured. Consequently, he felt threatened by the possibility of arrest by the KGB at any time. He wrote therefore in kaleidoscopic fashion, so that, if he were prevented from "finishing" his text, the outlines of what he wanted to say and the methodology of his investigations of the nature of Soviet society would be known. As it happened, he managed to complete *Ziiaiushchie vysoty* and have it smuggled to the West, where it appeared in 1976. It is noteworthy, however, that Zinov´ev has continued to operate his "generative device" even when the need for subterfuge has passed.

The device (a fuller description of which is to be found in Kirkwood 1993, 30-31) is simple, but remarkably powerful. It may not have been his invention, since it is highly reminiscent of the layout of such text-books as *Osnovy marksizma-leninizma* and other such compulsory pedagogical delights of the Soviet era. The two base elements are a short(ish) text and an accompanying title. Several texts can be grouped under one title, forming thereby a "strand" or "chain".[3] Alternatively, a strand may contain a series of texts which do not share a title, but which are thematically linked. These strands can be interwoven in various ways. For instance, a series of texts sharing the same title allows Zinov´ev to handle a topic in a number of textually different ways. Alternatively, he can highlight a number of different aspects of a question by varying the title on a series of thematically connected texts. Let us suppose, for example, that strand A consists of texts $a_1....a_n$, strand B of texts $b_1...b_n$, strand C of texts $c_1....c_n$. These texts can then occur in a variety of sequences, for instance $a_1b_1c_1a_2b_2c_2...a_nb_nc_n$. Zinov´ev also employs a wide range of literary and non-literary styles. Stylistic varieties could be differentiated with the use of superscripts. For instance: "prose" = 1, "poetry" = 2, "dramatic dialogue" = 3, and so on. If stylistic "labels" are attached to Zinov´ev's texts, the complexity and "richness" of his system is increased: $a_1{}^1b_1{}^2c_1{}^3a_2{}^2b_2{}^3c_2{}^1...a_n{}^nb_n{}^nc_n{}^n$. Often a text contains more than one stylistic variety: $a_1{}^{1/2}b_1{}^{2/3}c_1{}^{3/2/1}$, and so on. The patterning of a Zinov´ev work, thus, can become very complex indeed.

We can illustrate this point by considering the patterning and sequencing of texts of earlier work by Zinov´ev, such as *Ziiaiushchie vysoty* (1976) and *Zheltyi dom* (1980).

Ziiaiushchie vysoty

$a_1{}^1\ c_1{}^1\ c_2{}^1\ a_2{}^1\ a_3{}^1\ b_1{}^1\ [b_2{}^1/d_1{}^1]\ b_3{}^1\ d_2{}^1\ d_3{}^1\ d_4{}^1\ d_5{}^1\ d_6{}^1\ d_7{}^1\ c_3{}^1\ d_8{}^1\ d_9{}^1\ d_{10}{}^1\ d_{11}\ d_{12}{}^1$

The texts selected are the first twenty. The strands represented are: *a* ("social laws"): texts 1, 4, 5; *b* ("responses to *a*") : texts 6, 7, 8; *c* ("chats in the beer-bar"): 2, 3, 15; *d* ("aviator training school"): texts 8, 10, 11, 12, 13, 14, 16, 17, 18, 19, 20. Note that text 7 is common to both strands *b* and *d*, signified by the use of square brackets. The superscript denotes "prose" and indicates the stylistic uniformity of all twenty texts. But the stylistic uniformity is complemented by intricate patternings in terms of strands. The intricacy, however, is actually more complicated than has been so far shown, since in fact the strands themselves interconnect. Thus *b* is formed of "responses" to strand *a*, only part of which has features in the first twenty texts. But we can show by a system of bracketing further relationships between the texts:

Level 1: (1, 2), (1, 2, 3), (3,4), (4, 16), (5, 6, 7), (10, 11, 12, 13, 14, 15), (17, 18, 19, 20);

Level 2: ([1, 2,], 3, 5), ([5, 6, 7], 8), ([10, 11, 12, 13, 14, 15], [17, 18, 19, 20])

Level 3: (8, [{10, 11, 12, 13, 14, 15, 16}, {17, 18, 19, 20}])[4]

Zheltyi dom

If the example taken from *Ziiaiushchie vysoty* illustrates thematic intricacy, the following example from *Zheltyi dom* indicates stylistic intricacy. The texts in question are nos 61-78 of Part I of Volume I, pp. 82-92.[5] There are five discrete features which can be isolated, each one represented by an arabic numeral, as follows:

"narrative": 1
"verse": 2
"conversations between characters": 3

"Voices": 4 ("Voices" in this context refers to voices within the head of
the main protagonist, JRF)
"Himself'": 5 ("Himself' is a reference to the Voice which JRF regards
as his chief mentor)

We now show the eighteen texts in question in terms of their "stylistic"
variation, each variety being represented by a superscript. Where more than
one feature is present, a slash mark is used . Texts themselves are indicated
by lower case letters, x being used to indicate texts which do not form part
of thematic strands:

$$g_24 \; x^5 \; x^1 \; x^{3/4} \; f_8{}^2 \; e_4{}^1 \; x^5 \; i_2{}^3 \; f_9{}^2 \; h_2{}^4 \; f9_a{}^2 \; x^1 \; x^{2/4} \; f_{10} \;{}^2 \; g_3{}^4 \; f_{10a}{}^2 \; x^{1/5} \; x^{1/4/5}$$

As can be seen from the data, no two consecutive texts share the same
set of features.

These examples from *Ziiaiushchie vysoty* and *Zheltyi dom* illustrate the
simplicity and power of Zinov'ev's "generative device" for the production
of "texts" and the intricacy of their patterning. In the next stage of our
discussion we shall illustrate the extent and the flexibility of that patterning.

Let us begin by considering its extent. In an earlier study (Kirkwood
1987) I investigated the structure of *Ziiaiushchie vysoty* and showed that
450 of its 600 texts formed important strands which interwove to form the
fabric of the work. Many of the remainder could have been grouped into
smaller, less important strands. This analysis contradicted the impression
of some commentators that Zinov'ev's works are loosely structured. I had
previously engaged on a similar exercise with respect to *Zheltyi dom* and
there, too, patterning is extensive, accounting for at least fifty per cent of
its 824 texts (Kirkwood 1987).

Establishing the extent of the patterning in those works, however, turned
out to be essential for an appreciation of the flexibility of that patterning.
In 1991 the Soviet journal *Oktiabr´* published an abridged verson of
Ziiaiushchie vysoty (*Oktiabr´*, 1991 1: 36–97; 2: 23–82; 3: 59–81). Two
points were noteworthy. Firstly, the abridgement reduced the 600 texts of
the original to 168 — a very severe pruning, to say the least. Secondly,
Zinov'ev himself had carried out the abridgement and had left specific
instructions (*Oktiabr´*, 1991 1: 36) that not a word was to be changed.

The reason for Zinov'ev's concern was clear. No one who did not have
an intimate knowledge of the relationships connecting the six hundred texts
together would have had any chance of carrying out an abridgment which
would have been coherent. We can illustrate this point by considering the
following data, taken from *Ziiaiushchie vysoty* (ZV) and its abridgement
(ZV[1]) (Kirkwood 1992).

Strand	Designation	Number of Texts	
		ZV	ZV¹
1	"social laws"	15	7
2	"responses to 1"	11	1
3	"chats in the beer-bar"	10	2
4	"aviator training school"	32	16
5	"aspects of Ibansk history"	7	4
6	"battle for the journal"	14	2
7	"the ratorium"	13	12
8	"nature and role of the ideology"	13	7
9	"the Hog/Dauber relationship"	11	1
10	"Dauber's status as an artist"	4	0
11	"the views of Chatterer"	29	3
12/13	"beer-bar/Dauber's studio"	33	3
14	"art and its role in Ibansk"	17	0
15	"a wartime penal battalion"	14	0
16	"Journalist as the naive foreigner"	13	0
17	"Journalist and Neurasthenic"	12	3
18a	"a page of heroic history"	5	3
18b	"Ibansk history"	53	21
19	"liberals and reform"	9	1
20	"the story of Bawler"	27	0
21	"unity"	9	0
22	"truth-teller/Solzhenitsyn"	9	0
23	"Neurasthenic on the State, etc."	13	2
24	"Teacher's 'systems approach'"	5	0
25	"the theme of 'return'"	25	4
26	"Sub-Ibansk"	11	10
27	"Ibanskians on children, etc."	10	3
28	"'the queue' in Ibansk"	10	7
29	"Teacher's wartime experiences"	12	0
30	"Opposition in Ibansk"	10	0
	Total no. of texts	456	114

From this data we can see that Zinov´ev carried out his pruning operation in two ways: by eliminating strands altogether (there are no ZV¹ equivalents of strands 10, 14–16, 20–22, 24, 30); by reducing the length of the remainder, sometimes drastically (for example, strands 2, 3, 6, 9, 11, 12/13, 23, 25). In this respect it is useful to regard the strands as "chains", consisting of a varying number of "links", any number of which can be removed.

Further investigation of the texts themselves reveals that Zinov´ev has reduced the length of individual texts. The following texts in ZV¹ are shorter than their counterparts in ZV: 11, 12, 14, 20, 24, 26, 29, 32, 35, 52, 60, 88, 102, 108, 113, 122, 133, 154, 161, 165 (Kirkwood 1992, 442–43).

It is clear from this examination that Zinov´ev, in principle, could have reduced *Ziiaiushchie vysoty* to virtually any length he chose, while still retaining essentially the same structure. The version published in *Oktiabr´* is about one third the length of the original.

I conducted a similar exercise with *Zheltyi dom* in connection with a translation project. *Zheltyi dom* was originally published in two volumes, each containing well over 350 pages. I was invited to provide an English translation in one volume of about 400 pages, the result of which was *The Madhouse* (Zinov´ev 1986). Given my earlier analysis of the structure of the work, it was not in fact difficult to reduce the length by fifty per cent, for the same reasons as have been established in the discussion relating to *Ziiaiushchie vysoty*. Various "chains" were reduced in length, others were omitted, as was a number of "free-standing" texts which did not connect with any particular chain. Two points are worth noting, however. The first relates to the structure of *Zheltyi dom*. The second illustrates the ease with which the intricacies of Zinov´ev's structures can be overlooked.

The novel consists of four parts: 1) "Propadevtika" (Propadeutics), 2) "Apologiia nechistogo razuma" (A defence of impure reason), 3) "Apologiia prakticheskogo bezumiia" (A defence of practical unreason), 4) "Vechnyi mir" (Eternal peace). Parts 1, 2 and 4 are linked structurally. Part 3 is not. Indeed, its presence is potentially confusing, since it describes a period before the "action" of the other three parts, without any prior warning. The reason for its inclusion is buried in the "introduction" in Volume I. If a reader chooses not to read the introduction, part 3 appears from nowhere and without justification.⁶ On the other hand, it could have been excised entirely without the reader being any the wiser. But since it, too, contained chains of texts, I chose to prune it, rather than omit it entirely.

With regard to the intricacy of Zinov´ev's patterning, the following experience is salutary. I had submitted my translation of an abridged version of *Zheltyi dom* to the publisher and had received the page proofs. To my horror, I discovered that the penultimate sentence of the final text made no sense in my translation, because I had chosen to omit a much earlier text, to which that sentence alluded. I had, therefore, to translate the omitted text and make space for it by judicious pruning of other texts, in order not to disturb the pagination.⁷

But if it is a relatively simple matter (in principle, not in practice!) to reduce the length of a Zinov´ev work, it is also possible (in principle and in practice) for Zinov´ev to expand a work to any size, by lengthening chains of texts, by increasing the number of chains, by adding "free-standing" texts. As we noted above, this process is the one which Zinov´ev adopted at the outset of his career as a creative writer in response to the constraints imposed on him by the Soviet "juridical and institutional system".

The discussion above shows how Zinov´ev "made" his books under Communism. We now turn to a discussion of how he "makes" them under capitalism. In his memoirs, he alludes to plans for a "truly great book" which would reflect his "literary tastes" and his ideology (Zinov´ev 1990, 447–49). He had begun to write *Iskushenie* (Temptation) immediately after completing *Zheltyi dom*. The work was intended to have four parts: *Idi na Golgofu* (Go to Golgotha, 1985); *Evangelie dlia Ivana* (A gospel for Ivan, 1984); *Zhivi* (Live!, 1989). The title of the fourth part is not recorded in his memoirs (Zinov´ev 1989). However, for various reasons, the project did not come to fruition, and the three named parts were published as individual books (Zinov´ev 1985; Zinov´ev 1984; Zinov´ev 1989a). *Idi na Golgofu* is devoted to questions of religion. The "hero", Ivan Laptev, sets himself the task of founding a new religion, one that will be "adequate" in the context of scientific, materialist and atheistic society as represented by Soviet Communism. It represents, at least in chronological terms of the dates of publication, an attempt to formulate a specific set of precepts which will enable individuals to resist the power of the collective. Whereas the central hero of *Zheltyi dom* is incapable of conforming and intuitively performs acts and expresses opinions which set him apart (although he does not particularly want to be set apart), the central character of *Idi na Golgofu* develops a doctrine which will enable people to act like the hero of *Zheltyi dom* if they want to. *Evangelie dlia Ivana* (which appeared one year before *Idi na Golgofu*) is a publication entirely in verse devoted largely to the subject of drink. It contains, however, many "prayers", has a religious title and provides evidence for the view that one source of Russian spirituality comes via the bottle. *Zhivi*, by contrast, explores the lives and prospects of the "physically challenged" in the conditions of Soviet Communism, conditions which have changed for the worse under perestroika.

We shall now examine the structure of *Idi na Golgofu*, *Evangelie dlia Ivana* and *Zhivi* with a view to establishing the extent to which patterning in the form of chains and sequences occurs in these works. We shall then be in a position to demonstrate the ease with which these three works could have been combined to form the "great work" to which Zinov´ev refers. We begin with *Idi na Golgofu*.

The work consists of 205 texts and 183 pages. The average length of text is therefore less than one page. The vast majority of texts (virtually all of them) fit into one structural chain or another in a total of 23. Each chain has an informal descriptive "label", an explanation of which is given in the footnotes. The numbers in bold type indicate that the text in question appears in more than one chain. The high number of such texts indicates that the "texture" of *Idi na Golgofu* is complex and tightly interwoven.

1. *"Life in Ensk" texts*: 1, **9**, 178?, 206. These texts contain minimal information about the external context in which Ivan Laptev operates. The question mark after text 178 indicates doubt on my part as to whether it should be included in this chain or not.

2. *"Verse/prose" texts*: **2**, 3, **27**, **29**, **30**, **31**, **36**, 43, **50**, 65, 71, 73, **85**, **99**, 102, **110**, **123**, **137**, **148**, **161**, 173, **181**, **185**, 204. This is a relatively long chain which is important mainly for the stylistic variety it brings to the work. Texts containing both prose and verse are a hallmark of Zinov'ev's earlier work in particular.

3. *"Christ" texts*: **2, 7, 12, 13, 14, 16**, 18, 19, **22, 30, 31, 32, 33, 36, 38, 45, 50**, 51, 54, **55**, 57, **60**, 62. **65**, 69, **75**, 80, 94, 95, 98, **108, 126, 158, 181, 182, 183, 189, 190, 191**,197, **198, 200, 203**. This is an important chain containing many comparisons between Laptev's life as a Soviet Messiah and the life of Christ.

4. *"Title" links*: **4/5, 7/8/9/13, 9/42**, 43/**45**; **36/40/74**/80, **158/159, 33/181, 86/186**. These texts are linked via a common title. Most of the texts occur as members of other chains as well.

5. *"P"-texts*: **4, 6, 7, 13**, 27?, **32, 45, 60, 75**, 89, **98**, 113, **119, 126**, 127, **128, 129, 130, 131, 132**, 133, **134**, 135, 136, **138, 139**, 142, **144, 146?, 153, 158, 159, 169**, 180. P stands for "philosophy". The texts in this chain are devoted to discussion of various moral philosophical problems not necessarily in a religious context. Note, however, the number of texts which are common to chains 4, 7 and 8.

6. *"God" texts*: **4, 6, 7, 50**, 63, 68, **69,119,128,129,130**. These texts parallel the chain devoted to Christ, containing various comparisons of the problems facing God and Ivan Laptev.

7. *"Previous religions"* : **5, 8**, 17, **185**. These texts contain references to earlier religions, used by Laptev as a point of comparison with his own religion which is specially tailored to enable the non-conformist individual to cope with the conditions of life in the Soviet Union.

8. *"Chief of police" texts*: **5, 11, 55**. Laptev in text 5 has his first encounter with the local police chief. This latter character occurs in two other texts. The three texts form a chain, albeit a short one.

9. *"Word" links*: **6/7, 7/8, 8/9, 11/12, 14/15/16, 22**/23/24, 25/26, **27/28, 30/31, 33/34, 34**/35, **36**/37/38/39, 55/56, 62/64/71?, 67/68?, 92/96, **131/132, 143/144, 149/150/151, 162/163, 166/168, 170**/171. "Word" links are similar to "title" links in that the texts are associated via a

word or concept which is common to two or more individual texts. For example, texts 6 and 7 are linked by the word "Golgotha", texts 7, 8 and 9 by variants of the first person singular possessive pronoun "moi", etc.

10. *"Doctrine" texts*: **7, 29, 30**, 37, 52, **126**, 127, **138, 139, 142, 144**, 145, **146?, 148, 149, 150, 151**, 152, 154, 155, 156, 157, **159, 160, 161**, 164, **165, 167**. This is one of the most important chains in the book, containing as it does Laptev's "teaching".

11. *"Suslikov/Partgrad/Atom/Zhivi" refs*: **9, 10, 28, 33, 44, 55**, 59, 61, **65, 74, 110**, 113. The texts in this chain are important for their references to characters, places and events in other Zinov´ev works.

12. *"Ecclesiasticus" texts*: **9**, 20, **21, 22**, 76, 77, 78, 90, **101**, 104, 106, 107, 111, 117, 118, 121, 122, **123**, 141, **153, 175**, 177. The texts in this chain share common titles, each of which is (part of) a saying of Ecclesiasticus, such as "Vse sueta", "Sueta suet", "I tomlenie dukha". Texts in this chain tend to portray the futility of Soviet life.

13. *"Antipod" texts*: **10, 15**, 25, 36, 40, 70, 72, 74, 79, 92, 95, 100, 103, 105, **108**, 114, 120, **159, 160, 167**, 172, 173, **183, 200, 203, 204**. Possibly the most interesting chain in the book, it contains the texts devoted to Antipod, a friend of Laptev's who works in the field of ideology and who dreams of raising Soviet ideology to an intellectually respectable level, adequate for a highly educated population. These texts contain many interesting discussions on the relative merits and demerits of ideology and religion seen as sources of moral teaching.

14. *"Verse" texts*: 21, 140, **165, 179**, 201. A relatively short chain of texts consisting entirely of verse. However, taken together with chain 1, the number of texts containing verse is 29, or more than 10% of the total number.

15. *"Healing the sick, etc" texts*: **42, 44**, 48, **55**, 90. Laptev, like Christ, has the power to heal the sick.

16. *"Competitors" texts*: 46, **56**, 108. This short chain contains texts describing Laptev's "competitors" in the religious "market".

17. *"Goddess" texts*: 47, 53, 58, 81, 83, **85**, 96, **99**, 115, **166, 170**, 176, **179, 203**. Laptev is in love with a particular woman whom he adores from afar.

18. *"Miracle" texts*: **60**, 84. Like Christ, Laptev can also perform miracles.

19. *"Problem No 1" texts*: 61, 73, 82, 97, 109, 112, 116. This is an amusing series of texts in which Laptev trains the son of a bigwig in the arts of diplomacy, the son being destined for the diplomatic service. The title refers to the bigwig's "number one problem": how to educate his (extremely) thick son to the level necessary for entry into a highly competitive profession.

20. *"Interlocutor" texts*: 88, 91, **101**, 111, **169, 175**. These texts contain conversations between Laptev and a series of chance drinking-companions he encounters.
21. *"Chaotic thoughts" texts*: 89, 93, 98, **134**. This is a "title"-based chain containing a series of texts dealing with some very interesting topics such as the nature of "perfection".
22. *"The dream and the reality"*: **[link with "Goddess" texts]** 129, **137,143**, 147, 162. This chain forms a counterpoint to the "Boginia" chain. "Mechta" refers to Laptev's fantasy world of romantic love inhabited by himself and his Goddess and "real´nost´" to the world of sordid, loveless sex with a cynical "potaskukha".
23. *"School of sotsiioga" texts*: **181, 182, 183**, 184, **186**, 187, 188, **189, 190, 191**, 192, 193, 194, 195, 196, 198, 199, **200**, 202, **203, 204**. This is perhaps the longest, practically continuous, chain in the book in which the long drawn-out "denouement" is described. Zinov´ev uses it to work out a crude parallel between Ivan Laptev's journey from Ensk to Moscow and Christ's journey to Jerusalem. Christ's fate is crucifixion, Laptev's is worse: he is removed from society. Total: 192.[8]

If we examine the first twenty texts of *Idi na Golgofu* using the same notation as we did above for the first twenty texts of *Ziiaiushchie vysoty* we obtain the following result:

(1): a_1^1; (2): $b_1/c_1^{1/2}$; (3): $b_2^{1/2}$; (4): $d_1/e_1/f_1^1$; (5): $d_2/g_1/h_1^1$; (6): $e_2/f_2/i_1^1$; (7): $d_3/e_3/f_3/i_2/j_1^1$; (8): $d_2/g_2/i_3^1$; (9): $a_2/d_5/i_6/k_1/l_1^1$; (10): k_2/m_1^1; (11): h_2^1/i_7^1; (12):$c_3/i_8/^1$; (13): $c_4/d_6/e_4^1$; (14): c_5/i_9^1; (15): i_{10}/m_2^1; (16): c_6/i_{11}^1; (17): g_3^1; (18): c_7^1; (19): c_8^1; (20): l_2^1.

Each letter of the alphabet stands for a separate chain, the first (*"Life in Ensk"*) being *a*. We see, therefore, that some of the texts are simultaneously members of more than one chain. The more chains to which a given text belongs, the "denser" the texture of that particular text. *Idi na Golgofu* is clearly a very complex work.

Evangelie dlia Ivana by contrast is much less so. Its distinguishing characteristic is that is is written entirely in verse. It is composed of 186 separate texts and occupies 126 pages. These texts can, as usual, be sorted into chains, as follows:

Chains
1. *"war/post-war"*: 5, 6, 7, 8, 9, 10, 11, 12.
2. *"title" chain ("spivshiisia")*: 13, 14, 17, 20.

3. *"title" chain ("pokolenie")*: **20**, 21.
4. *"women"* : 30, **67**, 68, 69, 70, 71, 72, 73, 74, 75, 76.
5. *"title" chain ("itogi")*: 31, 32, 33, 34.
6. *"title" chain ("esli ... plokho")*: 44, 45, 46.
7. *"programme/policy" chain*: 48, 49, 50, 51.
8. *"religious" themes/titles/connotations*: 52, 53, 55, 57, 58, 59, 60, 61, 64, 65, 66, **67**, 110, 120, 122, 130, 137, **172, 173**.
9. *"title" chain ("molitva...")*: **59**, 87, **99**, 100, 101, 102, 104, 105, 106, 107, 108, 132, 133, 134, 135, 136, 138, 139, 140, 141, 142, 143, 144, 145, 146, 148, 151, **171, 176**.
10. *"friendship"*: 77, 82, 83.
11 .*"money"*: 84, 85, 86.
12. *"informer"*: 94, 95.
13. *"power"*: 97, 98, **99**
14. *"title" chain ("k liudiam/k bogam")*: 123, 124.
15. *"title" chain ("universal'noe ...")"*: 126, 127.
16. *"title" chain ("potom")*: 147, 153. Both link in with 131.
17. *"title" chain ("o boltovne/molchanii")*: 156, 157.
18. *"death and dying"*: 158, 159, 160, 161, 162, 163, 164, 165,, 166, 167, 168, 170, 171, **172, 173, 176**, 177, 178, 179, 180, 181.
    Total: 115

That the texture of *Evangelie* is far less rich than that of *Idi na Golgofu* is clear from two pieces of evidence. Firstly, there is a comparatively small number of numerals in bold characters. This means that relatively few texts are associated with more than one chain. Secondly, an examination of the sequences of the texts reveals that many of the chains do not "interweave" to anything like the same extent as they do in *Idi na Golgofu*. The *"war"* chain, for instance, is entirely contained in texts 5-12 inclusive. There is no interweaving whatsoever between this chain and others. The final chain (*"death and dying"*), one of the longest in the book, does not, however, appear until text 158 and continues with very few gaps right through to text 181. Admittedly, texts 171, 172, 173 and 176 also occur in other chains, but the point about the relative lack of interweaving remains valid. If we examine the first twenty texts using our notation, the result looks like this:

(1): x^2; (2): x^2; (3): x^2; (4): x^2; (5): a_1^2; (6): a_2^2; (7): a_3^2; (8): a_4^2; (9): a_5^2; (10): a_6^2; (11): a_7^2; (12): a_8^2; (13): b_1^2; (14): b_2^2; (15): c_1^2; (16): c_2^2; (17): b_3^2; (18): x^2; (19): x^2; (20): b_4^2.

We recall that x denotes a text which is not associated with a chain. We note, furthermore, that none of those twenty texts occurs in more than one chain.

There are obvious links between *Evangelie dlia Ivana* and *Idi na Golgofu*, quite apart from the religious connotations of the respective titles. In text 7 of the latter work (*"Moe uchenie"*, pp. 14–15) Laptev develops the theme of the *zabegalovka* ("pub") considered as a *khram* (cathedral) and his drinking companions as "disciples". He refers to his verses as *molitvy* (prayers) which fly round town and become known by the townsfolk as "Evangelie dlia Ivana". Chain number 10 in *Evangelie dlia Ivana* shares the general title of "Molitva" and, indeed, texts 137, 139 and 142 are entitled respectively "Preduprezhdenie vkhodiashchemu v khram" (A warning to those about to enter the cathedral), "Molitva pered vkhodom v khram" (A prayer before entering the cathedral) and "Molitva po vykhode iz khrama" (A prayer on leaving the cathedral). Common, therefore, to the two works are the associations between religion and heavy drinking, both of which are presented by Laptev as sources of spiritual succour, the latter being the more powerful.

It might be argued, therefore, that *Evangelie dlia Ivana* constitutes Laptev's impromptu verses gathered in one volume. However, the first and last texts make it clear that the "author" cannot be Laptev, since Laptev lives in Ensk, whereas the author of *Evangelie* lives in Moscow and then emigrates to the West. On the other hand, if these texts are omitted, the remainder could well have been composed by the provincial Laptev.[9] What is certainly clear is that the two works could have been interwoven without difficulty. The various chains of *Evangelie dlia Ivana* could be interwoven with those of *Idi na Golgofu* after text seven in the latter work entitled "Moe uchenie" (My teaching), in which reference is made to Laptev's "Evangelie dlia Ivana".

We turn now to a brief discussion of *Zhivi*, published in 1989, but written between 1982 and 1987. The three main characters ("Robot", "Slepoi" and "Teoretik") were born respectively without legs, eyes or arms, victims of the consequences of irradiation caused by a secret nuclear installation in the closed city of Atomgrad, near the provincial town of Partgrad. Much of the work is devoted to their discussions of moral and social problems relating to the difficulties of existing in Soviet society, this time from the perspective of those who have the least chance of ameliorating their circumstances by the usual means: bribery, connections, influence. What becomes rapidly clear is that these characters, while they may be physically badly deformed, compensate by being mentally and morally robust. Religious faith is ruled out as a possible source of moral sustenance, since faith can help only those who wish to live outside the system (Laptev, for instance), but not the majority who accept that they have to live in the environment in which they find themselves. Ultimately people have to make a choice: to be or not to be. As "Robot" observes, that question is of much greater immediacy to people like himself, "Slepoi" and "Teoretik" than to the occasional Danish prince. For "Robot" the answer is clear. No matter how deep on occasion might be his despair: live! Live the life you've been given, it is the only one you will get. Life is an eyeblink between nothing and nothing.[10]

Approximately two thirds of the total number of texts in *Zhivi* form chains as follows, some of them containing as few as two links:

Chains

1. *word link: ispoved´*: 1/2; *zhit´ ili ne zhit´*: 3/4/5; *ukhazher*: 5/7; *ona/ ee*: **5/8**; *pereryv*: **30**, 31. **42/43**: *klub*; *zhivi*: 50/**51**; *prazdnik urodov*: 53/54; *anonimka*: 64/65; *ideologiia...*: 69/70; *mir posle 3-ei mirovoi voiny*: 112/113/114; *smert´* : 125/126.
2. *temporal continuity*: **5, 6**, 7, **8, 9**, 10, 11, **12**, 13, 14, 15, **16**, 17, 18, 26, **27**, 28, **30**, 33?, 35, 38, 39, **40, 41, 42, 43, 49**, 50.
3. *"Buddha"*: **6, 9, 40**.
4. *characters*: **8**, 24, **27, 40**, 42, 43, 44, 45, 46, 47, 48.
5. *texts containing verse*: **12, 49, 102**, 115, 126.
6. *"worm" string*: **16**, 31, 55, 59, 67, 72, 109.
7. *"Fiancee"*: 24, 25, **41**, 60, 85, 107, 116.
8. *"R's invention"*: 28, 52, 77, 78, 79, 97, 106, [122?].
9. *"the club"*: **43, 49**, 99.
10. *title link: zhivi*: **51**, 71, 101, 111; *mnenie...*: **54/55**, *mysli...*:108/109.
11. *"Disabled day"*: **53, 54**, 55, 75, 95.
12. *"day out" chain*: 90, 91, 92, 93, 94.

Total: 83
Total no. of texts in *Zhivi*: 127

Noteworthy is chain 2. It is by far the longest in the work and, most unusually for Zinov'ev, describes a temporal sequence. The texts in chain 2 effectively constitute "a day in the life" of Andrei Ivanovich Gorev, alias "Robot", the first person narrator, whose "confession" is set out in texts 2-125. The kaleidoscopic effect which Zinov'ev achieves by juxtaposing texts from different chains is nonetheless preserved. This, as always, allows him to bring together different strands of argument, illuminate problems from a variety of angles, intersperse his prose texts with those containing verse. The texts in bold figure in more than one chain. Thus, interspersed with aspects of Gorev's description of an average working day (Chain 2) are texts introducing particular characters (Chain 4), Gorev's thoughts on Buddha (Chain 3), his yearning for "Nevesta" (Chain 7), and so on.

But there are also links to other works. "Robot" was born in Atomgrad, the secret town near Partgrad (text 1). We know that the factory where "Robot" works is in Partgrad. There are references to Novye Lipki, the neighbourhood where Ivan Laptev lives (texts 104, 127). Laptev and laptizm are discussed in text 6, in which we learn that Ivan Laptev's period when he believed he was God predates the time frame of *Zhivi*. Important Party and Government figures to whom allusion is made in the other works under discussion and who wield great power in Partgrad either directly or indirectly likewise receive frequent mention: Suslikov (texts 29, 36, 70, 93, 103); Mitrofan Lukich (text 37); Korytov (text 70); Krutov (text 88); Portiankin (text 123). Suslikov, Korytov and Krutov play important roles in *Katastroika*.

Another feature, present to a much greater extent in *Zhivi* than in any other work written by Zinov´ev is the use of proper names. Zinov´ev has usually given his characters sociological labels ("Sociologist", "Thinker", and so on) to emphasize the extent to which, in Soviet society, individuals have no intrinsic worth, other than as functional cogs in the Soviet machine. In *Zhivi*, although labels are still provided, they are nicknames which accompany names: Anastasiia ("Nevesta"), Sergei Pavlovich ("Romantik"), Iurii Chernov ("Teoretik"), and so on. Why has Zinov´ev chosen to do this? Does it reflect an ideological change in the status of the post-Soviet citizen: people are now individuals? Does Zinov´ev believe that if he gives his characters names, the reader will feel more sympathy for them? If so, his belief is naive. His characters remain as cypher-like as they ever did, mere vehicles for the expression of a variety of opinions on questions of politics, sociology and morality.

Idi na Golgofu and *Zhivi*, however, do not only share the same physical environment. The time-frame for both is the early period of Gorbachev's perestroika. The "action" in *Idi na Golgofu*, however, predates that of *Zhivi*, as we have seen with regard to Ivan Laptev. But there are important parallels. Thus, Laptev's discussions about Christianity in *Idi na Golgofu* have their counterpart in Gorev's reflections on Buddha and Buddhism in *Zhivi*. Laptev's discussions with Antipod on religion versus ideology have their counterpart in *Zhivi* between Belov and Chernov on the nature of a "healthy" society. It is not difficult to see how the respective strands of texts could be interwoven on a larger canvas.

But there are difficulties, largely connected with the mode of discourse of Zinov´ev's characters. They seem to share the same idiolect. It is consequently very difficult, if not impossible, to distinguish between Laptev's longing for his "Boginia" in *Idi na Golgofu* and Gorev's longing for his "Nevesta" in *Zhivi*. For the same reason it would be difficult sometimes to determine which of the first-person narrators was speaking on a variety of topics concerning aspects of Soviet life in which neither religion nor the plight of the disabled was discussed.[11]

We turn now to a consideration of *Katastroika*, the final work to be discussed in this paper. If the primary perspective of *Idi na Golgofu*, *Evangelie dlia Ivana* and *Zhivi* has been the "worm's eye view" of the respective narrators, in *Katastroika* the perspective is "top down", reflecting that of the "omniscient author". Moreover, in *Katastroika* the figure of Gorbachev appears, acting in collusion with Zinov'ev's personages who represent the Soviet "Party and Government", namely Suslikov, Korytov, Krutov and others. Thus *Katastroika* provides the over-all context of the Soviet Union in general and Partgrad in particular during the period of perestroika, within which unprotected individuals at the bottom of the social scale such as Ivan Laptev, Gorev, "Slepoi", "Romantik", have to struggle for survival.

The structure of *Katastroika* is relatively simple for a Zinov'ev work. It consists of 103 texts which can be loosely grouped together to form four separate sections, framed by a prologue and epilogue. Only forty of the texts are incorporated into chains, some of which are very short.[12] The prologue heralds the intention of the Partgrad authorities to turn provincial Partgrad into a "beacon of perestroika" and to promote it as a tourist attraction. The epilogue tells us that the project was successful. The four "sections" decribe repectively the nature of the project, the history of Partgrad, the implementation of Gorbachev's perestroika in Partgrad and the realization of the project.

The "chains" are as follows:

1. *"temporal continuity"* : 2, 3, 5?[13]
2. *"commentary"*: 4, 7, 12, 17[14]
3. *"title" chain: soveshchanie...*: 8/9; Partgrad...24/25[15]
4. *"history of Partgrad"*: 14, 15, 16, 18, 19, 20, 21, 33, 35[16]
5. *"liberalisation in Partgrad"*: 53, 54, 55, 56, 57
6. *"perestroika"*: 60, 61, 62, 65, 67, 68
7. *"tourist route"*: 81, 82, 83, 85, 87, 90, 92, 94, 96[17]

Total: 40

In quantitative terms, less than half of *Katastroika* is structured. Moreover, since none of the texts occurs in more than one chain, we can see that the density of structure is very 'thin' by comparison with other works, notably *Idi na Golgofu*. On the other hand, there are several texts which are important for the links they establish with the other works. These links can be tabulated as follows:

Suslikov:	2, 3, 4, 5, 6, 8, 22, 27, 34, 35, 74, 102
Korytov:	8, 11, 75, 78, 79, 90, 99
Krutov:	74, 76
Mitrofan Lukich Portiankin:	20, 27, 34, 35
Atomgrad:	23
Artificial limb factory:	63
Laptev/Laptizm:	71
"Bard":	72

Let us now review the basic data which we have assembled in order to demonstrate how Zinov´ev might have produced *Iskushenie*. The total number of texts of all four works is 621 and the total number of pages is 688. This is an accurate count, but the size of print varies a little from book to book. We are thus speaking of a book about the size of *Ziiaiushchie vysoty*. (That work contains 600 texts and occupies 591 pages, but the type-size is smaller.) The total number of chains is sixty, and these chains contain 430 texts or almost two thirds of the total number of texts comprising the four works. This proportion is well within the limits established for other major works, notably *Ziiaiushchie vysoty* and *Zheltyi dom*.

On the basis of the data presented in this article, there are many ways in which the various components could be combined. Perhaps the most obvious way would be to use *Katastroika* as an over-arching framework, within which the stories of Laptev and Gorev could unfold. Laptev's would come before Gorev's, and the various "prayers" in *Evangelie dlia Ivana* could easily be interwoven with Laptev's prose texts on religious, moral and pragmatic themes. The chains in Katastroika would allow the "project" to unfold gradually, within which framework the cynicism of the its authors (Suslikov, Gorbachev, Krutov) would be highlighted by the humanity of Laptev and Gorev, and the callous disregard for the welfare of ordinary citizens would be underscored by the hardship that Gorev and the other "worms" endure. "Worm" is Gorev's epithet, which he uses constantly with reference to himself and his unfortunate companions.

The result would be a book in the mould of *Zheltyi dom*. The hero of that work (JRF) would have his counterparts in Laptev and Gorev. JRF's companions like Teacher, Himself and Herself would have theirs in Antipod, "Slepoi", "Romantik", "Boginia", "Nevesta". There would also be contrasting themes, again reflected in various chains: Christianity/Communist ideology (*Idi na Golgofu*) interspersed with Buddhism/life on this earth (*Zhivi*); the nature of health/faith healing (*Idi na Golgofu*); the definition of health and its norms, both at the level of the individual and society

(*Zhivi*); the nature of possible moral codes in Soviet society: for non-conforming individuals (*Idi na Golgofu*), for the conforming, but underprivileged individuals suffering severe handicaps (*Zhivi*). The book would not merely replicate what Zinov´ev had done in *Ziiaiushchie vysoty, V preddverii raia, Zheltyi dom*. These works, allegorically or otherwise, described classical Soviet Communism. The four works discussed in this paper describe the transition to post-communism. Zinov´ev uses them to exemplify his long-standing thesis that Soviet Communism was the highest peak of social development to which the Russians could aspire. Beyond that lay only degradation.

In conclusion we might note two points of interest. The structure of *Idi na Golgofu* is much more complex than appears at first sight. We can quantify this observation by comparing the sets of data gathered for each of the four works discussed. The second, more interesting point is the exent to which textual study of Zinov´ev's works demonstrates how closely he exemplified Foucault's contention that an author is constrained by the "juridical and institutional system" within which he/she has to work. Zinov´ev has developed an approach to "écriture" which allows him to adapt with ease to whichever system he happens to find himself in. He can "make" books to any length, in any style or mix of styles. It is a nice irony that, having adapted to his new environment after his expulsion to the West by writing short, individual books, he can now witness their being reprinted in Russia as "long" books in various combinations, for instance, *Gomo sovetikus* (Zinov´ev 1991) and *Kommunizm kak real´nost´* (Zinov´ev 1994).

REFERENCES

Brown, E. J., 1987. "Zinoviev, Aleshkovsky, Rabelais, Sorrentino, Possibly Pynchon, Maybe James Joyce, and Certainly Tristram Shandy: a Comparative Study of a Satirical Mode", in L. Fleishman, G. Freidin, R.D. Schupbach and W.M.Todd III (eds), *Stanford Slavic Studies* 1: 307–25.

Foucault, M., 1988. "What is an Author", translated from the French by Joseph V. Harari, reprinted in D. Lodge (ed.), *Modern Criticism and Theory* (London: Longman), 197–210.

Hanson, P. and M. Kirkwood, 1988. *Alexander Zinoviev as Writer and Thinker: An Assessment* (London: Macmillan).

Kirkwood, M., 1982. "Elements of Structure in Zinoviev's *Zheltyi dom*", *Essays in Poetics* 7, 2: 108–10.

——, 1987. "Notes on the Structure of Alexander Zinoviev's *Ziiaiushchie vysoty*", *Scottish Slavonic Review* 8: 91–108.

——, 1992. "*Ziiaiushchie vysoty* and its Serialization in *Oktiabr´* ", *The Slavonic and East European Review* 70, 3: 420–52.

——, 1993. *Alexander Zinoviev: An Introduction to his Work* (London: Macmillan).

McMillin, A.B., 1988. "Zinoviev's Fiction in the Context of Unofficial Russian Prose of the 1970s", in P. Hanson and M. Kirkwood (eds), *Alexander Zinoviev as Writer and Thinker: An Assessment* (London: Macmillan), 61–70.

Oktiabr´, 1991 1: 36–97; 2: 23–82; 3: 59–81.

Zinov´ev, A.A., 1976. *Ziiaiushchie vysoty* (Lausanne: L'Age d'Homme).

——, 1978. *Svetloe budushchee* (Lausanne: L'Age d'Homme).

——, 1979. *V preddverii raia* (Lausanne: L'Age d'Homme).

——, 1980. *Zheltyi dom* (Lausanne: L'Age d'Homme).

——, 1984. *Evangelie dlia Ivana* (Lausanne: L'Age d'Homme).

——, 1985. *Idi na Golgofu* (Lausanne: L'Age d'Homme).

——, 1986. *The Madhouse* (London: Gollancz).

——, 1989a. *Zhivi* (Lausanne: L'Age d'Homme).

——, 1989b. *Mon Tchekhov* (Brussels: Editions Complexe).

——, 1989c. *L'Allegra Russia* (Milan: SugarCo Edizioni).

——, 1990. *Katastroika* (Lausanne: L'Age d'Homme).

——, 1990. *Les confessions d'un homme en trop* (Paris: Olivier Orban).

——, 1991. *Gomo sovetikus. Moi dom — moia chuzhbina* (Prilozhenie k zhurnalu *Lepta*), (Moscow: Kor-Inf).

——, 1994. *Kommunizm kak real'nost´. Konets kommunizma* (Moscow: "Tsentrpoligraf").

NOTES

1. Aleksandr Zinov´ev has expressed this opinion to me on more than one occasion in the course of private conversation.

2. As a matter of fact, Zinov´ev does occasionally engage in self-plagiarism and there are quite a few examples of this scattered through his vast *oeuvre*. Nevertheless, as a proportion of the total output, it amounts to probably less than one per cent.

3. In earlier work I used the notion of "strand", many of which "interwove" to form the "fabric" of Zinov´ev's works. However, a study of Zinov´ev's own abridgement of *Ziiaiushchie vysoty* showed me that, in fact, "chain" is a more useful metaphor, consisting as it does of "links" (individual texts), any number of which can be removed. For a fuller discussion of this see Kirkwood 1992, 420-52.

4.   For a more detailed discussion of the relationships indicated by the bracketing, see Kirkwood 1993, 81–83. Text number 9 is free-standing with respect to the other texts in the first twenty, but links in with a series of texts in Part III of *Ziiaiushchie vysoty* dealing with Chatterer's notes on Dauber and his art.

5.   This question receives fuller treatment in Kirkwood 1982, 108–10.

6.   It contains, however, some of the funniest writing in the entire book. In particular it contains Zinov'ev's description of the Soviet countryside and what made it "Soviet".

7.   The sentence in question "This time I'm leaving the Institute by the Escort Method", in *The Madhouse*, 141, refers back to the text entitled Ways of skiving off", *The Madhouse*, 76–79.

8.   This figure is sufficiently accurate for the purposes of this paper. It was computed by checking each member of each chain just once against a check-list of all the texts in the book numbered from 1–206 and then subtracting from 206 the number of texts in the check-list which did not feature in any of the chains. This was a complicated task and the possibility of slight error cannot be excluded.

9,   There are two further points about the title and content of the work under discussion. Several of the texts in *Evangelie dlia Ivana* appear in other works, notably *V preddverii raia*, *Zheltyi dom* and *Allegra Russia*. Indeed, the latter work consists entirely of verses taken from *Evangelie dlia Ivana* together with translations in French, English and Italian as "commentaries" on thirty of Zinov'ev's paintings. Secondly, the texts which first appeared in *V preddverii raia* were referred to as "evangelie ot Ivana". This, in my opinion, is a more appropriate title, since it suggests the "Gospel according to [St] Ivan". Why Zinov'ev changed it is unclear.

10. It is significant that Zinov'ev himself was apparently experiencing a moral crisis during the period when he was writing *Zhivi*. See Zinov'ev 1990, 420–26.

11. A similar phenomenon occurs in *Zheltyi dom*. In Part I the narrator is JRF, in Part III it is SRF. They both have practically identical views which they express in practically identical language. The reader knows who is speaking in Part III only because in that section of the novel JRF speaks in the third person. If the narrators of *Idi na Golgofu* and *Zhivi* were to appear on the same page of an amalgamated work, some such solution would have to be found.

12. For a fuller discussion of this work see Kirkwood 1993, 196–220.

13. This chain is very short in comparison with the corresponding chain in *Zhivi*. However, continuity is such a rare phenomenon in Zinov'ev's work that almost any example of such a chain merits inclusion.

14. These texts form a commentary to chain 1.

15. These texts share part of a common title.

16. The "labels" for chains 4–6 are self-explanatory.
17. So-called because these texts decribe the various "tourist routes" set up by the authorities which will present Partgrad to foreigners in the most favourable light possible.

THE DISSOLUTION OF REALITY IN SASHA SOKOLOV'S MEZHDU SOBAKOI I VOLKOM

Hanna Kolb

Sasha Sokolov's second novel, *Mezhdu sobakoi i volkom* (Between dog and wolf), written in exile and published in 1980, is not easily accessible to the reader: it is a complex mosaic of various linguistic levels comprising regional elements and the base language of the peasants, neologisms, the language of the Bible as well as everyday Soviet speech and Russian colloquial. Each word and idiomatic phrase may be understood literally and thus it may assume a new additional meaning or even develop a plot-building dynamic of its own. Sokolov plays with language and with the sound of words; similar sounds lead to extensive and ever-expanding chains of association.

Once this jungle of words has been fought through, the reader encounters new difficulties. Many figures present striking similarities, but they are not to be totally identified with each other. Many events are rendered in different versions. Each version is so anchored in the narrative as a whole that if one considers it a lie of the unreliable narrator, the whole section of the narration turns out to be false, and so on *ad infinitum*. The reader's situation may be compared to looking at one of M.C. Escher's picture-puzzles. There are three parallel narrative strands of equal status: the petition of the one-legged grinder Il´ia Zynzyrela, the story of the gamekeeper Iakov Palamakhterov, and the cycle of poems which, according to Sokolov, is the work of Iakov (Smith 1987, 327, n. 14).

The action takes place in the Upper Volga region, a mythical place inhabited by cripples and drunkards, a town with the telling name of Gorodnishche, where the poor of poorest live, and a place called Bydgoshch whose identity is as mysterious as the derivation of its name (perhaps taken from the Polish city of Bydgoszcz?). The most common causes of death are murder and suicide.

In this place something known as "Zaitil´shchina" is going on, a feud between the cripple Il´ia and the gamekeeper. The concept of "Zaitil´shchina" may be understood in various ways. Echoing the *Zadonshchina* epic which tells the story of the 1380 battle with Mamai, it is Il´ia's report of his feud with the gamekeepers: "Imenno s togo dnia est´-poshla eta smutnaia Zaitil´shchina, to est´ te nelady, radi koikh i razoriaius´ na kantseliarii" (136) (It was from that very day that this troubled Zaitil´shchina began, that is those disorders which have led to my being ruined in the department);[1] a report which, under this name, is being continued in several stages throughout the novel. The reference to a legendary fourteenth-century text indicates that the events described here are outside the teleological progress of history, in the timelessness of provincial Russia. Moreover, "Zaitil´shchina" may be understood in terms of space — the area beyond the Volga whose old Tatar name is Itil´, a mythical place, "not of this world". The use of the name Itil´ suggests that nothing has changed since the time of Tatar rule. Finally, Zaitil´shchina, in analogy to Pugachevshchina or Khrushchevshchina, is a certain state of being and way of life characterized by a "striving for a world beyond this world" on the one hand and hopelessness and stagnation on the other. There are unmistakable religious undertones, for the "striving" manifests itself in the passion of the Volga folk for a mysterious lady who recalls Blok's *neznakomka*, a kind of Hagia Sophia: "No vozliubili takzhe i damu prishluiu, i liubite bezzavetno, kotoraia vam nikto, i eto tozhe naravne s bezobraziiami i tat´boi nareku Zaitil´shchinoi" (p. 141) (But you have also fallen in love with a strange lady, and love wholeheartedly, who is no-one to you, and this as well as the disgraces and thieving I call Zaitil´shchina).

This "eternal life", this timeless, a-historical condition between life and death is not only manifested in the reflections and variations of constantly recurring motifs, but also in a number of activities — skating, hunting and drinking — which in their constant repetition and apparent lack of purpose are of an almost ritual, magical character. They are described by countless synonyms and paraphrases — linguistic variations of the never-changing. The deeply Russian credo of Zaitil´shchina is enacted and re-enacted: the futility of all human striving, the non-existence of any ultimate purpose, either in the life of the individual or history itself. The idea that man lives "not by bread alone" applied to the hunter Gurii, an inspired skater, becomes

"Khlebom, byvalo, ego ne kormi — dai razletet´sia po skol´zkomu" (12). (When, as happened, we didn't give him bread, he would fly about on the slippery surface.) The phraseologism wins back its literal meaning, for the Volga folk in fact prefer liquid to solid food, and scenes of eating are almost completely absent, while drinking is ubiquitous.

Skating is the favourite occupation of the Volga population. The intertwining circles and pirouettes of the skaters symbolize most graphically the repetitiveness of the eternal recurrences, the lack of linear chronology, and the net of interrelationships in which all the characters and events are trapped.

Like the permanent twilight, drinking, described with an abundance of synonyms and paraphrases, leads to a particular perception of reality, to the confusion between dog and wolf: "Pomalu ne p´esh´, / Ottogo-to sobaku / Svoiu volkom zovesh´" (117) (You always have a good drink / And that is why you call / Your dog a wolf). Like everything in Zaitil´shchina, drunkenness is in a dialectical relationship between on the one hand a kind of freedom and on the other self-destruction, misery and poverty.

Zaitil´shchina is a place suspended between life and death on the thin ice in the middle of the frozen river, but at the same time a state suspended between the futility of man's earthly existence and the unlimited, eternal freedom of another world. It is, however, completely static in its dialectical oscillation, and its inherent rejection of any teleology is frozen into the monotony and timelessness of the Volga world.

From the start Sokolov, who was born in Canada in 1943 as the son of a Soviet diplomat, but who was brought up in the Soviet Union, never submitted to Soviet literary conventions. Thus, his first book, *Shkola dlia durakov* (School for fools [Ann Arbor: Ardis, 1976]), could only be published abroad, and led to his emigration. The time he spent as a gamekeeper in the Upper Volga region (when he wrote *Shkola dlia durakov*), is clearly embodied in *Mezhdu sobakoi i volkom*. *Shkola dlia durakov* consists of a long monologue/dialogue of two narrators who are in fact one person, the "fool", a special-school pupil with an antagonistically split personality. In this poetic stream of consciousness built on a series of associations there are contradictions and inconsistencies too, deriving from the narrator's schizophrenia. In *Mezhdu sobakoi i volkom*, amongst other voices, is that of an adolescent who wishes to create the world to his own liking, in this case without schizophrenic motivation. In this novel, however, it is just one narrative mode amongst others in which Sokolov's heroes express their lack of interest in reality.

Placing Sokolov in the Soviet literary context is largely impossible — the differences are too great. Olga Matich is, however, right to suggest for *Shkola dlia durakov* the influence of Russian Youth Prose of the sixties, at the centre of which was youthful self-awareness with its subjective, rebellious perception of the world. *Mezhdu sobakoi i volkom*, on the other hand, is a reaction against the second main tendency in Soviet literature of the sixties and seventies, Village Prose (Matich 1987, 310). The spiritually healthy world of the village with its eternal Russian values is only a parodic backdrop; the depraved and unreal world on the Volga is completely different from the highly idealized and socially committed depictions of the *derevenshchiki*.

The third and latest novel of Sokolov, *Palisandriia* (1985) is an obvious satire. Disguised as science fiction, the book parodies memoir literature, popular with émigré writers, which was to come to the fore with *glasnost'*. The fictitious memoirs of Palisandr Dal'berg, a foster-child of the Kremlin, written in 2024, mock any concept of historical truth, any belief that the past can be reconstructed: "the past is even less knowable than the present day" (Sokolov 1985, 12). Alluding to Svetlana Allilueva's memoirs, intimate details of Kremlin life are related regardless of anachronisms (Palisandr is the great-nephew of Rasputin and the nephew of Beriia) "as it really was". Palisandr gives new versions of the deaths of Beriia and Stalin, he shakes up historical events and brings back to life layers of the Russian literary language buried by time and the Revolution. In recent Soviet times a comparable mistrust of history and time can be found only in the "bad" writing of Valentin Kataev's *mauvisme* (von Ssachno 1979, 208–19; Borden 1987, 247–63). The question of Nabokov's influence on Sokolov continues to be debated, although Sokolov strongly denies it (Johnson 1987, 153–62). The experimental approach to language refers us to the beginning of the century in Russia, to the word and world creative spirit of the avantgarde and to the poetic prose of Ornamentalism with its interest in the acoustic properties of words. Sokolov takes up with this interrupted tradition, and the categories developed for the poetics of the avant garde can be applied to him, as will be shown in this study.

Sokolov is plainly not interested in depicting an empirically credible reality, a historical truth. For him the literary world is nothing but the product of the artist's consciousness and does not cross its boundary (Sokolov 1989c, 195–202). This creative principle is transferred to his characters who create their own inner world through speech. Thus *Shkola dlia durakov* may be interpreted as the fantasy of the mentally sick hero, albeit modified by the interference of the "author" and the introduction of short stories into the text. In *Mezhdu sobakoi i volkom* many different voices are heard which may not be readily traced to a specific source. The displacements and condensations can no longer be explained by psychological blunders, as one was tempted to do with *Shkola dlia durakov*.[2] A realistic and satisfactory solution of the contradictions is impossible.

In the twilight Il'ia cannot distinguish "between dog and wolf" and thrashes the hunters' dog, which becomes the initial cause of his feud with them. Thus the novel's *siuzhet* arises from a phrase which is taken literally and unfolded. "*Mezhdu sobakoi i volkom*" is calqued from the Latin *inter canem et lupum* and denotes the hour of twilight, the intermediate period between day and night when a shepherd can no longer distinguish between a dog and a wolf. But such an intermediate state is ubiquitous in this text, not only for the relationship between day and night, but also between life and death, between past, present and future, between the two banks of the Volga, and between the different identities of the characters. Time, space and characters: these are the elements which make the telling of a story possible in the first place. In what follows I hope to show how these basic components of the story are dissolved in various ways, as if attacked by a corrosive acid, while at the same time language achieves the power to create a world of its own.

I. THE DISSOLUTION OF REALITY

"... i shchemiashchee oshchushchenie, chto vse vokrug v nashem nerazreshimom *zdes'* proiskhodit lish' iakoby, ne ostavlialo ego v oznachennyi vecher ne na minutu." (64)

(...and the oppressive feeling that everything around us in our incomprehensible *here and now* was happening only conditionally did not leave him for a moment on the evening in question.)

a. The dissolution of time

The "dating" of Il'ia's petition defies any attempt to establish a system of time: "Mesiats iasen, za chislami ne usledish', god nyneshnii" (9). "Mesiats iasen" (The moon is clear) can be read as either a (pseudo-) indication of calendar time ("the month is clear") or as a description of the moon's appearance ("the moon is [clear] light").[3] Like the old-fashioned use of *leta* for *gody*, mingling the concept of years with summers, the word play here denotes the origin of these measurements of time from nature's seasonal succession: in contrast to the linear time of dates and years is set the cyclical time of times of day, days of the week, months and seasons of the year; the Orthodox church year with its *Kanun, Sochel'nik, Sreten'e* and *Uspen'e*, with the namedays and feasts (*ot Paskhi do Pokrova*, 49) together with the Communist *pervomai* (142). Alongside the Latin names the months are called by such Russian names as *senognoi, listoboi, bokogrei* and *ledostav*,

which emphasize their close links to nature and at the same time appear
to derive from an archaic age.

In all Sokolov's books his characters express various theories about time
which, although they are not identical, nonetheless all discuss the chimerical
nature of a progressive, linear time that produces causality. The special
school pupil in *Shkola dlia durakov* constantly refers to his "problem with
time": "in general in our mind something is wrong with time" (Sokolov
1988, 22–23). His "selective memory" he regards as a defect, but also as
a privilege that allows him to live according to his own will. Calendars
with their ordering of days do not correspond to the time of the soul: this
time does not resemble a line but "a sheet of paper with a multitude of
dots on it" (Sokolov 1988, 34).

In *Mezhdu sobakoi i volkom* an individual theory of time is expressed
by the ancient hunter Krylobyl, "the wise serpent" (112), who was here
from the very beginning and who compares time to a river which flows
at different speeds in different places:

> davai s toboi ne vremia voz´mem, a vodu obychnuiu. A davai. I ostanovi
> vpechatlenie, tormoshit, v zavodi ona prakticheski ne idet, ee riaska dushit,
> trava, a na strezhne — stremglav; tak i vremia fiksiruet, ob´´iasnial, v
> Gorodnishche shustrit, makhom kryla strizha, priblizitel´no, v Bydgoshche —
> ni shatko ni valko, v lesakh – sovsem tish´ da glad´. (156)

> (let us take not time but ordinary water. Go on. And hold your impression,
> it agitates, in a backwater it hardly moves, it is held back by the duckweed,
> the grass, but in the main channel it runs headlong; that is how time works,
> he would explain: in Gorodnishche it races along, like the stroke of a martin's
> wing, more or less, in Bydgoshch neither this nor that, and in the forests as
> quiet as anything.)

This theory is "empirically" confirmed by the observation that in different
places there are different seasons of the year: autumn in the forest, winter
in Gorodnishche and spring on the Volga (89).

Because of the different speeds of time, the theft of Il´ia's crutches,
according to Krylobyl's words, has not yet taken place on the other side
of the river, and so the cripple crosses the river to recover them: "Prinial
ia eto k svedeniiu i zaezdil na budushchem chelnoke v pozaproshloe" (156–
57) (I took this into account and made a trip in a future boat into the
pluperfect).

This leitmotiv of repeated crossing of the river occurs at various points
in the text in past, present and future, recalling the dissolution of time
in the synchronicity of past, present and future tense in *Shkola dlia
durakov*. In the latter novel, too, all three are nothing but equal variations,

as the narrator makes a mythical and mystical journey on the river Lethe, transformed into a water-lily. The domination of time is abolished on the river: "Dear Leonardo, not long ago (just now, in a short time) I was floating (am floating, will float) down a big river in a rowboat" (34). On the other hand, the constant flowing of the river in *Mezhdu sobakoi i volkom* symbolizes the movement of time whilst on both banks time stands still and life is eternal (167). We obtain, on the one hand, a picture of incalculably (now quickly, now slowly) flowing time which destroys the categories of past, present and future, and, on the other hand, of the stagnation of human existence which is not in the least affected by this flow of time.

The river of time also symbolizes the boundary between life and death which can be crossed in both directions. The dead can recross the river and again mix with the living. The different metaphors for the passing of time, like the river of time, an hour-glass (53), the sieve through which the years pass (40), the grinding of a mill, all symbolize the transitoriness of human life and aspiration, and freeze into pictures of endless repetition.

Where there is no forward-moving, linear time, there can also be no history: "sensations have been abolished" and therefore "there are no newspaper boys" (100). The reference to the period of stagnation in the Soviet Union cannot be missed (if you believe *Palisandriia*, the passage of time was broken and replaced by a period of stillness in Russia when Beriia hung himself (!) from a hand of the Kremlin clock): the stagnation of the Brezhnev era and the timelessness of provincial Russia are henceforth inseparably linked.

Also chimerical are yesterday's sensations, to which they have to turn, since there are no present ones; the following mixture of newspaper stories from throughout the world are obviously pseudo-news mocking the sensation-seeking of historical thought, and mixing in anachronistic play the old, the new and the timeless: "In China they chopped off dogs' heads. Turkey smelled of coffee and tobacco [...] in Bulgaria the Bashibuzuki have murdered fifteen thousand! [...] The Siberian highway has been built" (101-02). Wars, revolutions and other political events are demonstratively not mentioned; their existence, however, is indirectly revealed through occasional details. The post-war period is indicated by many mutilated men and the popular wartime song, "Ia liubliu tebia moi staryi park" (I love you, my old park),[4] as well as the fact that the sailor had been evacuated in his youth (107). From this time derive the components of the imaginational matrix on which the text is based. This historical frame, however, lies outside the consciousness of the characters who move in a timeless space. The author's pointer is recognizable only by the reader who must co-operate in order to establish the frame, just as he must bring his knowledge of the

circumstances of Sokolov's life to bear, in order to understand the autobiographical references.[5]

b. The dissolution of space

According to Bakhtin every space (topos) has its specific time (chronos),
which may be placed in relationship to other chronotopes, for which he
gives as an example the "provincial town" (in Flaubert and others) with
its "cyclical everyday time" which provides the background for "temporal
sequences that are more charged with energy and event" (Bakhtin 1981,
247–48). This chronotopical principle is taken absurdly literally in *Mezhdu
sobakoi i volkom*. Insofar as that time in various places flows at different
speeds, and that at any time in any one place a different season may be
found, the inner, subjective perception of time to which Bakhtin refers
(cyclical time, biographical time) is revealed. The river symbolizes the flow
of time, and is itself a spatial factor; thus, all movements in space are at
the same time movements in time.

   This "overloaded" chronotope, in which each space really has its own
time, is only the most extreme expression of a general tendency in the novel
to produce independent space-time clusters, individual motifs of varying
extent which, whilst standing outside any chronology, are defined in terms
of space-time, in that certain events and places form firm constellations.
The chronotope is the basis on which the event materializes, and this
unfolding of the event, even without being fixed chronologically, is already
a temporal factor. The event-place combination is then repeated in manifold
reflections. Thus, there are various "places of promiscuousness": the park
with swings, and the place under the boat, whose reflection is the place
under the stairs. In these places various characters meet for love games:
Iakov, Il´ia with Orina/the feeble-minded girl, and groups such as the sailors
with Orina/the feeble-minded girl.

   The leitmotiv-like, repeated clusters produce individual, self-contained
chronotopes, of which the most striking is the crossing of the river. Even
more plainly separated from the text as a whole are the individual scenes
which are inserted into the text with a quite different time and place, as,
for example, in the hunting seat of one Ludwig (103) or "in the Indian
summer of 1916 in Bzura" (98). The "montage" effect of disparate "snippets
of reality" leads, as in *Shkola dlia durakov*, to what Felix Philip Ingold
has called "the relativization of spatial conditions and connections" (Ingold
1979, 116).[6] Associative imagination crosses the boundaries of space and
time and sets up chronotopic clusters in a new whole, according to its own
rules.

Like the indications of time, the names of places also lose any referential validity through disintegration into their component parts, synonyms, and distinctly relativistic, purely euphonic use. Although the text is teeming with topographical data, which are partially or wholly known from outside the reality of the novel, this information hinders rather than assists the building of a spatial image. The reader becomes the witness of the genesis and, on the contrary, the pseudo-etymological dismemberment of these names, as a result of which the places themselves forfeit their reality. The locality Vyshelbaushi appears, only to be immediately dissolved again in the witticism from which it arose: when the Drunken Hunter is asked whether such a "Vyshelbaushi" exists he replies "it is a homestead with three yards", but is mocked as "vyshe lba ushei ne mozhet stat´sia" (120) (ears cannot grow above the forehead).[7] The village name Mukomolovo is subjected to constant transformations and new meanings. It is introduced in two variants, of which the first sounds rather like a counting rhyme, "zhil on v Mylo, mozhno skazat´, Mukomolove" (10) (he lived in Mylo, one could say Mukomolovo), and then in speech disintegrates into its constituent parts: "Malokulebiakovo - malo li v Kulebiakove kto zhivet" (14) (Malokulebiakovo — who knows who lives in Kulebiakovo). The following Gogolesque discourse parodies both the Soviet practice of changing place names and the creation of sound associations which are challenged by the different "speaking" name variants:

...kakoe eto selo tut budet u vas? Ne obessud´, Malekulebiakovo, mol. A ia dumal – Mykomukomolovo tut budet u vas. Net, Mykomulolomovo – pesnia davniaia, Mykomulolomovym my prezhde zvalis´. Khm, a Milokurelemovo v takom variante zhe? Malokulelemovo, reche, v drugoi storone sovsem, u nas nikogda ne kulemali. (92)

(...and what's this village we have got here? Don't think about it, he says, it's Malokulebiakovo. But I thought, this Mylomukomolovo will be one of yours. No, Mykomulolomovo is old hat, Mykomulolomovo is what we were called before. Hm and where is Milokurelemovo, in such a version? Malokulelemovo, he says, is in a completely different direction, we have never done a little (*malo*) trapping [*kulemali* — an invented word, perhaps associated with *kulemka* — a trap for ermine, sable etc.])[8]

The variants of this chameleon-like ever-changing place name are reviewed in a different time dimension and convey to the reader the hopelessness of linking this name with a particular place. In one of the inserted passages, a traveller with Pushkinesque curly sideburns tries in vain to decipher the name of the place: "razobrat´sia dopodlinno — Malo-li-to-Kulebiakovo,

Mylo-li-Kulelemovo - ne dostaet pronitsatel´nosti" (105) (to sort it out properly — Who-knows-Kulebiakova, is it soapy Kulelemovo — I can't get to the bottom of it). The constantly changing spellings of names and the use of synonyms destroy the identity of places: there are four different spellings of Bydgoshch, and the Volga is also referred to as Itil´, Volch´ia (reka), Volka-rechka, and Valdai.

Symbolic space enters into competition with real experienceable space and overlays it, installing its own mythic-mystical order. "Zaitil´shchina" can be understood as both a place and a condition, and the ever-present twilight (*sumerki*) has a spatio-temporal extension (*v sumerkakh*) as well as a metaphysical implication of a mode of being between light and dark, good and evil, life and death: "Stranen krai tvoi na grani / Mezh svetom i t´moi" (116) (Your land is strange, at the border / Of light and darkness).

Two symbolic, metaphysical boundaries, the railway line and the river, cut through the space. Continuing the Lethe /Styx myth, the river is clearly a boundary between life and death ("Itil´" is a consonantal anagram of "Leta" [Lethe]: Witte 1989, 128) crossed by the drowning, and the railway tracks are the scene of death and mutilation.[9] The relationship between the two is again parallel: Orina's assignations with the railwaymen take place near the tracks, with the sailors by the river.

Here, on the railway line and on the river is found the central zone of the intermediate condition, the place of its highest concentration which radiates out to the nearby places like the riverside settlements and the railway station. Thus the entire topological organization of the Itil´ world is subjected to the laws of the symbolic.

c. *The dissolution of identity*

"...prosypaesh´sia, staraias´ poniat´: ty li eto ili kto-to drugoi prosypaetsia tut i ne znaet: on li eto ili kto-to drugoi" (98)

(...you wake up, trying to understand: is it you or someone else waking up here and not knowing: is it him or someone else)

Uncertain family connections, the relationships of fathers and brothers, false and assumed documents all rule out any purely external establishment of the 'civic' identity of the characters. Often in the text the characters express doubts as to the permanence of their own identity. Il´ia, for instance, asks who he is, and his various roles give him no answer to the question: "Kto ia, sprashivaetsia inogda, i komu. Brat i svat ia komu-to, komu-to kum, a byvaet, chto vovse znat´ - i ne dat´ i ne vziat´." (87–88) (Who am

I, I wonder sometimes, and to whom. I am a brother and matchmaker to someone, to someone a godfather, but sometimes I cannot tell which). This unalienable self, "being like you are", is an artificial act of violence imposed on man. Like the hunter's decoy duck, the travelling salesman is delivered up to his false and at the same time, imprisoning identity. He is subjected to fatal conditioning through the stars and trapped in his "supposititious" mask:

Подобно крякве подсадной,
Под дулом крякать обреченной
И бельевою бечевой
С охотником соединенной,
Навряд ли знает разъездной,
Какой он мог бы быть иной (127)

(Like a decoy duck,
Fated to quack under the barrel of a gun
And with a washing line
Tied to the hunter,
Hardly can the travelling salesman know,
How he could be other than he is.)

All possible strategies are used to escape the dictatorship of identity and to unmask it as mere appearance and deception. The people in the novel are splitting up into "forking characters" (Toker 1987, 354) or else flow together into a collective persona. All the women can be traced to a single source, the mythical incarnation of the eternal feminine, whilst the male characters show greater differences. They may be roughly divided into three groups: the group of narrators and heroes; the group of those who are unhappy in love, seduced and deceived, whose fate merely reflects that of the heroes; and, finally, the group of functionaries and fate-bearers. The latter — standing on another plane — are not subjected to the destructive linking of Eros and Thanatos, but seem to be far more in charge of both time and death: the ferryman and his wife, the miller (of time) and his assistant Alladin, the postman, and the hunter Krylobyl.

Between the group of main characters, the narrators and hunters, there exist (although, as always, nothing exists entirely certainly) blood relationships, such as son/father and brothers. Numerous points of correspondence in biography and characterization suggest that they are just variations on one and the same person.

The characters in the second group present even further weakened variants of the single narrator and hero figure, enacting the basic situation of love and death in various forms: as, for example, the hunter Manul, lover of the mysterious lady who meets his death, or Zimar´-man who murders his own wife.

Without any individuality are those characters which embody impersonal forces. The women are particularly affected: they all flow together into one single mythical personality representing the three ages of life[10] and the three forms of archetypal femininity: mother, saint, and whore. With the addition of the epithet *ta* (that), girl, woman and old woman are turned into the same person, as in *ta devochka, ta dama, ta bobylka* (that girl, that lady, that old maid). All the other woman characters may be easily recognized in them. Orina lives with her grandmother, was seduced in her youth, and now seduces others, like the (simple-minded) girl that Iakov loves. She becomes a mother, a phonetic and thematic variation of Iakov's mother Mariia; she disappears or dies, and eventually returns to the Volga in the form of the "lady". Il´ia has an affair with an old rag-picker and later with her backward granddaughter. Both he and Iakov live with a *bobylka* who, though unloved, provides nourishment and warmth.

The mother Mariia is clearly related to Pil´niak's "*mat´-syra zemlia*" (raw mother earth);[11] she surrenders herself to the train-driver-like rain, "receiving his insistent fine seed" (24), and, by the same token, reversed, the native land is personified as a mother: "...native land. Like a mother" (50). She is a *Rossiia-mater´* (little mother Russia) (65) in eighteenth-century language,[12] and a "she-wolf" (65) on which "we jump about like fleas" (65), and eating her flea-children like Chronos, instead of suckling them, as befits her Roman pedigree. She is the Volga, the wolf-river which gives them crayfish to eat and water to drink, a stone under their heads, but also a stone around their necks. In each of the only two women's names that occur in the text, Orina and Mariia, may be heard "*rodina*" (native land), as well as "*mat´*" (mother). Mariia is Iakov's mother and the mother of God, about whom Il´a speaks in his Christmas sermon: "there was born to the southern woman Mariia the Son of God" (140), both a mother goddess and the Mother of God. The lover Orina is raised in the figure of the Lady to sainthood, to the role of Blok's simultaneously life-giving ("Vechnaia zhizn´" [Eternal life]) and death-bringing ("Pogibel´" [Ruin]) "*neponiatnaia neznakomka* " (incomprehensible unknown woman) (115).

The novel's characters have no personal traits, but represent containers to be filled at will. The first description of Iakov Palamakhterov at the end of the text is rendered absurd by the emphatic lack of interest in the character's appearance, for what are we to make of "chelovek zauriadnogo rosta, obychnogo vozrasta i bez truda zabyvaiushchegosia litsa" (185) (a man of ordinary height, usual age, and an easily forgettable face)?[13]

The interchangeability of these characters and their fates is shown in the interchangeability of their names, like Fedor/Petr/Egor, or when two people suddenly exchange their first names and patronymics. With "Imiarekova" (66) and Bat´kovich (156) a name can be inserted or replaced at will.

The variants appear as if determined only by the different coordination of names and fates: individuals when they lose their name can no longer be attached to a particular identity. The symbolic and the typical triumph over the individual every time when, for instance, the ferryman is called Pogibel´ (literally, ruin) and the sailor Albatrosov.

Just as the place-name Bydgoshch changes constantly, so does Il´ia's surname Zynzyrela: place and personal names are both subject to the process of creation and disintegration which affects the identities of time, space and people.

The unusual formation of such names as Palamakhterov and Zynzyrela emphasises their "contrivedness" and the process and mechanism of their emergence. With the same purpose, the origins of the assumed names are demonstratively revealed: Orthodox Christian mythology with the prophet Il´ia; the apostles Petr and Pavel; and the martyrs Fedot and Iakov, Nikolai Ugodnikov, Foma, and Erema. Animal and place names likewise become personal names (Manul, Kaluga-Kostroma). The name Paklin may be derived from multilingual play on the words *klen*, *ne klen* and *pas klen*.

II. CREATING THE WORLD ACCORDING TO THE LAWS OF LANGUAGE AND THE SUBCONSCIOUS

"If we look at unconscious wishes reduced to their most fundamental and truest shape, we shall have to conclude, no doubt, that *psychical* reality is a particular form of existence not to be confused with *material* reality."

(Freud 1976a, 782)

a. Poetry and prose

The world on the Volga cannot easily be reconciled with our usual perceptions, but it is possible to discern a system behind this "topsy-turvy world". It is evidently determined by a system of laws that function differently from our usual instinctive and practical ways of thinking. I shall attempt here to find an entry to this particular type of fiction through the poeticality of Sokolov's prose and the dichotomy of "word art" and "narrative art". There is an inner coherence between the dissolution of reality and the form of the text which could be characterized as a kind of modern ornamental prose.

Sokolov himself has written of his desire to raise Russian prose to the level of poetry (Sokolov 1984, 185) and sums up this programme by the invented word "proeziia". "Proeziia" is what he calls the new way of writing of the SMOG group of writers who existed briefly in the sixties and to which Sokolov himself belonged (Sokolov 1989b, 68). Analogously, the father of ornamental prose in the twenties, Andrei Belyi, wrote of Gogol´'s "poeziia-proza" and of Maiakovskii's "prozo-poeziia".[14]

Sokolov's rejection of the presentation of reality and his creation of a new world is certainly more radical than was the case with the avant-garde at the beginning of the century. In the latter, behind the fictious world a real model can be recognized, even if the home is a stone-age hell and the oven is used for heathen sacrifice, as in Zamiatin's "Peshchera" (The cave).

The search for an individual language led at the beginning of this century, on the one hand, to the *skaz* form, and, on the other, to ornamental prose, which have been called "the forms of a particular 'non-classical' prose" (Kozhevnikova 1976, 55). Both these forms are used in *Mezhdu sobakoi i volkom*. The entire prose text is covered by a euphonic net of paronomasia by which Il´ia's discourse becomes a kind of ornamental *skaz*. Poetic euphony is, however, used most strongly in Iakov's text. In sentences like "Mariia shila. Shila Mariia. Masha ushivala mashinistu shinel´. Mashinist byl rad" (25) (Masha was sewing. The person sewing was Masha. Masha was sewing a greatcoat for the engine driver. The engine driver was glad), euphony becomes the only text-organizing principle, and on the level of both word and sentence the poetic principle of repetition, which is otherwise hidden in the recurrent sound combinations, is employed. In a first general, yet undifferentiated sense, the impression is created that the story derives from the words. In fact, Sokolov himself says that he proceeds not from an idea but from language:

Da, menia vedet imenno iazyk, iazyk pogruzhaet menia v kakie-to inye vremennye plasty, ia popadaiu v drugie leksicheskie vremena, a potom uzhe pridumyvaiu, kak eto poluchilos´. (Sokolov 1984, 180)

(Yes, I am led precisely by language, language immerses me in certain other lexical times, and then I begin to think up how this came about.)

This type of writing is related to the *écriture automatique* of the Surrealists who, maximally abandoning rational control, gave free rein to the associations produced by the word in order to release the creative potential of the subconscious. In their time the Russian avant-garde proclaimed (and practised) the freeing of the word from its subjugation to sense, grammar, and logical thought.

The poetic principle is inimical to plot. The characters and events in *Mezhdu sobakoi i volkom* are subordinate to language, as can best be illustrated by the treatment of personal and place names. The narrative and poetic principles are opposed. The text became a space in which the "principle of return" (Kozhevnikova 1976, 59) applies. It is mainly organized through repetitions and leitmotivs.

The poetic realization of the word finds its clearest expression in the treatment of names. It creates the basis for the identification with each other of bearers of the same or similar names in the text, the different Iakovs, Orina and Marina/Mariia, and also for the disintegration of identification through the dissolution of letters or the constant transformation of place and personal names (see above). The literary equivalence is transcended by magic identification: the person with the same name *is* the same person. The ferryman Pogibel´ *is* death. This linguistic thinking dissolves set combinations, poetic metaphors and idiomatic phrases by taking their component parts literally. Against the background of the figurative sense an "original" meaning containing a magic force is realized.

A potential of magic portent is also found in the Hunter's idiomatic reply to Il´ia's enquiry about his crutches: "zreli my tebia v grobu s tvoimi kostyliami" (133) (you can go to hell with your crutches; literally, we have seen you in a coffin with your crutches). Not only had the crutches, in one version of events, been placed in Gurii's empty coffin and buried instead of him (191), but the Hunters are after all Il´ia's murderers: they see him in his coffin. Moreover Il´ia's complaint that everything is hung on him, "vsekh sobak na menia sklonny veshat´" (191) (people are inclined to hang all the dogs on me), reveals a double truth: on the one hand, he will really have hung on him the dogs he has shot, and in this hanging, on the other hand, can be heard again the morbid promise of the Volga at the beginning of the text: "A kamyshek - khochesh´ pod golovu, khochesh´ - na sheiu dam" (21) (A stone, if you want, under your head; if you want, round your neck). The hints at linguistic logic invite the reader to fill in the gaps: have perhaps the murderers, to weigh him down, hung the dead dogs on or around Il´ia's neck? Omitted every time in the play of phrases is what is real and repressed: Il´ia's death.

Finally, the phrase about the dog and the wolf in the widest sense generates the whole text: it gives it its name, it functions as a leitmotiv-like constantly recurring instruction to the reader (not to look for "the truth"), and from it unfolds Il´ia's story. The dusky state between day and night is a metaphor for the dissolution of reality described in the first part of this article. The *siuzhet* discredits itself by displaying its idiomatic origin.

This is the "projection of a literary technique into artistic reality", as Jakobson said of Khlebnikov (Jakobson 1972, 37): the linguistic thinking discovered by the avant-garde converts linguistic facts into real ones.

b. Psychopoetics — the literature of dreams

The ever-present connection between the psyche and creative writing has been noted and used productively by modern literature (certainly not least thanks to Freud's discovery of the subconscious).[15] People's perception, their psychic disposition, has again taken possession of their environment, the subjective is made objective in the work of art, as can be seen most clearly in the paintings of the Expressionists. Modernist art was interested in the disturbance of perception in mental illness, in the reduced world view of the child, and the Surrealists sought to release the subconscious as a source of creative energy free from rational control.

In this development Sokolov marks an extreme point. The schizophrenia and puberty of the narrator, who invents for himself a child's playful dream world, provide a motivation in *Shkola dlia durakov* for the weakening of the reality principle, even if the metaliterary play with hero and author keeps the psychologism within bounds. In *Mezhdu sobakoi i volkom* the linking of the narration to one individual is far from being so strongly emphasized, but behind all the other narrator figures, whose common denominator is drunkenness, the world-creating consciousness of the Drunken Hunter Iakov may be recognized. Sokolov's poetic world-generation follows psychical laws in a way strikingly similar to the methods of Freud's dream-work. The difference from dreams is, of course, that Sokolov consciously creates this dreamlike unconscious text, by exploiting language's own dynamics. Language becomes a world-creational principle:

> Sasha Sokolov virtuosically dismembers continuous speech structures (phraseologisms, component lexemes, worn-out metonymies) and, by means of the energy thus released, moves in the direction in which he is thrown by the next solar flare. (Kuzminskii 1993)

Freud says in his study of dream-work: "the connecting paths which start out from *words* are in the unconscious treated in the same way as connections between *things* " (Freud 1976b, 235); "Words, since they are nodal points of numerous ideas, may be regarded as predestined to ambiguity" (Freud 1976a, 456). And this associative polyvalency of the word, the semantic potential which already exists in language, is used by Sokolov to create energy by word-splitting: "Language contains everything, all ends and beginnings. Language is in itself rich in feelings and ideas" (Sokolov 1989, 67). It is interesting to compare this type of writing with the *écriture automatique* of the Surrealists who, by giving free rein to their associations, wanted to let the subconscious speak. In Sokolov the same technique is proceeding towards the generation of an aesthetic text, the releasing of the beauty and dynamism inherent in the language. Associations, not subject to rational control but always following linguistic paths, are in both cases the motor for the generation of the text. This text is further developed by Sokolov without, however, hiding its origin.

The methods of poetry are also the methods of dream-work. Puns play a large role in dreams: "dream images [were] linked together merely through a similarity in the sound of words" (Freud 1976a, 125); phrases and metaphors are expressed in pictures. Thus dreams in their operations of condensation, displacement and symbolization use structures already present in the language.

The over-determining of the dream element in *condensation* is nothing other than the polyvalency of the poetic word. Alongside the homonyms introduced in the previous section, the formation of Gorodnishche from *gorodishche* (monstrous town) and *gorod nishchikh* (town of beggars) presents a classic case of word condensation. Likewise the name Zynzyrela is derived from the onomatopoeic *dzyn´*, the sound of skates on ice (10), and the name of the fairy-tale character Cinderella[16]. In the operation of condensation, a dream creates collective words and people, and can also, on the contrary, split the "I" into various persons.[17] Characteristic features are displaced from one figure to others: in *Mezhdu sobakoi i volkom* all the male characters are basically only split-personalities of the narrating I.

It is not my intention here to offer a psychoanalytical analysis of what happens in the text. It is, however, fully possible to explain the reflections of the text in this way: one basic, traumatic scene, when the child witnesses its parents having sex, is constantly and insistently repeated in various forms (it is notable, incidentally, that Mariia's congress with the train-drivers is described right at the beginning of the Iakov text [24–25]). Critics have already drawn attention to the Oedipus theme in Sokolov's fiction. In *Mezhdu sobakoi i volkom* patricide is indicated (as leader of the hunters, Iakov drowns Il´ia who is probably his father) and so sex with (a version of) the mother.

Because they are not graphically representable, the logical relationships between individual elements of a dream, causality and temporality, are destroyed by dream-work (Freud 1976a, 420). It is precisely the lack or the distortion of these categories that is the most prominent feature of Sokolov's text. Just as a dream changes "either/or" into "and", in *Mezhdu sobakoi i volkom* several mutually exclusive versions of one event are possible, which then produce an accumulatively readable, equally valid statement. This "stuck", not fully completed, condensation of a dream (in Freud) is in Sokolov clearly an artistic device of his "art of consciousness", which impressively demonstrates the primacy of imagination over reality. Since the subconscious knows the subjunctive as little as it knows the optative,[18] the "what if" becomes a fact. Equally little does a dream maintain a sense of before and after: experiences from the dreamer's childhood mingle with recent impressions. "In both [dream and psychosis] there is a complete lack of sense of time" (Freud 1976a, 164). Dates and, indeed, numbers altogether, are treated merely as material to which associations are attached; in the same way temporality is abandoned in *Mezhdu sobakoi i volkom*. That the category of time has no validity for men's lives is shown most strikingly in the return of the dead. For the dreaming and for children death is not a final phenomenon either, it means "approximately the same as being 'gone'" (Freud 1976a, 355), which idea is also expressed in fairy stories and folk tales. The dead are "away", they are in a different place (a different bank of the river) from which they can at any moment return. The "timeless" consciousness does not accept death.

One has to imagine the subconscious — like the literary text — as a space whose contents exist synchronically and are capable of any combination. In *Mezhdu sobakoi i volkom* we are provided with a "matrix of the imagination", a "pool" of ideas, and we are shown various propositions as to how to proceed with this material. The reader becomes a witness to the re-creation of the world according to the laws of the subconscious.

c. Sokolov's recycling poetics

Sokolov's text uses the principle of *Gschnas* adduced by Freud in his interpretation of dreams to characterize hysterical people who "build up frightful or perverse imaginary events [...] from the most innocent and everyday material of their experience" (Freud 1976a, 310):

> I need not explain to a Viennese the principle of the *"Gschnas"*. It consists in constructing what appear to be rare and precious objects out of trivial and preferably comic and worthless materials (for instance, in making armour out of saucepans, wisps of straw and dinner rolls) — a favourite pastime at bohemian parties here in Vienna. (Freud 1976a, 310)

Things are removed from their original context and provide the building material for a new world. A dream undertakes much the same, reproducing thoughts "exclusively or predominantly in the material of visual or acoustic memory-traces" (Freud 1976a, 650-51) which remain recognizable as such, but now endowed with far from harmless connotations. A *Gschnas* in reverse is also conceivable, when what is valuable and exalted is used for low purposes. Important for the effect to the *Gschnas* is that the individual elements — exalted or low — do not deny their origin. They bring with them their own ready-made context which stands in humorous contrast to their new use. The subject ill-treated in this way is given a complete review, its self-evidentness is placed in question. Thus, Sasha Sokolov is praised by Tat´iana Tolstaia as a renovator, an expander and restorer of the Russian language:

> His Russian language is amazingly flexible and rich, as if he had discovered in it dark alleys, had wiped the dust from shades and tints that we have not noticed, had discovered registers which have vegetated in neglect; he has thrown open the doors of halls and box rooms and underground passages of meaning. (Tolstaia 1988, 20–21)

Sokolov draws indiscriminately from the entire fund of language, literature and art, taking in new meanings from foreign texts: hence the polyvalency of every single element. Every statement contains countless allusions which go far beyond the context of this individual work — Sokolov's works as a whole are, after all, *one* text[19] — and they strive, finally, to escape centrifugally from this context into the world text of maximally universal intertextuality. This "metonymic" intertextuality on the one hand activates entire sense horizons which are not to be found in the text itself, but it is also a disrespectful "deconstructional" intertextuality which does not continue the *Gschnas* rags, does not integrate them according to instructions, but instead unmasks them as pure set-scenes. They are only building material for the world of language. The quotation, the figure of speech, the image is "filled anew" according to the requirements of the one who speaks: "Not so well-read, so experienced, you did not vouch for the accuracy of any borrowing, and therefore you shook it up, unfettered and uncorked it, filling it with your own ideas" (Sokolov 1991, 179).[20] This comment of Sokolov leads us directly to the recycling poetics practised in *Mezhdu sobakoi i volkom*. The metaphor of an uncorked vessel of liquid is used here also: "Let us roll out the barrel of our narration into God's earth and knock out the bung at last" (28). With nice symmetry the bottle is again closed shortly before the end of the text: "Tuzhe zatkni sivoldai / Probkoi iz mestnoi gazety" (182) (Stuff up tight the raw vodka / With a bung from the local paper). The genie is back in the bottle. The whole text, as the fiction has it, has come to the reader in a bottle: "I have composed these Notes; here they are, / In a bottle that has been washed up to you" (184).

It is worth tracing other uses of the *bochka* (barrel) in the text. It leads us to a meta-meaning of the constant drinking theme. If the "cooper" is the producer of literature, drinkers are the consumers of this product: "I kagor na dvore u bochkarnika / P´et kogorta mladykh kustarei" (31) (And in the cooper's yard red wine / Is being drunk by a cohort of craftsmen). That such a link is not completely remote may be seen in the Russian expression *chitat´ zapoem* (to read avidly) — compare *pit´ zapoem* (to be a heavy drinker). The "patching up of a barrel" also contains an additional meaning which is particularly probable in that these lines come at the end of the text:

Предзимье застало за штопкой мешка,
Починкой мережи и бочки,
Но знаю — набухнут исподтишка
И лопнут настырные почки!

Попробуй пожги только, дурья башка
Мои гениальные строчки. (194)

(Late fall found me mending a burlap sack,
Repairing my nets and my barrels,
Yet I know full well that those tough little buds
Will swell on the sly, then burst open!

Go ahead, just you try it, you dunderhead,
To set fire to my brilliant verses.) (Smith 1987, 345)

It will not escape the careful reader a/ that the harmless hunters' activities of mending nets and barrels are followed by a political allusion (hope for a Thaw), and b/ the proximity of the rhyming words *bochki* and *strochki*. According to the logic of rhyme and to the barrel metaphors, the text thus ends with hope for the publication of the barrel of lines. But what the mending of the barrel means on the metaliterary level should become clearer from what follows. With an instruction which can easily be deciphered as a theory of poetics,[21] the Drunken Hunter addresses Il´ia: "Is it not wrong, he insists, to pour this year's wine into an old barrel, it will burst it at every joint, it will deform it, and, worst of all, the wine will run away" (88). In this way the question of new content (wine) and old form (barrel) is here brought into the text. Il´ia, however, wonders where the new wine is going to come from:

It is good, good advice, you can't deny it. The only trouble is it is no good for us, for our modest Zaitil´shchina, for how can we get enough of this wine to fill the barrel up at one go — it doesn't matter whether it's a new one or not — with whose, if you'll pardon my doubts, money. (88)

Il´ia considers that the Drunken Hunter's next "lesson" is better suited to Zaitil´shchina with its poverty:

> There is no point, he teaches us, in putting whole patches onto torn rags — it doesn't look good. And in any case why tear up a whole piece. Now that, that concerns us, that we understand. But you have to say that this advice is no good in reality either. After all we don't have anything new amongst our old rubbish. (88)

Thus we find ourselves with the second chain of metaphors which applies to creativity and takes issue with the question of new form and old content — the application of new patches on an old base. Now it becomes evident: there is nothing new! This truth established at the latest in the postmodern period (and celebrated by it eclectically and with relish) applies to the Volga world in a completely literal sense. The imagery itself comes from the reference to new patches on old clothes and new wine in old bottles in the New Testament (Matthew 9.16-17) — yet another example of adoption of ready-made materials. Everything in this text is in a constant state of reutilization, under the slogan "Is not something thrown to the ground by one beggar a treasure for someone else?" (45). The recurrent theme of stealing and borrowing objects, of begging and scrounging, the repairing and mending of defective goods all fall under this general denominator. When Il´ia and Iakov after their stay in a sanatorium put on the clothes of the dead, wear a clownish jumble of different garments and stolen boots (56), they are doing nothing different from what the text they are in is doing. Here people go about in patched and re-patched clothes (164). Creation means "recycling" used material. This idea is subtly introduced in the poem "Kak budto sol´iu kto..." (As if someone with salt...), which plainly refers to Pushkin's famous "Zima. Chto delat´ nam v derevne? Ia vstrechaiu..." (Winter. What is there for us to do in the country? I meet...", 1829), especially when the following lines come after the reference to Pushkin and boredom:

> Шлафрок ли старый, тесноватый,
> Велеть изрезать в лоскуты,
> Чтобы были новому заплаты,
> Задать ли в город лататы? (41)

> (If your dressing-gown is old, tightish,
> Should you have it cut into strips,
> To have patches for the new one,
> Or dash off to the town?)

In the light of what has been said, the old, tight dressing-gown is, of course, the old poetic form, but the image here is turned around: is there any sense cutting something old into rags to patch something new? The return to the old appears to have its justification. We understand better why at the end of the text the Drunken Hunter is mending a sack, repairing nets and barrels — objects which have in common that they are "containers": the old form is renewed and improved, and the old material is combined to make a new structure.

The borrowing of names, as, for instance, when the characters bear the names of biblical personages, turns into the economical re-using of raw materials After the disappearance of the original owner of a name it is taken by another: "ne dal, nazyvaetsia, dobru propast'" (14) (waste not, want not, as they say). The name becomes a thing, which is singular. It cannot be multiplied but it can be passed on. On the other hand a letter can arise from a thing: Il´ia's broken grinding wheel makes, with a cross in the middle and the two sides of the wheel on either side, the letter "ж", whose intelligent further use is suggested by the old Krylobyl to Petr: "I do not want to teach you to pick up other people's property, you know how to do that yourself, I want to teach you something else..." (45). The noise "zhe-zhe-zhe" made by the grinding has been materialized in the broken parts of the grinding wheel, and a "ж" as a letter of the alphabet had to be brought by Petr for his nephew along with yeast (drozhzhi — NB the same "zhe" sound here) from the town. The lesson of this absurd fable is the material nature of a letter (or the literality of the material thing). The letter too becomes an item in the material cycle of the Volga world.

There is no difference between letters and things in this text, and there is no difference between "life" and "art", which are equally important as sign-bearers. Looking out of a window or looking at a picture are equivalent; in both cases the frame creates the same distance. The boundaries between "remembering" and "creating" blur, "drawing from memory" becomes "according to the artist's whim". The narrators are only superficially people who remember, they are "world-creators": "prophet" and "magician", "painter" and "poet". The text takes no trouble to conceal its invented nature, and out of the "remember" arises a fairy-tale:

Вспомни о ком-нибудь и,
Сдвинув на брови мурмолку,
К дереву по пути
Сказку придумай. О волке? (182)

(Remember someone and,
Pulling your hat over your brow,
On the way to the tree
Think up a fairy-tale. About a wolf?)

The text lays open the principles by which it was created, and does not hide the origins of the materials from which it is built. Striking details which return in different combinations suggest that the fund of imagination from which this work has been created is limited: for example, the "admiral's sky-blue riding breeches" (56) which Il´ia "inherits" from one of the corpses in a morgue soon return as the "uniform of sky-blue colour" (61) of one of the actors in a Gogolesque scene from the last century. Thus the re-utilization of clothes goes beyond the individual stories of the text. The reappearance or metamorphosis of a motif raises the question of its origin. There seems to be an original stratum of acoustic or visual impressions from which — as in a dream — entire associative and imaginative chains of motifs are generated. This imaginational matrix is closely related to the consciousness of the hero Iakov who, looking out of the window, builds his new world on the perceptions of what he sees there. It is here that the only realistic footholds in the text are to be found, but they are not enough to form the basis of a full psychological interpretation.

In the poems, particularly, an ironical attitude is taken towards the Russian nineteenth-century classics, but in Iakov's narration "high culture", particularly the nineteenth-century classics, are thoroughly exploited too. The discussion of place names has already shown it to be feasible that the imaginational matrix moves almost exclusively in the realm of things Russian. Those, however, who, like D. Barton Johnson, speak in this connection of the work's "deep roots in the Russian tradition" (Johnson 1984, 216) are misled by the text's self-production and have not grasped the autoreflexive and artificial character of this "Russianness". The pre-condition of creating a world, about which one may say in the words of Kreid, "zdes´ russkii dukh, zdes´ Rus´iu pakhnet" (Kreid 1981, 215), determines precisely which type of imaginational matrix is chosen, and which the characters then have at their disposal. The most varied stages of Russian literature, of Russian culture — as it is fixed in the language — are worked into the text, beginning with the Old Russian monuments (see the first chapter, "Zaitil´shchina"). Freely drawing from this reservoir should not be confused with "influence", which is the most frequent mistake of scholarly "influence hunters". The main sources of literary parody are undoubtedly the verses with their references to Krylov, Tiutchev, Fet and Nekrasov (Johnson 1984, 213; Smith 1987, 322; Toker 1987, 352). Indisputably the most important source of literary discourse in *Mezhdu sobakoi i volkom* is, however, Pushkin,

as *the* representative of the Russian literary language. His *Evgenii Onegin*
is the source of one of the epigraphs, and the subject of playful references
in the thirty-second poem, "Ekloga":

...Эклога
Слагалась сама. Бормоча,
Достигнул поленовской риги
К саврасовской роще свергнул
И там, как в Тургеневской книге
Аксаковских уток вспугнул. (178)

(...The eclogue
Formed itself. Muttering,
I reached Polenov's threshing barn
Turned to Savrasov's grove of trees
And there, as in a book by Turgenev,
Frightened up Aksakov's ducks)

The aesthetic world-view which lies at the basis of the text is caught in
a nutshell in these lines. "Art" lays claim to an equally real status as "life".
There is nothing original, and perception is pre-formed by art and literature.
One may recall the dictum of that professed aesthete Oscar Wilde that
London fog only began when Turner painted it. Likewise, the Russian barns
and woods do not simply exist by themselves but needed to be painted by
such *peredvizhnik* painters as Polenov and Savrasov and then to become
re-usable set-scenes for intra-cultural discourse. The duck hunting does not
go back to the experience of the Drunken Hunter or even to the author's
own wandering about in the reeds, but to Turgenev and Aksakov (with his
Zapiski ob uzhen´e ryby [Notes on the catching of fish,1847] and *Zapiski
ruzheinogo okhotnika orenburgskoi gubernii* [Notes of a hunter in the
Orenburg province,1852] Russia's leading writer about hunting and fish-
ing).

Thus the strategy of recycling includes pictures, just as dreams work in
scenes witnessed during the day without being any longer recognizable.[22]
The detailed account of the hunters' return (26–29)[23] is nothing other than
a description of Pieter Bruegel the Elder's "The Hunters in the Snow
(January)", and from here comes a large proportion of the whole book's
properties and thematic threads (Johnson 1984, 209). Just as in Bruegel,
the hunters are descending into a valley where a river, a pond, a village
and, far away on the other side of the river, a town are to be seen, the entire
contents of the Volga world at a glance. Down below people are skating,
and on the hill stands a tavern in front of which, following Bruegel's model,
a suckling pig is being "singed". The hunters are carrying a fox they have

killed, the source of the story of Cinderella's fur slipper. According to his report, Iakov hangs back: "in order not to attract the attention of gawpers and not to spoil the picture by my awkward, still urban gait, I am staying at the back of the procession" (24).

This same scene is depicted by Il´ia from his perspective by the river:

> A s kholma, s kholma vysochaishego, slovno gosudarev o poblazhkax ukaz, prebol´shaia okhota valila vdol´ kubare, retiruias´ iz chutkikh chashch: Krylobyl na khrebtine kakuiu-to tushku nes, a strelki, chislom po dvenadtsati, — vepria trup. (139)

> (And from the hill, from the very high hill, like a monarch's decree about allowances, a huge hunt was streaming alongside the tavern [equivalent to Bruegel's tavern — HK], withdrawing from the sensitive groves: Krylobyl was carrying some carcass along the brow of the hill and the hunters, twelve in number, the corpse of a wild boar.)

In Bruegel's painting only three huntsmen can be seen, although an un-limited number could be keeping outside the frame of the picture, in order, like Iakov, "not to attract the attention of gawpers". Twelve is, however, also the number of the biblical apostles: the texts to which Sokolov's book refers cross and intercross.

In the formula of the inhabitants of Itil´, who must for their hard human existence *liamku tianut´* (to tow; figuratively, to toil and sweat [12, 112]), there may well be a reference to one of the best-known Russian pictures of the 19th century, Repin's "The Volga Barge Haulers" (1870–73), which might serve as a good illustration of the situation of Zaitil´shchina.

For the levelling activity of the recycling poetics the Book of Books is also just one book among many. The Gospels and especially the Sermon on the Mount with its "blessed are the poor in spirit: for theirs is the kingdom of heaven" (Matthew 5.2) is one of the pre-texts for Zaitil´shchina. The message that the last shall be first, the healing of the cripples, blind and lepers, and the call to renounce all worldly goods create a suitable background for Il´ia's story. The cripple Nikolai's sharing of his stolen fish with the poor (15–16) can be seen as a miserable re-enactment of the feeding of the five thousand with food from the Volga. The reference to the New Testament justifies theft, too, when Nikolai says in a biblical gesture, "all this belongs neither to me nor to you" (15).

The Sermon on the Mount is also a pre-text for the genuinely Russian phenomenon of the *iurodivyi* or fool in Christ. Deficiency, the inability to achieve anything in the world, becomes a positive quality, a sign of being a chosen one. In *Mezhdu sobakoi i volkom* physical disability (of the cripples) as well as mental disability[24] (of the feeble-minded girl) are a special form and even opportunity for human existence: not only *"invalid"* and *"individ"* (individual), but also *"kaleka"* (cripple) and *"kalika"* (minstrel) (85) become one. The temptation of a metaphysical interpretation is indeed present. Oleg Dark (in the spirit of post-Communist Russia) sees here an adaptation of the philosophy of Vladimir Solov´ev and Nikolai Fedorov: "His eschatological impatience and 'practical' religious utopianism give Sasha Sokolov a place in the tradition of Russian teleological thought" (Dark 1990, 227).[25] But Orthodox Christianity and the Russian middle ages only present one possiblity for discourse and one linguistic dimension of this text. The reviewer in *Novyi mir*, Andrei Zorin, is more accurate, writing of the "fragmented pieces of great myths" (Zorin 1989, 253) which are strewn about the text, be this the myth of Oedipus, of the Hagia Sophia, or the murderous Sirens.

   Its eclectic use of quotations and self-referentiality show *Mezhdu sobakoi i volkom* to be a typical postmodern text. Sokolov finally entered postmodernism with *Palisandriia*, a book which won him the — quite questionable — recognition of both its leading Russian prophets, Boris Groys (Grois 1987, 171-78) and Igor´ Smirnov (Smirnov 1987, 127-43). The price to be paid is, however, dear. The high degree of reflexivity can only be achieved at the expense of losing immediacy and forfeiting the reader's identification with the text. The judgment of one critic is symptomatic: "a paradoxical situation is created when Soloukhin [...] writes badly, but interestingly, and, say, Sasha Sokolov [...] writes well, but uninterestingly" (Vasilevskii 1990, 11). The procedures of "putting reality in brackets" contain the danger of a certain sterility. Withdrawn from the world, the self-referential space of the text which enables the word games to exist in the first place can very easily become a prison — or a straightjacket.

   In my opinion, however, Sasha Sokolov in *Mezhdu sobakoi i volkom* maintains a balance between the pleasure principle and the reality principle. The oscillation between reference to the world outside and play within the text also makes up the fascination of *Shkola dlia durakov*. And precisely in the dissolution of reality that is the secret of *Mezhdu sobakoi i volkom* lies the truth of the world on the Volga, expressing sublimely the stagnation and hopelessness of the departing Soviet era, but also the freedom that lies in the imagination.

Translated by Arnold McMillin

REFERENCES

Bakhtin, M. M., 1981. *The Dialogic Imagination* tr. C. Emerson and M. Holquist (Austin and London: University of Texas Press).

Belyi, A., 1969., *Masterstvo Gogolia*. Reprint from the Moscow 1934 edition (Munich, Slavische Propyläen, LIX).

Dark, O., 1990. "Mir mozhet byt´ liuboi. Razmyshleniia o 'novoi' proze", *Druzhba narodov* 6: 223–35.

_____ , 1992. "Mif o proze", *Druzhba narodov* 5–6: 219–32.

Freud, S., 1976a. *The Interpretation of Dreams* (Harmondsworth, The Pelican Freud Library, IV).

_____ , 1976b. *Jokes and Their Relation to the Unconscious* (Harmondsworth, The Pelican Freud Library, VI).

Gogol´, N. V., 1994. *Sobranie sochinenii v deviati tomakh* (Moscow: Russkaia kniga).

Grois, B., 1987. "Zhizn´ kak utopiia i utopiia kak zhizn´: iskusstvo sots-arta", *Sintaksis* 18: 171–78.

Hansen-Löve, A., 1978. *Der russische Formalismus. Methodologische Rekonstruktion seiner Entwicklung aus dem Prinzip der Verfremdung* (Vienna: Österreichische Akademie der Wissenschaft).

Ingold, F. P., 1979. *"Škola dlja durakov"*. Versuch über Saša Sokolov", *Wiener Slawistischer Almanach* 3: 93–124.

Jakobson, R., 1972. "Die neueste russische Poesie (Noveishaia russkaia poeziia)", in Jurij Striedter (ed.), *Texte der russischen Formalisten* (Munich: W. Fink), II, 18–135.

Johnson, D. B., 1984. "Sasha Sokolov's *Between Dog and Wolf* and the Modernist Tradition", in Olga Matich and Michael Heim (eds), *Russian Literature in Emigration: The Third Wave* (Ann Arbor: Ardis), 208–17.

_____ , 1986. "Sasha Sokolov's Twilight Cosmos: Themes and Motifs", *Slavic Review* 45, 4: 639–49.

_____ , 1987. "Saša Sokolov and Vladimir Nabokov", *Russian Language Journal* 41, 138-39: 415-26.

_____ , 1989. "The Galoshes Manifesto: A Motif in the Novels of Sasha Sokolov", *Oxford Slavonic Papers* 22:155-79.

Kozhevnikova, N.A., 1976. "Iz nabliudenii nad neklassicheskoi (ornamental´noi) prozoi", *Izvestiia Akademii Nauk SSSR*, Seriia literatury i iazyka 35: 55–66.

Kreid, V., 1981. "Zaitil´shchina", *Dvadtsat´ dva* 19: 213–18.

Kuzminskii, B., 1993. "Langol´ery, ili Russkaia kukhnia v izgnanii", *Segodnia* 23 (8 June).

Matich, O., 1987. "Sasha Sokolov and His Literary Context", *Canadian-American Slavic Studies* 21: 301–18.

Pil´niak, B., 1988. "Mat´ syra-zemlia", in Boris Pil´niak, *Tselaia zhizn´. Izbrannaia proza* (Minsk: Mastatskaia litaratura)

Schmid, W., 1992. "Ornament — Poesie — Mythos — Psyche. Einleitende Thesen", in Wolf Schmid, *Ornamentales Erzählen in der russischen Moderne. Čechov — Babel´ - Zamjatin* (Frankfurt am Main: Peter Lang), 15–28.

Simmons, C., 1986. "Cohesion and Coherence in Pathological Discourse and Its Literary Representation in Saša Sokolov's *Škola dlja durakov*", *International Journal of Slavic Linguistics and Poetics* 33: 71–96.

Smirnov, I.S., 1987. "Nepoznavaemyi sub˝ekt", *Beseda: Religiozno-filosofskii zhurnal* 6: 127-43.

Smith, G. S., 1987. "The Verse in Sasha Sokolov's *Between Dog and Wolf*", *Canadian-American Slavic Studies* 21: 319–39.

Sokolov, S., 1976. *Shkola dlia durakov* (Ann Arbor: Ardis).

———, 1980. *Mezhdu sobakoi i volkom* (Ann Arbor: Ardis).

———, 1984. "Ia khochu podniat´ russkuiu prozu do urovnia poezii", *Dvadtsat´ dva* 35: 179-86.

———, 1985. "Beseda s Sashei Sokolovym: Nuzhno zabyt´ vse staroe i vspomnit´ vse novoe...", *Russkaia mysl´* 3571: 12.

———, 1988. *A School for Fools*, translated by Carl R. Proffer (New York: Four Walls Eight Windows).

———, 1989a. "Amerikantsy ne mogut poniat´ — o chem eto mozhno govorit´ dva chasa", *Iunost´* 12: 66.

———, 1989b. "Obshchaia tetrad´, ili Gruppovoi portret SMOGa", *Iunost´* 12: 67–68.

———, 1989c. "'Vremia dlia chastnykh besed...'", *Oktiabr´* 8: 195–202.

Ssachno, H. von, 1979. "Valentin Katajew und Sascha Sokolow", in G. Lindemann (ed.), *Sowjetliteratur Heute* (Munich: Beck), 208-19.

Toker, L., 1987. "Gamesman's Sketches (Found in a Bottle): A Reading of Sasha Sokolov's *Between Dog and Wolf*", *Canadian-American Slavic Studies* 21: 31–61.

Tolstaia, T., 1988. Introduction to excerpts from *Shkola dlia durakov*, *Ogonek* 33: 20.

Vasilevskii, A., 1990. "Na perelome? Kuda ischez literaturnyi protsess?" A round table on Russian prose in 1989 with A. Arkhangel´skii, G. Gordeeva, A. Nemzer and E. Shklovskii, *Literaturnoe obozrenie* 1: 9–29.

Witte, G., 1989. *Appell — Spiel — Ritual. Textpraktiken in der russischen Literatur der sechziger bis achtziger Jahre* (Wiesbaden: O. Harrassowitz)

Zorin, A., 1989. "Nasylaiushchii veter", *Novyi mir* 12: 250–53.

NOTES

1. There exists no printed translation of this deliberately illiterate and parodic text (except for a selection of verses from the novel made by Gerald Smith: Smith 1987, 337–45), although unsuccessful attempts have been made more than once at the far more obscure prose sections. The "literal" English

versions which appear here are entirely the responsibility of the article's translator. All page references to unpublished translations refer to the Russian text.

2. This is a temptation to which Cynthia Simmons has succumbed. Comparing the discourse of the special school pupil with that of schizophrenics she comes to the satisfying conclusion that the writer has been very successful in simulating this discourse for his character: "We can affirm that *Škola dlja durakov* is a creditable reproduction of a particular kind of pathological discourse" (Simmons 1986, 94). The present study is intended as an alternative to this type of psychologism.

3. Compare the increasingly confusing references to time in Gogol''s *Zapiski sumasshedshego* (Notes of a madman), where the word *mesiats* (moon/month) is also taken literally: "Chisla ne pomniu. Mesiatsa tozhe ne bylo. Bylo chert znaet chto takoe" (Gogol' 1994, III, 162). Similarly, the following words seem like a model for the restitution of "the inner soul's time" in *Mezhdu sobakoi i volkom*: "Martobria 86 chisla. Mezhdu dnem i noch'iu" (Gogol' 1994, III, 160).

4. These observations come from Kreid 1981, 214. Kreid believes that close reading can establish the exact year of the action in the novel, but does not make such an attempt at dating himself.

5. As is not difficult to establish, the temporal frame outlined here encompasses Sokolov's lifetime, and thus as a whole forms an autobiographical reference.

6. See in general Ingold's valuable analysis of the correspondence of the dissolution of space and time in *Shkola dlia durakov* : Ingold 1979, esp. 114–17.

7. This is one of the poems from the novel translated by Gerald Smith: Smith 1987, 338–40.

8. Amongst other obvious points of comparison with Gogol' may be mentioned the play with Akakii Akakievich Bashmachkin's name in *Shinel'* (The greatcoat), and, particularly, the discussion about the name Manilovka / Zamanilovka in *Mertvye dushi* (Dead souls) (Gogol' 1994, V, 24).

9. The theme of death on a railway track recalls *Anna Karenina*. It has also been noted as a reference back to *Shkola dlia durakov* (Johnson 1986, 646; Witte 1989, 105) where space is organized similarly through the railway line and station, and the pond and river (Lethe) beyond.

10. Compare the "generational triad" of the women characters in *Shkola dlia durakov* (Witte 1989, 127).

11. Pil'niak's story "Mat' syra zemlia" is related to Sokolov's work in a number of ways: Matich 1987, 311-13.

12. Compare the epigraph of Radishchev's *Puteshestvie iz Peterburga v Moskvu* (Journey from Petersburg to Moscow): "chudishche oblo, ozorno, ogromno, stozevno i laiai". In Sokolov (65) we find, "Rossiia-mater' ogromna, igriva i laet, budto volchitsa vo mgle": Smith 1987, 321.

13. This, of course, recalls the famous description of Chichikov at the beginning of Gogol''s *Mertvye dushi* (Gogol' 1994, V, 11).

14. Whilst Gogol', according to Belyi, smashed prose, turning it into "poeziia-proza", Maiakovskii freed poetry from "academic verse" thus creating "prozo-poeziia": Belyi 1969, 227.

15. In this connection see Schmid 1992, esp. 23, and Hansen-Löve's observation on the "perplexing methodological and teminological analogies between the formalist theory of puns (*Kalauertheorie*) [...] and Freud's theory of jokes (*Witztheorie*)" (Hansen-Löve 1978, 161ff).

16. For further discussion of the Cinderella theme see Johnson 1989, 164.

17. "There are also dreams in which my ego appears along with other people who, when the identification is resolved, are revealed once again as my ego": Freud 1976a, 435.

18. "The dream repressed the optative and replaced it by a straightforward present" (Freud 1976a, 683).

19. Compare the striking similarities of topography between *Shkola dlia durakov* and *Mezhdu sobakoi i volkom* with their rivers, ponds, cemeteries, parks and railways, but also the concurrence of details such as the songs and counting rhymes which are referred to in both texts: for example, the song of the chrysanthemums, and the variants on "Vyshel ezhik iz tumana, vynul nozhik iz karmana" or the folk curse, "Merzni, Merzni, volchii khvost".

20. This is precisely the intertextuality of a dream, its way of quoting: "However much speeches and conversations, whether reasonable or unreasonable in themselves, may figure in dreams, analysis invariably proves that all that the dream has done is to extract from the dream-thoughts fragments of speeches which have really been made or heard. It deals with these fragments in the most arbitrary fashion" (Freud 1976a, 545).

21. Compare Leona Toker's interpretation of this point: "Sokolov's version of the respectably time-worn truth about new content demanding a new form". She also notices the connection between the "barrel of the narration" and the "cooper" without, however, seeing the further implications of the use of that literary principle in this text: Toker 1987, 347, 351.

22. Thus the setting of one of Freud's dreams recalls "a reproduction of a woodcut inserted in an illustrated history of Austria" (Freud 1976a, 556).

23. The description is a response to the "special commission"'s enquiry "about the circumstances accompanying the *return of the hunt* (my emphasis — HK) from the battue" (25). This is another example of Sokolov's method, to show what is covert openly, in order that no-one notice it; in Iakov's words "because a thing is lying in view, — it lies most discretely of all" (90).

24. Mental illness, "abnormality", as an opportunity for inner freedom and an escape from society's obligations is, of course, much more clearly expressed in *Shkola dlia durakov*.

25. It is interesting that two years later another published article by the same critic is without any reference to "Russian teleological thought". In the later work he suggests more convincingly that Sokolov's first two books are linked novels "about how man was replacing the Creator": Dark 1992, 224.

RUSSIAN VILLAGE PROSE IN PARALITERARY SPACE

Kathleen Parthé

From Valentin Ovechkin's first instalment of *Raionnye budni* (District routine) in 1952 up to the present day, writers, critics, and ideologues have seen the post-war narrative of rural Russia as anything but neutral territory. Paradoxically, as the village signified increasingly less in the real world, it began to figure more prominently on an abstract plane.[1] The literary village and its inhabitants achieved a much higher and more politicized profile than did cities and urban dwellers, factories and workers, or battlefields and soldiers — other familiar settings and characters in Soviet Russian literature from the early fifties to the mid-eighties. And while writers of canonical Village Prose (roughly 1956–1980) generally raised issues of social or political importance at the level of metaphor, character, setting and dialogue, a number of critics — along with some of the writers themselves after 1985 — used these metaphors as ideological stepping-stones. As it evolved, Village Prose and the debates surrounding it, entered what Rosalind Krauss — in another context — has called "paraliterary space": ". . . the space of debate, quotation, partisanship, betrayal, reconciliation . . . not the space of unity, coherence, or resolution that we think of as constituting a work of literature" (Krauss, 292–93).

When analysing the politicization of rural prose, it is important to remember that we are accustomed to following the evolution of literary careers, styles, themes and genres, but are apt to forget that "codes of reading" evolve as well. For post-Stalinist literature about the countryside it is possible to identify a number of distinct "codes of reading":

(1) from the early "Thaw" period (with some stirrings already evident in 1952);
(2) from the late fifties to the end of the Brezhnev period;
(3) during the early *glasnost'* years (c.1985–89);
(4) during the post-*glasnost'*, post-Soviet period (which began in late 1989 before the official end of the Soviet Union).

After a brief discussion of the first two codes, this article will concentrate on the last two categories, which were only briefly mentioned in my 1992 book, *Russian Village Prose: the Radiant Past*, completed as the last code was evolving.

During the Thaw, there is a reading "forward": in 1952, rural literature meant the novels of Simeon Babaevskii and Galina Nikolaeva, some of the most barren works of socialist realism; against that background, Ovechkin's *Raionnye budni* and the subsequent school of reform *ocherki* (essays) represented an obvious change for the better to most readers. Ovechkin was no dissident; he worked well within the "space" of the kolkhoz and Communist Party directives while lobbying for administrative reform in life and more accurate descriptions in literature.[2]

Some critics recognized in these rural essays a deliberate challenge to the prevailing literary representation of the countryside, but in general their reading of Ovechkin was no different from that given Thaw literature as a whole, and they compared the new writing to canonical works of socialist realism. Vladimir Pomerantsev shattered the spell of a ritualized literary-critical nexus with his 1953 essay, "Ob iskrennosti v literature" (On sincerity in literature), which he could have easily called "On Sincerity in Criticism". Pomerantsev's goal was not just to expose the bankruptcy of the kolkhoz novel, but also to recognize and encourage writers — above all Ovechkin — who were attempting a more honest, interesting and effective narrative of rural life. Essays by Fedor Abramov, Sergei Zalygin, Efim Dorosh, Vladimir Tendriakov, and others — many of them writers themselves — followed in a similar vein, with witty, at times trenchant, commentary on the shortcomings of kolkhoz literature. They warned younger writers that replacing the *rozovaia kraska* (rosy colours) of court bards with the darkly critical tones of investigative reporters would not by itself improve the aesthetic quality of literature. Their list of suggested models for younger writers was heavily weighted in the direction of pre-revolutionary figures, a number of whose works were republished in the mid-fifties (for example, Aksakov, Bunin, Leskov, and Dal'); this list in itself was a not very well-hidden commentary on the artistic value of canonical Soviet literature.

The Party was looking to writers of critical and artistic prose to aid the speedy post-war recovery of the countryside, to suggest improvements and to mobilize energies. But the countryside was still not a place where the Party's control of either literature or agriculture could even be implicitly challenged; editors were sacked and writers kept from publishing when the suggestions were too bold, or the tone too sarcastic.

It was works like Efim Dorosh's *Derevenskii dnevnik* (Rural diary), stories by Iurii Kazakov and Vladimir Tendriakov, and Vladimir Soloukhin's *Vladimirskie proselki* (Vladimir country roads) that helped shift the centre of attention from the contemporary Soviet countryside to the timeless, traditional Russian village — a major change in chronotopes — and from young agronomists full of new ideas to old peasants full of memories. These essays and stories of the later 1950s — along with Abramov's first novel *Brat'ia i sestry* (Brothers and sisters, 1958) — quietly prepared the ground for a work that although written during this decade did not appear until January 1963, namely Solzhenitsyn's "Matrenin dvor" (Matrena's home). It was the response to this latter story, along with Abramov's "Vokrug da okolo" (Round and about) and Iashin's "Vologodskaia svad'ba" (Vologda wedding) — published at the same time — that set the tone for critical discussion throughout the rest of the Village Prose period, that is, until the end of the seventies.[3] This was one of the liveliest and most protracted literary discussions on a single topic in Soviet Russian literary history.

There is a surprising variety in the responses to this new direction in rural literature that — contrary to the tenets of socialist realism and the ethos of Soviet life — privileged the past, old people, village life, spiritual depth, eccentricity, traditional ways, and a strong Russian national identity. The very term *derevenskaia proza* (village prose) became an object of contention on both the political level (it emphasized differences between rural and urban life that were supposed to have been eliminated, and it promoted a Russian — even a local — loyalty over Soviet patriotism) and on the artistic level (it was claimed that there were so many divisions of literature that the process of typology was becoming meaningless). The predictable reaction was that this was so *non*-Soviet a literature as to be approaching something *anti*-Soviet, and its appeal to pre-revolutionary values and a Russian identity could have a dangerous effect. An extended polemic over rural literature flared up in 1963, at the end of the sixties and the seventies, as well as at other times around specific important works. One of the most controversial responses came from Aleksandr Iakovlev in a 1972 article called "Protiv antiistorizma" (Against anti-historicism). His impassioned defence of Soviet patriotism over a rural-based nationalism ought to have earned him the thanks of a grateful Party, but instead he was sent to Canada for ten years, out of the fray.

The response to Iakovlev's broadside is only one of many pieces of evidence that Village Prose was never subject to a monolithic condemnation by the Party. There were times when that view was in the ascendancy and depictions that foregrounded the importance of religion, the excesses of collectivization, or "the glory that was Russia" were subject to severe criticism, as were the journals in which they had appeared; as with all Soviet literature, much of the problematic material was weeded out before permission was given to publish. But throughout the "stagnant years" there is abundant evidence that a certain level of Russianness was not only tolerated, but rewarded. The nationalization of Bolshevism that had begun after 1934 was strengthened by the War; it was virulently present in 1949, and was fully in evidence during the Brezhnev period. The transcript of a 1977 meeting of writers, critics and students of Moscow State University (MGU) at the Central House of Writers (TsDL) that was published in Russia only fourteen years later, shows Kuniaev, Kozhinov, Lobanov, Seleznev, and Palievskii expressing chauvinist views in an unsubtle way, attacking Meierkhol´d, Babel´, modernism and innovation in literature and theatre, and questioning the "credentials" of non-Russian critics and directors.[4] Lip service was still paid to the multi-cultural nation, but the pro-Russian faction in the Party had to have been fairly strong for it not only to tolerate, but to reward the nationalist — although not yet chauvinist — rural literature of Belov, Rasputin and other writers. They were still subject to censorship and occasional reprimands but they were allowed to deviate to a surprising degree from classical socialist realism, whose theoreticians tried to accommodate the rural writers as best they could under the flexible rubric of *zrelyi sotsrealizm* (mature socialist realism).

So while Village Prose was openly criticized by some as being not Soviet enough, it was implicitly praised by others for displaying a Russian patriotism that was not implacably anti-Communist. It was important in an era when so much interesting writing came out only in samizdat to salvage something of quality for gosizdat (state [that is, official] publication). There was a broad readership for Village Prose among members of the urban intelligentsia, with — and this is based on anecdotal evidence — most readers having a favourite writer or group of works, but few embracing the entire canon.

During the early *glasnost´* years there was a sense of relief as constraints on literature and other forms of discourse loosened with each passing day, and of unity as the different strands of Russian literature — émigré, samizdat, delayed and repressed texts — joined the best of the Soviet canon. The *derevenshchiki* were praised as having been a significant factor in keeping alive the "moral-philosophical 'nucleus' of Russian literature" in the post-Stalinist period by ignoring Soviet models and linking themselves directly to the pre-revolutionary tradition.[5] All past cultural resistance to socialist realism was for a brief period seen as a single enterprise, what has been called "a single anti-world" (Belaia 1992, 4), in which Village Prose had played an important and honourable role. In the post-Stalinist period where one text, above- or underground, often dominated literary-political discussions until it yielded to the next "one text", the *derevenshchiki* had supplied many stimuli for debate, especially during the ten years between the appearance of Belov's *Privychnoe delo* (An ordinary matter, 1966) and Rasputin's *Proshchanie s Materoi* (Farewell to Matera, 1976).

By 1989, this briefly unified post-revolutionary Russian literature began breaking up in earnest at raucous sessions of various branches of the Writers' Union. The newly identified literary camps began to be analysed seriously in 1990, the hallmark of which was Viktor Erofeev's deliberately provocative essay, "Pominki po sovetskoi literature" (A funeral feast for Soviet literature) (Erofeev 1990). Despite the efforts of respected commentators at home and abroad like Galina Belaia and Naum Korzhavin to salvage the aesthetic — and to some extent moral — reputation of canonical *derevenskaia proza* for the sake of historical accuracy and fairness, the post-Stalinist rural canon was subjected to two different but ultimately related political readings, as (1) a Soviet literature of compromise, if not collaboration, and (2) as a proto-chauvinist, even proto-fascist Russian literature, as *natsrealizm* (nationalist realism) (Zviniatskovskii 1992, 233–37).

What was the historical role of Village Prose? Was it a subtle force helping to undermine the Soviet state and its mandated culture? Or was it a literature that helped that state to flourish, its writers generously compensated for their services while other brave and steadfast *literary* had to choose between no audience at all and the dangerous space of samizdat or tamizdat, to be "rewarded" with poverty, prison camp, exile, or emigration. Erofeev's essay and the many responses it stimulated raised awkward and ultimately unanswerable questions about the ethics and politics of a literary career in an oppressive state.

The vulnerable writer of "dangerous texts" is such a powerful cultural myth in Soviet Russia that writers who enjoyed public success — in the form of large and frequent editions of their works, state awards, and prominent positions on the boards of journals and branches of the Writers' Union — before 1985 have been subject to intense scrutiny. Was it better to have published a censored — but still valuable — text or to have either hidden it or sent it abroad? Is a writer's failure to defend another writer in political trouble the moral equivalent of joining the attack? Does joining the Party count as heavily against people in the literary world in the Thaw year of 1956 as it would in earlier — or later — years? Can a rural writer whose parents were repressed during collectivization or died in World War II compete in suffering with an urban writer whose true-believer parents were swept away during the Stalinist purges and who was himself pressured to emigrate? "Competitive suffering" was very much a factor in the rereading of literary history and writers' biographies that began as the Soviet period came to an end.[6]

In the light of this post-totalitarian interest in the legitimacy of success versus the legitimacy of suffering, one can easily come up with two opposing views of a *derevenshchik* like Fedor Abramov. His native region and family were seriously weakened by collectivization, the War, and Stalinist repression in general; the writer himself was severely wounded and evacuated from a besieged Leningrad. Abramov had to put many stories "in the drawer"(Village Prose writers tended not to release works to underground or émigré publishing networks), and was silenced for several years after his essay "Vokrug da okolo" appeared in 1963. Abramov published a substantial number of stories and novels that were very well received by the reading public, and he defended rural Russia and its inhabitants on every possible occasion. But he also worked in the Soviet counter-intelligence system from 1943 to 1945, joined the Party at the end of the War, and then advanced very quickly to become head of the Soviet Literature Department at Leningrad State University; he received awards and occupied positions of responsibility during the Brezhnev period, and was allowed to travel to the West (as were a number of urban writers like Trifonov and Aksenov). The story "Kto on?" (Who is he?), fragments of which were released by the writer's widow in 1993, is an apt title for Abramov's biography, or in fact for the biography of any of the prominent Village Prose writers.

To this politicized appraisal of Village Prose and its creators an even more damaging charge was soon added. The disturbing rise of chauvinism in the years after 1985 was in part a result of the freeing up of public discourse to include the whole range of political beliefs and agendas; the high profile of the Pamiat´ organization in the late 1980s stimulated a search for the origins of chauvinism in the literary world, a search that soon led to Village Prose. The evidence that groups like Pamiat´ had actually arisen among urban members of the technological intelligentsia from the 1960s on and that many of its members or sympathizers — urban and rural — took inspiration from pre-revolutionary tracts such as "The Protocols of the Elders of Zion" and from official Soviet anti-Zionist material, was obscured by the fact that a number of the erstwhile writers of Village Prose expressed very strong nationalist — and at times chauvinist — opinions after 1985, stepping out of the frame of artistic literature altogether into the impassioned world of *publitsistika*. Rather than inspiring the rise of chauvinism, they seem — and this is not to their credit — to have been inspired by it.[7] In 1990, Galina Belaia analysed what she called "the tragic paradox of Russian culture today — the degeneration of yesterday's opponents of the regime into reactionary ideologists blocking the nation's way out of the abyss" (Belaia 1992, 3).

By 1980 Village Prose had pretty much died out as a viable school, which is not surprising for a movement that began in the second half of the fifties. Village Prose writers fell silent for personal reasons (the deaths of Abramov, Kazakov and Tendriakov, and Rasputin's severe injuries in the first half of the eighties, along with the earlier demise of Shukshin, Rubtsov, Ovechkin and Dorosh) and for political reasons (the censorship of the fundamental criticism of collectivization by Belov, Mozhaev, Soloukhin and others). The writers had lost clout among readers and critics although several of them still played an active role in the Writers' Union. But with the publication in rapid order of new works by Rasputin, Astaf'ev and Belov in 1985 and 1986 rural writers began to regain a place in the literary-political life of the country which soon mutated into a primarily political role. That at least Astaf'ev — by the early 1990s — and Rasputin — by the end of 1994 — acknowledged their mistake in actively entering the political fray is an interesting but largely moot point, since they had already aided and abetted the re-reading and even mis-reading of their previous works.

Astaf'ev, Belov and Rasputin and their conservative and far-right urban colleagues in literature, criticism and political journalism attracted attention both in Russia and abroad for comments about harmful, alien forces in Russian history, especially in the Soviet period, highlighting the role of Jews. They made these comments in speeches, essays, public letters, and less often in works of fiction (for example, Astaf'ev's *Pechal'nyi detektiv* (A sad detective/story, 1986), Belov's *Vse vperedi* (The best is yet to come, 1986), and *God velikogo pereloma* (The critical year, 1989).

They have claimed Dostoevskii's works — especially *Besy* (The possessed) and *Dnevnik pisatelia* (A writer's diary) as an inspiration, but one would be hard put to find passages in which they have outdone their mentor on this subject, except that they had the advantage of concrete historical events to point to whereas Dostoevskii relied more on fears of what the future would bring. Although Gary Saul Morson, the leading Western authority on *Dnevnik pisatelia*, has stated unequivocally that the anti-Semitic portions of that work "were, even by the standards of the day, particularly poisonous", the anti-Semitic charge against Dostoevskii, although raised periodically and even analysed at some length, has never seriously affected the critical or popular reputation of this writer. He is, as Joseph Frank counsels us, to be given "the benefit of the doubt" about such a charge (Frank 1990, 166, note 8).[8] It is interesting to contemplate briefly the irony in the fact that the chauvinistic comments of writers like Belov, Astaf'ev and Rasputin have been given a much less benign reading.

The explanation of the critic Ekaterina Starikova is that, unlike Dostoevskii, post-Holocaust chauvinists are fully aware of the possible consequences of such remarks, how they contribute to a climate of intolerance that can easily lead to violence (Starikova 1986, 87/18–19);[9] this is a point well taken. Another explanation is that although Dostoevskii is no less chauvinistic than, say, Vasilii Belov, he is — to risk a gross understatement — much more the writer. *Dnevnik pisatelia*, with its anti-Jewish diatribes, complicates our view of Dostoevskii, and troubles a Dostoevskii enthusiast, but it does not diminish his great talent or cause many readers to search the Dostoevskii canon for evidence of chauvinism or to refuse to read Dostoevskii altogether. But when Belov, Astaf´ev, and Rasputin embrace the philosophy of *Dnevnik pisatelia*, and take their inspiration from its darkest pages, they are severely diminished in the eyes of many readers and critics, and their works from earlier years are subject to a fundamental re-evaluation or even a simple dismissal. The lesson is a predictable one: a great writer — by common agreement irreplaceable in the canon — can afford to write political obscenities that would destroy the reputation of a lesser talent. Morson (1983, 311) was reminded of Freud's comment that Dostoevskii's "narrow Russian nationalism [was] a position which lesser minds have reached with smaller effort", a comment almost tailor-made for the case of the erstwhile *derevenshchiki* (Freud 1962, 98).

This fourth reading of Village Prose, that began in 1986 and grew in strength as the eighties waned, involved either searching through stories from the sixties and seventies for the roots of chauvinism, or simply making the assumption that chauvinism was present, obviating the necessity for a search. Much attention was paid to metaphors of rural literature that were ripe for misuse; Galina Belaia described the "romanticized world" of the traditional village, whose depiction in Village Prose "was fraught with hidden dangers" (Belaia 1992, 5). She identifies the moment when the "artistic-philosophical metaphor[s]" mutated into a "philosophy of history", and nostalgia became part of a political agenda promoting a return to the past (Belaia 1992, 8, 16).

Is the Village a Dangerous Place?

Are there, as Belaia claims, "hidden dangers" in the village of Village Prose? Is this literature utopian, and, if so, does it give a falsely idyllic picture of rural life that can be used to dangerous ends? By examining these questions, we can better understand the politicized readings given to *derevenskaia proza* after 1985.

Utopian is a problematic term as applied to Russian Village Prose; if we accept Auden's opposition of the Arcadian vision of a past Eden to the Utopian vision of the future New Jerusalem, then the rural narratives of

Rasputin, Belov, Abramov and other *derevenshchiki* could most accurately be called Arcadian.

> Eden is a past world in which the contradictions of the present world have not yet arisen; New Jerusalem is a future world in which they have at last been resolved. [. . .] the backward-looking Arcadian knows that his expulsion from Eden is an irrevocable fact. [. . .] The forward-looking Utopian [. . .] necessarily believes that his New Jerusalem is a dream which ought to be realized.
>
> (Auden 1968, 409–10)

The Utopian's future vision, says Auden, "[must] include images [. . .] not only of the New Jerusalem itself but also images of the day of judgment" (Auden 1968, 409–10).

Of course, "Utopia" is more often used in the much broader sense of an idealized, imaginary realm, a place that exists primarily in visionary or impractical thought. In that meaning, the Russian literary view of the countryside and the peasant has been to a great extent "Utopian" for the past two hundred years, beginning most notably with Karamzin's *Bednaia Liza* (Poor Liza), extending through the nineteenth-century gentry novel and some turn-of-the-century works by Chekhov and Bunin, the peasant Utopias of Esenin and Kliuev, and the Utopias of collectivization. Another — and distinctly secondary — line of rural literature presented a much bleaker picture of peasant life.

The reform essays of the early fifties — what might be called "proto-Village Prose" — were in fact a reaction to the false idyll of life on the collective farm. The movement itself, though, became as lyrical as it was critical, and if one is to call it "Utopian" that is only to say that it corresponded to the most common approach to the rural theme throughout modern Russian literary history. Canonical works of Village Prose are both **anti**- and **ante**-kolkhoz literature. In setting themselves in opposition to the false idyll of the collective-farm novel, they drew on prior literary idealizations; the difference was that this time the author was himself from the countryside, which lent a greater credibility to his observations. The rural childhood he described was his own childhood, the colourful old female character was his grandmother, and the hard-working peasant who did not return from the War closely resembled his father.

The past in Village Prose is bathed in the radiance that one expects from any nostalgic, elegiacal view, especially one that stands in opposition to the false illumination of socialist realism's "radiant future". Time is slow, cyclical, focused on everyday life, and the past — both of the writer, his extended family (*rod*) and of peasant Russia as a whole — looms large as a source of beauty and value. The location is usually a specific village or cluster of villages — a *malaia rodina* (native realm) — of which the author has detailed, personal knowledge, although the exact name may have been changed according to the conventions of artistic prose. There is a naturally arising radiance surrounding the "remembered village", a place which may no longer be inhabited by the time the story is written. And each village was the centre of the world for its inhabitants, who for generations rarely ventured far beyond its periphery, and who saw people from outside their *malaia rodina* as *chuzhie* (alien). It was a virtually complete world, with its own oral history, lexicon, and "cognitive map".[10]

While there is nothing inherently dangerous about the depiction of the *malaia rodina* of one's childhood, it is also a chronotope that can be easily adapted to the needs of a strong nationalist or even chauvinist world-view. Each of these "native realms" can be seen as a *zapovednik* (reserve) of "genuine" Russian life, and the decline or disappearance of the author's home village can stand for the loss of a traditional, agricultural *Russian* Russia, its place usurped by a more cosmopolitan, Western-influenced society. The distilled portrait of Russian village life in a work like Vasilii Belov's *Lad* (Harmony), can give the illusion of a perfectly ordered society, whose exit from history becomes all the more lamentable.

There are a number of distinct areas of Russia represented in *derevenskaia proza*, for example, the central regions of Vladimir and Orel, and the far North of Arkhangel´sk and Pomor´e. But it is the Siberian village and the Siberian expanse as a whole which figure most prominently as emblems of the nation, rapidly acquiring a political function in the paraliterary space that came to surround Village Prose. The *derevenshchiki* had made it clear that the further one travelled from Moscow the more one could see the roots of a village Russia that had not been entirely destroyed; in the minds of some of the more ardent nationalist commentators it was Siberia, distant and relatively uncontaminated by Moscow, St Petersburg, or — heaven forfend! — the West, that came to be seen as the ideal location for a post-Soviet Russian state. A century before, in the final entry of *Dnevnik pisatelia* (for January 1881), Dostoevskii had suggested that Asian Russia may be the place where the old European Russia would be restored and resurrected. Village Prose was not born of the cultural-ideological myth of Siberia, but it fed off and in turn strengthened that myth and the sense of a strong, unadulterated Russian identity whose continued existence is guaranteed by Siberia more than by any other region.

By the late 1980s, the ultra-nationalist press was proposing that Russia's capital be moved to Omsk, pointing out that Russia's centre has migrated steadily eastward over the centuries, from Kievan Rus´ to Muscovy to the Siberian taiga. According to this line of thinking, the parameters of Russianness stay the same, while the centre of Russia can shift to a more remote and defensible place.[11] This move is generally described not in terms of an advance, but of a strategic, nation-preserving withdrawal, like Kutuzov before the French advance on Moscow in 1812. Siberia, especially as it is depicted by the *derevenshchiki*, can stand for the new Russia because it is demonstrably non-European, and — despite mismanaged resources and environmental damage — it is still a land of great natural beauty and economic potential.

The most striking and potentially powerful image of the Siberian village came from Valentin Rasputin, Siberian patriot, ardent environmentalist, one of the best-known writers of *derevenskaia proza*, and the rural writer who was most deeply involved in the political sphere after 1985. The finale of *Proshchanie s Materoi* was read in 1976 as an affectionate — if somewhat melodramatic — leave-taking of thousand-year-old rural Russia. The island village of Matera would sink beneath the waves of the new hydroelectric dam's reservoir, and Dasha Pinigina and her neighbours would drown with it, unwilling to abandon the remains of their ancestors. But the novella's ending was ambiguous, and a reading in the 1990s leaves one with the feeling that possibly it is Dasha's son Pavel and the other men adrift in the foggy Angara (having been sent to take the villagers to the mainland) who will perish because they have lost their roots, their sense of a nation, and have found nothing to replace it. The Siberia-as-Russia motif is re-inforced by Rasputin's series of essays on the history of that region, and by his 1985 story "Pozhar"(The fire), which ends with the hero's retreat from the corrupted society of a logging settlement into the forest.

Matera can easily be read as a latter-day Kitezh, the Russian city that legend says "sank uncorrupted to the bottom of a trans-Volga lake at the time of the first Mongol invasion" and which cannot be discerned by any foreigner (Billington 1970, 368, 540). The true kingdom is not lost, but exists in a state of suspended animation, awaiting *svetoprestavlenie* (the end of time), when it will just as magically appear to the righteous, that is, to genuine Russians. Vladimir Lichutin, another ruralist who has ex-pressed strong political opinions in the newspaper *Den'* and its successor *Zavtra*, wrote of his fervent wish that the village would not die, but fall into a deep sleep which would preserve it until the day when its message could once more be heard (Lichutin 1989, 233). The critic Igor' Zolotusskii characterized the late Fedor Abramov's prose as an attempt to rescue in writing a village world that could not be saved in reality: "It is the peasant Atlantis, which has already sunk to the bottom of the ocean . [...] Of course it is a poetic illusion [...] but it is one that is difficult to abandon" (Zolotusskii 1990, 3).

There was genuine ideological potential in poetic, occasionally apoca-lyptic, images of a lost Russia that could — like Kitezh or Atlantis — be resurrected under the right conditions. Just enough of the "once and future kingdom" was written into the Arcadian village of the 1960s and 1970s to allow it to be read two decades later as the homeland of the New Jerusalem. And some *derevenshchiki* took the opportunity to exploit their own past metaphors in an effort to reinvent themselves as prophets of the post-totalitarian age.

RE-READING VILLAGE PROSE: THE RADIANT PAST, THE UNCERTAIN PRESENT, AND THE OMINOUS FUTURE

In his 1994 book *Narrative and Freedom: The Shadows of Time*, Gary Saul Morson shows how we most often see both real-life and literary narratives — as well as the broad expanse of history — through the prism of either "foreshadowing" or "backshadowing". In the case of foreshadowing, our retelling of past events adds "backward causality" (Morson 1994, 48), the shadow of things to come, such as a storm as an omen of a subsequent tragedy. Time is closed off and "choice becomes illusory", since everything is already "written down" (Morson 1994, 49). Backshadowing draws a direct line from the past to a supremely confident present, the key formula contained in the phrase "He should have known" (Morson 1994, 236). The privileged present (for example, Soviet Russia from 1917 to 1985) justified everything that brought it about and everything that kept it in place. Morson quotes an Eastern European saying to the effect that "Communism is a system in which the future is known but the past always changes" (Morson 1994, 263). Time is again closed down as all important choices have already been made; the only necessary action is to recognize (usually by rewriting historical accounts) the line that leads from there to here.

Morson offers a third view of time and choice called "sideshadowing", which "conveys the sense that actual events might just as well not have happened" (Morson 1994, 118). A "shadow" is cast on the narrative from the other possibilities that existed simultaneously alongside the one that was eventually embraced; contrary to the other temporal constructs, with sideshadowing there were real decisions to be made at the time in question.

Morson's categories help us formulate questions about the political legacy of *derevenskaia proza*. In terms of foreshadowing, we should ask ourselves whether, as we read *forward* through the canon from Ovechkin's first essays to the last major works of the late 1970s, we can see clear indications of extreme nationalist sentiment, and of intolerance towards non-Russians, and especially of Russian Jews. How should we read the criticism of the time, some of which accused the writers of a dangerous return to the values of patriarchal Russia? Are these critics talking about chauvinism, or about the value the *derevenshchiki* placed on family, local, and regional identity, rural life, folk customs, Russian Orthodoxy (including the faith of the Old Believers), nature, and on a past which in their works often seemed "radiant".

The concept of backshadowing leads us to ask whether one can draw a clear line from the more extreme varieties of Russian nationalism that have surfaced in Russia since 1985 back to the Village Prose movement of 1956-80. If we feel that we can draw that line, what do we do about the virulently chauvinistic samizdat material from those years which is of urban origin? And the anti-cosmopolitan and anti-Zionist campaigns of the government? Or peasant poets of the 1920s like Esenin and Kliuev? Or right-wing anti-Semitic tracts from the early part of the twentieth-century? Or Dostoevskii's *Dnevnik pisatelia* ? We will find ourselves drawing many lines from present to past, if our search is a thorough one.

Finally, the idea of sideshadowing leads us to ask whether it was inevitable that Village Prose would be linked to the rise of chauvinism. And, more importantly, was it inevitable that some of the leading rural writers, whose openly non-Soviet stories held great significance for members of the urban intelligentsia during the "period of stagnation", should have damaged the reputation of their own past works by their political behaviour after the end of totalitarian constraints? Were they like "country bumpkins" from a Shukshin story, who did not know how to act in Moscow? Were they angry at losing their central role in the country's literature? To cite one example, did Rasputin and Belov think it was acceptable to sign an open letter that, among other noxious statements, accuses Jews of complicity in the pogroms and the Holocaust? Was the anger in their literary and extra-literary writings of the second half of the 1980s newly-felt or had they simply suppressed it in the past in order to get past the censors? And was it inevitable that the newly unified Russian canon of the 1980s would split along ethnic and generational lines, with extreme nationalists denouncing the cosmopolitan avant-garde in Russian literature, while younger critics and postmodernists devalued the legacy of their literary "fathers", including the *derevenshchiki*, because it was all — in their eyes — either pro- or anti-state, and devoid of genuine aesthetic value? How can we sort this all out in order to arrive at a reading of Village Prose that is neither alarmist nor naive, that is politically aware without itself becoming politicized?

From the 1950s until *glasnost´*, when first the kolkhoz and then the village became controversial literary subjects, the evidence cited in critical articles came from the literary texts themselves. Since the late 1980s, the paraliterary space has come to surround the by now largely historical genre of *derevenskaia proza*. The evidence used in critical arguments most often comes from *outside* the texts themselves, and is based on the authors' extra-literary comments or on works written outside the parameters of Village Prose (for example, Belov's *Vse vperedi*). The original texts are **re**-labelled without being **re**-read — or without being read at all. The paraliterary space framing Village Prose includes not only literary criticism within Russia, but also scholarship outside Russia: conference papers, book reviews, exchanges of letters in journals, even manuscript evaluations at university presses have all become part of this process.[12] Despite the subsequent retreat from political confrontation claimed by Astaf´ev and Rasputin, it is unlikely that this paraliterary expanse will shrink in the near future.[13] Village Prose will remain in the space so aptly characterized by Krauss as marked by "debate, quotation, partisanship, betrayal, [and] reconcilia-tion" and not in "the space of unity, coherence, or resolution" that its authors and first readers hoped it would be. It is still, as was said in 1981, not so much an object of literary-critical study as "an occasion for argument about the most important contemporary problems" (Petrik 1981, 66). But, as Krauss reminds us, "the paraliterary cannot be a model for the systematic unpacking of the meanings of a work of art that criticism's task is thought to be" (Krauss 1985, 293). It is a challenge for scholars to chart an objective path through the sometimes "dangerous" space in and around Russia's literary village.

REFERENCES

Anastas´ev, N. and Iu. Davydov, 1989. "Liubov´ k blizhnemu cheloveku", *Literaturnaia gazeta* 22 February: 2.

Auden, W.H., 1968. "Dingley Dell and the Fleet", in *The Dyer's Hand and Other Essays* (New York: Vintage), 407–28.

Belaia, G., 1992. "The Crisis of Soviet Artistic Mentality in the 1960s and 1970s", trans. Lesley Milne, in Sheelagh Duffin Graham (ed.), *New Directions in Soviet Literature. Selected Papers from the Fourth World Congress for Soviet and East European Studies, Harrogate, 1990* (New York: St Martin's Press), 1–17.

Billington, J., 1970. The *Icon and the Axe. An Interpretive History of Russian Culture* (New York: Vintage).

Bol´shakova, A., 1995. "Teoriia avtora u M. Bakhtina i V. Vinogradova (na materiale derevenskoi prozy)," from *Book 1* of the Seventh International Bakhtin Conference, 26-30 June, 1995 (Moscow: Moscow State Pedagogical University), 151–57.

Davydov, Iu. and N. Anastas´ev, 1989. "Chto takoe russkaia literatura?", *Literaturnaia gazeta* 1 March: 2.

Emerson, C., 1994. "Kathleen Parthé, *Russian Village Prose: The Radiant Past*", *Slavic Review* 53:2 (Summer): 652.

Erofeev, V., 1990. "Pominki po sovetskoi literature", *Literaturnaia gazeta* 4 July: 8. Trans. as "A Funeral Feast for Soviet Literature", *Soviet Studies in Literature* 26: 4 (Fall): 10–18.

Frank, J. 1981. Foreword to David Goldstein, *Dostoevsky and the Jews* (Austin: University of Texas Press), ix-xv.

––––––. "Approaches to *Diary of a Writer*", in Joseph Frank, *Through the Russian Prism* (Princeton: Princeton University Press), 153–69.

Freud, S. 1962. "Dostoevsky and Parricide", in René Wellek (ed.), *Dostoevsky: A Collection of Critical Essays* (Englewood Cliffs, NJ: Prentice-Hall), 98–111.

Iakovlev, A., 1972. "Protiv antiistorizma", *Literaturnaia gazeta* 15 November: 4–5.

"Klassika i my", 1990. [A discussion at Tsentral´nyi dom literatorov, 21 December 1977], *Moskva* 1: 183–200; 2: 169–81; 3: 186–96.

Krauss, R. 1985. "Poststructuralism and the Paraliterary", in *The Originality of the Avant-Garde and Other Modernist Myths* (Cambridge: MIT Press), 291–95.

Lichutin, V., 1989. "Tsep´ nezrimaia", *Druzhba narodov* 8: 231–47.

Morson, G. S., 1983. "Dostoevsky's Anti-Semitism and the Critics: A Review Article", *Slavic and East European Journal* 27:3 (Fall): 302–17.

––––––., 1994. *Narrative and Freedom: The Shadows of Time* (New Haven: Yale University Press).

Murav, H., 1993. "Kathleen Parthé, *Russian Village Prose: The Radiant Past*", *Slavic Review*, 52:4 (Winter): 878–79.

Parthé, K., 1992. *Russian Village Prose: the Radiant Past* (Princeton: Princeton University Press).

––––––, 1994. "Introduction: Vulnerable Writers and Indestructible Texts", and "Afterword: What **Was** Soviet Literature". "FORUM: Russian Literature in the Soviet Period: On the Margins of Literary History", *Slavic and East European Journal* 38:2 (Summer): 217–23 and 290–301.

––––––, 1995. "The Empire Strikes Back: How Right-Wing Nationalists Tried to Recapture Russian Literature", *Nationalities Papers* (at press).

Petrik, A. P., 1981. "'Derevenskaia proza': Itogi i perspektivy izucheniia", *Filologicheskie nauki* 1: 65–68.

Soloukhin, V., 1990. "Eto byl boets, voin, rytsar´... K 70-letiiu so dnia rozhdeniia Fedora Abramova", *Moskva* 2: 167–68.

Starikova, E., 1986. "Kolokol trevogi". *Voprosy literatury* 11: 80–99. Trans. as "The Alarm-Bell", *Soviet Studies in Literature* 24:4 (Fall): 13–30.

Vil´chek, L., 1987. "Derevenskaia proza", in A. Bocharov and G. Belaia (eds), *Sovremennaia russkaia sovetskaia literatura* (Moscow: Prosveshchenie), 51–88.

Zolotusskii, I., 1990. "Tropa Fedora Abramova. K 70-letiiu so dnia rozhdeniia", *Literaturnaia gazeta* 28 February: 3.
Zviniatskovskii, V., 1992 "Partiinaia literatura bez partiinoi organizatsii", *Znamia* 2: 226–37.

NOTES

1. In the nineteenth century the Slavophiles and *Pochvenniki* were more focused on the peasant and the commune rather than on the village as a physical space.
2. Liliia Vil'chek's term is *kod prochteniia* (52–53).
3. In an attempt to write a revisionist history of Village Prose, Soloukhin stated in 1990 that the Ovechkin-style *ocherk* had actually been harmful to literature, because its writers accepted collectivization, and merely wished that the kolkhozes were run more efficiently (Soloukhin 1990, 167–68).
4. The Solzhenitsyn and Tendriakov stories came out in *Novyi mir,* and the Abramov story in *Neva*.
5. "Klassika i my" 1990, 1–3. My thanks to Natal'ia Ivanova, who was present at the 1977 meeting, for bringing this to my attention.
6. Davydov and Anastas'ev 1989, 2 (the quote is from Davydov).
7. I address this topic in my contributions to the Forum in Parthé 1994, and at greater length in my forthcoming book *Dangerous Texts: The Russian Canon in Paraliterary Space.*
8. "Competitive suffering" will be covered in greater detail in *Dangerous Texts.*
9. Larisa Vasil'eva, Russian poet and author of *Kremlin Wives*, confirmed this in an interview at the University of Rochester on 20 October 1994. Soloukhin, Kunaev and other conservative nationalist writers and critics are her long-time neighbours and she often sees them at the nearby market; she recalled that during the early *glasnost'* years they were excitedly passing around the "Protocols" and other turn-of-the-century materials of that nature, which were suddenly much easier to obtain.
10. Frank also took a non-alarmist view in his Foreword to David Goldstein's *Dostoevsky and the Jews*, ix–xv, taking comfort in the observation that Dostoevskii seemed to feel guiltier about his anti-Semitic views than about his antagonism for the Poles, French, Germans, and English.
11. The page references are to the Russian and English versions respectively.
12. Culturally-generated mental maps of Russia are the subject of what will be my third book: *'Unreal Estate': Cognitive Maps of Russia and Their Cultural and Ideological Significance.*
13. On culturally-based concepts of Russianness among right-wing nationalists, see Parthé 1995.

14. Alla Bol´shakova, a scholar at IMLI, has spoken of the "polemic over Village Prose, that developed in the Western press in connection with the appearance of Kathleen Parthé's monograph" (Bol´shakova 1995, 154). While controversy over the political legacy of Village Prose actually arose at the end of the 1980s, it did have an impact on the nature of the book's reception; see, for example, the evaluation in Murav 1993 the response in Emerson 1994.

15. This information comes from a telephone conversation I had with the *Chicago Tribune*'s Moscow reporter, Jim Gallagher, on 5 December 1994; Gallagher said that he had recently conducted a two-hour interview with the writer.

RUSSIAN LITERATURE AND IMPERIALISM: THE LATE SOVIET AND EARLY POST-SOVIET PERIODS

Ewa M. Thompson

In 1992 there appeared in St Petersburg a booklet entitled *Rossiiskaia imperiia: slovar´-spravochnik*. Its contents were lifted from the Efron-Brokgauz *Malyi entsiklopedicheskii slovar´* (1907–09), but in such a way as to present a resplendent image of what Ryszard Kapuścinski has called the *Imperium* (Kapuścinski 1994). The book lists in alphabetical order all the regions and major cities of the Empire, except Helsinki and Warsaw. Scores of non-Russian territories have been included, thus contributing to the perception that they have no histories of their own, no separate coherence, and no languages in which to tell their stories, even if they had stories worth telling. In this little book, they are dissolved in the sea of Russian identity, and they become invisible as separate entities; they are merely parts of *rossiiskaia imperiia*, somehow like the West's colonial territories in Asia and Africa, or the "white colonies" of America and Australia which had once been forced to exchange their own identity for that of an appendix to the English people. But while the British Empire dissolved with the changing times, the *Imperium*, this little book suggests, is in existence even today and will be in existence tomorrow regardless of the wishes of the mute peoples it has embraced. It is this imperial wish of the Russian elites, nurtured by books like *Rossiiskaia imperiia*, as well as by countless literary works, that I wish to address.

My paper is indebted to Edward Said's *Culture and Imperialism* (Said 1993). Said commented upon Joseph Conrad, Jane Austen, and Albert Camus, writers who are not customarily charged with imperialistic tendencies, but whose writings nevertheless reflect that peculiar point of view from which the *militarily* successful nations face the defeated. Said also spoke of such articulators of American destiny as Walter Lippmann and George Kennan, who assumed the tone of pragmatic observers, but who also reflected that readiness to *classify* which characterizes imperial thinkers. Said referred to the Russians only briefly, indicating an awareness of parallelisms between them and the other colonial powers, but he did not analyse Russian writers at all. His subject matter was Western imperialism and the endless classifications and hierarchies which it has introduced in regard to itself and its dominions.

Were my choice of countries not different from Said's, my paper would be a plagiarism. I use this word deliberately to soften the shock of those who have never made the discovery of the colonial nature of the present day "Russian Federation", let alone of the Soviet Union of yesteryear. In my paper, the suggestions of cultural parallelisms between Russia and the West do not refer to the influence of one writer on another but rather to that drive to conquer which the Russians have never satiated. Perhaps one reason for the failure of scholarly vision in regard to this subject is the contiguous nature of Russia's colonies. The Western colonial empires had their dependencies overseas, whereas Russia kept conquering its immediate neighbours. For over two centuries until 1914, the Russian Empire expanded at a rate of fifty-five square miles a day. This rate of expansion guaranteed that the annexed territories would not be fully russified, thus making the Empire perpetually unstable. On the other hand, Russia avoided being labelled imperialistic precisely because neighbourly disputes tend not to be equated with colonial conquests but rather with security interests. The colonization and incomplete russification of lands and nations adjacent to the Russian heartland has been poorly understood,[1] and the powerful ideological system which acts against the appropriation for scholarly enquiry of Russia's numerous acquisitions is still in place.

Said rightfully acknowledges Joseph Conrad's irony and scepticism concerning England's imperial conquests, and he is well aware of Jane Austen's "moral discriminations" (Said 1993, 84). His book examines those English writers who can by no means be called jingoists and who articulated the imperial vision in all its presumed innocence. Conrad spoke with a forked tongue: while presenting Africa or Asia "from the outside", he managed to distance himself from the most vulgar imposed hierarchies of imperial rule. Similarly, Jane Austen touched only lightly on the realities of having possessions overseas, and she was unsparing in passing moral judgments on the characters' behaviour back home. While Walter Lippmann and George Kennan nurtured a profound sense of American superiority, they both despised chauvinism (Said 1993, 285). Russia has had no such writers. The imperial consciousness in Russia has generally been untouched by a realization that *succès* (if not *noblesse*) *oblige*. Not a single Russian writer of note has questioned the necessity or wisdom of using the nation's resources to subjugate more and more territory for the Empire, or to hold on to territories that are not Russian, and not even Slavonic. The notion of reparations, should it ever be articulated by a Russian intellectual, would probably (initially at least) endanger that intellectual's life and limb. The idea of colonial dependency, and the cost of it to the conquered nations, has not yet penetrated Russian national discourse. While many Russian writers have excelled in making moral discriminations, they have written only from the inside of their imperial house, like those British people who agonized over the just spending at home of income derived from overseas possessions. There is much compassion in Russian literature for the Akakii Akakieviches or, more recently, for the Ivan Denisoviches and Andrei Gus'kovs, but no awareness whatever that these miserable characters have acted as tools of the mighty in appropriating for Russia a dozen or so major nations, and scores of minor ones, while the natural resources of these nations have been used "for the good of the Imperium". Neither Russian writers nor Russian intellectuals have acknowledged the realities of Russian imperialism; indeed, they tend to respond with indignation to suggestions that their literature is filled with imperialist rhetoric.[2]

My paper deals with those contemporary Russian writers who write about *Imperium* as if it were Russia, who confuse *Imperium* with Russia.[3] Like their West-European counterparts in the nineteenth and early twentieth centuries, these writers perceive the unassimilated lands of the Russian Federation (or, earlier, of the Soviet Union) as rightfully Russian, never once entertaining the idea that they have blackened out the background to the colonial story, somewhat like those Soviet specialists who "retouched" photographs to blot out the recently arrested members of the party elite. Thus Siberia becomes Russia, and its history and peoples disappear. Siberia becomes a "white" colony, comparable to that of Britain's America or Australia where native populations were scarce and easy to silence. It is seen as a place where exiles are sent and prisons are established, and where Russians can emigrate if it becomes hard to make a living in the Fatherland. Remember the good Mrs Khokhlakova's advice to Dmitrii Karamazov to seek his fortune in the "gold prospecting" region of Yakutia? What a parallel between that and Mr Micawber seeking to improve his fortunes in Australia. The details of how the Russians compelled the Yakuts to reveal to them the location of the gold-bearing territories, indeed the very fact that such compulsion was central to the history of the Yakut gold, are blotted out. From Dostoevskii's account in *Brat'ia Karamazovy* (The brothers Karamazov) one might get an impression that the Russians themselves discovered the gold-bearing territories in Yakutia-Sakha and Kolyma, while the Yakuts did not even know what they possessed (see Cieslewicz 1985, 1–4). In Russian literature, Siberia became an extension of the Russian landscape and mores, as if Russian geography and countryside could be moved eastward at will. Siberia's (or the Volga's or the Caucasus's) non-Russian peoples are belittled by such representations whose centre is invariably Moscow or St Petersburg. If the native peoples appear at all in Russian novels, they are on the verge of russification, standing at the door of that Imperial House which is the writer's (and the presumed reader's) centre of attention. But while Conrad's or Austen's (or Dickens's) social space was firmly secured by the as-yet-unshaken empire that enveloped them, Aleksandr Solzhenitsyn, Anatolii Rybakov, and Valentin Rasputin composed their works at a time when the Russian Empire trembled, faltered and partially imploded. In the 1990s, a novel such as Solzhenitsyn's *Rakovyi korpus* (Cancer ward, 1968), where no distinction was made between Russian and non-Russian lands of the Soviet Union, would perhaps be less likely to appear. In the 1990s in the capital of Uzbekistan, a hospital owned by Moscow would be perceived by local inhabitants as a *foreign* hospital, one serving the Russian minority, a reminder of the colonial domination or (most unlikely) one established by a Russian charity. To impose a Russian perspective on the land of the Uzbeks, as Solzhenitsyn has done, puts this writer in the same imperial camp to which those English writers who presented Africa with paternalistic arrogance belonged (Said 1993, xviii). But in regard to the Russian Federation, such awareness has not yet appeared, indeed there is no indication that it is about to appear.

While the English have ultimately learned to make distinctions, Russian writers continue to place their characters in various spots in the Russian Federation with innocent brutality, and they impose themselves onto the social space that should be at least partially filled with native voices reflecting native visions. The interpreters of the fall of the Soviet Empire have not yet confronted the model of Russia as a stubbornly imperialistic state that has depopulated the Russian mainland to plant Russians in various parts of Asia and the Caucasus where they hardly belong. While the so-called "union republics" of the USSR have been let go at least nominally (although Russian presence in Tadjikistan indicates otherwise), the non-Russian "autonomous republics" of the Russian (*rossiiskaia*) Federation continue to be treated as Russian private property from which gas and oil can be extracted and where the most pollution-prone industries can be set up. The model of the Russian Federation which is still being taken for granted by Russian writers in the 1990s resembles the model of the world during the Cold War, as seen by such theorists of American power as George Kennan.

For Russia's imperial writers, Siberia is an extension of Russia. The native peoples of the region are marginalized in ways that suggest that the very geography of the place works against their importance. In Rasputin's "Vek zhivi - vek liubi" (You live and love, 1981), fifteen-year-old Sania, a Russian, sees Siberia in terms of Gogol´'s *Vechera na khutore bliz Dikan´ki* (Evenings on a farmstead near Dikan´ka). The sombre atmosphere of Siberian nights is rendered in Gogolian terms, or reinterpreted through another variety of colonial terminology (for Gogol' too wrote of Ukraine rather than Russia). The works of Nikolai Gogol´ act as a solvent in which cultural boundaries between Russia and Siberia vanish, thus pre-empting native self-definition. What one generally sees in Rasputin is not a description of Siberia but rather an *ascription* of Russianness to Siberia. In Anatolii Rybakov's *Deti Arbata* (Children of the Arbat, 1988) and *Strakh* (Fear, 1990), Sasha Pankratov's Siberian exile becomes an extension of his Moscow life, or a brutal and challenging version of it. Rybakov's Siberia is peopled by persons like himself, Russians from the mainland whose cultural centre is Moscow, and who assume that everyone else in the narrative trajectory feels likewise. Seeing events and happenings through Muscovite eyes only, they deign to notice the "natives" only indirectly, by using geographical terms that go back to pre-Russian times: *Podkamennaia Tunguska*, or *Evenkiiskii natsional´nyi okrug*, or *Taishet*.

Sasha Pankratov and his Moscow colleagues were exiled to an area east of the Enisei River. The area is inhabited by the Evenki, or Tungus, who numbered between ten and fifteen thousand in the 1930s, when the action of the novel unfolds.[4] The area was virtually free of Russians at that time except for exiles and concentration camps, and thus its native inhabitants should have figured prominently in Sasha's extensive travels through the region. Not only do they not, but their very identity is confused with Tatar identity.[5] Zida, Sasha's casual lover, is lumped together with the "natives" (as opposed to Russians) by the narrator, who in this respect is Sasha's *alter ego*.

The treatment of Zida is symptomatic of Rybakov's colonial attitude. While he lacks Joseph Conrad's depth and frustrated sympathy for the "natives", he displays in abundance that impenetrability to local history and society which characterizes colonialist writers. Zida is introduced to the reader by means of her first name and patronymic, as if she were Russian. Her father's Muslim name is distorted into a form that sounds ridiculous to Russian ears: a put-down against which the Turkic and Ugro-Finnic peoples of Siberia have had no recourse (an offshoot of this are the "Chukchi

jokes" — comparable to Irish jokes in England and Polish jokes in America
— which avail themselves of the fact that the name of this remote tribe
sounds funny to Russian ears).

Zida is the only representative of the "natives" to acquire an extended
presence in Rybakov's book. Even though she plays an important role as
Sasha's helper and entertainer, she has no voice and no aspirations of her
own (except the netting of Sasha). She appears from nowhere and disappears into nowhere; it is suggested that people like her have no story to
tell, they are just appendices to Russian history. Zida emerges through the
narrator's, and Sasha's, Russian voice. She falls madly in love with Sasha,
like a Madame Butterfly of Siberia, but unlike her Japanese counterpart
she does not even complain when Sasha leaves her. She is entirely dis-
posable, like a dog who does not dare to whine when her master punishes
her. "She was gone for good, vanished from his life as mysteriously as she
had entered it", says the narrator (139). She risks her own life and freedom
many times to save Sasha, and she conceives of a way to wipe out his
"criminal" record by offering to marry him and let him assume her name.
This devotion Sasha Pankratov compares to the actions of a cockroach.

The final irony and humiliation of Zida comes in the narrator's disclosure
of her profession. She is a teacher of Russian. The intellectual energies of
this representative of the "natives" are harnessed to advance the good of
the Empire, just as her sexual and moral energies are employed to bolster
Sasha's well-being. All this bias is taken in his stride by Rybakov's narrator
and, one suspects, by the author as well, just as it has been by dozens of
other Russian writers who wove Siberia into their narratives. Here and
elsewhere, Siberia serves as a backdrop for stories that might as well have
been told in Moscow, for it is Moscow's voice that resounds in them, not
the voice of the region.

Other mentions of the Tungus/Evenki people in Rybakov's novel suggest
that they are hunting savages (452), that they are fat and uneducated
drunkards (340), syphilitic (354) and crazy (356). While Sasha and his
fellow Russians rob the native forests by indiscriminate hunting, the "natives" are consigned to both criminality and marginality. As was the case
with Lermontov's "evil Chechens", Rybakov's natives are defenseless and
voiceless. Any ascription can be attached to them. They are seen through
the eyes of their adversaries. General Aleksei Ermolov, who conquered the
Caucasus for the Russians in the nineteenth century, said that the Chechens
could not be pacified but only exterminated (quite a parallel with the most
recent attempt to exterminate the Chechens in the 1994–95 Russian-Chechen
war). Rybakov implies that the culture of such "natives" deserve no better.
They have to move over to make room for the *Imperium*, and they should
feel grateful for an opportunity to become russified. The riches of Siberia

are Russian and not Tungus; they are to be used by Moscow rather than sold by the native peoples to the highest bidder. The strategy of power and violence undergirds the plot of Rybakov's novel.

The bounty of Siberia may be "renewable", as in Valentin Rasputin's "Vek zhivi — vek liubi" where three Russian colonists compete with the wildlife for food, or it may not, as in the mines of Solzhenitsyn's *Arkhipelag GULag* (The Gulag archipelago). Rasputin's narrator says that if they did not collect berries, a forest animal might, and then of what use would the berries be? Nature in the colonies is treated as the property of the colonizers. Rybakov mentions a Russian trapper who in a good year would trap or shoot as many as twenty thousand animals. One wonders whether this still falls into the category of renewable resources. In *Arkhipelag GULag*, Solzhenitsyn mentions prisoners who mined precious metals for the *Imperium* somewhere on its non-Russian outskirts. Characteristically, the realization that he was speaking of double exploitation did not enter Solzhenitsyn's mind at all. He remained indifferent to the fact that these riches were being mined in the colonies. He would be satisfied, it seems, if the Russian state brought "free" peasants from the mainland to work in Siberia's mines, in the same way in which it resettled entire Cossack villages in the Caucasus to make trouble for the "natives" in the nineteenth century. Solzhenitsyn's Ivan Denisoviches were exiled *to the colonies*. As Said points out, for all his amiability and helplessness, Mr Micawber in Australia was also an imperialist, and his imperial advantage consisted in the possibility of emigrating overseas and settling there, an opportunity which the colonial peoples did not have. When they began to demand such equal opportunity and chose the British Isles to settle, they were greeted with chagrin, anguish and dislike at best, and with violence and discriminatory laws at worst. The treatment in post-Communist Moscow of people from the colonial periphery is part of the same pattern.[6]

At one point in Rybakov's novel a sarcastic remark is uttered that a certain ranking member of the secret police has "an Eskimo face". While it is comforting to know that not only Jews can be blamed for the Russians' misfortunes, it is disturbing to find in Rybakov, a writer of Jewish background, a replay of the convenient suggestion that the Russian secret police was run by non-Russians, as if such a thing were possible in a sovereign country. On the other hand, the absence of Eskimo faces on the Arbat is taken for granted, affirmative action not being part of the Russian or Soviet traditions.

The literary and artistic texts of the late Soviet and post-Soviet period reinforce the imperial posture and continue to assume the centrality of the imperial vision. One can repeat after Said that [Russian] "culture is exonerated of any entanglements with power" (Said 1993, 57). A pretence is maintained that Sasha's coming from the centre of empire did not empower him in Siberia, that he and Zida could have swapped places in society, that the Buriats were not crowded out by the arrival of families such as the Gus'kovs in Rasputin's *Zhivi i pomni* (Live and remember, 1975). Yet Zida on the Arbat would be one of those "Eskimo" or "Caucasus" faces so suspiciously viewed by the Muscovites in the 1980s or 1990s. But Sasha's presence in Siberia is construed as "normal" by the narrator.

In Soviet Russia, those Siberian writers who reinforced the imperial viewpoint were generally favoured, just as the native voices were crowded out. Foremost among the beneficiaries of this treatment was Valentin Rasputin. His powerful invocations of Mother Russia in the depth of Siberia ring hollow to a reader attuned to the massively emerging self-consciousness in postcolonial areas of the world, but they have been favourably received by Soviet Russians. Rasputin can be compared to Il'ia Glazunov, Russia's beloved contemporary painter, who is likewise a master of the pictorial strategies by means of which Russia's artistic imagination continues to appropriate colonial territories (Berezina 1989).

Soviet statistics for the year 1979 say that there were 353,000 Buriats in the Baikal area, where the action of most of Rasputin's novels and stories takes place. Like so many other nations and tribes that have been victims of empires, the Buriats have been partitioned between the Soviet Union (now the Russian Federation) and Mongolia. It is reasonable to expect that the Buriats, many of whom were ousted by Russian settlers, might have some grievances against their conquerors, and that writers dealing with Siberia would face up to this emotional issue. Not Rasputin. Unlike Americans who have undertaken a tortuous soul-searching in regard to the American Indians, Rasputin and other Russian Siberian writers refuse to recognize the problem, let alone deal with it.

A device that facilitates this imperial obliviousness is the type of narrator whom writers like Rasputin employ. He is well familiar to the readers of Russian literature, having made his appearance in Gogol' and Leskov. The *skaz* narrator is simple-minded (though not without cunning), poor, uneducated, and funny. He is certainly not militant; he in no way resembles those V-Day troops marching in Red Square in May 1995. One cannot expect this kind of narrator to deal with the business of Russia's being a military superpower and a territorial glutton. Rasputin's and Astaf'ev's *skaz* narrators screen away from readers Russia's territorial and military dilemmas. The rural metaphors which they employ deflect the readers' attention from Russia-as-imperial-bully to the self-image which Russians so cherish, of Russia-as-the-meek-victim. Like a Russian Rip Van Winkle, such a narrator bypasses situations that are beyond his ability to describe and interpret. But unlike Rip, he manages to persuade Russian and foreign readers that he represents Russian cultural identity, rather than being a cover-up for the imperial establishment which his village voice conceals.

Rasputin's *Zhivi i pomni* is a story told by this kind of narrator, about an army deserter who managed to get back to his native Siberian village to which he could not return legally; so he hid in an old bathhouse and communicated secretly with his wife, who got pregnant in the process and eventually perished in the hunt for the deserter which ensued. One would imagine that if a writer were to make a patriotic appeal to the reader on the basis of this tragic story, he would call for a resolve to abolish the system that institutionalized the victimization of persons like Nastena and her husband Andrei for the sake of the power of the state. But instead, Rasputin exhorts his readers to "live", or to preserve Russia biologically; and to "remember", or to preserve the tribal memory. If we were dealing here with Estonians or Latvians whose group survival is at stake, we could understand this tribal anxiety. But the title refers to Russians who are certainly not threatened with extinction. For a Russian to make this kind of appeal suggests the author's desire that Russians "survive" in Siberia at any price. Rasputin urges his readers not to rebel and not to fight for a dignified life, but to remain alive and preserve the tribe.

The interpretation of Rasputin above has been suggested by Viktor Astaf´ev, who commented on Rasputin's novel thus: "Live and remember, o man: in misery and turmoil, during the harshest trials your obligation is to remain part of your nation. Any kind of separation from your nation, caused either by weakness or by a misuderstanding, imposes new burdens on your fatherland and therefore on you."[7] This is a far cry indeed from Tolstoi's "living for God and for one's soul".

Another example of this sentimental imperialism is Rasputin's story "Pozhar" (Fire, 1987). The story deals with a group of downtrodden peasants who were told to leave central Russia and settle in Siberia. A peasant named Afonia, a righteous man, declares that the village of Egorovka from which he came worked "for Mother Russia", and that he would like to commemorate that fact (Rasputin 1986, 376). Two things are worth noting here: first, the collective and non-anthropocentric nature of this Egorovka; we are talking here not about people, not about Ivan and Masha and their families, but about "the village of Egorovka", a communal entity that is an element of state organization. Second, this impersonal anthill is said to have worked for the state, not for themselves, and not for the sake of a moral ideal such as God's commandment or dedication to the good of other human beings. When Afonia is asked what the community should do after the fire, he answers, "We shall live" ("Zhit´ budem"). In the context of the story, this determination to live is, again, advocated not for the sake of individuals, or for the nurturing of families, certainly not for God or one's soul: but for the tribe, for Russia. If Afonia had said "I worked so that others after me could have a better life", one might perceive him as a generous and unselfish person. If he said "I worked for my family", or "I worked for myself", we could understand that. If he declared his willingness to live for his soul, we would class him together with the spiritually alive peasants in Tolstoi. But working for the tribe? And a successful tribe at that, not threatened with extinction like some of the conquered ones. The treatment of Russians as pegs in the national machine is evident in so-called Village Prose. Great Britain managed to maintain a distinction between domestic liberty and repression and terror abroad,[8] but the Russian Empire did not offer its titular nationality freedom from suppression by the state. I see in writers like Rasputin and Astaf'ev a regressive quality, a confirmation of Russia's imperialistic goals achieved at the expense of the population, rather than the search for a way out of the dulling morass of the collective farm. The inability to distinguish between the interest of the individual and the state, that perennial blind spot of Russian politicians, is amply present in the last "school" to emerge out of socialist realism.

All this does not mean that the Russian colonialist experience is somehow uninteresting, or that the works which convey that experience are deprived of artistic or humanistic value just because their authors see the world through imperialist spectacles. This reservation is particularly important in regard to Solzhenitsyn, whose *Arkhipelag GULag* remains a key to the Soviet period of Russian history, even as it records a special kind of colonialist intervention: making the colonies into a vast archipelago of prisons and death camps. Solzhenitsyn's achievements as an anti-totalitarian writer are considerable, but so are his imperialistic habits. In *Arkhipelag GULag* and elsewhere, he has presented the moral pollution of the conquered land, but not as one more insult dealt to the periphery by the centre, but rather as another injustice meted out to long-suffering Russia. The very word "Siberia" (unlike, say, "Alaska") resonates throughout the world as an invocation of cruelty and horror. The creation of Siberia's grisly reputation has been part of the Russian colonial experience. The native peoples of Siberia were subjected to the injustice of having their homeland besmirched in the memory of the world, and not because they were particularly odious but because the conqueror so willed. It has apparently never occurred to Solzhenitsyn that the Russians did to Siberia what the Nazis did to the town of Auschwitz: they wrote a history of it against the wishes of the local people. Similarly, the Russians implanted in the world's memory the notion of Siberia as a land of repression.

Western literary history has been combed through by critics like Said for major and minor examples of imperial self-assertion and colonial marginalization. The native writers of postcolonial Africa, Asia and Latin America added more insights, and Wole Soyinka and Derek Walcott received Nobel prizes in the process. The former "white colonies" of European powers such as Canada, New Zealand, the United States and Australia developed their own distinctive voices in literature, politics and social life. But the vast areas of Russian-controlled Asia, the Volga region and the Caucasus are still battlegrounds between colonizer and native, between centre and periphery. The Russian-Chechen war has been a grim reminder of this contest. In the Russian equivalent of "white colonies", the development parallel to that in which Canada gained independence from Great Britain was stifled by Soviet censorship proclaiming the unity of centre and periphery. Russia's "white colonies" are still in the stage of dependency on Moscow, although some of them have attempted to win sovereignty recently. In 1994 the governor of the Far East, Evgenii Nazdratenko, openly spoke of Russian colonial rule and his desire to bring independence to his region. This was labelled by Moscow as criminal, in a way resembling the language Moscow has used in regard to the Chechens.[9] In 1995 Governor Eduard Rossel's electoral victory in Ekaterinburg (he won against the centre's candidate) demonstrated separatist tendencies in the Russian-speaking Urals. In regard to her colonies, Russia is still at a stage preceding that of the American Revolution. The assertion of separate identity by America and Australia has not yet been followed in Siberia, the Urals, the Caucasus and the Far East. To prevent history from repeating itself, attempts are made to saturate Siberia ideologically with Muscovite experience, while crowding out native presence and experience. To secure the identity of empire over vast territories, Russian writers like Rasputin and Solzhenitsyn race against time and perpetuate a vision of Siberia as being *inside* the Russian mainland, albeit on the margins of cultural space. In their books, the Russian super-subject maintains a privileged position as the imperial spokesman, and his monologue makes the imperial intervention in geographical and cultural periphery invisible. The socially desirable and empowered space in the empire's centre informs the attitudes of writers towards the periphery, which is seen in terms supplied by the centre, as in Sania's vision of Siberian nights which he borrows from Gogol´. This choreographed movement for 'unity" between ethnic Russia and her remote colonies has been a persistent feature of Russian literature in the late Soviet period.

Walker Percy once said that language is a living organism subject to certain organic ailments. The Russian language today remains insensitive to the concepts which have developed, for instance, in American English, such as equal opportunity, minority participation, affirmative action, bilingual education, ideological appropriation and the like. Those Russian writers who deal with Siberia as if it were a storeroom for the Russian mainland are writing in the classical imperialist tradition created by Western writers who once looked at Africa and Asia as antechambers and storerooms of the British or French empires. Unwittingly perhaps, Russian writers engage in perception management with regard to their country's cultural politics. Contemporary Russian literature and the press display an inability to recognize, let alone discuss, the problems which have been part of the Western intellectual agenda for over half a century.

In the late 1980s and early 1990s, Russian cultural periodicals such as *Literaturnaia gazeta* and *Ogonek* (and, at the other end of the political spectrum, *Literaturnaia Rossiia*) conducted lengthy discussions about Russian identity, but without identifying the problems outlined above. The discussion was kept within the parameters of imperial vision, even though its participants were among the most resolute democrats in Russia today. While some of them went so far as to question the concept of *edinaia i nedelimaia* (single and indivisible), none attempted to devise a vocabulary that would launch the post-imperial period in the Russian language.[10]

A feature of all imperialisms is a desire for land, but in addition to that desire, a tendency of Russian imperialism has been the proclivity to call all the appropriated land "Russia". In a lecture delivered at the Kennan Institute for Advanced Russian Studies on 27 November1989, Russian legislator Galina Starovoitova said that Russians base their national consciousness not on their historical heritage but on the idea of territoriality, whereby whatever is conquered is called *rossiiskii* and translated into English, French and German as *Russian*, leaving the speakers of these languages unaware that there is another word, *russkii*, that corresponds more accurately to the English word "Russian", while *rossiiskii* should rather be translated as "Russian-dominated". In regard to Russia, the issue of imperialism and language is a fertile field of study. The Russians call their lands *rodina*, *otchizna*, *matushka Rossiia* regardless of whether these lands are ethnically Russian or not.

Dostoevskii once said that all Russian writers came from under Nikolai Gogol´'s overcoat. In the twentieth century, one might say that a good part of Russian literature has as its patron saint the figure of Shatov in Dostoevskii's *Besy* (The possessed, 1872). In a significant conversation with Stavrogin, Shatov said that he believed in Russia, and as to God, well, he... would believe in God; the implication being that he might believe in God because believing in him would strengthen his belief in Russia. This placing of the nation above all values has been a temptation to which many contemporary Russian writers have succumbed. Through their novels, stories, and articles, they have inscribed in the Russian language a sentimental vision of Russia *über alles*. They have further implied that the source of significant action and life within the Russian Federation is Russia, and that the native cultures have willingly submitted to Russia's paternalistic guidance; in fact they are grateful to Russia for the many benefits they have received from her. With very few exceptions, contemporary Russian historians have applied a fixing solution to this version of reality. The rhetoric of power routinely used in Russian literature is accompanied by the rhetoric of benevolence towards the conquered territories. It is not the "natives" but Russians who suffer because of territorial appropriations, as Rasputin suggests in his descriptions of the Russian settlements in Siberia. This is an innocent vision of imperialism, one that lacks an awareness of its own misdeeds. The issue of colonial dependency and the price which the conquered peoples have paid for being so dependent, is totally blotted out. If Joseph Conrad's Negroes and Orientals remained mute, there was at least a suggestion in the narrator's tone that they might have a story to tell. Not even a hint of such a suggestion is present in Rasputin or Rybakov or Astaf'ev. In regard to Russia's imperial possessions, the Russian reader today faces a linguistic and literary scene dominated by the monologue of power unaware of itself. The Russian language is now at a stage where it excludes, organically rejects as it were, concepts and ideas incompatible with the full acceptance of Russia as *Imperium*.

REFERENCES

Cambridge Encyclopedia, 1982. *The Cambridge Encyclopedia of Russia and the Soviet Union* (Cambridge: Cambridge University Press).

Cieslewicz, W. J., 1985. "A History of Russian Gold Mining", *The Sarmatian Review*, 5,4 : 1–4.

"Diktator Primor´ia", 1994. "Diktator Primor´ia", *Novoe vremia*, 40: 12–15.

Entsiklopedicheskii slovar´, 1964. *Entsiklopedicheskii slovar´ v dvukh tomakh* (Moscow: Sovetskaia entsiklopediia).

Berezina, I.I., 1989. *Il´ia Glazunov* (Leningrad: Avrora).

Kapuściński, R., 1994. *Imperium* (New York: Alfred A. Knopf).

Lane, C., 1981. *The Rights of Rulers: Ritual in Industrial Society — the Soviet Case* (Cambridge: Cambridge University Press).

Parkhomenko, V.P. 1992. *Rossiiskaia imperiia: slovar´-spravochnik* (St Petersburg: Izdatel´stvo imeni A. S. Suvorina).

Rasputin, V., 1986. *Poslednii srok, Proshchanie s Materoi, Pozhar* (Moscow: Sovetskaia Rossiia).

———, 1987. *Uroki frantsuzskogo. Povesti i rasskazy* (Moscow: Khudozhestvennaia literatura).

Rybakov, A., 1988. *Children of the Arbat* (Boston: Little, Brown and Company).
Said, E., 1993. *Culture and Imperialism* (New York: Alfred A. Knopf).

NOTES

1. The following books reflect a growing awareness of the problems which incomplete russification has caused: Alan W. Fisher, *Crimean Tatars* (Stanford: The Hoover Institution Press, 1978); Azade Ayse-Rorlich, *The Volga Tatars* (Stanford: The Hoover Institution Press, 1986); Martha B. Olcott, *The Kazakhs* (Stanford: The Hoover Institution Press, 1987); Audrey L. Altstadt, *The Azerbaijani Turks: Power and Identity under Russian Rule* (Stanford: The Hoover Institution Press, 1992).

2. My personal contacts with the spokesmen for Valentin Rasputin at the Fourth World Congress for Soviet and East European Studies, Harrogate, 1990 alerted me to this phenomenon. My subsequent conversations with Russian intellectuals such as Alla Latynina, Evgenii Khramov, Aleksandr Panchenko, and Vladimir Uspenskii persuaded me that such attitudes are widespread.

3. The English usage is unhelpful here, as it confuses ethnic Russia with the Russian Federation.

4. *Evenkiiskii natsional'nyi okrug* numbered 11,000 inhabitants in 1963, mainly the Evenki. Other Evenki (14,000) lived in surrounding areas. *Entsiklopedicheskii slovar'* 1964, 2: 683. In the 1970 census, the Tungus/ Evenki numbered 25,000. *The Cambridge Encyclopedia* 1982, 72.

5. Rybakov speaks of a "Tungus, Tatar grin" on the face of Lukeshka, a native girl from the village in which Sasha Pankratov resides (Rybakov 1988, 355). All subsequent page references are to this edition.

6. Vanora Bennett of Reuters wrote in February 1995 that in Moscow, non-Russians from the *Imperium* are routinely treated as "guilty until proven innocent".

7. V. Astaf'ev's review of *Zhivi i pomni*, quoted in Valentin Kurbatov, "V tebe i vokrug: Predislovie", Rasputin 1987, 7. This interpretation is confirmed by Lane 1981, 23.

8. This is how Bernard Semmel and Irfan Habib described the relation between Jamaica and Great Britain. Quoted from Said, 130, 345.

9. "Diktator Primor'ia" 1994, 12-15. *Dal'nevostochnaia respublika* was formed in 1921 and it acquired a constitution of its own. For a copy of the constitution see the Hoover Institution Archives under *Dal'nevostochnaia respublika*.

10. In *Literaturnaia gazeta* of 18 April 1990, Alla Latynina questioned the desire of Russians to hold on to the non-Russian nations of the Soviet Union. A similar view was expressed by Elena Bonner in a MacNeil-Lehrer interview,

15 May 1990. On 9 May 1990 in *Literaturnaia gazeta*, Sergei Chuprinin wrote cogently about the Slavophile-Westerner controversy, its re-emergence in present-day Russia, and the presumptions of some of the participants in these discussions. The Russians, said S. S. Averintsev in *Novyi mir* (January 1989, 195), "do not trust that freedom which is guaranteed by institutions". "One cannot understand Russia by rational discourse alone", echoed *Literaturnaia gazeta* on 5 April 1990. Recently, D. S. Likhachev expressed an opinion that St Petersburg is a world cultural treasure and that it is the world's obligation to help restore it (*Clarinet News*, 9 January 1995). Imagine Irving Kristol saying that Washington, DC is an architectural pearl and the world owes it subsidy. In keeping with these views, Likhachev's article in *Literaturnaia gazeta* on 11 April 1990 (entitled "Narod dolzhen imet´ svoi sviatyni") implies that only Russian churches and monasteries that had been taken over by the Soviet State are worth restoring. Insofar as the Soviet Union was only half Russian, Likhachev's statement is symptomatic of the unselfconscious imperialism so characteristic of Russian intellectual life.

BLUES AT FORTY: THE PLAYS
OF VIKTOR SLAVKIN

Robert Russell

Viktor Slavkin, who was born in 1935, belongs to the so-called "new wave" of Russian dramatists who emerged in the late 1970s and the 1980s and who include Aleksandr Galin, Liudmila Razumovskaia, and Liudmila Petrushevskaia. Slavkin was educated at the Moscow Institute of Railway Engineers, but worked as a staff member of the journal *Iunost'* from 1967 until 1984. At *Iunost'* he was responsible for the regular satirical and humorous section and most of his one-act plays are amusingly sceptical visions of a life that is essentially absurd.

Slavkin himself considers that his career as a dramatist began on 28 April 1979, the date of the première of his first full-length play *Vzroslaia doch' molodogo cheloveka* (A young man's grown-up daughter) at the Moscow Stanislavskii Theatre (Slavkin 1986b, 98). Before that date his plays had been short pieces written with a student company in mind, namely "Nash dom", the Moscow University Variety Theatre Company ("estradnaia studiia"). By implication, Slavkin appears to minimize the significance of his one-act plays, preferring to concentrate attention on the full-length works, but the short pieces deserve some consideration, both in their own right and as a stage in Slavkin's development as a dramatist.

Plokhaia kvartira (The bad apartment, 1966), *Moroz* (Frost, 1966), and *Orkestr* (The band, 1966) are concerned with serious issues such as lone-liness and the essential absurdity of the human condition, yet they are saved from any hint of portentousness by an infectiously cheerful good humour. The inhabitants of the bad apartment in *Plokhaia kvartira* were forced to move from their previous home when it literally fell down and they have been re-housed in the only space available in an overcrowded city, which happens to be behind the targets in a shooting gallery. The members of the family have had to learn to dodge the bullets as they go about their daily lives. Much of the humour derives from their matter-of-fact acceptance of their situation, especially in contrast to the terror of a distant relative who is a first-time visitor to the apartment:

Nephew: Bullets! There are bullets! Get down! Somebody is shooting at us! Why are you standing? Get down! Down!
Mother: I'll just go and set another place at the table. (*To the prone nephew*) You are going to eat aren't you?
Nephew: You'll get killed any second!!!
Mother: That's no reason to turn down a meal. (*Plokhaia kvartira*: Slavkin and Petrushevskia 1983, 8)[1]

The husband and wife who live in the apartment have a long conversation, punctuated by the sound of gunfire, in which they fantasize about their future children. After a particularly prolonged bout of firing there is a pause, whereupon the husband says:

Husband: Listen, I've been thinking, and I can see that our apartment's no good for a child.
Wife: Why not?
Husband: A child just couldn't live here.
Wife: Rubbish!
Husband: Do you mean to say that you don't understand what I'm talking about?
                              A shot
Wife: No, I don't understand.
Husband: Don't pretend!
                     A series of rapid gunshots
Wife: What are you on about?
Husband: I've told you a hundred times. It's like banging your head against a brick wall.
Wife: What?
Husband: The flies! The house is full of flies. (14)

Their problem is solved when a letter arrives from the Housing Department offering them different accommodation. On hearing the address Mother recognises it as a bathhouse. She is delighted: "It's a very nice building, high ceilings, clean. It's a little damp, but there is absolute hygiene and there are no flies" (28). The owner of the shooting gallery tries to dissuade them from the move because his customers have grown used to firing at live targets, particularly female ones, and will stop coming to the gallery if there is nobody to fire at. But the family have made up their minds and they leave. The owner looks out into the audience and begs people not to leave, but without success. Then he puts on one of Mother's old dresses and declares that he is a target. Slowly the customers come back in and the firing starts up again. The owner is ecstatic, and as the curtain goes down his head is the last in a line of targets which are being shot down one by one. There are just a couple of ducks to go before it is his turn.

Moroz, which is virtually a monologue in that it consists of one side of numerous telephone calls, begins with a much more firmly realistic premise than *Plokhaia kvartira* but eventually becomes a vehicle for a similarly grotesque vision. In a bare room a man plays telephone chess, explaining to his unseen opponent that it is far too cold to leave the house. Between moves he makes other calls, including several in which, identifying himself simply as Number 173, he appears to take part in a telephone trivia quiz, using a system of filing cards to come up with the correct answers; or perhaps this senseless stream of useless facts is his sole form of education. Throughout the play the trivia answers act as an absurd background to the man's personal calls which reveal his lonely and meaningless existence.

The calls involving telephone chess and trivia questions are realistic enough, but one of the protagonist's other calls soon slips from reality into grotesque, leaving the reader or audience uneasy about the play's genre. The man calls his wife and finds out that the child which she has recently borne is a boy. He asks her to put the receiver to the child's head so that he can talk to him. At first he talks as to a baby, trying to get the child to say "Papa", but in the course of a few lines on the page or a few seconds in the theatre the child grows older and older. It is obvious from the man's answers that the boy has asked why there is summer and winter; then that he is alone in the house as his mother has gone off on holiday; and finally that he has become a university student. The speech is simultaneously amusing and disturbing, as is a later telephone conversation with the protagonist's mother. She tells him that she is seriously ill and might never see him again, but although he promises to come to her straight away he is so concerned about catching a chill that we understand that he will not leave the room. He promises her that when the weather improves they will go out together and he will buy her some candy floss. Then the text lurches into the absurdity that underlies the whole play: "And you will...Why won't she? Who am I talking to? Her former doctor? Why former? Her former doctor...(*Pause*) Where was she buried? I would have come with some flowers, but where can you get flowers at this time of the year?" (*Moroz*: Slavkin and Petrushevskaia 1983, 40)

No sooner have the implications of this section of the monologue sunk
in than the mood shifts again in the direction of the farcical. The protagonist
makes use of the fact that he is speaking to a doctor to seek advice on
the best way to perform an appendectomy on himself since, of course, he
cannot leave the house in such cold weather. He goes off to get a knife
for this purpose and by the time he rings the doctor again for detailed
instructions someone else is on the other end of the line informing him
that the doctor has died.

The man decides that life has lost all meaning, so he cuts the telephone
wire and sits immobile, wrapped up in numerous scarves, cardigans and
shawls. Just when it appears that the play must end with this affirmation
that the single protagonist is alone in the world, a second character enters:
a fit young athlete exuding health and energy who turns out to be the man's
son. He explains that it is hot outside and persuades his father to cast off
the warm winter clothing and come out with him. The older man agrees
and goes off to change and the son sets about mending the telephone wire
while he waits. The absurd world of total isolation seems to have been
defeated by human warmth and sympathy, but in the final lines of the play
the young man rings up a friend and starts a game of telephone chess and
the play has come full cycle.

In *Orkestr* a member of a small band turns up late for rehearsals and
cannot take part because he has lost the key to his strangely shaped instrument case. Neither he nor any of his colleagues can say what his
instrument is. Each member of the band has been concerned only with
himself: the violinist, for example, thinks of nothing but his own supposed
greatness; the drummer rushes directly from rehearsals to whatever sporting
competition is being held; and the mandolin player dreams of retirement.
Although he has sat beside them for months none of the other members
has ever noticed the latecomer.

From inside the mysterious case a rustling sound turns out to be caused
by some mice. The musician is in despair lest they eat up his instrument:
"...and I will be left with nothing. I will never be able to find out what
it was that I devoted my whole life to and I'll never get to do what I am
able to do. There is no other instrument like that in the whole world.
Tomorrow I'll have to start life from zero, from the beginning" (Slavkin
1990, 20-21). Unexpectedly he finds the key and opens the case which turns
out to be empty apart from some white mice which run out onto the stage
as the curtain goes down.

Slavkin has described *Plokhaia kvartira*, *Moroz*, and *Orkestr* as "grotesque [and] metaphorical" (Slavkin 1986b, 98). A fourth one-act play,
Kartina (The picture, 1966), appears to be very similar, but Slavkin distinguishes it from the others because, apart from one unrealistic premise,

"the rest, as they say, is taken from life" (Slavkin 1986b, 98). *Kartina* is set in a hotel room. The two characters are the man who is staying in the room and an artist called Alapat´ev whose only painting of any worth has been bought by the hotel and hangs in that particular room. He visits frequently in order to see the painting and talk about it to whichever guest happens to be in the room at that time. The two characters are by turns friendly and aggressive, but in the end they quarrel seriously and the guest destroys the painting. Appalled at the possible consequences of what he has done, he makes Alapat´ev promise to work all night on a replacement.

It would be quite possible to interpret Slavkin's early short plays as Aesopian commentaries on various aspects of Soviet life. *Plokhaia kvartira*, for example, was written in the mid-1960s, when the housing shortage was acute, and, yes, one did have to keep one's head down in the Moscow of the Brezhnev period because there were plenty of people trying to shoot it off. The critic Marianna Sorvina writes: "Slavkin's plays, which at first sight appear to be absurd, are in fact nothing other than true-to-life. Our people have to live everywhere - in a bathhouse, in a shooting-gallery, on a firing-range. They move into apartments with no doors, no windows, no ceilings" (Sorvina 1991, 55). But tempting as a socio-political reading might be, it would not do full justice to Slavkin's miniatures. As with the work of Kharms, the socio-political reality is not fundamental but adds a further element to a vision which is essentially absurdist. The plays are concerned in different ways with the nature of human life rather than Soviet life, and it is in that sense that they are "metaphorical" works (to use Slavkin's own term) or "parables and fairytales and poetic sketches" (Arbuzov 1990, 3). Apart from the probable influence of Beckett and Ionesco, they bear some resemblance to the work of Kharms and Erdman. In places, particularly in *Moroz*, Slavkin captures the absurdity of the human situation with a bleak comic touch which justifies his description of the plays as "grotesque". In general, though, they are shot through with a good-humoured optimism which distinguishes them from some of the absurdist works to which they bear a formal resemblance.[2]

Apart from the question of loneliness and isolation, which is examined in all of these plays, an important recurrent theme which was also to be significant in Slavkin's full-length plays of the late 1970s and 1980s is that of self-reappraisal in middle age and the search for self-definition. The musician in *Orkestr* fears that with the loss of his instrument the entire flow of his life has been stopped and he has been forced to begin again "from zero, from the start". Likewise the artist in *Kartina*, faced with the destruction of his "masterpiece". Yet painful as the loss is, it opens up possibilities for self-renewal. He thanks the hotel guest for destroying the picture, because that act has given the artist freedom:

Guest: At last I am free! I am nothing!
Host: A nonentity, more like.
Guest: Nice words you choose. A nonentity. Just so. Oh, you don't un-
         derstand how good it is to feel that one is a nonentity. Everything
         lies ahead. It's as if you hadn't been born yet, as if you were just
         standing at the entrance door to the world. All great things start
         from the feeling that you are a nonentity, a speck of dust before
         the Universe, the truth! (*Kartina*, 73)

The feeling which the artist expresses here is the consciousness of being
half way through life, able to look back at what has been done, but free
to look forward to the second half. For the artist in *Moroz* that freedom
comes through the destruction of his sole achievement.

For the central characters of Slavkin's three full-length plays of the late
1970s and 1980s letting go of their youth so as to be able to enjoy their
later years is no easy task. Only Prokop in *Vzroslaia doch´ molodogo
cheloveka* has been able to accept that he is no longer young. He advises
Bems, the hero of the play, to put his past on the shelf: "I have put my
past on the shelf [...] Like the first volume of my life. It stands there and
I admire it" (Slavkin 1990, 167; further references to this play are to this
edition and given in parentheses in the text). But such an uncomplicated
acceptance of the passing of time is beyond Slavkin's heroes, and their
attempts to cope with being forty-something are at the centre of what has
turned out to be a trilogy.[3] Writing of the three plays collectively, Slavkin
has said:

> Middle life crisis [*sic*: Slavkin's English] is the subject of my three plays.
> From a point in the middle of life's journey I cast three glances: back, forward,
> and into myself. *Vzroslaia doch´* is a glance backwards, *Serso* [Cerceau, 1982–
> 85] a glance forwards, and *Mesto dlia kureniia* [The smoking room, 1988]
> a glance inwards (Slavkin 1988, 12).

Vzroslaia doch´ molodogo cheloveka, the "glance back", is a play which
is infused with Slavkin's love of jazz. Bems's daughter is called Ella after
Ella Fitzgerald (and if his child had been a boy he would have been named
after Louis Armstrong). Bems himself was famous as a student for his
passionate singing of the Glenn Miller number "Chattanooga Choo Choo",
which on one occasion had resulted in serious trouble with the college
authorities. In 1954 the only way of getting hold of a jazz record was to
make an illegal pirated copy on an X-ray plate, giving rise to the expression
that was current at the time that jazz was "na kostiakh" (on bones). In a
detail to be discussed more fully later, Bems declares that if he had to choose
a particular place in which to live out the whole of his life it would be

in between two particular notes - the "ti" and the "ta" - of Ellington's "Mood Indigo".[4] But the significance of jazz in *Vzroslaia doch'...* runs deeper than this kind of detail. Bems lives his life as if it were a jazz piece and he were performing it like Armstrong, Fitzgerald, or Ellington. Individualistic and passionate, he is also part of an ensemble upon which he depends. According to the critics Mariia and Vladislav Ivanov the textual basis for considering jazz to be central was further reinforced in Vasil'ev's production. They write: "The architectonics of psychological relations are realised by [Vasil'ev] in a musical fashion. The characters are combined into a harmonious jazz 'head arrangement' which becomes the basis for improvisation." The Ivanovs assert that the actors and audience are united by the flow of "the musical river" which carries them all along "according to its own laws" (Ivanova and Ivanov 1987, 250).

Bems is the universally-used nickname of Kupriianov, a forty-four-year-old engineer in a modest job who lives with his wife Liusia and daughter Ella. He and Liusia are visited by an old friend from student days, Prokop'ev, nicknamed Prokop, who has come to Moscow from Cheliabinsk with his son Tolia in order to try to secure the latter's entry to the same institute that he and Bems attended. For this purpose they have invited to dinner the pro-rector of the institute, Ivchenko, who was their contemporary. But whereas Prokop and, especially, Bems were rebels at college - *stiliagi* - Ivchenko was a conformist, a leading member of the Komsomol. Bems and Ivchenko were once rivals for the same girl - the pretty Liusia, a singer in the local cinema. To make the relationship between them even more complicated, Elka (Bems's daughter) is now a student at the institute, and, like her father before her, she is a rebel in trouble with the authorities (although Ivchenko does not know whose daughter she is). In the 1950s Bems and Prokop wore tight trousers, thick crepe-soled shoes, and a "*stiliaga*" quiff in their hair, while Elka and her friends are 1970s hippies — beautiful flower people — but in essence history is repeating itself. On the day of the play's action Elka has been involved in a demonstration against an elderly lecturer and, as a result, is threatened with expulsion.

Using the framework of these events and relationships, Slavkin creates a free-flowing drama focused on the themes of middle age and the passing of time. By turns melancholic and comic, tense and farcical, the play explores the state of mind of a man who has reached the halfway point in his life, or beyond, but who still sees himself as the carefree *stiliaga* of his student years. The paradox in the play's title (how can a genuinely young man have an adult daughter?) points to the central feature of Bems's psychology: despite all the evidence to the contrary, in his own mind he remains a youth standing on the threshold of life. Interestingly, the title which encapsulates the central problem of the play was not Slavkin's own. He originally called the work *Doch´ stiliagi* (Daughter of a teddy boy), but the use of the word *stiliaga* in the title did not please the censor and the play was held up. When Vasilii Aksenov heard about the difficulties he suggested an alternative: *Vzroslaia doch´ molodogo cheloveka*, which Slavkin gratefully accepted. In a generous tribute to Aksenov, Slavkin has asserted that his friend's influence on the play was much deeper than simply that of supplier of the title. Aksenov was himself a *stiliaga* in Kazan´, a lover of jazz, "the first bard of this generation", and "the whole play is full of him [propitana im]" (Slavkin 1991c, 76).

The universal theme of nostalgia for one's youth is examined in the specific context of Moscow student life of the 1950s, which gives the play a social resonance which Slavkin has emphasized in several articles. Speaking about the first review of the Vasil´ev production, a positive one in *Pravda*, Slavkin writes:

> But, strange as it may seem, it was in *Pravda* that the political aspect of the play and the production was most clearly revealed: the word "*stiliaga*" was mentioned [...] it was pointed out that people were given a hard time for wearing narrow trousers and dancing in the modern style. I mention this because the authors of most later reviews and articles tried to say as little as possible about the historical significance; they wrote about "sincerity", "purity", and "nostalgia", about these abstract human and theatrical concepts, and hesitated when it came to explaining what that "sincerity", "purity", and "nostalgia" was all about (Slavkin 1991a, 161).

For Bems and Prokop, as for young people of every generation, the search for their own voice, for their own way in the world, took the form of fashion, music, and literature which were frowned upon by the establishment. As Bems says: "What was it that you and I wanted then, Prokop? What did we want? Not so very much...We wanted clothes that were a little brighter, we wanted to walk with a springy step, we wanted jazz, we wanted to read Hemmy" (129). But in the Soviet Union in 1954 wearing bright clothes, sporting a moustache or a *stiliaga* quiff, listening to jazz, and reading Hemingway represented much more of a political threat than the corresponding signs of youthful self-assertion in other generations and other societies. And when Bems says that what they wanted was not all that much he is being disingenuous. Ivchenko suggests to Prokop that he and Bems could have given their performance of "Chattanooga Choo Choo" without getting into trouble if only they had agreed to allow their number to be given an anti-American title such as "Their morals" or "Pictures by Uncle Sam" ("Diadia Sem risuet sam"). But for Prokop and especially Bems that would have been an impossible compromise. Instead they performed their song without authorization at a student concert and paid the price for doing so: Bems's degree was awarded, but professional recognition as an engineer (*dopusk*) was withheld.

Bems seems to resent the fact that those things for which he fought and which cost him so much have now become, as it were, common property. Chiurlionis and Picasso are recognised as geniuses; the record shops are full of Louis Armstrong records; Duke Ellington has given a concert in Moscow; everyone has now read Hemingway. Particularly galling is the fact that Ivchenko, who kept his head down in the 1950s, now has a degree of access to those same things which is denied to Bems. Ivchenko speaks casually about foreign travel, whereas Bems dreams of being able to look at a map of the world and say, "I've been there and I've been there. I haven't been there yet". Ivchenko has two copies of a rare recording of "Chattanooga Choo Choo" brought from abroad. Most crushing of all, Ivchenko has travelled through Chattanooga on the train on his way to an academic conference; he has been to Shangri-La, whereas the furthest Bems has been is Bulgaria.

It is tempting to see Ivchenko as a Glebov-type figure. Like the anti-hero of Trifonov's *Dom na naberezhnoi* (The house on the embankment, 1976), Ivchenko has progressed from orthodox student of the late Stalinist and early post-Stalinist period to successful Soviet academic of the late Brezhnev era, able to enjoy the fruits of his earlier caution. In a draft of the play Ivchenko was portrayed in an uncompromisingly negative light, reflecting Slavkin's own warmth towards Bems. But a friend to whom he showed the draft persuaded him that the play would benefit greatly if the two protagonists were to be portrayed in an even-handed manner, and the final version is much more sympathetic to Ivchenko, "not in order to whitewash a Soviet functionary, not in order to ease conflict but, on the contrary, to increase it through dramatic complexity. After all, if one character is known to be completely right and another hopelessly wrong in advance then what have they got to talk about for three hours and what is there for the audience to watch?" (Slavkin 1991a, 158).

Bems has always resented Ivchenko, partly out of jealousy over Liusia and partly because, as a student leader, Ivchenko had inevitably been involved in the decision to expel Bems following the unauthorized perform-ance at the New Year concert. That decision had later been rescinded, and Bems had been reinstated, but his professional difficulties began at that time, and he had always held Ivchenko partly responsible. Stung into defending himself, Ivchenko contemptuously compares Bems's hothead-edness with his own cool appraisal of the situation. By abstaining in the vote on expulsion he might have appeared to have betrayed Bems, but his abstention meant that he was able to get the Dean to reverse the original decision on expulsion. As he says: "The fact that I had abstained gave me the chance to have a word with the Dean, old 'Expel 'em'. He'd cooled down a little by then and when he was considering the thing again I was able to have my say. But if I had gone against him at the meeting that would have been it, they would have decided the matter without me" (136).

In the matter of Elka's possible expulsion for the "flower power" demonstration Ivchenko shows himself to be equally flexible. Although initially enraged and ready to argue for expulsion, he later concedes that the students have a point, that the elderly lecturer (the selfsame "old Expel 'em") should be asked to retire, but insists that this needs to be done delicately rather than by open conflict. To the maximalists like Bems and Elka's boyfriend Igor´, Ivchenko's political pragmatism reeks of self-serving careerism, and the fact that Ivchenko is in a position to enjoy that emancipated future of foreign travel and jazz concerts which Bems fought for, while Bems himself remains stuck in a 140-rouble-a-month dead-end job with only retirement to look forward to, seems bitterly unfair. Yet Ivchenko clearly impresses Prokop and Liusia as a mature and reasonable man, one who — as he says himself — has changed over the years as the times themselves have changed. Bems, on the other hand, has not moved forward, preferring to look back with nostalgia on his heroic days as a *stiliaga* in the 1950s. Slavkin has stated explicitly that these two responses to the passage of time are equally valid, although when he wrote the play his sympathies lay with Bems (Slavkin 1991a, 158).

In Bems's refusal to change, to move with the times, to place his past on the shelf and admire it, there is something infantile, and the concept of the infantile (*infantil´nost´*) is one which has preoccupied Slavkin for many years. As Konstantin Rudnitskii has said (speaking about the characters of *Serso*): "It is important to realize that it is not old age that frightens them. Old age is still a long way off. It is maturity that they are afraid of. It is frightening to become an adult, to cross that threshold beyond which the questions end and the answers begin. They are infantile" (Rudnitskii 1990, 388-89). As Rudnitskii goes on to point out, in *Vzroslaia doch´ molodogo cheloveka* Bems's extended infantilism is linked to the fact that his youth coincided with the Thaw of the Khrushchev period which raised hopes that were later dashed. Bems and, to a lesser extent, Prokop, like their creator, are typical "sorokaletnie" figures.

Bems's infantilism, which is, of course, not a negative characteristic, is seen most clearly in his wish to live out the whole of his life between two of the notes of Duke Ellington's "Mood Indigo":

> If someone were to ask me right now what I would want if the most fantastic thing were possible do you know what it would be? To perch myself some-

where between two notes, for example in Duke Ellington's "Mood Indigo", to perch myself and to get warm, and I wouldn't need anything else, as long as I lived I wouldn't need anything else. In "Mood Indigo" the Duke's got one place "ti - ta", and I think I could squeeze right in there, between the "ti" and the "ta", get perched and just curl up and get warm while the tune flows past you, round you, and you are carried along by it, and you feel good. You wouldn't need anything else as long as you lived. (142)

Ivchenko responds ironically to Bems's fantasy, but for Liusia it provides a glimpse of the sensitive Bems of the past, and she asks whether there might be room for her too in the space between the two notes of "Mood Indigo".

Like Bems, the central figure in *Serso* is a forty-year-old man who has never stopped regarding himself as young. Slavkin's original title for the play was *Mne sorok let, no ia molodo vygliazhu* (I am forty, but I look young), which refers to the way in which the protagonist thinks of himself. He is an engineer called Petr Viacheslavovich, but like Bems he is universally known by a nickname, in this case Petushok. As one of the other characters says; "You'll always be Petushok, even if you do have a house in the country now" (Slavkin 1986a, 102; further reference to this play are to this edition and are given in parentheses in the text). The elegiac tone which pervaded sections of *Vzroslaia doch´* here extends to the whole play and the Vasil´ev production, the theme of which, as Slavkin has pointed out, "turned out to be loss" (Slavkin 1986b, 99).

Petushok has been left an old country house by an elderly relative, Elizaveta Mikhailovna, and he and a group of acquaintances arrive on a Friday evening to spend the weekend there. Each of them knows Petushok, but they do not know each other, and have little in common. Vladimir Ivanovich is a colleague of Petushok's, his immediate superior; Valia is an old flame with whom he had broken up many years earlier, telling her curtly that he "could see no prospects in [their] relationship" (104); Pasha is a historian by training and an art lover who now works in the more lucrative field of home improvements (he upholsters apartment doors); Lars is a mysterious stranger whom Petushok appears to meet by chance and who claims at different times to be from the Baltic republics and from Sweden, but who speaks perfect Russian. These four characters are Petushok's near contemporaries, all in their forties. The final member of the group, Nadia, is younger: a twenty-six-year-old neighbour who regularly meets Petushok on the stairs as they are putting out the rubbish. What they have in common is, above all, loneliness, a condition which is beginning to frighten Petushok as he contemplates the onset of middle age:

Petushok: I got you all together because we've got something in common.
     You're all...each of you...and me, we're all — alone.
Nadia: What do you mean? There's one, two three, four, five, six of us.
[...]
Petushok: There are six of us now. We're together now. But as soon as
     we split up we'll all be — each of us will be — alone. (106–07)

With their loneliness and their sense of having lost something essential these
characters are all typical of the "sorokaletnie". Their equivalents can be
found in the writings of Slavkin's contemporaries such as Makanin. Even
the younger Nadia sits alone watching television and eating sweets all
evening, dreaming that her prince in the shape of an artillery man will come
and rescue her. So desiccated is her existence that she has no rubbish to
put out; when she meets Petushok on the stairs she is just getting rid of
sweet papers. Even her cat has deserted her. Some of the older characters
have had the opportunity of family life, but all have either lost it or spurned
it. They are "outsiders who have been left behind, who have lost their sense
of perspective" (Gerber 1987, 83).

Petushok's intention in gathering the group together is to propose that
the house becomes their joint property, that they become a "circle of
friends", a *kompaniia*, which will meet here at weekends and provide for
each other the communal support which they each lack during the week:
"A person can live either a family life or a bachelor existence. But there's
also a third way: a circle of free adults, we're not dependent on each other,
but it's interesting when we're together" (107).

If this group is to form itself into a *kompaniia* then it must seize this
opportunity, for, as Petushok says: "We're already forty. It's time to think
what we'll be like at fifty and sixty and seventy" (107). At first the five
guests feel cheated because Petushok has lied to each of them in order to
get them to the dacha. In Vasil′ev's production they stayed near the walls,
as if unwilling to commit themselves to the house and to the others in the
group. But gradually the atmosphere of the house begins to affect them,
and as Petushok plays boogie-woogie on the old piano they come into the
centre of the room, and begin a dance which gets increasingly energetic
and eventually ecstatic. At its height Vladimir Ivanovich notices an old man
who, unseen by the others, has made his way into the dacha. His name
is Nikolai L′vovich Krekshin - Koka - and he had once been in love with
the former owner of the house, Elizaveta Mikhailovna.

In the long and solemn second act the "colonists", as Slavkin calls them,
discover a collection of love letters written by Koka and Elizaveta
Mikhailovna in 1916. The tender love, preserved in the letters, seems to
be in stark contrast to the uncommitted lives of the "sorokaletnie". Koka

quotes a Blok poem about lovers dying together ("Ty vsegda mechtala, chto, sgoraia, dogorim my vmeste - ty i ia, chto dano, v ob˝iat´iakh umiraia, uvidat´ blazhennye kraia") and adds "they don't write like that nowadays", to which Valia adds, "they don't love like that nowadays" (109). In every respect, it seems, the authenticity of the past is juxtaposed to the superficiality of the present. Koka explains that he and Liza were separated during the summer months because in those days the summer was a time for visiting parents, "for their pleasure and comfort", as he quaintly expresses it. To the self-obsessed forty-year-olds the idea of filial duty overriding all other considerations must seem strange indeed. Similarly, when Koka describes how Liza's eyes shone with pleasure when she opened a present that he had given her, Nadia remarks that she buys her own rings and brooches at a tobacconist's kiosk where they are cheap and she can change them frequently. "Recently they put out a brooch with a picture of Esenin on it. One rouble ninety-seven. My favourite poet." (110) The love between Koka and Elizaveta Mikhailovna was not perfect — one of the letters reveals her pain on hearing of his infidelity - but the letters and the feelings which they reveal are far removed from the isolation of the younger "outsiders".

Under the influence of the letters, as well as that of the house with its oval dining table, pure white table cloth, candles in brass candlesticks, and tall glass goblets, the "colonists" become the people that they might have been: open, emotional, vulnerable. After passing around the letters of Koka and Elizaveta Mikhailovna they compose and read out their own "letters" to each other, in which nobler, more direct personae can be glimpsed. The language of these letters, taken directly by Slavkin from the letters of real people, including Ol´ga Knipper and Tsvetaeva, has an old-fashioned elegance which encapsulates the change in the colonists. For example, Vladimir Ivanovich's earlier, vulgar sexual pursuit of Nadia is replaced by the respectful adoration of his letter to her. It is as if, through the influence of the house and the wonderful love letters of Koka and Elizaveta Mikhailovna, the modern city-dwellers have been put magically in touch with a less prosaic world which has now vanished. The realism of the first act has now been replaced by a Maeterlinck-like atmosphere of mystery, and the characters' earlier physical concerns have been transformed into a spiritual quest for the selves who might, in another age or in other circumstances, have existed.[5]

If the letters are one expression of a past age which, through their elegance and authenticity, transform the characters, then the old game of cerceau, the play's central metaphor, is another. Cerceau is a French game which used to be played in the house when Koka and Elizaveta Mikhailovna were young. One player places a ring on a wooden sword and flips it high into the air and the others try to catch it on their swords. The wooden rings and swords have been preserved in the attic, and the colonists go out to the garden and play the game. Rudnitskii gives the following description of the scene:

> The light hoops fly right across the stage, across the dacha roof. The women in their white dresses and the men in white suits run from behind the table and deftly catch these hoops on wooden swords. And here a miracle takes place: it is clear that none of the characters has ever played the game before or, indeed, even heard of it. But now, at the moment when their dream shoots up towards heaven, when, from the mists of other people's youth the noble images of poetic love descend on them they all play cerceau absolutely wonderfully, ecstatically. (Rudnitskii 1990, 392)

The point of cerceau, and the reason for its central metaphorical position in the play, is that it involves contact between two players. One throws a ring into the air and it is caught by another. It is impossible to play cerceau without companions. And if, for the wooden rings of the real game, one substitutes the words and feelings of the metaphorical game then its significance becomes clear. In the first act the characters spoke, but did not communicate. Alla Gerber writes: "They speak like you would play ping-pong. Only in this form of the game one person serves and so does the other. No one receives service. No one returns. The table-tennis-ball-words leap up, fall, and roll into the void" (Gerber 1987, 82).

In the second act everything is transformed. The atmosphere of the old house, the elegant clothes, the beautiful words of the letters all combine to release the characters from their isolation and they come together in their letters to each other and in the balletically graceful game of cerceau. But the mundane world of the 1980s reasserts itself. Koka reveals to Pasha that he married Elizaveta Mikhailovna in 1924 and they lived together for just over a week before he went back to Siberia and never returned. He is the legal owner of the house and has a dog-eared marriage certificate to prove it. Now he needs money to look after his granddaughter and the child which she will soon bear. Pasha sees the opportunity to obtain the house he has always dreamed of, and persuades the old man to sell it to him. As Valia says, Petushok appears to have lost the game of cerceau.

The third act is "sad and gloomy" (Rudnitskii 1990, 392). The magical transformation has been reversed, and as the weekend draws to a close and the characters prepare to return to their daily lives their speech reverts to its form of the first act: monologues which slide past and cut across each other. The curtain rises on a damp and foggy garden in which Lars and Petushok are sitting, one on each side of the house. Each reads aloud, Lars from a Thomas Cook travel brochure and Petushok from a book of ancient Oriental poetry. The prosaic details of train arrival and departure times appear to contrast shockingly with the elevated exotic tone of the verse, but in fact the two texts are harmonious rather than cacophonous: for Lars and Petushok respectively they represent an unattainable dream which is about to be dispelled by the return to normal city life. In this third act the characters face up to who they really are; the various masks which they have been wearing are discarded. For example, Valia is not Simone Signoret or Jeanne Moreau, she is a middle-aged Russian librarian whose humdrum life is about to recommence. There can be no going back to what might have been, no holding on to the beautiful yet fragile intimacy of the cerceau game. So when Petushok tells Valia that he has kept a photograph of her taken when they were lovers she contradicts every detail and then says:

Valia: [...]. But nothing like this ever existed.
Petushok: That's right, I made it all up.
Valia: You never had a camera, and the man you asked to take our picture
    at VDNKh never existed, and that photograph doesn't exist.
Petushok: No.
Valia: No.
Petushok: No. There never was such a photograph.
Valia: There is no such photograph.
Petushok: There's no such photograph. No.
Valia: That's that, then. When you get home, tear it up, and that'll be the
    end of it. (126)

Pasha tells everyone that they can come again next weekend, they can even leave some of their things in the dacha rather than carting them back to the city, but they continue to make preparations to leave. In any case, the dacha is not Pasha's; Koka has changed his mind and destroyed the marriage certificate, so the house still belongs to Petushok. Pasha, who is driven by the need to possess everything he comes into contact with (books, antiques, a car, above all a house), makes one final bid. Casually, in the flow of conversation and in the presence of all the others he asks Nadia to marry him. At first she pretends not to have heard or understood, but he persists, to everyone's embarrassment.

As they leave for the car it gets dark and cold, and the rain starts to fall. Nadia says that she once missed an eclipse of the sun because she was sitting in the cinema. It is the play's final image, and despite its apparent inconsequentiality it is an effective closing metaphor. In Vasil´ev's production Petushok suddenly goes back into the house and plays the piano; not an elegaic piece in keeping with the sombre mood of the play's closing section, but a driving boogie-woogie tune which adds complexity and openness to the ending.

In some respects *Serso* must be regarded as an example of postmodernism in Russian drama. It is deliberately eclectic, with constant intertextual references to other works of art, notably the plays of Chekhov. In an interview recorded in Stockholm in 1990 Slavkin commented on the place of eclecticism in drama at the end of the twentieth century: "I think that success awaits the dramatist who can combine in one play political, psychological, and aesthetic elements. There is no definite line; instead you've got to mix a cocktail" (Slavkin 1991b, 11). Slavkin could be describing *Serso* here. His "cocktail" combines the psychological and aesthetic, and even — obliquely — the political, in that his group of alienated town-dwellers have been moulded during the late Soviet period and bear all the hallmarks of that particular socio-political group. Like the characters of Petrushevskaia's *Svoi krug* (Our crowd, 1979, published 1988), they attempt to create for themselves a new grouping — the "kompaniia" or "krug" of like-minded people — to replace the traditional family and social structures which have crumbled. This is the generation for whom Okudzhava's texts are of major significance, and it is not in the least surprising to hear some of Okudzhava's words echo in the first act: "Voz´memsia za ruki, druz´ia, chtob ne propast´ poodinochke". This is the generation which gathers in small groups in kitchens, people who cling together so as not to be picked off one by one. In his letter to the "colonists" Petushok muses on the meaning of the word "native land" (*otechestvo*). As a child he had loved parades on national holidays, delighting in the feeling of oneness with so many people, but as the years have gone by there are fewer and fewer people around, and now there is nobody except this group which he wants to weld into a *kompaniia*: "Who have we got left except ourselves?.. And here we sit, a few people under one roof...Perhaps that's what our native land is now?" (117).

As has already been said, *Serso* is very much a self-consciously literary work which plays on the reader or viewer's knowledge of other texts. In other words, intertextuality is a major feature of the play. We have already noted the fact that parts of the letters in the second act are drawn directly from the real letters of famous figures from nineteenth- and twentieth-century Russian culture and that Okudzhava's words are used. The most extensive example of this kind of cross-referencing is Slavkin's use of Chekhov. Situations, speeches, sound effects, characters are all used to refer the reader to particular moments in works by Chekhov. When Petushok repeatedly asserts that he is forty he could be Uncle Vania proclaiming that he might have been a Dostoevskii or a Schopenhauer. In several respects Lars is another Charlotta Ivanovna, a comic character with an uncertain past, even of uncertain nationality, who performs conjuring tricks learned in childhood. When Pasha offers to buy the dacha he could be Lopakhin triumphantly obtaining an estate of his own after the indignities of his childhood. Valia, the intelligent, alienated lady in black brings to mind Masha Prozorova. In the final act when Vladimir Ivanovich, suddenly looking much older, sits wrapped in a rug and rambles on about his poor childhood and about rice, potatoes, and bread he seems to turn into the Serebriakov of Act Two of *Diadia Vania* (Uncle Vania, 1897). When, a little earlier, he declares: "Everything in a person should be fine — face, clothes, thoughts, apartment, where to go in the summer, where to get medicine, where to get a tasty meal" (127) he is first quoting and then parodying Astrov. Nadia's long speech near the end of the play conjures up notions of her as the lady with the little dog as well as of Kashtanka (130).

When the love letter of Koka and Elizaveta Mikhailovna are being read in Act Two they are accompanied by "the tender sound of a little bell" (111), unmotivated on the realistic level but essential in creating the atmosphere of the scene, much as the sound of the breaking string does in *Vishnevyi sad* (The cherry orchard, 1903). Finally, Slavkin's text contains a great many pauses during which a level of action goes on above the verbal level, in a way which is recognisably Chekhovian.[6]

Slavkin does more than make the odd reference to Chekhov; he uses the reader/ viewer's presumed knowledge of Chekhov to add a level of meaning to his work. Our understanding of Petushok, for instance, is made more complex by our awareness that there is much of Uncle Vania in him.

The handling by Slavkin and Vasil´ev of time and space is a major factor in the success of the play and the production. The work is framed by two long parallel scenes in which the "colonists" first literally break into the boarded-up dacha and then spend a long time boarding it up again. The house is thus more than simply a setting; it becomes a theatrical metaphor for the closed and boarded-up lives of the six "colonists", and when at the end they spend a very long time securing the house again we understand the full significance in terms of their return to isolation and loneliness (see Rudnitskii 1990, 387).

Time is handled by juxtaposing the weekend, or "prazdnik", when the weather is fine, to the cold, autumnal weekday world of work and the city. Once again the metaphorical significance is clear: the weekend at the dacha provides the opportunity for the human contact of the cerceau game only because it is, as it were, removed from the flow of everyday time. When the clock begins to tick again and the rain begins to fall then the game must be put away.[7]

Despite the fact that it ran for only a few performances on the small stage of the Taganka, *Serso* became one of the major theatrical events of the 1980s. From the very beginning, however, critics voiced the opinion that the play was weaker than the production. To Slavkin and Vasil´ev, on the other hand, the work of author and director was not easily separable. It is clear that for Slavkin the Vasil´ev company was *his* company, and that the long preparatory work on *Serso* was regarded by him as joint work (Slavkin 1989). Vasil´ev has pointed out what Slavkin, perhaps, did not care to, namely that when *Chaika* (The seagull, 1896) was first performed some critics praised the director and actors but everyone condemned the play. Vasil´ev says he does not wish to make direct comparisons, but it is clear that he believes that Slavkin's play was underestimated in a similar fashion (Vasil´ev 1986, 99).

More than ten years have now gone by since the opening of *Serso*, and while the Vasil´ev production has so far overwhelmingly dominated its production history, the play continues to arouse the interest of literary critics and theatre professionals alike, not only in Russia but throughout Europe and in North America. Writing in 1985, Anatolii Smelianskii tentatively suggested that the play might be ephemeral: "Does Slavkin's play have an independent literary significance? I don't know. [...] Given its scenario-like quality, [it] is probably doomed to an early death" (Smelianskii 1985, 216). In terms of new productions of the play Smelianskii may well prove to be right, but the Vasil´ev production will certainly retain its significance in the history of the Russian theatre, while the text of *Serso* can now be seen to be one of the major contributions to Russian dramatic literature of the 1980s.

REFERENCES

Arbuzov, A., 1990. "Eti dvoe", in Viktor Slavkin and Liudmila Petrushevskaia, *P´esy* (Moscow: Sovetskii pisatel´), 3–4.

Gerber, A., 1987. "Peizazh na asfal´te", *Literaturnoe obozrenie* 3: 81–86.

Ivanova, M. and V. Ivanov, 1987. "'Nastroenie indigo'. Tema i variatsii", *Sovremennaia dramaturgiia* 4: 248–58.

Reissner, E., 1992. *Das Russische Drama der Achtziger Jahre: Schmerzvoller Abschied von der grossen Illusion* (Munich: Otto Sagner).

Rudnitskii, K., 1990. *Teatral´nye siuzhety* (Moscow: Iskusstvo).

Seemann, K.D., 1992. "Zur Deutung von Viktor Slavkins *Serso*", *Zeitschrift für Slawistik* 1: 7–18.

Slavkin, V. and L. Petrushevskaia, 1983. *P´esy* (Moscow: Sovetskaia Rossiia).

Slavkin, V., 1986a. *Serso, Sovremennaia dramaturgiia* 4: 100–31.

———, 1986b. "…Kotoromu ia doveriaiu" (Preface to *Serso*), *Sovremennaia dramaturgiia* 4: 98–99.

———, 1988. "Vse i srazu", *Sovetskii teatr* 4: 12.

———, 1989. "Riadom s p´esoi", *Sovremennaia dramaturgiia* 3: 176–85.

———, 1990. *Vzroslaia doch´ molodogo cheloveka: P´esy* (Moscow: Sovetskii pisatel´).

———, 1991a. "Bems - i net starushki", *Sovremennaia dramaturgiia* 4: 156–66.

———, 1991b. "Beseda, v kotoroi uchastvovali: Nina Sadur, Viktor Slavkin, Lars Kleberg, Staffan Ete, i Barbru Smeds", *Teatral´naia zhizn´* 14: 10–12.

———, 1991c. "'Rasskazhi, o chem toskuet saksofon'", *Iunost´* 6: 70–79.

Smelianskii, A., 1985. "Pesochnye chasy", *Sovremennaia dramaturgiia* 4: 204–18.

Sorvina, M., 1991. "Kto zhivet v etom dome?", *Literaturnoe obozrenie* 4: 54–57.

Vasil´ev, A., 1986. "…Kotoromu ia doveriaiu" (Preface to *Serso*), *Sovremennaia dramaturgiia* 4: 99.

NOTES

1. This and all subsequent translations are my own.
2. See Arbuzov 1990, 3, where the suggestion is made that the essential optimism of Slavkin's one-act plays accounts for their popularity with young audiences.
3. Eberhard Reissner describes *Vzroslaia doch´ molodogo cheloveka*, *Serso*, and *Mesto dlia kureniia* as a "Trilogie der Selbstprüfung". See Reissner 1992, 193.
4. G.S. Smith has suggested to me that it is more likely that Bems has in mind two notes from Ellington's "Creole Love Song" rather than "Mood Indigo". I am grateful to Professor Smith for his assistance with jazz terminology.
5. The similarity to Maeterlinck is noted in Smelianskii 1985, 216.
6. The Chekhovian references in *Serso* have been examined in Seemann 1992, 13–16. The issue of *Zeitschrift für Slawistik* in which Seemann's article is published also contains several other articles on *Serso*.
7. For a detailed discussion of the handling of time in the play and the Vasil´ev production see Ivanova and Ivanov 1987, 255–58.

KAVALEROVS AND COFFINS: URBAN PROSE OF THE EIGHTIES

Sally Dalton-Brown

The city has [...] turned the city dweller into a shadow.[1]

A. Belyi, Gorod (1907)

They were not fortunate enough to have a
Destiny [...] They were born when time stood still.

V. Bondarenko on urban writers (1989)

The city, as Malcolm Bradbury has noted, is closely associated with the entire modernist movement; "urban sensibility" has come to stand for "modern sensibility". The urban topography is an apposite object correlative for one of the central paradoxes of modern times, being both a place of lost innocence, and a birthplace for new ideas. Through their depictions of city life modern writers can express their ambivalence towards progress and technology by creating images both of the "new Jerusalem", expressing humankind's belief in its ability to create monuments to its own ability as well as a perfect social order, and also images of dystopia, expressing a sense of self-disgust, post-Lapsarian guilt at the fact that instead of Utopia humankind has built an edifice of inhumanity and destruction. The sensuous city of Baudelaire, the alienated urban wasteland of Eliot, or Verhaeren's "villes tentaculaires", are powerful images of modern man's predicament in a world he has proudly created but in which he remains profoundly dissatisfied.

The urban theme has a distinguished genealogy in Russian literature. The so-called "Petersburg tradition" established itself in the literature of such nineteenth-century notables as Pushkin, whose *Mednyi vsadnik* (The bronze horseman) offered a "vision of the madness on which it (the city) is based" (Berman 1982, 181), or Gogol´, in whose *Peterburgskie povesti* (Petersburg stories, 1835–42) Nevskii Prospekt is a place of marvels, of fragmented vision, a place of unreal light which "always lies" ("Nevskii Prospekt", 1835). In St Petersburg, that "most abstract and intentional city on earth" according to Dostoevskii's underground man (1864), the paradoxical image of the city as a place both of dream and despair, of humanity's achievement and barbarism (built to propel Russia forward, its foundations resting on the bones of the many who died while building it), was created. At the heart of this paradox lies the question of power. The city is man's creation, and yet it is a topography of chaos, not control.

The loss of power has often been expressed through the theme of irrationality: the logical, rectilinear streets of Andrei Belyi's well-known *Peterburg* (Petersburg, 1913–14), become warped by the illogical, tormented and inherently anarchic minds of the inhabitants. The straight line, worshipped by the city governor Ugrium-Burcheev in Saltykov-Shchedrin's *Istoriia odnogo goroda* (The history of a town, 1869–70) as the hallmark of his ideal city, its rigid and "unnatural" logic an expression of man's evolutionary progress, cannot be maintained. The city becomes instead a place of labyrinths and spiderlike alleys, confused, chaotic and doomed, like Andrei Belyi's Moscow in the text of the same name (I, 1926–27, II, 1932), in which the city is described as a self-destructive arachnid.

To Belyi, as to Aleksandr Blok, or to Valerii Briusov, who has been called the forerunner of Russian urban literature (despite Chukovskii's claim that Bal´mont should hold this title), the city is both a place of endless potential and tremendous failure. Influenced by Verhaeren, who dreamed of writing an epic of human destiny situated in the city of the future, but whose early work also incorporates a vision of the city as a place of tragedy and decadence, Briusov's city is a place either of fall or ascent. Man is told that he is no more than an "atom" in the blood of the city, which, itself, will live for centuries. The city may be a place in which humanity's mortal power is demonstrated, as in Aleksandr Blok's *Gorod* (The city, 1904-08) cycle of poems (influenced by Briusov's *Urbi et orbi*), where Peter the Great is described with a dominating sword held out over the city, but it is also a place of madness, of loss of control. Peter's city is "closely associated with vice and evil and an all-pervading feeling of profound solitude" (Donchin 1958, 162); bloody with the sun's red rays, or suffused with dark and swimming light, its streets "drunk from cries" ("ulitsy p´iany ot krikov")

(Blok 1960, 159), it becomes a place of excess, of exhaustion and confusion, prefiguring the apocalyptic scenes of Blok's later work.

The "end of universal history" postulated by Andrei Belyi in an article "Apokalipsis v russkoi poezii" (from *Lug zelenyi* [The green meadow], 1910), influenced by Vladimir Solov'ev, incorporated the idea of the Antichrist's attempt to turn the city, potentially a new Jerusalem, into a "dark capital". The "super-Solov'evans" (Nikolai Berdiaev and Sergei Bulgakov being the best known) who ran the significantly titled *Novyi Grad* (The new city) journal in Paris from 1931 to 1939 developed a type of "novogradstvo" which endorsed the concept of Apocalypse as the preface to the establishment of the kingdom of heaven on earth, symbolized by the New Jerusalem.

Even to the Acmeists, to whom the city was primarily an emblem of cultural survival, a place of beauty, eternity written in the granite and marble of its buildings, the urban topography has been one of ambivalence. Even Anna Akhmatova's beloved Petersburg cityscape embodied "the image of a Cosmos never wholly free from the incursions of that Chaos from which it was wrested, a sense of the precariousness of human existence in the face of overwhelming historical and natural forces" (Leiter 1983, 5). Osip Mandel'shtam described the city as a powerful animal, or as a "Nero" and human life as a "tale without plot or hero, made of emptiness and glass, from Petersburg's influenza delirium" (*Egipetskaia marka* [The Egyptian stamp], 1927).

After the Revolution this hallucinatory vision of the emotionally charged *urbs* took on a new appearance. In Konstantin Fedin's *Goroda i gody* (Cities and years, 1924), St Petersburg is a dark, windy place, a symbol of post-revolutionary stress, even of frenzy, but is also a place of discipline and socialist fervour. In post-revolutionary prose, with its excessively hubristic belief in Soviet man as a godlike creator, the image of the city *per se* was not of particular significance; what was prominent in this socialist realist literature was the concept of building, of controlling and developing nature. Unsurprisingly, two central genres in which a sense of doubt at the positive nature of such building emerged in the post-war period, genres which have been given the name of village and urban prose. About the first literary trend and its practitioners, there is little debate, for the genre, with its evocation of traditional village values and love of nature, has established its canons firmly. Urban prose is another matter.

In the late seventies and eighties a new type of literature, understated, ambivalent, and one which dealt with everyday city life, appeared to have grown out of sixties prose such as Iurii Trifonov's *byt* texts and the *zhenskaia proza* of writers such as Natal'ia Baranskaia and I. Grekova, in which problems of family life and career security were discussed with a refreshing,

albeit often depressing, new realism. Urban prose is the natural outcome
of the post-Thaw drive towards a greater literary honesty, a movement
attended by a cynical and weary focus on a sense of individual limitation
and lost innocence. Urban prose, the literature of post-Thaw *tristesse,* is
the prose of the depressingly prosaic, of the evocatively boring, the bland,
and the beaten. In Russian urban literature we find a modern return to the
Gogolian urban landscape of the "little man", yet one unattended by the
sparkle of fantasy, or by Dostoevskian intensity; modern urban Russian
literature is like a faded photographic print of the nineteenth-century cityscape.

The new generation of eighties writers attracted several labels. The term
"urban" is often supplanted by titles such as "the Moscow school", as most
of these writers are resident in Moscow (although some write about towns
other than the capital), or that of the *sorokaletnie* (as they were all in their
forties when critics began to write about them in the 1980s). A further
nomenclature has been noted by critics who, writing on urban prose in
respect of the debate around the theme "man-city-literature" which was
conducted in *Literaturnoe obozrenie* during 1984–85, have debated the term
"ironic" literature. If the terminology appears confused, the identity of
urban writers appears to be even more so, for there is little critical consensus
on which of the writers of the eighties might be included under these new
rubrics, or, indeed, whether these terms should be limited to the forty-year-
old generation or not.

In the eighties, the label of *byt* prose, used so frequently during the
seventies, appeared to have been abandoned by critics who turned to a
discussion of what they claimed was a new generational phenomenon. The
critics Vladimir Bondarenko, Igor´ Dedkov and Evgenii Sidorov, and the
writer Anatolii Kurchatkin, all writing in 1980, offered the term *sorokaletnie,*
perhaps the most widely used of the four, to define the new literary trend
(Kurchatkin 1980, 26–30; Bondarenko 1980, 5; Sidorov 1980, 4; Surganov
1980, 202–12). Kurchatkin, writing about the style of seventies prose and
discussing the "new stream" to which he himself belonged, gives little
detail. He does include the names of Vladimir Makanin and Anatolii Kim
amongst others such as Vladimir Lichutin (although he has to make a case
for this writer as not a village writer), or the little-known writers G. Abramov
and B. Vasilevskii. Other listings expand indefinitely to include almost any
writer active during the eighties, from the well-known to the second-rate;
P. Roll´berg has asked not without reason whether the idea of a *sorokaletnii*
group is not merely an artificial critical construct (although he then goes
on to list Vladimir Makanin, Anatolii Kim, Vladimir Krupin, Ruslan Kireev,
Anatolii Kurchatkin and Anatolii Afanas´ev as *sorokaletnie*); it is no wonder
that Vladimir Kardin has argued that "urban prose" in the pure sense does
not exist (Kardin 1989, 40).

Vladimir Bondarenko, discussing the new wave of writers in a subsequent article in 1985 listed the following: Vladimir Makanin, Anatolii Kurchatkin, Anatolii Kim, Vladimir Lichutin, Ruslan Kireev, Aleksandr Prokhanov, Georgii Bazhenov, Timur Pulatov, Sviatoslav Rybas, Anatolii Afanas´ev, Vladimir Gusev, Vatslav Mikhalskii, Iurii Arakcheev, Vladimir Krupin, Viacheslav Shugaev, as well as other writers who are even less well known, such as the following also named by Bondarenko: Alekseev, Krasnov, Poptsov, Mirnev, Skalon, Antropov, Bazhenov, G. Abramov, Kokoulin, Gangus, and Bashkirova (Bondarenko 1985b, 79-115; Bondarenko 1985a, 2; Sokolov 1985, 3). Thankfully, by 1989, in an article which reviewed the position of the *sorokaletnie* at the end of the decade in which they had come to prominence, Bondarenko appeared (if not altogther conclusively) to have narrowed the group down to twelve: Andrei Bitov, Anatolii Kurchatkin, Vladimir Gusev, Ruslan Kireev, Anatolii Kim, Vladimir Makanin, Vladimir Orlov, Afanasii Afanas´ev, Sergei Esin, Vladimir Krupin, Aleksandr Prokhanov, and Vladimir Lichutin.

In what way can these twelve, on whose primacy as urban writers there is as yet no firm agreement,[2] be linked together? The arguments offered — namely that they are linked by generational *Weltanschauung*, by their Moscow-centricism, or by their particular themes or style — all have something to recommend them, but only to a limited degree. The first two of these arguments in particular have been acknowledged as inadequate. The attempt to classify them as a generation has not been welcomed by the writers themselves, nor did these "forty-year-olds" all begin publishing at the same time: Makanin (born in 1937) had his first novel, *Priamaia liniia* (A straight line) published in 1965; Kim was born in 1939 but began to publish only in 1973, as did Kurchatkin (born 1944);[3] whereas Kireev (born 1941) began earlier, in 1958. Anatolii Bocharov, reacting critically to the concept of a new group of forty-year-old ("young") Moscow neo-realists, has preferred to call them the "Moscow school" (he has also suggested the term "the sidelined generation", (Bocharov 1981, 246). However, the fact of their common Moscow location does not necessarily have any particular significance As N. N. Shneidman has argued in a ruthlessly definitive paragraph on the subject, they are not all Muscovite:

> To the outside observer, the only thing they have in common is that, at present (1989), they all reside in the capital. In fact many are not Moscow natives, and their past reflects their thematic and artistic interests. Thus the works of Vladimir Lichutin and Vladimir Krupin are in the tradition of village prose. The writings of Vladimir Makanin and Ruslan Kireev are closer to city, or *byt* literature. Aleksandr Prokhanov deals with a variety of topics, most recently issues of international politics. The prose of Anatolii Kim is grotesque and surrealistic. Anatolii Kurchatkin, Georgii Bazhenov, Anatolii Afanas´ev, and others belong to the same generation. (Shneidman 1989, 57)

Makanin, Kireev, and Afanas´ev may be postulated as a core group of urban writers, Afanas'ev's prose line being developed by Makanin and Kireev in the eighties, when the genre (now supplanted by the new "dark" and more avant-garde prose), had its final flowering. Traces of the urban prose can be found more frequently in texts by other writers during the mid-seventies to eighties (such as Granin, Zalygin, Semenov and Rybas), but these three are the most apposite in terms of the similarity of their themes and style.

MORIBUND MALES AND THE MID-LIFE CRISIS: URBAN THEMES

What are the "urban" themes which distinguish these writers' work? The theme of the town itself has not, surprisingly, been particularly to the fore, as it was in the work of Trifonov, despite the arguments of Igor´ Dedkov, who in a 1981 article wrote of the *sorokaletnii* interest in

> ... a panorama of opening reality, its space, its borders: the southern town of Svetopol´ with its directors, teachers, artists... (R. Kireev); the little town near Moscow of Fedulinsk with its scientific workers, policemen, war veterans... (A. Afanas´ev); the provincial towns with their journalists, correspondents, institute teachers.... (A. Kurchatkin, V. Gusev); the regional little town with its workers... (V. Mirnev), and, finally, Moscow .... with its journalists, writers (V. Makanin, V. Gusev, V. Mirnev, A. Kurchatkin, L. Bezhin and others). (Dedkov 1981, 22)

According to Dedkov, in the work of these writers, with a few exceptions, such as Gusev's old Russian provincial town of Spasskoe-Lutovinovo, or Rybas's Starobel´sk, what we see is "a strange city... As if the city is something featureless (*bezlikoe*) and without memory, a placard on a bare wall, announcing the place of an event" (Dedkov 1981, 23). Dedkov appears to suggest the standard modernist idea of the city as a dehumanized locale, but his argument is inherently contradictory, for the town as he understands it from *sorokaletnii* writing is not a topography, but a community of people. The urban writer is primarily concerned not with the *gorod* but with the *gorozhanin*. This attitude is summed up by Anatolii Afanas´ev in his *Privet, Afinogen!* (Greetings, Afinogen!, 1979) in which the author pays lip service to the idea that locale is significant, mentioning Fedulinsk ("an ordinary peripheral industrial little town, where people are born, study, work, suffer, love, go on pension", Afanas´ev 1979, 7) frequently, but emphasizing its human component: "Oh, Fedulinsk, city of lovers, disappointed wanderers, the quietest rebels, individuals with undefined desires, educated children, merry women, builders, drunkards, realists and eccentrics..." (Afanas´ev 1979, 232).

In the work of other Moscow writers the city is a background, not a character. To Vladimir Makanin Moscow functions only as a contrast to the Urals home towns of his characters in *Starye knigi* (Old books, 1976) or *Na pervom dykhanii* (At first breath, 1976), for instance; his characters muse on the *poselok* which they have left behind and compare it to the life of the *barak* which they often inhabit. Ruslan Kireev's Svetopol´ is also a constant but unremarkable component of his texts, which could be set in any provincial town; as in the work of Trifonov, the city functions as the object correlative of his characters' sense of the drabness and hopelessness of life.

Although writers classified as "urban", *sorokaletnie*, or as members of the "Moscow school" are reticent on the question of Trifonov's influence on their work, there seems little doubt that Trifonov set the paradigm for the urban text. The *gorozhanin*, in the work of Makanin, Kireev, and Afanas´ev, is very similar to the typical Trifonov "hero", whose lineaments were definitively traced by that author in his Moscow cycle of five *povesti*. A morally weak man dominated by an aggressively materialistic and often bored wife, living with offspring with whom he cannot communicate, and faced with the need to make ethical compromises in order to succeed at work, he was the focus for Trifonov's analysis of a particular kind of limited human being. This was the type of man who had committed and who continued to commit minor transgressions, not out of deliberate malice, but through a form of cowardice which he could, or would, not — and herein lay the horror of it to Trifonov — understand. A type of human being irrevocably damaged by the time and place in which he lived, the descendant of Stalinist mores, he was a person living a dual life; the actual and the one his limited vision permitted him to see.

It is no wonder that the city dweller does not wish to comprehend fully the truth of his life and situation. Anatolii Bocharov has defined *sorokaletnii* prose as "not so much the prose of 40-year-old writers, as that of forty-year-old heroes" (Bocharov 1985, 127), a comment which aptly defines the core concern of urban literature: the mid-life crisis. The protagonist is usually a male in his forties; ageing, with flabby muscles, often unwell (heart complaints are particularly prevalent). He is an essentially ordinary person (in strong contrast to the heroes of socialist realist literature), with a professional job such as work in an institute, writing, journalism; he is not particularly well-off or handsome. Essentially, he is a *malen´kii chelovek*, a victim or failure; the city is a place of *neudachniki,* as Trifonov once categorized his characters, not of *pobediteli*. Herein lies one of the central, yet unstated, ironies of urban prose; for the city, the place of man's failure, is paradoxically man's finest creation, the immense "home" he has built for himself.

The theme of the would-be "victor" who discovers that he is only a little man is a staple concern of Ruslan Kireev, who began publishing in 1959, and who is best known for his tale *Peschanaia akatsiia* (Sandy acacia, 1985) and the (loosely defined) trilogy *Podgotovitel'naia tetrad', Apologiia* and *Pobeditel'* (Preparatory exercise book, Apologia and The victor). His locale is usually the southern town of Sevastopol' (or the holiday resort of Vitta some 80 kilometres away, to which he addresses the odd apostrophe, as in *Apologiia*). In these three seminal texts, Kireev concentrates on heroes with delusions of grandeur, who are in fact rather uninteresting types doomed to end up as failures: Karmanov in *Podgotovitel'naia tetrad'* is a *neudachnik,* Girkin in *Apologiia* a second-rate poet with the "face of a clerical rat" (Kireev 1989, 202), and Riabov in *Pobeditel''* an egotistical womanizer. In the first of the three texts, the thirty-seven-year-old Viktor Karmanov is a typical urban hero; a little man who believes he can be a great writer, despite being bluntly told by an editor that he is "the most ordinary failure" (Kireev 1989, 13). When he does meet a "great man" of sorts, one Svechkin, the factory administrator who can fix all problems, Viktor is at first admiring, but then deeply envious.

This situation is very common to urban prose, deriving possibly from the opposition of the *neudachnik* with the pragmatist which forms the central dilemma of Trifonov's *Obmen* (The exchange, 1969), in which the Dmitrievs, intellectual yet impractical, are contrasted to the more materialistic types who "know how to get things done", the Luk'ianov family. In *Podgotovitel'naia tetrad''*, Svechkin is another Luk'ianov figure, one who continues the debate implicit in Trifonov's carefully non-judgmental depiction of the family in *Obmen* fifteen years earlier. Whereas Luk'ianov was definitely not a "great man", merely one more adapted than the old-fashioned Dmitrievs to the new age of materialism which Trifonov snidely depicts, Kireev's Svechkin (whose very name suggests light) may actually be a great man, for according to one definition presumably offered with some irony, greatness lies in "answering the needs of the time" (Kireev 1989, 68).

Like Trifonov's heroes when faced by those with talents they do not possess, Karmanov takes the route well trodden by Dostoevskian and Gogolian protagonists: that of envy and revenge. A complicated *obmen* (a motif popularized by Trifonov's 1969 text in which the exchange of living space stands as a metaphor for the exchange of principles for negative emotions), causes Viktor to lodge temporarily with Svechkin. He lures the latter's bored, materialistic wife into an affair, and attempts to instil in Svechkin a fear of death in order to destroy his confidence (Kireev 1989, 115); this leads to one bizarre scene in which he sends a skull to this man he so admires and dislikes.

The *neudachnik* as a type is descended from the downtrodden yet inherently spiteful underground man, who despises those whom he envies, and from Gogol´'s secretly resentful and ambitious "little men". He is, to use a more modern and apposite example, a Kavalerov type (from Iurii Olesha's *Zavist´* [Envy], 1927), mocking the practical Andrei Babichevs of this world, and yet unable to tear himself free of his fascination with the powerful and acclaimed. Suffering from the "Kavalerov syndrome", the *neudachnik* dreams of being a handsome and romantic figure, a "cavalier", yet remains largely unloved and unlovable even to himself, for his actions slowly poison the wellsprings of what self-respect has not been leached away by the demands of job and family. Another of the *sorokaletnie*, Sviatoslav Rybas, offers a neat formulation of the problem: the hero, the young engineer Morozov, who inhabits an uneasy textual space between the socialist realist novel and a *byt* text in *Varianty Morozova* (Morozov's variants, 1982), reads a newspaper report about the heroic feats of a mine team, and feels a "degrading jealousy": "Nothing of the kind had ever happened to him. But someone else's glory underlines his mediocrity, that was what it was all about. He could see all the rest of his life ahead of him...he was weighed down by the terrible contradiction between what he had wanted as a young man and what he had achieved now..." (Rybas 1982, 11).

In *Podgotovitel´naia tetrad´*, jealousy proves futile, envy impotent; ultimately Karmanov realizes that he cannot win; Svechkin remains impervious to Karmanov's actions, but when pushed, delivers a neat punch to his tormentor's face and walks casually away (Kireev 1989, 186), leaving Karmanov both homeless and defeated. Kireev lacks the lightness of Trifonov's writing style, but his work is a clear reflection of many of Trifonov's themes, gathered into the urban melody of regret and defeat, the swan-song which gives urban prose its tired air. Svechkin, like the practical Luk´ianovs in Trifonov's *Obmen*, stands for the reality with which the *neudachnik*, with his half-formed dreams of being great, loved, talented, in some way "special", collides and is defeated.

Rivalry between a man who knows how to "get on", and a less talented, but perhaps more principled, "friend" is a theme common to several urban texts. Iurii Trifonov's first novel, *Studenty* (Students, 1950), followed this plot line, describing the narrator, Vadim Belov, and his more dashing, yet immoral, friend, Sergei Palavin. The first novel published by Vladimir Makanin has some similarities with *Studenty*. *Priamaia liniia* (1965), describes two mathematician friends, Volodia Belov and Kostia Kniazogradskii, who are working on a project which ends with the death of a man after an explosion at the test site. Volodia is not necessarily at fault, and more of the blame would appear to attach to his more brilliant, but less academically meticulous, friend Kostia, but the latter arranges matters so that Volodia becomes the scapegoat. The text ends with Volodia dying rather inexplicably, presumably as a result of stress and lost innocence, from the realization, perhaps, that he is less fit for this reality than manipulators and pragmatists such as Kostia.

In urban texts, the plot is usually not highly dramatic, as the tension of events is less important to the author than the "internal plot", that is, the swings in his protagonist's moods, tension between characters, and the deflation of that tension by the defeat of the *neudachnik*. Writers of urban prose follow a Chekhovian line in the development of plots around very simple, often rather dull events, or events which have somehow lost their significance; although there is very often a death to be noted, it passes quietly. Death and other changes, often quite minor, are central to the city dweller's mid-life crisis; his Kavalerov syndrome is based on a belief that there is still a chance to change his life radically, and job crises, marital tension, an ethical dilemma, or the death of a relative serves as the catalyst for the crystallization of the hopes of the *neudachnik* for transformation.

One subject which brought Iurii Trifonov to fame was that of the exchange of apartments. To Trifonov, in *Obmen*, the exchange entailed profiting at another's expense; the Dmitrievs' larger flat can only be achieved through the exploitation of Kseniia Fedorovna, Dmitriev's mother, dying of cancer. In Makanin's "Polosa obmenov" (A chain of exchanges, 1979), the Tkachevs, upwardly mobile yet naive people, find that they, too, will only fulfil their desire for a three-roomed apartment by profiting from other people's sorrow. The only people likely to be interested in their two-roomed flat will be the impoverished, or widows, such as Gelia (Angelina), the prospective exchanger who does turn up, and whose husband was killed in a plane crash a year ago. Staring gloomily at the portrait of Gelia's husband, Tkachev meditates on life's unfairness; he will shortly both have the dead man's apartment, and possess the body of his wife Gelia, who has agreed to become his mistress. Tkachev dimly understands that he is capitalizing on misfortune; but his sorrow is, Makanin tells us, "not severe" (Makanin 1989, 358). Tkachev comforts himself that he is simply trying to live better, following a natural social law. All Kavalerovs end up, ultimately, like Olesha's "hero", in bed with the vulgar and profaned (the widow in Olesha's text), their own indifference the manifestation of their own inability to confront the conflict between their ideals and the reality which has vanquished them.

The protagonist usually has a difficult choice between principles and pragmatism, and in the majority of cases opts for the latter, usually influenced by something which he vaguely senses as the "pressure of circumstances". Alternatively, he gives in to pragmatism because he, like Kavalerov while living with Andrei Babichev, senses its power. The need of the neu*dachnik* to be part of the world which the practical inhabit is the theme of Makanin's *Chelovek svity* (A man of the entourage, 1982), in which the forty-year-old Rodiontsev and the thirty-five-year-old Vika are privileged members of the inner circle established by Aglaia Andreevna, secretary to the director of a Moscow institute. Aglaia gives them a sense of being important, needed, a sense of life, without which, as Vika believes, life would be drab indeed (Makanin 1987, 173). For those for whom "daily life is grey", there is the comforting illusion of knowing "*that* life", namely the power-filled life of influential people, and "even the illusion of participation in it" (Makanin 1987, 192–93). For Rodiontsev, excluded from the circle after a tactless remark, life without Aglaia and the status the acquaintance conveys on him, is meaningless; he feels himself to be "nothing". Both he and Vika are replaced by younger workers, and although Rodiontsev is told that he should consider himself fortunate to be free of the circle or entourage, the last the reader sees of this urban hero is Rodiontsev drunkenly asleep in the street, out in the cold.

The urban "hero" often gives in out of apathy, believing that his struggle is irrelevant or unlikely to be crowned by success, or he succumbs to his own feelings of futility, sensing approaching mortality and the collapse of romantic hopes. The motif of defeated love is another constant in urban prose, beginning with Trifonov's tales of disappointing marriages in which husband and wife coexist through habit or the need to support children, rather than through love or respect. Love affairs are usually described with an emphasis on the inevitable disillusionment which will result. Afanas´ev's "Bez liubvi" (Without love) subtitled "Zapiski gorozhanina" (Notes of a city dweller), depicts a cautious desire, describing the unsuccessful love affair between the book-keeper Kolia and a certain Nina, who are both "meek, cautious" and "like mice", and whose love is distinguished not by passion but by secrecy and quietness (Afanas´ev 1976, 188). Nina, of course, eventually finds another man, and Kolia realises that he is indeed a "little man", one unlikely to experience a grand passion.

In Daniil Granin's *Dozhd´ v chuzhom gorode* (Rain in a strange town, 1973), the protagonist, Chizhegov, embarks on a love affair with a woman named Kira, who lives in the town of Lykovo, where he often goes on *komandirovki* (a rather Chekhovian plot, reminiscent of his "Dama s sobachkoi" [The lady with the little dog]). Chizhegov may be undergoing the usual Trifonovian mid-life crisis, or, like Chekhov's Gurov, he is merely bored in a strange place. However, Kira soon grows tired of being the "other woman", and after bitter scenes the relationship is ended. With time the whole story of passion and bitterness becomes amusing, an "ordinary story" (Granin 1980, 277) with no particularly strong feelings attached to it, as in the love affair Dmitriev from *Obmen* has with Tania, for whom he later feels nothing at all. Urban protagonists seem incapable of sustaining love when it is offered to them, or of making the commitment necessary to develop the emotion. In Vladimir Makanin's *Otdushina* (Safety-valve, 1976), for example, two men, the furniture-maker Mikhailov, and the mathematician Strepetov, both married, compete for the affections of Alevtina. Strepetov is hampered by his caution, and natural apathy; it is rather easier to live under the thumb of his doctor wife, who physics his body and his soul with merciless firmness.

Mikhailov wins, proving himself better than the "clever and handsome" opponent; however, it is indicated that for this unlikely lover, who is fortyish and fat, winning is the important thing. In his desire to prove himself better than Strepetov, he induces Alevtina to depend on him and on his ability to "get things done", that is to obtain cassettes, to find someone who owes him a favour to repair her tape recorder, and, principally, to provide cheap, attractive furniture (reminiscent of the arch-philistine Glebov's pursuit of furniture in Trifonov's *Dom na naberezhnoi* [The house on the embankment, 1976]). Mikhailov even goes so far as to to ask his rival, Strepetov, to coach Mikhailov's sons for the entrance examination to Moscow University. Having transformed himself from an unhappy man (distinguished by his inertia and sense of life being over) into a "victor", Mikhailov severs his connection with Alevtina (Makanin 1987, 97). In such a victory lies a great defeat, however, for Mikhailov refuses to admit the depth of his love for her. At the end of the story he is shown on his hands and knees, crawling drunkenly up the stairs leading to his apartment, where his wife awaits with her usual reproaches for his inebriation. This is a sorry end for the "victor" in the field of love. An even messier end to a great love story occurs in Kireev's *Apologiia,* in which one Kesha Mal´ginov, a married man, is horrified to discover that his beloved mistress, Faina, is pregnant. Forcing her to agree to an abortion at a dangerously late stage, he becomes the indirect cause of her death.

Relationships with wives and mistresses are usually shown in urban prose to be based on power-plays rather than on genuine and altruistic affection. Perhaps influenced by Trifonov, who rather misogynistically portrayed the wives of his male protagonists as domineering philistines, other urban writers tend to show wives as people who attempt to dominate and mould them, like Makanin's Dashen´ka in the story of the same name, who reduces the handsome and talented Andrei to the level of a helpless child. Urban male (and, less frequently, female) protagonists are therefore frequently shown as attempting to escape from their spouses (and from their usually difficult teenage children). Trifonov's Moscow tales, with their motif of the "ubeg", or escape, encapsulate this desire, as does Granin's *Dozhd' v chuzom gorode,* in which Chizhegov realises that he has a chance to change his life, and that before he met Kira he had "been asleep".

In Trifonov's *Predvaritel'nye itogi* (Preliminary conclusions, 1970) the "hero", Gennadii, runs off to the south to escape the pressures of his life and finds comfort in the arms of the young Valia; however, he soon slinks back to his wife and family. In Sergei Zalygin's *Iuzhno-Amerikanskii variant* (The South American variant, 1987) the forty-five-year-old Irina Viktorovna has always dreamed of a "better life", symbolized by the concept of a *iuzhno-amerikanskii variant,* referring to a man whom she once met on a train. Vikentevskii, thereafter immortalized in her memory as a "knight" who might save her from her boring life, was on his way to a diplomatic posting in South America, and could have taken her with him, had she abandoned caution and her fiancé. This pleasant belief in the possibility of escape keeps Irina going until one cruel day when she realizes that he has died, and all possibility of escape has vanished too. The mid-life crisis always passes without the protagonist being able to escape, to begin a new life.

DREARINESS, DISAPPEARANCE AND DEATH: THE "COFFIN" STYLE OF URBAN PROSE

The *gorozhanin* is in reality attempting to escape mortality; this is the essence of the fear which the forty-year-old protagonists (and at times, even younger "heroes") experience as life begins to close in around them with its dreadful monotony. Mikhailov, crawling up the stairs to his apartment in *Otdushina,* is not merely drunk, but unwell, and afraid of his illness.

The emphasis on death and on the swift passing of time so apparent in urban texts is part of the authorial intention to deflate the characters' pretensions to greatness; life is shown to be repetitively, deadeningly dull, as in Kurchatkin's *Sem' dnei nedeli* (Seven days of the week, 1977), which describes a week in the life of his journalist protagonist. In Rybas's *Varianty Morozova,* in which Starobel'sk (in actual fact known for its unsavoury past, its mass graves) is shown to be boringly provincial, Rybas's hero, Morozov, begins to wonder whether the lack of variation in the city buildings does not represent a lack of variation amongst people: "The coarse solidarity of the pre-war buildings, the chilling majesty of the structures dating back

to the fifties, and the utilitarian simplicity of the contemporary house —
such were the features of the city. There were no others. 'Perhaps we don't
vary so much ourselves', thought Morozov" (Rybas 1982, 105).

Monotony, a sense of limitation, and fear of mortality — these aspects
mark out the style of the urban prose text as a "coffin" style in which the
author's intent is to diminish his characters, placing them in situations
which induce a feeling of helplessness. The *neudachnik* develops a philosophy of the "full-stop"; as Afanas´ev's protagonist in *Privet, Afinogen!*
puts it, "Life isn't always right. Life entices welcomingly with its personal
boundlessness and then suddenly places a full-stop in the most unexpected
place" (Afanas´ev 1979, 463). In his text *Operatsiia* (The operation, 1976),
Afanas´ev's main character offered a similarly disillusioned view: "Almost
to the age of twenty there was no limit to my sight... I could imagine
Moscow entire, like a plate with unfinished porridge. But... then I understood that everything has its boundaries" (Afanas'ev 1976, 201–02). It is
in such brooding moments that the urban tone is clearly heard. The narrator
wonders why he has come to such a full stop; in *Privet, Afinogen!* he mutters
forlornly that whereas at twenty he felt himself to be a genius, now he is
only an ordinary worker. He adds that "the transition from genius into
ordinary worker – it's the same as moving from a bright palace to a cellar
room without a toilet" (Afanas´ev 1976, 399).

The sense of the full stop comes with age and with pain, as in *Operatsiia,*
in which Afanas´ev's protagonist, Volodia Bersenev, cannot comprehend
why pain and illness have struck him down. Urban writers, examining the
reactions of their protagonists to mortality (as in another of Afanas´ev's
stories, "Pozdno ili rano" [Sooner or later], which deals with a woman
attempting to come to terms with her husband's death), depict characters
who shy away from the realization that time has transformed them from
young, active and optimistic boys into flabby, paunchy old men with heart
problems, domineering wives, and adult, incomprehensible offspring. The
urban author's irony lurks like a mugger, about to reduce the "great man"
to nothingness, reminding him of the ultimate "disappearance", of which
Makanin writes in his evocatively named "Reka s bystrym techeniem" (The
swift-flowing river), in which the river of time has swept over one Ignat´ev,
who realizes with some shock that not only is his wife deceiving him, but
that she is fatally ill. Ignat´ev goes on a drinking binge, unable to deal with
the threat of approaching annihilation.

In his *Krovli dalekogo goroda* (Roofs of a far town, 1986), Kireev writes
of the urban past of the narrator and his particular and admired friend, one
Sania Grushko, who dies, and this fact, mentioned early in the text, sets
the tone of regret and surprise at the swift passing of time which is the
dominant mode of Kireev's novel: "How can it be! For these people were

here just now, alongside, on this side of the window... And then...they are no longer. They have disappeared forever, although the window was tightly shut" (Kireev 1986, 16). Kireev adopts for a moment a distinctly Trifonovian mode, "disappearance" being one of Trifonov's most frequently used words, one which sums up the *gorozhanin*'s helplessness in the face of time and mortality.

Kireev has recently adopted a brief, meditative style, in his "pozdniaia proza" (late prose), short pieces about families and acquaintances often linked by the same narrator, one K-ov (Karmanov, possibly), who is described a victim of circumstances, which are "always or almost always stronger" (Kireev 1993, 74). His protagonist has given up the attempt to topple great men, or to attempt greatness himself. He merely waits for the darkness "on the other side" of the window. Kireev's use of imagery taken from the interior of a house to refer to man's existential, ephemeral condition, is a favoured conceit of urban writers. Characters are depicted surrounded by objects, dragged down by domestic needs, the claustrophobic confines of the average city apartment an apt metaphor for the coffin which awaits them, the grey walls of the cramped rooms, rather like the grey fence in Chekhov's "Dama s sobachkoi", a symbol of drab life. At times the image used to express existential angst is a strong one, as in the Kurchatkin story "Labirint" (The labyrinth), in which the protagonist finds himself eternally trapped in a maze from which he cannot escape.

Urban prose is a prose of quiet defeat, of bathos, of regret, of no way out, clutter and confusion. It is literature which, as Bondarenko has suggested, prefers the microscope to the telescope; urban writers' concern with minutiae, with cramped rooms, distinguishes the urban genre from the often epic landscape of the *derevenshchik* text (Bondarenko 1985b, 98). Iurii Trifonov's "hermetic world", as it has been called (Hughes 1980, 470), the world of his prosaic and defeated texts, dominated by materialistic objects, a "cage with a television", as Anatolii Kim has called it in a story of that name, is a tightly sealed world of limitations, and for the *gorozhanin* there never is any way out, any possibility of glorious transformation. Urban prose is a complex form of literature, laconic, unornamented and grey, noted for its flatness and starkness, the so-called *strogaia* or *bednaia* prose of Makanin being one such example.[4] It is essentially the prose of the prosaic, a carefully modulated form of literature with a quiet, often rather weary, Chekhovian irony running through it; the genre is that of the wry smile hiding itself within the sagging jowls of the increasingly flabby forty-year-olds. For this reason, several writers often called "urban", such as Anatolii Kim, with his exotic locations and eccentric characters,[5] or Andrei Bitov, with his travel texts, his metafictional *Pushkinskii dom* (Pushkin house,

1978), or his cities in which odd events often occur, are not writers of urban prose.[6]

Part of the prosaic understatement so typical of the urban style has been revealed through its paradoxical concern with ethical problems combined with a distinct lack of censure, following the non-didactic line for which Iurii Trifonov was so criticized in the seventies. Urban prose writers have succeeded in analysing the "Kavalerov" disease while at the same time suggesting that a world divided into materialistic victors and depressed *neudachniki* allows no-one the elevated stature of judge, jury or executioner. This fact was clearly acknowledged by Trifonov when he argued that writers were infected with the illness they depicted; namely, that of disliking to see the truth of their life and actions. In the words of the underground man, "my vse bol'ny" (we are all sick).

In Makanin's *Portret i vokrug* (A portrait and around, 1978) the author describes a "man of the sixties", one Starokhatov, who abuses his position as a well-known scriptwriter and producer to sign his name to scripts written by novice authors. The main character in this novel, Igor´ Petrovich, involved in the Starokhatov case, finds himself unable to take any action against the man; Starokhatov tells Igor´ that he "sees himself" in Starokhatov. For Igor´, laying charges against this man would be like indicting himself; and he cannot accept his own criminality. The sense of communal guilt which Makanin and Trifonov both depict is also a theme of Kireev's *Apologiia*, in which Kesha Mal´ginov, accused of the death of his mistress Faina, is put on trial. He announces that all those in the courtroom are as guilty as he is, and Kireev hints that Faina's other lover, Girkin, may also be at fault. As Kireev suggests in the beginning of the text, although this is an apologia, no-one is really guilty, and yet all are. Authorial reticence is combined with a deep sense of the protagonists' guilt, conveyed, as Konstantin Kustanovich, who discusses the *sorokaletnie* under the heading of "confessional prose", has argued, through a "Trifonovian technique": "Vladimir Makanin, Tat´iana Tolstaia, Liudmila Petrushevskaia, Ruslan Kireev, Sergei Esin, Nina Katerli, and Iurii Poliakov are among those writers who, by using a Trifonovian technique, force pragmatists to unmask themselves in their confessions" (Kustanovich 1991, 980).

The situation is too complex for such easy judgements; the hero is left "in a neutral position" (Kireev 1986b, 205). After all, time is the real judge, jury and executioner; the coffin metes out an even-handed justice. Trifonov's technique required the protagonist to suffer the faint pangs of memory, coupled with an awareness of the difference between the then and the now, between innocence and health, between middle-age and cynicism. Even if urban prose protagonists fail to see the great divide between what they would like life to be, and what it is, namely, a messy failure, time has a way of pointing this out to them as it details the changes and the ethical erosion which has accompanied the physical. Time indicates this erosion gently, and without reproach. The fact of its occurrence is enough.

REFERENCES

Afanas´ev, A., 1976. "Bez liubvi", "Pozdno ili rano", in *V gorode v 70-kh godakh* (Moscow: Sovremennik).

_____, 1979. *Privet, Afinogen!* (Moscow: Sovremennik).

Berman, M., 1982. *All That Is Solid Melts Into Air. The Experience of Modernity* (London: Verso).

Blok, A., 1960. *Gorod*, in *Sobranie sochinenii v 8-i tomakh*, II (Moscow: Khudozhestvennaia literatura).

Bocharov, A., 1981. "Rozhdeno sovremennost´iu", *Novyi mir* 8: 227–47.

_____, 1985. "Kak slovo nashe otzovetsia?", *Voprosy literatury* 11: 86–129.

_____, 1988. *Literatura i vremia* (Moscow, Khudozhestvennaia literatura).

_____, 1989. "The Courage of Living Without a Destiny", *Soviet Literature* 10: 4–20.

Bondarenko, V., 1980. "Stolknoveniia dukha s materiei", *Literaturnaia gazeta* 5 November: 6.

_____, 1985a. "Velenie vremeni", *Literaturnaia gazeta* 7 August: 2.

_____, 1985b. "Avtoportret pokoleniia", *Voprosy literatury* 11: 79–115.

Bradbury, M, 1976. "The Cities of Modernism" in M. Bradbury and J. McFarlane (eds), *Modernism* (New York: Penguin).

Chuprinin, S., 1981. "Zhizn´ vrasplokh", *Literaturnaia gazeta* 4 February: 5.

Dedkov, I., 1981. "Kogda rasseialsia liricheskii tuman", *Literaturnoe obozrenie* 8: 21–33.

_____, 1986. "Skol´ko budet dvazhdy dva?", *Literaturnoe obozrenie* 1: 32–35.

Dmitrievskaia, E., 1985. "No v pamiati takaia skryta moshch´...", *Literaturnoe obozrenie*, 7: 95–98.

Donchin, G., 1958. *The Influence of French Symbolism on Russian Poetry* (The Hague: Mouton).

El´chin, V., 1982. "Byt´ samim soboi", *Literaturnaia gazeta* 21 April: 3.

Fanger, D., 1977. "The City of Russian Modernist Fiction", in M. Bradbury and J. McFarlane (eds), *Modernism* (Aylesbury: Penguin), 467–80.

Gibian, G., 1978. "The Urban Theme in Recent Soviet Russian Prose: Notes Towards a Typology", *Slavic Review* 37, 1: 40–51.

Glazunov, V., 1985. "Lad slova i kamnia", *Literaturnoe obozrenie* 2: 89–93.

Granin, D., 1980. *Dozhd´ v chuzhom gorode*, in his *Sobranie sochinenii*, III (Leningrad: Khudozhestvennaia literatura).

Howlett, J, 1985. "Petersburg-Moscow-Petropolis", in *Unreal City. Urban Experience in Modern European Literature and Art*, E. Timms and D. Kelley (eds), (Manchester: Manchester University Press), 158–77.

Hughes, A.C., 1980. "Bol´shoi mir ili zamknutyi mirok: Departure from Literary Convention in Iurii Trifonov's Recent Fiction", *Canadian Slavonic Papers*, 22, 4: 470–80.

Kardin, V., 1989. *Po sushchestvu li eti spory?* (Moscow: Sovremennik).

Kim, A., 1985. *Progulka po gorodu*, in *Vkus terna na rassvete* (Moscow: Molodaia gvardiia).

Kireev, R., 1986a. *Krovli dalekogo goroda, Zvezda* 8: 3–106.

————, 1986b. "Ubyvanie geroia?", *Voprosy literatury* 7: 201–06.

————, 1989. *Avtomobili i dilizhansy* (Moscow: Molodaia gvardiia).

————, 1993. "Iz pozdnei prozy", *Znamia* 4: 70–86.

Klitko, A., 1983. "Litso, kharakter, sud´ba", *Literaturnoe obozrenie* 2: 21–26.

Kurchatkin, A., 1980. "Bremia stilia", *Literaturnoe obozrenie* 12: 26–30.

————, 1993. "Labirint", in *Zapiski ekstremista* (Moscow: Moskovskii rabochii).

Kustanovich, K., 1991. "Monologue of the Anti-Hero: Trifonov and the Prose of the Last Decade", *Slavic Review* 50, 4: 978–88.

Lanshchikov, A., 1981. "Trevogi nashikh dnei", *Literaturnaia gazeta* 13 May: 4.

Leiter, S., 1983. *Akhmatova's Petersburg* (Cambridge: Cambridge University Press).

Makanin, V., 1987. *Chelovek svity, Otdushina*, in *Izbrannoe* (Moscow: Sovetskii pisatel´).

————, 1989. *Utrata* (Moscow: Molodaia gvardiia).

Preston, P., and Simpson-Housley, P. (eds), 1994. *Writing the City: Eden, Babylon and the New Jerusalem* (London: Routledge).

Roll´berg, P., 1990. "Proza sorokaletnikh — izobretenie kritiki ili iavlenie literaturnogo protsessa?", *Zeitschrift für Slawistik*, 35, 3: 388–94.

Rybas, S., 1982. *Varianty Morozova* (Moscow: Moskovskii rabochii).

Shneidman, N. N., 1989. *Soviet Literature in the 1980s: Decade of Transition* (Toronto: Toronto University Press).

Sharpe, W., and L. Wallock, 1987. "From 'Great Town' to 'Nonplace Urban Realm': Reading the Modern City", in W. Sharpe and L. Wallock (eds), *Visions of the Modern City* (Baltimore/London: Johns Hopkins University Press).

Sidorov, E., 1980. "Zhivaia voda i kriticheskaia zhazhda", *Literaturnaia gazeta* 24 December: 5.

Sokolov, V., 1985. "Nachinaetsia s publitsistiki", *Literaturnaia gazeta* 16 January: 3.

Strelkova, I., 1989. "Ozhidanie neozhidannogo", *Literaturnaia gazeta* 1 February: 3.

Surganov, V., 1980. "Porog zrelosti", *Oktiabr'* 1: 202–12.

Tait, A., 1993. "The Russian Disease: Kurchatkin's Diagnosis", *Slavonic and East European Review*, 71, 1: 14–34.

Tolstaia, T. and K. Stepanian, 1988. "...Golos, letiashchii v kupol", *Voprosy literatury* 2: 78–106.

Trifonov, Iu., 1981. "Gorod i gorozhane", *Literaturnaia gazeta* 25 March: 5.

Varshavskii, V., 1976. "Chevengur i Novyi Grad", *Novyi zhurnal* 122: 193-213.

Zalygin, S., 1987. *Iuzhno-Amerikanskii variant* (Moscow: Moskovskii rabochii).

NOTES

1. All translations in this article are my own.

2. Irina Strelkova, in a 1989 article which focuses on those urban writers "who have been classified as the *sorokaletnie*", has suggested the following names: Ruslan Kireev, Aleksandr Rusov, and Andrei Bitov ("thanks to whom the concept of urban prose finally crystallized") as well as Iurii Nagibin, Georgii Semenov and Tat'iana Nabatnikova (Strelkova 1989, 3).

3. Kurchatkin has argued that the "*sorokaletnie*" label is a useless one, but has admitted a kinship with Makanin, Kireev and Kim.

4. K. Stepanian has argued that Makanin's prose seems almost to be non-literary writing: Tolstaia and Stepanian 1988, 80.

5. Only Kim's stories collected under the heading *Progulka po gorodu* (Strolling around the city) may be called urban, in particular, his "Kletka s televizorom" (A cage with a television), "Diagnoz" (The diagnosis), about an unfaithful husband, and "Liubov'" (Love), about two materialistic people.

6. Comparing the list of urban writers suggested in Strelkova's list to the names referred to by George Gibian in his article on the "hostile urban environment" — Bitov, Vitalii Semin, Trifonov, Natal'ia Baranskaia and Anatolii Gladilin — one sees that only Bitov appears on both; he is, however, a markedly different writer to both Makanin and Trifonov: Gibian 1978, 40–51.

VLADIMIR SOROKIN AND
THE NORM

David Gillespie

The work of the Russian writer Vladimir Sorokin is shocking, grotesque, some would say irredeemably reprehensible. Boris Groys describes him as "a cruel talent" (Groys 1992, 99), while in his recent book Robert Porter likens him to Iuz Aleshkovskii as a writer offering "shock therapy" to Soviet and post-Soviet readers (Porter 1994, 33). Especially in the last few years, though, Sorokin has become fairly well known in the West, at least in academic circles, due in large part to his being shortlisted for the 1992 Russian Booker Prize. His chosen subject-matter does not make for easy reading: murder, mayhem, indiscriminate slaughter, cannibalism, sexual deviance and abuse, coprophagy, summary mutilation, torture, sadism, masochism and extraordinary verbal violence all feature to greater and lesser degrees in his work. Stylistically, he favours the absurd and irrational, the grotesque and parody, all the while giving the impression that he is testing the reader's squeamishness threshold. To be sure, reading Sorokin is often an aesthetic ordeal, with one atrocity worse than the preceding one, and the cumulative experience is mentally shattering. However, the very nature of the violence and the apoplectic irrationality of human behaviour as shown in his works offer a statement on life and the psychological make-up of society in the twilight years of the Soviet regime. For Sorokin is a writer who is deeply part of his time and his society, indeed, a society where reality has often been more shocking and absurd than anything in his writings.

Vladimir Georgievich Sorokin was born in 1955, and trained as a chemical engineer in Moscow. Apart from writing prose and drama, he has worked as a graphic artist and stage designer. His first novel, *Ochered'* (The queue), appeared in Paris in 1985, and, judging by its subject-matter, was written in the early 1980s. His other main works include *Roman* (A novel) (the Russian title means not only "novel", but also the name of the main character), written between 1985 and 1989, *Tridtsataia liubov´ Mariny* (Marina's thirtieth love) and "Serdtsa chetyrekh" (Four stout hearts). He has also published a novella, *Mesiats v Dakhau* (A month in Dachau), and a book of short stories. His novel *Norma* (The norm) was written between 1979 and 1984, but was published in full for the first time only in 1994. A particular feature of his writings is that they are published in obscure journals or small editions (*Norma* has a circulation of 5000, whereas *Roman* has an even smaller one: 2000); indeed, some works seem available only in manuscript form.[1] Often it appears that Sorokin is deliberately challenging the concept of a commercial, market-oriented literature by making his book editions as obscure or difficult to obtain as possible. However, it is with the novel *Norma* that this paper is primarily concerned, as it is not only a stylistically accomplished work, but also offers a statement on the Soviet collective and individual psyche in the last years of Soviet power.

The novel consists of eight parts, all stylistically and thematically distinctive and independent of each other. Part One is a series of vignettes, each one no more than a couple of pages long, representing various aspects and layers of Soviet society, and human life in general. Everyday situations depicted include a father's conversation with his son, lesbian lovers about to make love, heterosexual lovers in the throes of passion. These latter two episodes illustrate perfectly Sorokin's predilection for breaking sexual taboos. More specifically Soviet situations include a well-placed bureaucrat coming home to a well-furnished flat and doting family, various representatives of the cultural and artistic intelligentsia, and their discussions over what can be published in journals or produced on the stage. We are also introduced to the lower rungs of society: a murderer on the loose in Moscow, killing a taxi driver and stealing his car; and thugs battling it out with their fists in a forest clearing to settle some difference. What unites these different levels of society, the preoccupations and interests of these very different people, is their consumption of the *norma*. This is human excrement served in a cellophane wrapper which, we understand, is the staple diet of this society, and to dispose of one surreptitiously is regarded as a heinous crime (one of the episodes concerns just such an undesirable, reported to the police after being seen throwing his ration into the river). The best *norma* is produced by small children, and, indeed, one sketch depicts a class of schoolchildren depositing their waste in a pot to be collected for the benefit of the State. In this, the opening part of the novel, one thing is clear: the *norma* of Soviet society is excrement, on which everyone is fed, and the vast majority of the Soviet population love it.

Part Two, on the other hand, is thematically and stylistically very different. It simply consists of twenty or so pages of vertically arranged columns of nouns, all preceded by the adjective "normal" (*"normal´nyi"*). The list covers about a thousand nouns, usually linked only by the subjective association of the author, but the list begins with birth and ends with death. Here, for example, are the lines that bring the chapter to an end:

> normal time
> normal responsibility
> normal operating theatre
> normal specialist
> normal anaesthetic
> normal operation
> normal condition
> normal blood pressure
> normal pulse
> normal breathing
> normal fibrillation
> normal adrenalin
> normal coma
> normal discharge
> normal massage
> normal death. (Sorokin 1994c, 98)[2]

In this chapter, as well as later in Part Six, we see the graphic designer at work, where the structure of the text on the page strikes the eye before any sense is gleaned from the words. The boundaries of literature as the written word, and communication as a visual art form, become blurred. Moreover, by so arranging his nouns and their one common and unifying adjective, Sorokin begs questions about the nature of meaning, or rather meaninglessness. Here, as elsewhere in his fiction (his novella *Mesiats v Dakhau*, for instance) the author plays with notions of the power of communication and the truth of the word.

Part Three is by far the most complex in the novel, and begins in a manner recognizable as beloved of Russian Romantics, especially those associated with the "Village Prose" movement of the 1960s and 1970s:

> The ravine began to get wider and more shallow, the bushes were creeping outwards and soon were clustered all around, sweeping to the left and the right, the thick, tall, yellowed grass crunched under his tread, mercilessly soaking his grey wool trousers. Anton threw his cigarette butt into a bush, glanced to the right and suddenly felt his heart begin to pound: the path. It was overgrown and barely discernible in the unmown sun-baked and rain-drenched grass, leading into a mist, winding its way along the bends he knew

since childhood, it called after him, drew him and lured him towards it.

He stepped up his pace, no longer feeling weary after his two-day journey, no longer feeling his wet knees and frozen arms.

The past was something fatally sweet, somewhat bitter, and came alive with each step he took, growing out of the mist, rising to the left in the dark pine forest, to the right in the three dense lime trees, and in the middle, in the middle...

Anton slowed down.

The house.

Still the same.

Their house. His house. The house of his childhood. The house of his youth.

(101)

Once he has found his old family home, now abandoned and dilapidated, Anton sits by an apple tree and, consumed by nostalgia, drinks vodka and recalls his youth. His memories of a rural childhood, hunting trips, and first love accord perfectly with the elegiac pathos of the works of Valentin Rasputin, Vasilii Belov, Vladimir Soloukhin and others. Indeed, in the passage quoted Sorokin shows a gift for lyrical evocation and for vivid nature description which equals, if not excels, that of his "village prose" brethren. Anton goes on to reflect on Russia and the sense of kinship with the Russian land, and Russian national identity. But then, as sentimentalism threatens to overcome the narrative, the narrative changes, becomes disrupted as other voices intrude. Anton finds a manuscript buried in his garden which turns out to be a collection of letters by the nineteenth-century poet Fedor Tiutchev, and it dawns on him that he may be a descendant of the poet. But then another voice, seemingly from outside the text of the novel, interrupts, ordering the author, in the style of a Soviet editor, to alter the manuscript and make the plot more interesting. As a result of this intrusion, we are presented with "Padezh" (Livestock plague), a novel within a novel that is as devastating and harrowing an account of the consequences of collectivization as Vasilii Grossman's *Vse techet* (Forever flowing) or Andrei Platonov's *Kotlovan* (The foundation pit).

"Padezh" is the alternative text to Tiutchev's letters that Anton finds, and reads. It is set in the late 1940s, that is, two decades after the collectivization of agriculture. The Party regional secretary, Kedrin, and the secret police chief, Mokin, arrive in a village, purportedly to inspect its agricultural and social facilities. Tishchenko, the collective farm chairman, accompanies them on their rounds. However, rather than simply inspecting and taking note of the state of the farm, Kedrin and Mokin systematically burn down buildings, beat up peasants, destroy the grain collection, and finally set Tishchenko himself on fire by pouring petrol over him. This in itself may be an absurdist yet powerful symbolic representation of the desolation of the rural community by the power of the Party, but Sorokin leaves the most grotesque aspect to the end. Tishchenko has informed Kedrin and Mokin that all the livestock has died from foot-and-mouth disease, and they go to check. The dead animals are actually people, enemies of Soviet power or from a "hostile" social background, all lying in the sheds normally reserved for animals. Their bodies are in various stages of decomposition, half-eaten by rats, with swarms of flies around the eyes and mouths. The "Padezh" of the title, therefore, refers not to the massive loss of livestock in the aftermath of collectivization, but to the conscious extermination of people.

By thus turning the brutality of collectivization and the Party's belligerent attitude towards the peasants into a grotesque combination of metaphor and metonymy, Sorokin creates both an anti-aesthetic, based on grotesque, and an anti-novel, showing true horror and real death. Sorokin has dismantled the socialist realist myth of collectivization to reveal the tragedy in its actual human cost, the horror augmented by the revolting physiological detail. Moreover, he has also rewritten the literary representation of collectivization, not only in subverting its socialist realist affirmation in works such as Sholokhov's *Podniataia tselina* (Virgin soil upturned). The grotesque surrealism of the dénouement intensifies the theme of human catastrophe. Through its callous brutality, and the sheer viscerality of the narrative, "Padezh" is ultimately more immediate, and thus more horrifying and disturbing, than the philosophically oriented novels of Grossman or Platonov.

Part Four is subtitled "Vremena goda" ("Seasons of the year"), and consists of twelve poems, each one devoted to one of the months. The very fact of their subject matter is immediately reminiscent of Russian nature poetry, in particular that of Tiutchev, and so this chapter continues the link with Part Three. However, there is more here than simply lyricism. The poems are all in different styles, from political bombast in true Stalinist fashion, to quiet lyricism, from a populist glorification of the sporting ethos, to full-blown pornography.[3] Consider, for instance, these two seemingly polarized 'months':

> March. The sky. Hands
> > and the moist trusting wind...
> Again the soft
> > sad, incisive sound of music...
> Again your face
> > is incorporeal, trusting and light...
> No! Our lips shall not be parted,
> > our entwined arms shall not be unfrozen!

> No, on our bodies
> > the bloodless flesh shall not be broken.
> In our souls
> > the water of life has long since found its source.
> We cannot be thoroughly ressurrected
> > nor thoroughly destroyed.
> In this grey, ominous sadness
> > you and I are one forever...
>
> You and I will be carried
> > by this evil, hump-backed violin
> These strings, these pegs
> > this Mozart in the grey wig.
> And the distance will stretch out
> > like the Mona Lisa's exhilarating smile
> And our faces will flash by
> > in the troubled, overflowing river... (151)

The tone here is restrained, with allusions to classical music and art reminiscent of the Acmeist traditions of Anna Akhmatova or Osip Mandel´shtam, and the treatment of love and nature recalling the verses of Boris Pasternak. Yet this is in stark contrast to June:

> June, the end, the fucking twat!
> Shit on Volobuev's arse!
> Fuck whores in the cunt and in the mouth!
> Shove shit down everyone's collar! (154)

It is unlikely that there are Russian poetic precedents of this celebration of *mat*. The effect of the rhyming couplets, given their abusive, scabrous content, is actually humorous, if the reader is prepared to overcome his or her natural aversion to the use of such words in such a purportedly elevated genre. Common profanities, the kind scrawled on walls as graffiti, and the extraordinary sexual verbal abuse, are elevated to the status of poetry. As these two examples testify, and as often occurs in Sorokin's works, the lofty and pretentious is juxtaposed with, and thus subverted by, the base and the scurrilous. Sorokin here reveals his gift for imitating the style of the classical idiom, and his ear for the everyday obscenities of the street.[4]

Part Five is written in the form of a series of letters from an unnamed writer to a certain Martin Alekseevich. There is surely an allusion here to Dostoevskii's novel *Bednye liudi* (Poor folk, 1846), which also takes the form of a correspondence, not least because the hero of Dostoevskii's novel has a name similar to that of Sorokin's addressee: Makar Alekseevich.

Sorokin's writer is an elderly villager who is looking after Martin Alekseevich's dacha, and the early letters simply reflect the day-to-day life of the village, and the writer's jobs and duties in maintaining the dacha in its owner's absence. As Dostoevskii's novel progresses, Makar Devushkin becomes increasingly more desperate at his worsening material situation. Here, too, as the letters go on, the writer becomes more and more angry and embittered. He feels indignation and then hatred towards this young, affluent representative of the urban intelligentsia, so much so that eventually all syntax and grammar collapse. We get a hint of the coming apoplexy when the writer at first reels off a string of obscenities, and punctuation becomes arbitrary, but the last few letters are sheer nonsense, with a succession of absurd vowel and consonant sounds culminating in three pages consisting of nothing more than line after line of the despairing cry "aaaaaaaaaaa".[5] Devushkin also runs out of ideas and words, but Sorokin's letter-writer, together with his syntax, suffers what looks like a terminal breakdown.

Part Six again sees the graphic artist at work, as each page consists just of one line of text, which itself consists simply of one hackneyed phrase or Soviet-style slogan. Thus, we get "I have fulfilled my norm!" (190); "Have you fulfilled your norm?" (193); "With Petia and Liuba everything is normal" (195); "The aria of the norm is virtuosic" (201); "Tariff norms have been observed" (205); "A glass is Serega's norm" (210); "The city of Norm grows and is being built" (214) and "The sports complex Norm grows and is being built" (215). Again, as in Part One, there is little connection between any of these phrases other than the word and concept of "the norm". The norm here is a meaning-less, context-less phrase, typical of the empty bombast of officious rhetoric.

In Parts Seven and Eight the reader is brought closer to the actual over-riding theme of the novel, that is, the subversion and destruction of the truth of the word in a totalitarian state. Part Seven begins in the form of a prosecuting counsel's indictment speech, except that it is peppered with obscenities. The indictment is not so much against a person, other than that he is a follower of Western modernism, but rather against that person's texts, and these texts are duly integrated into the narrative. The indictment contains lists of authors, artists and philosophers, mainly from the twentieth century, who are said to have influenced the author, and many of whom were proscribed at one time or another by the Soviet cultural authorities.

The texts themselves subject to ridicule that most solemn Soviet insti-tution, the armed forces. Sorokin is not only keen to parody the official myths of the Soviet armed forces during the war, but also to literalize clichés and slogans. Thus, when a sailor wishes to "make a present of his heart" (234) to his girlfriend before leaving, he literally presents her with his heart wrapped in a stocking, crowned with an anchor-shaped tattoo. Similarly,

a girl called Osen´ (Autumn) is shot by the counter espionage agency
SMERSh at the end of August, and the next day the first snows fall. Both
the army and the navy are shown here as incompetent and unthinkingly
brutal, their officers foul-mouthed and thick-headed, and these individuals
are portrayed through typically grotesque or surreal narrative twists. Sorokin's
indebtedness to the stock situations and personalities lionized by socialist
realism is also demonstrated in his particular debunking of the sentimental
convention of a soldier or sailor parting with his loved one, as in the
example above. Stalin's favourites (Beriia, Zhdanov, Voroshilov, Budennyi,
Lysenko, Kosior), and Stalin himself, are also mocked and their personal
habits derided.

Part Eight, the final chapter of the novel, is subtitled "Letuchka" ("An
emergency meeting"), and is set in the editorial offices of a literary journal.
Sorokin's satire of the literary world, and the socialist realist falsification
of reality, is here at its bluntest. The language of the narrative is standard
literary Russian, but the speech of these arbiters of cultural and ideological
norms is pure nonsense. Sorokin does not mock their ideas or their adher-
ence to a censorship-based ideology, but simply puts into their mouths a
mixture of words that we recognize as standard Russian, and absolute
gibberish that would be untranslatable in any language:

> — Ia lish´ vkratse arorvnrk eg´ora poreornra Semenovoi. Eto loarokr egonon
> prostye arorenrkpepv proshedshie proanrkr i lishenii. I v etom prostom apevakau
> shchofshoeno vakau srazu ugadyvaetsia. Derevenskie aorovrts fukaveak rispia
> dushe kazhdogo, a aroraepkek spmapmk egogoen nel´zia ne zabyt´. (250)

Here, as elsewhere, Sorokin literalizes the pretensions of the Soviet authorities to truth. The representatives of the media speak and communicate in
an unrecognizable idiom, as if they were from another planet and only they
understand their common gobbledygook. Ordinary human language, the
basic means of all communication and intercourse, is all but irrelevant to
these official cultural arbiters.

The eight parts of the novel are framed, both at the beginning and the
end, by a subplot beginning with the arrest of a certain Gusev and his
apparently subversive manuscript perused by a KGB "expert" all of thirteen
years old. Gusev is Sorokin the author, the manuscript is the novel we have
just read, and the KGB's "expert" appraisal is that it is only moderately
dissident. Sorokin thus mocks not only the system, and the dissident movement of the 1980s, but also his own role and status as a writer. Ultimately,
the whole relationship of reader and writer, text and its reception, the word
and its deformation, constittute the main theme of the novel. The bonds
between people in the Soviet Union of the 1980s have irretrievably broken

down, and the ultimate consequence is a nation of imbeciles, incapable of communication, rational behaviour or creative impulse.

Norma is a fundamental work of the 1980s, although it spent much of that decade underground. It obviously accords with notions of the postmodernist text, with its fractured structure and its full-blooded assault on the reader's aesthetic sensibilities. The "acceptable" becomes replaced by an anti-aesthetic, the novel is an anti-novel where even parody is ultimately reduced to apoplexy and gibberish. Sorokin himself is only now emerging from this underground, and reveals himself to be both an erudite observer of a culture collapsing in on itself, and a highly original and free-thinking writer. In the novel Sorokin asserts the independence and autonomy of art, and his public prosecutor from Part Seven is undoubtedly speaking on the author's behalf when he contrasts "science", so beloved of Soviet ideologues, with the avant-garde:

> For the first time in history science has eclipsed philosophy, and has claims on its role. However, it has not managed to play this role in full because of the coarse and restricted nature of scientific methods and language. On the other hand, the avant-garde art of the twentieth century, born in great pain, has been able to assume on an equal footing the place of a philosophy that is now both decrepit and irrelevant. (222)

Sorokin thus identifies himself with the avant-garde in art and literature, and strives to establish the place of the avant-garde in modern Russia, where science has had its day, verbal communication is no longer adequate, and human actions are no longer governed by reason or emotional need.

If anything, Sorokin is a sculptor of words, for in all his writings the devices of the graphic artist are in evidence. His supreme gift is parody, and "Padezh", his rewriting for the modern age of Platonov's *Kotlovan*, may yet prove to be the definitive literary statement on collectivization. After all, Platonov wrote his novel before mass murder as a means of government was widely known; Sorokin writes for a country that has seen countless crimes committed by the rulers on the people for over half a century, and where under the Bolsheviks the concept of "atrocity" became a legitimate weapon in the class struggle.

But there is more to Sorokin than mere parody or satire. Certainly he is adept at travestying official concepts and norms, and he can combine the most ferocious verbal abuse with evocative lyricism within a single page or even paragraph. Like his contemporaries Liudmila Petrushevskaia, Evgenii Popov or Nina Sadur, Sorokin describes a society staring into the abyss, but he goes further than these writers in charting in grotesque, absurd and surreal colours the various stages of degradation and breakdown as the abyss is confronted. Sorokin is not a realist in the same way as the three aforementioned writers, but rather a conceptualist whose literary works are planned, arranged and executed for the utmost graphic effect. He brings to the foreground the most basic and everyday in human life: faeces, urine, sperm, vomit, decay, pus. Furthermore, he is not interested, despite his love of the bodily lower stratum, in a Bakhtin-inspired carnivalesque celebration of life and the upsetting of hierarchical "norms" for future regeneration and rebirth. Sorokin explores ends, not beginnings. He is out above all to repel and disgust. His naturalistic use of what is commonly accepted as foul and obscene language reproduces the oaths and profanities of colloquial Russian as spoken on every street corner, unlike its usage by Aleshkovskii, where *mat* is the source of elegant wit. His treatment of sex is often intended simply to disgust, unlike its depiction by that other *enfant terrible* of the Russian literary scene, Eduard Limonov, who sets out consciously to break taboos.

So what is Sorokin's norm? Clearly, the norm of Soviet society is a kind of conformist behaviour on the part of individuals (especially the cultural intelligentsia), but it is, above all, the "normal" Soviet use of language that is here so mercilessly travestied. Sorokin reduces Soviet-speak to nonsense, official slogans and platitudes are deprived of a context and so here both look and sound empty and absurd. He uses aleatory writing to fragment the text and create a sense of dislocation, chaos and breakdown. The literalization of clichés and stock literary parameters also makes those concepts hollow and ridiculous. Yet even his final narrative trick, a sly chuckle at the status of his own novel as text, reveals the novel's awareness of its own fictionality. *Norma* can thus be seen as a work of metafiction in its subversion of conventions and its reliance on parody. It works on the reader's awareness of stock Soviet literary and social concepts in order to destroy the legitimacy of those concepts.

In many ways *Norma* can be seen as an anti-novel, for it has no coherent structure or plot, and its "message", if that is the right word, is confined to what is "normal" in a society where language no longer means anything. Sorokin profanes, ridicules, often rubs the reader's nose into the pus and gore of the atrocities he depicts, but he offers a fundamental challenge to the Soviet reader accustomed to easily palatable platitudes and assumptions. He subverts, ridicules, travesties, parodies and finally destroys all vestiges of pretence, bombast and falsehood. Sorokin is not ready to construct anything on the social and cultural debris he has amassed; rather, he revels in filth and violence to reach catharsis, and breaks down language, words and syntax in order to seek language's lowest common denominator. Sorokin challenges us all to reject the old aesthetic, but does not offer a replacement. However, in the literary market-place of modern Russia, he also reminds us all that the writer today still occupies a particular place, and still sees himself as the real moral heart of the nation.

REFERENCES

Gillespie, D., 1997. "Sex, Violence and the Video Nasty: The Ferocious Prose of Vladimir Sorokin", *Essays in Poetics*" 22: 158–75.

Groys, B., 1992. *The Total Art of Stalinism: Avant-Garde, Aesthetic Dictatorship, and Beyond,* trans. Charles Rougle (Princeton: Princeton University Press).

Kenzheev, B., 1995. "Antisovetchik Vladimir Sorokin", *Znamia* 4: 202–05.

Porter, R., 1994. *Russia's Alternative Prose* (Oxford and New York: Berg).

Sorokin, V., 1992. *Sbornik rasskazov* (Moscow: Russlit).

_____, 1994a. *Roman* (Moscow: Obscuri Viri i izdatel'stvo "Tri Kita").

_____, 1994b. "Serdtsa chetyrekh" in *Konets veka*, ed. Aleksandr Nikitishin (Moscow: "Konets veka").

_____, 1994c. *Norma* (Obscuri Viri and "Tri Kita").

_____, 1995a. *Ochered'* (Paris: Sintaksis).

_____, 1995b. *Tridtsataia liubov' Mariny* (Moscow: Izdanie R. Elinina).

_____, n.a. *Mesiats v Dakhau* (Gräfeling).

Vail', P., 1995. "Konservator Sorokin v kontse veka", *Literaturnaia gazeta* 1 February: 4.

NOTES

1. For a more general survey of Sorokin's writings, see Gillespie, 1997.
2. This and other translations are my own.
3. Petr Vail' discerns stylistic affinities in these poems with Pasternak, Esenin, Bagritskii, Isakovskii, Evtushenko and Shchipachev (Vail' 1995).
4. Bakhyt Kenzheev notes: "Sorokin is undoubtedly an artistic writer, with an unsurpassed talent as an imitator. This talent gives him the opportunity to imitate practically unerringly a whole gamut of styles — not only socialist realism [...], but lyrical prose à la Nabokov, the vernacular of the crowd, and the somewhat obtuse preachiness of village prose" (Kenzheev 1995, 202).
5. Boris Groys notes of this chapter: "This indignation gradually becomes so intense that it can no longer be expressed by ordinary words, and the old man's anger pours forth in a kind of transrational language. His letters begin to resemble the transrational texts of the Russian avant-garde, so that Khlebnikov's poetic inspiration suddenly becomes the equivalent of a kind of verbal foam on the lips of a narrow-minded philistine driven by life into a fit of hysterical frenzy" (Groys 1992, 100). However, Khlebnikov's "transrational" language was intended to re-generate the basis of language and create new universal meaning; Sorokin abuses and degrades language to destroy the false reality on which that language is based.
6. There is a clear punning reference to Bellini's opera *Norma* here.

INDEX

A

Abramov, F.A., 226, 227, 230, 231, 233, 235, 240n.4; *Brat'ia i sestry* (Brothers and sisters), 227; "Kto on?" (Who is he?), 230; "Vokrug da okolo" (Round and about), 227, 230

Abramov, G., 282, 283

Abramovich, S.L., 19, 30n.15, 30n.18; *Predystoriia poslednei dueli Pushkina* (The prehistory of Pushkin's last duel), 30n.15, 30n.18

Afanas'ev, A., 282, 283, 284, 285, 289, 292; "Bez liubvi" (Without love), 289; *Operatsiia* (The operation), 292; "Pozdno ili rano" (Sooner or later), 292; *Privet, Afinogen!* (Greetings, Afinogen!), 284, 292

Aikhenval'd, Iu.I., 113

Aizenberg, M., 2, 3, 79,107-23, 127; "A mozhet, ty poshel nazad" (Perhaps you went back), 119; "Govoriu vam: mne nichevo ne nado..." (I tell you, I need nothing...), 120; "Razdelenie deistvitel'nosti" (The division of reality), 120; *Ukazatel' imen* (An index of names), 107, 108

Akhmatova, A.A., 49, 79, 84, 87, 101n.18, 148, 281, 304; "Predystoriia" (Prehistory), 84; "Severnye elegii" (Northern elegies), 84, 101n.17

Aksakov, S.T., 216, 226; *Zapiski ob uzhen'e ryby* (Notes on the catching of fish), 216; *Zapiski ruzheinogo okhotnika orenburgskoi gubernii* (Notes of a hunter in the Orenburg province), 216

Aksenov, V.P., 69, 230, 266

Alekseev, M., 283

Aleshkovskii, Iu., 299, 308

Alexander I, 30n.19

Allilueva, S., 196

Amert, S.I., 102n.20

Andreev, L.L., 170n.8; *Noveishii Plutarkh* (The latest Plutarch), 170n.8

Andropov, Iu.V.,165

Annenskii, I.F., 53, 112

Antonii, Metropolitan, 60

Antropov, Iu., 283

Apuleius, 173

Arakcheev, I., 283

Archpriest Avvakum, 150

Arkhangel'skii, A., 169n.4

Armstrong, Louis, 264, 265, 267

Arndt, W., 104n.35

Aronzon, L., 59

Arzhak, N. (Daniel', Iu.M.), 148, 149, 165

Asarkan, A., 113, 114, 115